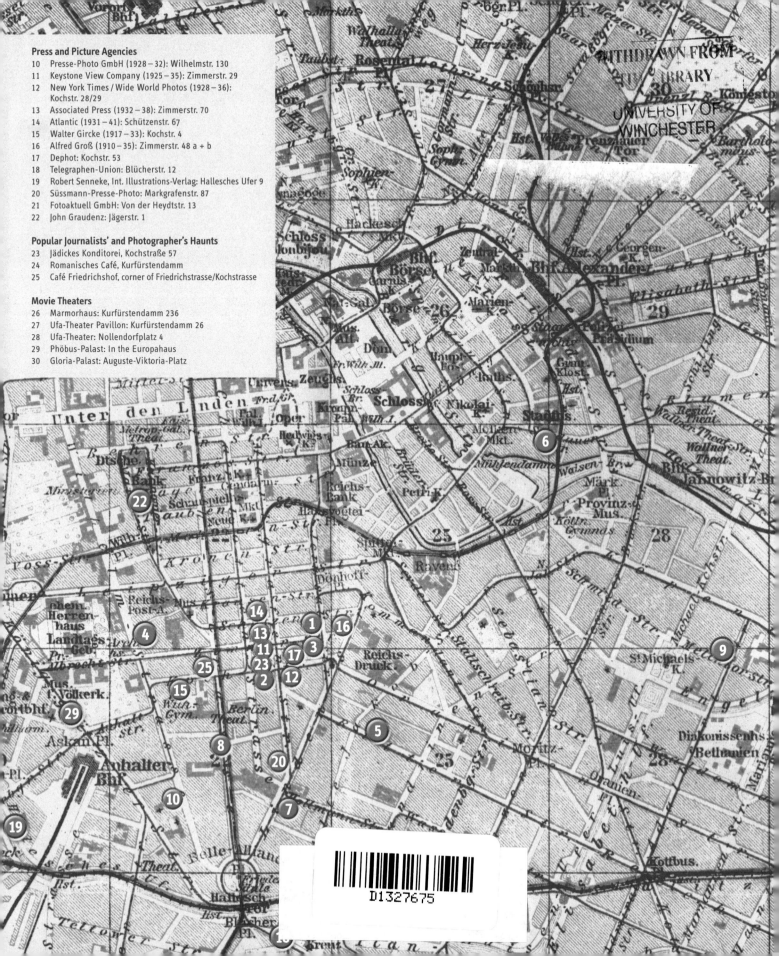

Press and Picture Agencies

10 Presse-Photo GmbH (1928–32): Wilhelmstr. 130
11 Keystone View Company (1925–35): Zimmerstr. 29
12 New York Times / Wide World Photos (1928–36): Kochstr. 28/29
13 Associated Press (1932–38): Zimmerstr. 70
14 Atlantic (1931–41): Schützenstr. 67
15 Walter Gircke (1917–33): Kochstr. 4
16 Alfred Groß (1910–35): Zimmerstr. 48 a + b
17 Dephot: Kochstr. 53
18 Telegraphen-Union: Blücherstr. 12
19 Robert Senneke, Int. Illustrations-Verlag: Hallesches Ufer 9
20 Süssmann-Presse-Photo: Markgrafenstr. 87
21 Fotoaktuell GmbH: Von der Heydtstr. 13
22 John Graudenz: Jägerstr. 1

Popular Journalists' and Photographer's Haunts

23 Jädickes Konditorei, Kochstraße 57
24 Romanisches Café, Kurfürstendamm
25 Café Friedrichshof, corner of Friedrichstrasse/Kochstrasse

Movie Theaters

26 Marmorhaus: Kurfürstendamm 236
27 Ufa-Theater Pavillon: Kurfürstendamm 26
28 Ufa-Theater: Nollendorfplatz 4
29 Phöbus-Palast: In the Europahaus
30 Gloria-Palast: Auguste-Viktoria-Platz

The Weimar Republic

To Maya in memory of Berlin

Copyright © 2000 Könemann Verlagsgesellschaft mbH
Bonner Strasse 126, D-50968 Cologne

Publisher and Art Director: Peter Feierabend
Project Management: Kirsten E. Lehmann
Project Coordination: Britta Harting
Glossary: Patrick Bierther
Editor: Dr. Nils Havemann
Translation from the Swedish: Maike Dörries
Reproductions: typografik, Cologne

Original Title: *Die Weimarer Zeit in Pressefotos und Fotoreportagen*

Copyright © 2000 for the English edition
Könemann Verlagsgesellschaft mbH

Translation from German: Peter Barton, Mark Cole and Susan Cox
Editing: Susan James in association with Cambridge Publishing Management
Typesetting: Cambridge Publishing Management
Project Management: Jackie Dobbyne for Cambridge Publishing Management
Project Coordination: Alex Morkramer
Production: Mark Voges
Printing and Binding: Reálszisztéma Dabas Printing House
Printed in Hungary

ISBN 3-8290-2697-8
10 9 8 7 6 5 4 3 2 1

The Weimar Republic

through the lens of the press

IDEA AND CONCEPT: TORSTEN PALMÉR
EDITED BY: HENDRIK NEUBAUER

KÖNEMANN

The Age of the Image

Whereas the 18th century is known as the Age of Enlightenment, the 19th century is seen as a time of relentless scientific and technical progress. The 20th century resists such simplified definitions: the first half saw the collapse of Germany and Japan while it was the turn of the Soviet Union in the second half. Could it be described as America's century? Or should it be remembered as the century of genocide and mass exile?

Whatever labels can be applied to it, the 20th century was first and foremost the age of the image. Whatever ghastly events were occurring, people were subjected to a flood of photographs and filmed footage that brought current events to the attention of a mass audience. The daily flood of images which we perceive consciously and subconsciously started with the development of the mass media in the 1920s. Whereas, before 1900, press reports and photographs trailed events by weeks and months, after the First World War this gap was gradually reduced to days and even hours.

The abolition of censorship in Germany initiated a veritable Renaissance of the press in the Weimar Republic. While the political struggles did not exactly unfold on the streets during the first German democracy, they did take place in the newspapers on a daily basis. Photography assumed a completely new role and readers developed an irrational collective gullibility in their attitudes to photographs: it's a press photograph, so it must be true.

Photo-journalism in Germany developed out of the illustrated reporting of the Weimar period. The photograph assumed a central role in magazines: the pictures themselves told the story and were accompanied only by brief explicatory texts and commentaries. The photo-journalists presented a panoramic view of society in their photo essays. Armed with their recently invented 35 mm cameras, they discovered life on the streets and in the court-yards, producing "warts and all" portraits of statesmen, and daring to go behind the scenes in the lives of the rich and famous. The great magazines of the Weimar period developed a style of reporting that continues to influence the visual idiom of major magazine publications to the present day.

This book gives an account of the history of the Weimar Republic from 1918 to 1933 from the special perspective of photo-journalism. It addresses the following central question: How did the Weimar period portray itself? The press photographs and photo essays from the Swedish Television Archives, *SVT Bild*, are presented as original documents with translations of the original captions and accompanying texts. Hence the key events and trends of the time as perceived by the photo-journalists are brought to life. These original documents are accompanied by extracts from newspapers, speeches, memoirs, and songs, which all bear witness to the personalities who dominated the social scene during the era of Germany's first democracy. In general terms, the book provides an insight into the way in which the media depicted life in the first German Republic .

Today, we are all too aware that pictures can "lie." In the course of the 20th century, politics and wars were increasingly tested for their "aesthetic" qualities before being transmitted or printed. From the mid-1920s, National Socialist propaganda attempted to influence the public in the same way – albeit at a completely different level in view of the limited technology available.

In order to demonstrate the ideological nature of the interaction between words and images, the texts introducing each chapter outline the main events and concerns behind each individual period and topic. The photographs are also accompanied by contemporary comment where explanation was deemed necessary.

Hendrik Neubauer, December 1999

Right: *Symbolic Depiction of Work. The Reporter*
Previous page: *Reich Chancellor Hermann Müller during an address to the [...] 'Black-Red-Gold' Reichsbanner meeting in Magdeburg. 22 May 1925*   (Original captions)

Contents

AND AS YOU SEE...

Swarms of photo-journalists traced the political genesis and development of the Weimar Republic in their capital city of Berlin. This photograph was taken on 1 April 1930 during the presentation of the new presidential cabinet under Reich Chancellor Heinrich Brüning following the downfall of the Grand Coalition. The original caption stated: "This is how a government starts out. An army of cameramen and photographers bombards the new government during its official presentation." Beyond the world of politics, photo-journalists in the 1920s developed an intense interest in all aspects of society both at home and abroad. Kurt Korff, editor of the *Berliner Illustrirte* magazine, summed up the importance of photography for the press in 1919, as follows: "Press photography gives the people of the world a microscope with which they can view the events of their time. The photographer travels the world on your behalf [...] And as you see, you are informed."

1

The Liberation of the Press

Together with New York, London, and Paris, Berlin was a leading "newspaper city" of the "roaring twenties." Between 1924 and 1929, the daily newspapers, tabloids, and magazines expanded rapidly and grew into mass media with circulation figures in the millions. The success of the magazines in particular was based on new aesthetic standards, attracting readers with portrayals of contemporary reality in photographs and photo essays. In the early 1930s, there were over four million people living in the capital of the German Reich, which provided both the domestic and foreign reporters with a continuous flow of political and cultural fodder.

As the new "old" capital, Berlin experienced a political and economic boom in the late 20th century. However, it has not yet re-established itself as a press metropolis. Today, it is difficult to find any trace of the former heart of the "newspaper city." The press quarter was located between Potsdamer Platz and Anhalter Bahnhof railway station. The main publishers were based in Zimmerstrasse, Kochstrasse, Hedemannstrasse and Jerusalemstrasse, and it was in these streets that the barricade fights of the January revolt of 1919 took place.

The 1920s was an exceptional period in the history of the press. However, its variety and complexity was demolished in one fell swoop when the Nazis suspended the freedom of the press in 1933. The little that remained of the press quarter after the bombing raids of the Second World War was razed to the ground during the reconstruction of the city in the post-war years.

Mass Media in the Weimar Period

The europhoria that accompanied Berlin's re-establishment as a capital city in the 1990s was inevitably accompanied by the rebirth of the myth of Berlin as a "newspaper city." Holger Böning made the following comment on this phenomenon in an article in the weekly newspaper *Die Zeit* in 1999: "... anyone who is familiar with the history of the press in Germany will remain skeptical. ... the sandy soil of the Mark Brandenburg has never yet provided a fertile ground for a successful and vibrant national press." From this perspective, the history of the press in the Weimar Republic must be seen as an exception. The 1919 armed revolt and the abolition of censorship in 1918 surged through the press in the German Republic like a liberating tornado. The deafening noise of the rotary presses spewing newspapers at an incredible speed became a symbol for the modern city. In the early 1920s, 47 newspapers were published every morning, afternoon, or evening in Berlin. And a further 33 daily local newspapers, approximately 50 weekly publications, and 18 magazines were also published in the capital.

The myth of "Berlin, the newspaper city" still lives on in memories of the great newspaper houses. The liberal Jewish publishing houses of Mosse and Ullstein as well as the highly conservative Scherl-Verlag were all located in the Berlin press quarter. The venerable *Vossische Zeitung* (founded in 1704), the left-wing middle-class *Berliner Morgenblatt* and Theodor Wolff's liberal *Berliner Tageblatt*, the conservative to reactionary dailies *Berliner Lokalanzeiger*, *Der Tag*, and the *Deutsche Allgemeine Zeitung*, the Catholic journal *Germania*, the tabloid *Tempo*, the Social Democratic *Vorwärts*, and the Communist *Die Rote Fahne* were all published in this small area. With the exception of the party political publications, none of these publications achieved any nationwide significance during the Weimar period.

The Flood of Images in the Post-War Period

The magazines did, however, succeed in reaching an audience far beyond their city of publication. As early as spring 1919, when the Republic's economy was still in the doldrums of post-war depression, German publishing houses were struck by acute expansion fever and over 100 new magazines were launched between April and June of that year. However, most of them did not survive the inflation crisis. Thanks to their extensive circulation,

Spellbound by the newspaper – Photo essay
The photo essay emerged as a new form of expression in the late 1920s. The photographer was not normally credited.

Left: *A stockbroker devours the stock listings.*
Above: *Two people read their papers and a third spies over their shoulders.*   (*Original captions*)

Spellbound by the newspaper – Photo essay (continued)
Left: *The reporter scans the pages of the newspaper for his article.*

Right: *Rather than stop reading, he risks breaking a leg.*
Right page: *New today, everything new today!*   (*Original captions*)

the major magazines published in Berlin and Munich enjoyed rapid success after 1923. The cultured middle-class weekly magazine *Berliner Illustrirte Zeitung* (*BIZ*), which was founded in 1891, reached its heyday in the 1920s. In 1924, however, it faced serious competition from the *Münch(e)ner Illustrierten Presse*, which was popularly referred to as the *MIP*. From 1925, the design of these two publications was greatly influenced by the *Arbeiter-Illustrierte-Zeitung* (*AIZ*). The *AIZ* not only promoted the rise of Socialist photo-journalism, it was also viewed as an avant-garde model for all publications of this kind. The enormous popularity of the photographic image in the 1920s is easily explained: the magazines' main source of competition was the film industry, which attracted audiences of millions. For the price of a ticket, visitors to shabby suburban and plush downtown movie theaters alike were entertained with a weekly newsreel, a supporting movie, and a main feature. Photography was also becoming a common feature of advertising.

This collaboration between journalists, artists, entrepreneurs, and politicians created a unique atmosphere in the city. The annual Press Ball held on the third Saturday in January was the high point of the social season. Similar events abounded, but journalists also liked to keep to themselves at times. The latest gossip from the press scene in particular and society in general could be heard around the clock in Jädickes Konditorei, the café in Kochstrasse that became a notorious haunt for newspaper people. The legendary "Romanisches Café" near the Kaiser Wilhelm Memorial Church and the Kurfürstendamm was the regular haunt of philosopher Walter Benjamin, "rampaging reporter" Egon Erwin Kisch, and many other intellectuals. Press photographers met for bowling in Café Friedrichshof at the corner of Friedrichstrasse and Kochstrasse.

Illustrated News

Between heaven and earth: all in a day's work for the photo-journalist. Left: *Highlights from the second conference in The Hague. The Romanian delegation in the camera crossfire.* Right page: T*ied to a balloon – and always on the scene – a press photographer floats above the crowds at the air show in Staaken in April 1928.*
(Original captions)

Press photography originated with the development of the printing process known as half-toning in 1882, when it became possible to reproduce photographs in printed matter. The British and American daily newspapers, such as the *New York Tribune* in 1887 and the *Daily Graphic* in 1891, were the first to use this new technology, and they were followed in 1902 by *Der Tag* in Germany. Photographs soon became a standard component of journalism for newspapers in the USA and England, and special photo-editing departments and archives were set up. In contrast, up-to-date press photographs were a rarity in the German daily newspapers. German press photography was still in its infancy and the newspapers and magazines depended on the work of foreign photographers and picture agencies. Around the turn of the century, the major German newspapers began to publish up-to-date press photographs in illustrated weekly supplements printed on better quality paper, as the paper used for the standard edition was barely suitable for the reproduction of photographs. One of the forerunners in this trend in 1892 was the Social Democratic newspaper *Vorwärts*, which published a supplement called *Die Neue Welt*, renamed *Volk und Zeit* in 1919. The Mosse publishing house issued its *Welt-Spiegel* as a supplement with the *Berliner Tageblatt* for the first time in 1896. The *Berliner Lokalanzeiger* followed suit in 1909 with its supplement *Bilder vom Tage*, and the *Vossische Zeitung* issued its supplement, *Zeitbilder*, in 1914.

Photography Gains Ground

The illustrated newspaper supplements were created by the daily newspapers in response to the competition from the illustrated weekly magazines. These were targeted at a mass audience in the major towns and cities. The magazines used photography to catch the eye of readers, who were lured by lavish full-length photos and numerous double spreads as they leafed through them at the news stands. The weekly *Berliner Illustrirte Zeitung* (BIZ) was published in Berlin from 1891. In 1894 it was taken over by the Ullstein publishing house and, under the management of its editor-in-chief Kurt Korff, it became Germany's most important magazine. In 1914 it had a circulation of

one million and by 1932 this had almost doubled. Among the photographers who became famous for their work in the *BIZ* before 1914 were Walter Gircke, Alfred Gross, Robert Sennecke, and Willi Ruge.

In order to compete with the Jewish liberal publications of Ullstein and Mosse, the conservative publisher Verlagshause-Scherl launched *Die Woche* in 1899. This magazine was specifically dedicated to current affairs coverage.

The transformation of the press around the turn of the century and its growing need for photographs prompted the German photography market to turn professional. In 1900, amateur photographers Karl Delius, Heinrich Sanden, and Martin Gordan founded the *Berliner Illustrations-Gesellschaft*, which specialized in press photography. This marked the beginning of the heyday of press photography in Berlin and just ten years later there were some 20 press picture agencies in the city. This development was, however, interrupted by the First World War when the press was subject to censorship and the press photographers sent to work on the war front: Robert Sennecke, for example, was stationed in Turkey, and Willi Ruge served as the official photographer of the *Luftwaffe*.

Social Crisis

The turbulent post-war years provided sensational material for the press photographers, from the January revolt in Berlin in 1919 to the Hitler Putsch in Munich in 1923. The press reacted to these events by publishing special

illustrated editions. A special 24-page edition of the *BIZ* was dedicated to the documentation of the 1919 revolt by photographers Walter Gircke, Georg Pahl, Willy Römer, Willi Ruge, and Robert Sennecke. For the next three years, the Weimar Republic teetered on the brink of civil war and suffered a severe economic crisis. During this period the fate of the magazines, proved irrevocably linked with the country's economic fortunes, and even successful titles like the *BIZ* lost over one million of its readers. The last edition of the *BIZ*, issued before the introduction of the *rentenmark* in November 1923, cost exactly one trillion marks.

This fall in demand for magazines also plunged press photography into a crisis. Despite this, nonetheless, 50 new picture agencies were established in Germany after 1919. In the early 1920s there were approximately 40 such agencies in Berlin, each employing up to ten full-time photographers and approximately 70 freelance press photographers. In the hopeless economic climate of the post-war years, many amateur photographers tried their luck in this business, which required relatively low initial capital outlay. Even though there were so many photographers making a living from the industry, the circulation and size of the German magazines declined. The foreign market also collapsed because publishers in New York, London, and Paris expressed little interest in the events unfolding in the Weimar Republic. In the aftermath of the First World War, Germany was far from center stage on the world political scene.

Storms of Fire

During the First World War in Germany, film and photography assumed not only strategic but extreme propagandistic importance. The general public believed wholeheartedly in the heroic poses and victorious reports presented to them in the weekly newsreels and special newspaper supplements.

After the end of the War, many Germans were faced with a rude awakening. With the lifting of censorship, the press was flooded with confusing, contradictory, and uncensored images. In addition to the usual positive images of soldiers in action, resting, eating, and smiling, the people were for the first time also confronted with pictures of death. The horror of the war machinery was presented, with examples of both individual fates and abstract, almost artistic, aerial shots. When the real extent of the destruction that had been wreaked in vast areas of Europe became known, many observers lost their faith in humanity and became supporters of a global

pacifism, whose objective was to save man from himself. Yet many militarists, such as Ernst Jünger, felt their theories had been proved right and regarded the devastation and misery as "storms of fire" which merely discharged the survivors to face their existence with even greater resolve. The question as to whether the First World War represented a tragedy or an heroic epic firmly divided the German nation into two camps.

The Photographs as Proof

Photography provided yet another insight into the ethical–moral experience of world war. Hundreds of thousands of photographic documents, in which German soldiers, officers and official reporters, newspaper and agency journalists, and civilians on visits to the front recorded their impressions with their cameras, reinforced the notion that only film and photographs could show it "as it really was."

Chiang Kai-Shek's troops fought the Red Army in the Chinese Civil War.
The Chinese people flee. The latest photos from the war in the Far East. An elderly Chinese woman flees to safety on a primitive cart with her meager possessions. 1931.　　　　　　　　　(Original caption)

This idea was not new; it had been around since the advent of photography. However, it was becoming more popular: the press and its audience increasingly demanded photographic evidence to substantiate the events described in the newspaper copy. In 1919, the *Berliner Illustrirte Zeitung* redefined the professional profile of the photographer, whose job until this point had been to provide background material for the text, as a journalist in his own right: "Press photography gives the people of the world a microscope with which they can view the events of their time. The photographer travels the world on your behalf and brings it closer to you. He stands on the edge of an erupting volcanic crater, cuts through the current of Niagara in a boat, climbs to the

It was only after the end of the First World War that the full extent of the horror of the war became known. The events took on a new dimension when pictures like this one of German soldiers on the Western Front in 1918 were published.

From the World War. Our troops move into an enormous mine crater immediately after the explosion.

(Original caption)

top of skyscrapers, flies over the Himalayas in an airplane, allows himself to be buried in a trench, stands in the line of fire between Spartacus and the government troops. And all this so that you can be in places where you've never been, so that you learn to see this world inside and out, from every perspective. And as you see, you are informed." (Kurt Korff)

The Weimar generation of photographers, editors, and readers had an unshakable belief in the accuracy and quality of journalistic photography. This popular stance was, however, opposed by contemporary theoretical debate. Expressionism completely rejected it and the "New Objectivity" (*Neue Sachlichkeit*) movement saw all attempts to present social reality as a construct which at best could only come close to reality. Only the so-called "image theorists" assumed that with sufficient effort reality could be adequately translated into any medium.

The Quest for Truth

It is difficult to reconstruct the precise details of attitudes to the press in the early years of the mass media, but it is plausible to assume that the general public perceived photographs as synonymous with truth and authenticity. Such common perceptions were often reflected in the typical sayings of the time, for example, "one picture says more than a thousand words."

And as cultural philosopher Arthur Liebert wrote in 1926: "Does not the fact that illustrations are increasingly replacing the shortest of texts prove that the absolute minimum has been reached in terms of 'representation'? The increase in such depictions using images ... is completely in tune with the dynamic spirit of our times. A picture is shorter than the shortest text and is more powerful than the most forceful formulation of words."

The Republic's Illustrated Broadsheets

From their inception, the magazines and illustrated newspaper supplements provided a weekly supply of pictures of the current events which the newspapers reported on a daily basis. The population of the Weimar Republic changed its attitude not only to reading but to life in general. Social taboos were faltering and sexuality became a subject for open discussion. Once the economic crisis was overcome, from 1924 onwards there was a pervasive sense of a new beginning, which seemed both exciting and frightening at the same time. The mass media presented glamour, style, stars, and celebrities while glossing over the inescapable social misery.

Printed Cinema

The magazines made it possible for their readers to escape in their limited leisure time from the grim reality of daily life in the Weimar Republic to an illusion of the big wide world.

The editor-in-chief of the *BIZ*, Kurt Korff, coined an apposite comparison: "It is no accident that the development of the cinema and the development of the *Berliner Illustrirte Zeitung* ran roughly parallel. The public grew increasingly accustomed to receiving a stronger impression of world events from pictures than from written reports." The magazine was neither a newspaper nor a journal; as a mass medium it most resembled the weekly newsreels which from 1910 provided a continuous chronicle of world events and were shown in most movie theaters before the main feature. Also, "the subjects of the film reports are for the most part similar to those in the magazines [...] and present viewers with a most universal range of options: politics, catastrophes and the latest innovations in technology, science, art, and fashion" (Jest van Rennings). People saw the new weekly newsreels in the movie theaters at weekends and bought the magazines hot off the presses on the streets and in newspaper kiosks. They provided pictures for the reports people had already read about in the newspaper or heard about on the radio, which also gradually developed as a medium from 1923 on.

The Big Wide World

Numerous magazines were published in the Weimar Republic in the mid-1920s. According to press historian Otto Groth, their full front page photographs had the following function: "the picture on the first page had to pull, draw, attract: a distinguished head, a figure, a scene from current political or social life, and – particularly popular – the portrait of a male or female film or sports personality, or a person otherwise in the spotlight, the face of a beautiful girl, scantily clad females, swimming, dancing, playing sports." Putting images of the female body on magazine covers was a marketing strategy used by the mass media as early as the 1920s. There were double page spreads

Social life was a recurrent topic in the magazines.
Film Ball in the Berlin Zoo. On Saturday 16 November the Film Ball was held in the festival rooms of the Berlin Zoological Gardens. Apart from personalities from the world of film, politics and the police were represented. Our picture shows the former Reich Chancellor Dr. Wirth (left), Vice President Dr. Weiss (center), and the Bavarian envoy in Berlin, Dr. Preger.
(Original caption)

with photographs on specific topics elaborately laid out on glossy paper. These photo essays were generally composed by the editors from the archived work of several photographers. Photo essays featuring the work of a single photographer were rare at first.

As a rule, the photo essays were dominated by timeless and exotic topics such as: travel reports from other continents, snapshots from galas and matinees, and tales from the lives of the European royal families. Technical innovation came to represent the epitome of a new German self-confidence. The grim reality of day-to-day life in the Weimar Republic had nothing in common with this world picture. The texts that accompanied the photographs were short and pithy if the editors deemed the content of the report familiar enough. In general, the lines written by the reporters said more about their subjective viewpoints than about the topic in question.

The Competition for Readers

A lot of the magazines established a relationship with their readers by publishing novels in serialized form. These frequently dealt with the eternal topic of romantic love and provided a literary testing ground for the new gender roles and sexual morality of the Weimar period. Vicky Baum's novel, *stud. chem. Helene Willfüer*, dealt with the problems faced by a single mother and is said to have boosted the *BIZ*'s circulation by 200,000 in 1928. The *BIZ* had also given the Weimar Republic a cult figure in 1921 with Theo Matejko's satirical drawings of the war profiteer "Raffke." Raffke, the personification of the uncivilized parvenu whose wealth had been accumulated from the misery of others, was a regular feature in this magazine for many years. The editorial comment in numerous magazines launched after 1924, such as *MIP, Deutsche Illustrierte, Hackebeils Illustrierte*, and *Kölnische Illustrierte Zeitung* also reflected the moral and political concerns of the time.

After 1925/26, photographs also became an increasingly common feature in the daily newspapers. The richly illustrated tabloid newspapers based on the American models, such as Scherl's *Nachtausgabe*, Ullstein's *Tempo*, and Mosse's *8Uhr-Abendblatt*, blazed the trial for the daily broadsheets. In this way, the magazines gradually relinquished their original function as providers of illustrated news. Providing images of current affairs up to one week after the event was no longer in tune with the *zeitgeist* and with the status of technology. This development resulted once again in the depoliticization of the magazines, which were then free to dedicate themselves completely to reporting on contemporary social topics as well as sensational and catastrophic events.

Photo-sensitive 35 mm cameras, such as the Ermanox and the Leica, made it possible to take unconventional close-up photographs like this portrait of an old fisherman from Friesland in Northern Germany.

Have a good journey, Allah bless you! – Photo essay
Travel reports were a favorite feature of the magazines. This
series of 35 mm photographs from a journey through
Macedonia on the "smallest state railway in the world"
aimed to bring life in the Balkans closer to German readers.

Above: *The journey in the small stuffy carriage and the
Macedonian heat takes its toll – a sleeping cleric.*
Left: *Into the bend.*   (Original captions)

The medicine man speaks – Photo essay
Photographer Walter Süssmann presented a living anachronism in progress-enthralled Weimar times – the herbalist extolling his remedies in rhymes. The traditions of yesteryear were quickly transformed into a gimmick by the speed of life in the big cities.

*Ladies and gentlemen, this will give you a new lease of life!
It's the very best thing for your bladder and liver
rheumatics, sciatica, consumption, and shiver.
This is g-a-r-l-i-c, the great cure-all.
Give the bottle a shake and take twenty drops,
it will soothe the sick heart that races and hops,*

*You'll be jumping around like a kid on your feet,
and no one will say you're as white as a sheet!
No matter
Whether you're coughing, sweating, or hobbling on sticks –
Other kinds of onions in your soup you can mix!
But they won't do you much good!*   (Original caption)

The Fasci- nation of Image

The inclusion of photographs in daily newspapers marked a dramatic change in the German photography market. The increased demand for photographs attracted new suppliers and resulted in the introduction of new sales and distribution channels. The leading Anglo-American picture agencies raced to open offices in Berlin: Keystone View Company in 1926, Wide World Photos and Associated Press News Photos in 1927, and Pacific & Atlantic in 1928. With their substantial economic resources, global networks, low prices, and fast delivery rates, the international picture agencies finally gave the German press access to photographs from current events all over the world. From 1926, the invention of telegraphic picture transmission made it possible to transmit photographs from every corner of the world to the major press centers.

Initially, the local competition was no match for this new speed and efficiency. The German press photographers were still too accustomed to the weekly publication cycle of the magazines, for which prompt delivery was not an issue. They still thought in terms of the weekly editorial deadline. However, there was no way of halting progress and by 1928 photographs regularly accompanied the text in some 600 to 800 of a total of 4,000 newspapers.

The New Way of Seeing

The magazine editors like Kurt Korff (*BIZ*) and Stefan Lorant (*MIP*) were forced to look for a new niche in the market for their product. In fact, all they had to do was take a careful look around them. Avant-garde ideas abounded in the "roaring twenties." Bauhaus artists such as Renger-Patzsch experimented with photography and strove to go beyond traditional patterns of perception. From 1925, the Socialist magazine *AIZ* consistently developed sophisticated methods for visual and textual narration which provided sharp social criticism in "essay" form. John Heartfield also published his photomontages in the *AIZ* in the

late 1920s. The avant-garde movement distrusted photography and questioned its apparent objectivity. Siegfried Kracauer summarized the avant-garde distrust of photography in 1927 as follows: "Never has a time known so much about itself, if knowing about itself means having an image of things that is like

them in the photographic sense." With the flood of images that became available in the 1920s, mass media like the *BIZ* and *MIP* contributed to the very perception of photography by the general public that Kracauer is criticizing here. Just a few years earlier, in 1919, the *BIZ* had come up with the slogan

The Photo Essay

Photo-journalism provided the magazines with completely new visual narrative techniques. Unlike the individual shots that had previously been standard in press photography, in photo essays the photographer presents a topic or tells a story using a series of photographs. New forms of photo-journalism emerged with the help of 35 mm cameras which made it possible to produce close-ups, unusual perspectives, interior shots and "candid camera" effects. Cinematic sequences showed images photographed in rapid succession from varying positions, and everyday topics documented over longer periods. The photographs were laid out in coherent sequences in the magazines, usually in the form of a double spread with a minimum of text. The image became the focus of interest and the text was secondary. In 1927, Korff commented on the pictorial strategy of the *BIZ* once it had been liberated from the constraint of presenting weekly news: "The *BIZ* adopted the editorial principle that all events should be presented in pictures with an eye to the visually dramatic and exclude everything that is visually uninteresting. It was not the importance of the material that determined the selection and acceptance of pictures, but solely the allure of the photo itself."

The Mass Media Market

This period saw the emergence of the competition between the printed word and the image that continues to the present day in the competition between the press and the electronic media. And then as now, the object of this competition was not merely that of winning public favor. It was also very concerned with attracting advertising revenue for the medium in question. In the course of the 1920s, the magazines developed into a mass product with high production costs which could not be covered by subscriptions and street sales alone. Profit margins could only be guaranteed by solid and consistent advertising revenue.

"And as you see, you are informed." Now Kurt Korff and Stefan Lorant were digging around in the avant-garde's bag of tricks and adapting the structure of the photo essay. However, the iconoclastic avant-garde movement itself had no part in this process of adaptation. And just how convinced the magazine readers were of the objective nature of photography was demonstrated by the hundreds of letters received from readers in response to the annual April Fools' jokes. These generally involved deliberately faked or retouched photographs and the readers were taken in by them in droves.

The Techno-logy Revo-lution

A 1935 advertisement for the Ermanox 35 mm camera reads "You can now take photos during the show at the theater – short exposure times and snapshots. The Ermanox is small, easy to use, and discreet."

A technological revolution was underway in photography, but in the mid-1920s most press photographers were still working with heavy and awkward bellows cameras which had plate magazines for the glass negatives. Each plate magazine held 12 glass plates. Photographers who were traveling around and compiling photo essays could hardly carry more than five of these magazines, which meant that each photograph had to be carefully planned and executed. However, one advantage of the glass plates over the 35 mm cameras was that the photos taken with the latter had to be enlarged. With glass plates, contact copies could be made immediately from the plates and sent to the newspaper offices without delay. Speed was often the key weapon in this highly competitive market.

The press photographers' equipment also included a heavy wooden tripod for the camera and, in big cities like Berlin, a standard household ladder which the photographers used to take photos over the heads of the crowds at mass public events. The consistent quality of photographs taken using this method is impressive, but it was impossible to provide comprehensive documentation of events using this equipment. The photographers had to summarize the situations in a few shots and their mobility was severely hampered by the heavy and awkward equipment they had to carry. This explains why the press photographers could only provide individual shots to publishers.

The Participating Observer

Various 35 mm cameras became available on the market in the mid-1920s: the Leica with its perforated 35-mm roll film, the Plaubel Makina, and the handy medium-format Rolleiflex. The innovation that really made headlines, however, was the Ermanox which

The camera helps with construction. Europe's biggest neon sign is being installed on the Europahaus in Berlin. Our photo shows a scene on the 98-foot-high scaffold.
(Original caption)

was produced in 1925. This was a miniature camera with a particularly fast lens which made it possible to take photographs without a flash in extremely poor light. It even enabled photographer Dr. Erich Salomon to take photos inside courtrooms and conference halls. Readers were enthralled by the direct and natural feel of these photos, which gave them a new "fly on the wall" experience. Salomon and his candid camera became famous throughout the world and his photographs would become icons of photo-journalism. But the Leica soon became a favorite

with photo-journalists as well. André Kertész had fond memories of his first Leica, which he bought in 1928 and which enabled him to take snapshots and sequences of photos for his work on photo essays: "I could finally react with the camera as quickly as my feelings did without missing a beat or being restricted and delayed by technical problems. I suddenly had the very physical feeling that I was finally completely free to express myself."

Witnesses of their Time

The newspaper photographer at work. On horseback. The newspaper photographer stands on the Quadriga of the Brandenburg Gate in Berlin to record the arrival of a distinguished personality in the Reich.   (Original caption)

The generally stagnant labor market in the Weimar Republic had little to offer, particularly to young, academically well-educated men. However, the invention of the photo essay by the popular magazines provided some of them with new and sometimes unexpected opportunities. For example, the Gidal brothers, Tim and Georg, came into contact with the *MIP* as young students and amateur photographers. Tim published "Hi Buddy!", his first photo essay about young dropouts in 1929. Georg's "Eight hours in the lecture hall," for which the student secretly photographed the well-known anatomy professor Siegfried Mollier, appeared the same year. Ethnographer Wolfgang Weber went on a field trip to Kilimanjaro in the mid-1920s before starting to work as a photo-journalist in 1929 compiling photo essays on daily life and the world of work. Erich Salomon, who had a doctorate in law, left Ullstein's advertising department to become a freelance photo-reporter, exploiting his legal background for material to use in his new profession. He became an overnight star with his photographs of the Kranz murder trial, which were published in the *BIZ* edition of 19 February 1928.

A New Profession

Many paths led to the job of photo-journalist. Most of these men came from formerly well-to-do families whose savings had been eroded during the inflation crisis. Others were attracted to the press metropolis from other major cities like Vienna or Budapest. They were all highly cosmopolitan and often multilingual. Usually left-liberal in their political leanings, they were well informed about contemporary social problems and cultural issues. Unlike the traditional press photographers, they developed a new and individual "journalistic eye for the characteristic features and nature of things and events." According to Willy Stiewe, they were also required to have a "journalistic feel for the interests of readers." But it was not just the young talent that succeeded in the new profession; old experts like Willi Ruge also succeeded in transferring to the photo-journalists' camp.

Magazine editors like Korff and Lorant, who did not employ any permanent photographers, were surrounded by a permanent circle of 15 to 20 photographers who, up until 1933, produced photo essays on a freelance basis. This small creative group also included the directors of the Deutscher Photo Dienst agency and Weltrundschau agents Simon Guttmann and Rudolf Birnbach. They specialized in supplying complete photo essays with images and text, inspired photographers with their ideas, and mediated between the publishers and the photo-journalists.

In the following years up to the "seizure of power" by the National Socialists in 1933, these young enthusiasts traveled the world, out to discover it with their miniature cameras. In terms of style, their work was inspired by the Bauhaus and contemporary Soviet-Russian photography with its expressionistic and visual idiom. In addition to the abovementioned photographers, the circle of well known photo-journalists included Umbo (Otto Umbehr), Felix H. Man (real name: Hans Baumann), Kurt Hutton (Kurt Hübschmann), Alfred Eisenstaedt, Martin Munkásci, Robert Capa (André Friedmann), Walter Bosshard, and Harald Lechtenperg.

Ideals and Reality

Photo-journalists like Tim Gidal enthuse in their memoirs about the creative chaos that was so characteristic of this era. Ideas were generally implemented hours or, at the latest, days after their inception. However, their work was not entirely devoid of premeditated idealistic intent. "The decisive element was the human attitude of the photo-reporter, the honest reporting of what he saw whether positive or negative, attractive or not. This kind of direct reporting made it possible for readers and observers to access areas in the lives of fellow human beings that had previously been concealed, a privilege provided by the modern photo-reporter who completely respected the boundaries of intimacy," recalls Tim Gidal. He continues with some reservations: "However, it must be said that in most cases these photo essays did not show situations so that they would be prevented, but just as they were. As in real life, it was open to the observer to choose how to react individually."

The photo-journalists had no say in the ultimate layout and design of the photo essay in the magazines. Even if they supplied the text and captions for the pictures, the editors had the final word and decided on the overall tone and message of the contribution. Press historian Wilhelm Marckwardt is very matter-of-fact in his evaluation of the self-image of the early photo-journalists, and suggests that it was for the most part dictated by the capitalistic market conditions under which they worked: "The image became a commodity; anything that was potentially profitable was photographed and no questions were asked about the buyer's purpose or political intentions." Without dismissing Tim Gidal's memories as pure self-delusion, it must be pointed out that there is a clear discrepancy here between the reporter's idealistic claims and the reality of the magazine market.

Left: *The Hague Conference has started. The foreign delegates have been hotly pursued by the press since the minute they arrived.*
Top: *A press photographer on the trail of the VIPs driving along in the car. He must get a shot of them and tries to do it while driving alongside his subject's car.*
Above: *They pounced on every representative! Our photo shows the press photographers posted in front of the entrance to the Reichstag ready to spring into action as each representative arrives.*
Berlin 13 October 1930.

(Original captions)

A Visitor in the White House – Photo essay
The photographer Dr. Erich Salomon accompanied the French Prime Minister, Pierre Laval, on a visit to the American President, Herbert Hoover, in November 1931. Salomon was exceptionally at ease while moving and working in the top echelons of society. His contemporaries were particularly impressed by the natural and intimate feel of the photographs he took with his 35 mm camera.

Top: *Prime Minister Pierre Laval (left) and President Herbert Hoover during their seven-hour meeting in the library of the White House.*
Left: Prime Minister Pierre Laval (second from right) in conversation with the French and German ambassadors during lunch in the White House with the American President and his wife.
Right page: Prime Minister Pierra Laval (left) and the American Secretary of State, Henry L. Stimson, at lunch on the train to Washington. *(Original captions)*

AND AS YOU SEE...

For the Entertainment and Instruction of Readers

Around 1929, photo-journalism became an established feature of not only the *MIP* and *BIZ*, but other magazines too. In addition to the Dephot and Weltrundschau picture agencies, many others, such as Presse-Photo, Pressebericht, Keystone, and last but not least Willi Ruge's Fotoaktuell, started regularly supplying their subscribers with photo essays on specific topics. The issue of the *MIP* published on 17 March 1929 clearly demonstrates the commercial nature of photography at this time: it contains a photo showing six linen baskets full of photographs. The caption indicates that this is the normal volume of photos received by the publishers in one week. The photo editor, Stefan Lorant, who from 1928 spent one day a week in Berlin and then returned to his office in Munich, was guided by a single principle when selecting articles and photos from the copious supply: "It was my aim to educate, to inform, to entertain. In general, I put the magazine together so that it should hold people's attention and give them something they had not seen before, to teach them, to amuse and interest them."

The forms of expression and topics featured in the magazine may have changed with time, but when compiling the *MIP*, Lorant was faithful to the motto of 19th century family magazines like *Gartenlaube* ("Garden Arbor") and *Daheim* ("At Home"): "For the entertainment and instruction of readers."

The Special Angle

An overview of the photo essays published at the time shows that while the familiar faces from public life were still of interest in the late 1920s, the photo-journalists concentrated on providing a look at them behind the scenes, be it backstage or in the celebrity's own home. The "special angle" was important even when it came to the portrayal of spectacular public events and sensations. The reporters were also beginning to discover the broad canvas offered by everyday life, which had previously been neglected by conventional press photography. The magazines now featured series of photographs accompanied by short texts exploring life in workplaces, on the streets, in the

Street roulette. The photo-journalists assume a representative function: everyone can participate visually in events from everyday street life without crossing any social boundaries.

markets, schools, sports arenas, hospitals, and prisons. The topic "Night in the Big City" promised intimate and shocking insights, with snapshots of revelers and tales from nightclubs, cabaret venues, and vaudeville theaters. The pictorial narratives in the magazines moved between erotic behaviour at tea dances and the exotic nature of circus life, between the fast buck at the race course and the poverty of the city slums. Another popular angle was that of "the press photographer and his camera" whereby photo-journalism focused on itself as the topic of "a new way of seeing." Photographer Willi Ruge, for example, believed in the camera image as the message and developed a particularly idiosyncratic visual idiom.

Analyses of the content of the photo essays in the *MIP* and the *BIZ* clearly demonstrate that in adopting the motto of the old family magazines – "For the entertainment and instruction of readers" – the new style magazines also adopted their yearning for social

harmony and an idyllic life. Contemporary political events and social injustice did feature as topics of the photo essays – the following headlines from the *BIZ* in the emergency year of 1932 speak for themselves: "Unemployed between 14 and 21," "Cave Dwellers near Berlin," "A Roof for the Night" – but the texts and images in such essays repeatedly tended to try to tone down the social problems they tackled. The magazines were aimed at a broad readership and depended on the constant approval of their advertisers. Direct social criticism was a nonstarter in this kind of mass product from its inception.

The Magazine Bag of Tricks

However, the magazines were not merely entertaining pictorial broadsheets which left the judgment of events up to the reader, as suggested by Tim Gidal. As a printed record of world events, the magazine also created in words and images an apparently objective,

cism from many politically aware contemporaries, such as sports reporter Curt Riess: "A lot more could be said about the press in Germany at the time, about the Ullstein publishing house which, in addition to major newspapers and many magazines, published the *Berliner Illustrirte* which was probably the most important magazine in Germany but was, alas, apolitical and remained so even when danger was clearly visible."

Roulette on the Street – Photo essay
Photo-journalists explored the broad canvas of everyday life in the cities for the magazine readers. Georg Gidal photographed these workers gambling on the street around 1930.

Left page: The primitive equipment is completely adequate for the needs of these gamblers.
Left: *"Faites votre jeu!" [...] Callused workers' hands place their coins, usually hard-earned cash.*
Below: *"Rien ne va plus" the ball starts to roll – on the street.*   (Original captions)

consistent world picture which provided readers with an idyllic counterpart to the highly political and conflict-ridden nature of daily life in the Weimar period.

The lowest common denominator of a politically and socially heterogeneous readership – a magazine like the *BIZ* was ultimately aimed at an audience of millions – could only be satisfied by a strict focus on sensational events and topics of general human interest with the emphasis on superficial rather than analytical presentation. Publications of this kind ultimately reduced general social events in an increasingly complex life and world of work to their most arresting and happy moments. (This of course did not apply to politically motivated magazines, including the National Socialist *Illustrierter Beobachter* and KPD-aligned *AIZ*.)

Readers responded to the formula adopted by the successful mainstream magazines with an attitude summed up as follows by Egon Erwin Kisch in *Ein Reporter wird Soldat*: "'Complete invention' remarked my brother. 'There was no mention of it in the newspapers.'" From the inception of the mass media in the Weimar period, the issue of the empirical truth of a statement was less relevant than the fact that it had been published and hence provoked a reaction. Thus, the magazines appear to have reflected a common attitude of readers by closing their eyes to the existential problems of the Weimar Republic, despite criti-

No Eye for Misery

The Presse-Photo picture agency compiled a photo essay in 1930 on the Berlin working-class slum "Meyerhof" at 132 Ackerstrasse in the Wedding neighborhood. This was one of the slum complexes which were particularly characteristic of the Berlin working-class neighborhoods and dated from the Gründerzeit, the period of rapid industrial expansion between 1880 and 1890.

The photographs give a frank and unembellished portrayal of the rundown environment, the flaking plaster on the façades, the dark corners, the inhabitants prematurely aged by hard physical work, and the children who spent their days in the dim cobbled courtyards. However, the text that accompanies the photos transforms the scene into a romantic idyll. The words completely sentimentalize the misery portrayed in the photographs. The decay is elevated to an artistic dimension, and – despite their difficult circumstances – the people are portrayed as good-humored, patient, and contented petit-bourgeois who seem to have jumped straight off the pages of Heinrich Zille's popular cartoons. The "Meyerhof" photo essay shows that, in the entertainment industry of the magazines and their suppliers, there was a constant conflict between the ambition of the journalists to provide an objective account of their subjects and the aim of a picture agency to produce the photo essay in an entertaining form acceptable to the market.

This photo essay was also offered to *Volk und Zeit*, the illustrated supplement issued with the Social Democratic newspaper *Vorwärts*. The latter published the uncut original text in 1930 with the following commentary:

"This is the article which the photo agency sent us with these disturbing pictures. It finds romanticism in this dreadful decay, the misery of which is truly breathtaking. We do not believe that a demagogic intention lies behind the accompanying text. It seems to us that it is a shocking example of common upper-middle-class attitudes which simply have no eye for misery as it exists in its most obvious form."

"No eye for misery" – this is something of an oversimplification of the attitude behind the reporting in popular mass circulation magazines. It would be more accurate to say that the magazines developed a special angle on misery. Although it did not dominate the thematic content of the magazines, numerous photo essays reporting on the social aspects of life in the capital city and the rest of the Weimar Republic were actually published in the *Woche*, the *BIZ*, and even in the *MIP*. Some of the more serious photo essays actually provided completely realistic accounts of the desperate situations faced by certain social groups and showed representatives of the middle and upper-middle classes providing help and relief. There was a clear political message here: the inadequacies of the Weimar welfare state could only be compensated for through private charitable action.

The Meyerhof – Photo essay
The misery of the Berlin slums was given a strong romantic slant in the accompanying text by the Press-Photo picture agency:

1500 people in a single complex. A veritable idyll in the vast residential quarter of the cosmopolitan city of Berlin.
Left page: *Little light penetrates the narrow windows.*
Above right: *The stairways are dark and narrow.*

Above left and below: The 'good old days' live on in Ackerstrasse 132 in the heart of Berlin.

(Original captions)

Entertainment for Millions

Was the magazine reader of the Weimar period an unknown quantity? There is little empirical evidence to support the assumption that the movie theaters were a particularly popular source of entertainment among the working classes and white-collar workers, while the illustrated journals and weeklies were read mainly by more senior employees and civil servants. The theory that the structures of the old class-based society were gradually eroded by the consumer oriented mass culture of the 1920s is supported by the clear parallels between the film and magazine media. Unfortunately, it is only possible to speculate about this as relevant social–scientific data and studies are not available.

The history of the publishing houses is, however, well documented in numerous monographs and, in particular, the publishers' archives. However, these historical accounts merely touch on the mass media such as the magazines and do not provide a detailed analysis of their content over several years. The labeling of the *BIZ* and *MIP* as "middle-class" seems quite inadequate to anyone who is familiar with the political history of the Weimar Republic and is aware that the middle class virtually disappeared there in the 1920s. The term "middle-class" is only appropriate here insofar as it can be applied to differentiate the popular magazines from the Socialist magazines. Harry Pross stated that "The *BIZ* was best at focusing on center conformism." This raises the question as to where exactly this "center" was located.

The magazines were part of the entertainment industry in the Weimar Republic. Photography was purchased by this branch of the press as raw material for processing by the magazine editors. A quick glance behind the scenes in the publishing arena gives some indication of the political orientation of the major publishers who were the key players in press sector of the Weimar Republic.

Ullstein Verlag

In the volume published to celebrate the 50th anniversary of the Ullstein publishers, court reporter Paul Schlesinger, who was known under the pseudonym "Sling," described the business philosophy of this liberal Jewish establishment in 1927 as follows: "It is a

Newspaper readers – Photo essay
Place of business. Our greengrocer also has to keep informed about politics. (Original caption)

major industrial concern with firm, strong, and serious commerical principles, and with the experience, statistics, and bureaucracy that goes with this. But what is produced is not boot polish or benzene, it is entertainment for millions, sometimes heavy and enduring, sometimes light and ephemeral. An intellectual battle is fought in this house, and not just with outside forces on the front against those of a different political persuasion. But this external and internal fight is not dictated by egotistical hate. Behind it is the love of something. And this is something we all agree on: entertainment. From the boss right down to the last messenger ..." None of Ullstein's publications reflected this philosophy to the same extent as the *BIZ* and no daily newspaper or journal reached its circulation figures. There can be no doubt that this mass entertainment medium was not engaged in the fight against those of a different political persuasion. However, neither did it contravene the liberal

democratic ethos of the company which, unsurprisingly also had interests in the film industry. The opposite was true of Ullstein's daily newspapers and journals: the political fight was their preserve. Thus, for example, the partial journalism that was typical of the Weimar period was definitely a feature of Ullstein's *Vossische Zeitung* newspaper and the journal *Querschnitt*.

From its launch in 1923, the *MIP* was intended to compete with the big Berlin magazines published by Ullstein. It ran into severe financial difficulties at the beginning which were instantly resolved when its publisher, Knorr & Hirth, teamed up with the Hugenberg conglomerate and Rhenish–Westphalian heavy industry. Historians now refer to this media consortium, which was built up from 1914 by former Krupp director and subsequent leader of the German National People's Party (*Deutschnationale Volkspartei – DNVP*), Alfred Hugenberg, with profits from heavy industry, as the "first modern multi-media concern" in Germany. The Weimar Republic's second biggest news agency, the Telegraph Union, and a company which provided Germany's provincial general gazette press with pre-printed reports and commentaries, were also part of this concern, whose ideological orientation was nationalistic and anti-democratic. It also included the Scherl-Bilderdienst picture agency, newspaper libraries, and newspaper consultancies. In this way, the concern controlled German opinion in the regions outside Berlin without actually being active in publishing.

In 1927, Hugenberg added the financially vulnerable Universum Film AG (UFA) film production company to the consortium and hence gained control of the Weimar Republic's most important supplier of weekly newsreels and feature films. He also owned the Scherl-Verlag publishing house in Berlin, publisher of the influential *Berliner Lokalanzeiger*, which up to November 1918 was the only newspaper which could be presented uncensored to Kaiser Wilhelm II by his press officers. The Berlin magazine *Die Woche*, which was also published by Scherl, was very successful up to the mid-1920s and had a circulation of up to 320,000. However, it lost ground with the rise of the more modern *BIZ* and *MIP*.

Newspaper readers – Photo essay
The large format is no obstacle to the enthusiastic newspaper reader. He carelessly unfolds his favorite paper in the hustle and bustle of the tram, to the horror of those who stand within reach. (Original caption)

"Pressa," the international press exhibition, took place in Cologne from May to October 1928, and attracted 1,050 German and 450 foreign exhibitors. The exhibition on the Rhine, with contributions covering the world, offered visitors a historical overview of the press from beginnings of news reporting to the great diversity of press products of the 1920s.

Hugenberg's Empire

There can be no doubt about the political leanings of media owner Alfred Hugenberg. His career in the Reichstag as a DNVP representative and subsequent initiator of the Harzburg Front speak for themselves. However, the Hugenberg concern's many publications resist such easy classification. In political terms, for example, the *MIP* falls well within the above-described framework. An example is Felix H. Man's contribution on Mussolini, which was published in 1931. The front page promised that "This essay does not present the dictator as we are used to seeing him but focuses on the creative man – the mentor of the fascist revolution." (*MIP*, 1 March 1931)

Photo-journalist Tim Gidal complained that he was unable to sell any more photo essays to *MIP* editor Stefan Lorant after 1932 due to the latter's rigidly chauvinistic Bavarian editorial line. Despite this, however, the *MIP* should be classified as one of the more politically neutral of the concern's major sources of profit, as not every publication reflected the reactionary spirit of Alfred Hugenberg.

The Red Hugenberg

The third biggest player in the publishing industry was the conglomerate established in Berlin by Communist Willy Münzenberg, which united book publishers, newspapers, journals, and the film industry under one roof. Münzenberg was denounced by contemporary dogmatic KPD members as "The Red Hugenberg." Under his management, the

Arbeiter-Illustrierte-Zeitung reached a circulation of almost 500,000 copies in 1930. "The *AIZ* differs fundamentally from all other illustrated newspapers. It is completely aimed at the life and the struggle of workers and all other employed classes." (Kurt Koszyk)

The key to the concern's social success was Münzenberg's undogmatic approach. He was not afraid to include the middle-class tabloids in his empire. He saw all these activities as the means to the end of extended revolutionary agitation. His film newsreel which was distributed from 1930 was a political counterpart to the UFA productions that adopted an increasingly nationalistic tenor under Hugenberg's influence. Münzenberg recognized the importance of good images: "an illustrated book is easier to read and buy and an illustrated newspaper is a more entertaining read than the leading article in a political daily newspaper. The photography attracts the human eye, the events are played over in the mind with no need for complicated reflection."

The NSDAP Press

The extreme right wing had its *Illustrierte Beobachter*, which was founded by the National Socialists in 1925 and started out with a modest circulation. After the electoral successes of the

The strangest printing press in the world – Photo essay
Above: *Three generations at work in the Glückstadt printing press.*
Below: *'We print in all languages here.' 300 years of German book printing in Glückstadt on the Elbe. Setting an Arabic catalogue.* (Original captions)

The modern production methods of leading London newspapers. Behind the scenes in the famous Fleet Street – the center of the universe. A machine operator inserts a printing plate. We can see why the plate is produced in semi-cylindrical form. A scene from the offices of the Daily Express. *(Original caption)*

NSDAP (National Socialist German Workers' Party [Nazis]) from 1930 to 1933, the *IB* reached a circulation in excess of 300,000 while the circulation of all the Nazi dailies increased to approximately 3.2 million. The party magazines were dominated by photographs by Heinrich Hoffmann, who initially also acted as editor-in-chief. In terms of layout and design, the *IB* faithfully reflected the standards set by the other magazines.

The photomontages in which Hitler featured regularly, surrounded by his crowds of supporters, were a conspicuous feature of the *IB*. Heinrich Hoffmann later became Hitler's "court photographer" and his archive provides detailed documentation of the rise and fall of the man who in Hoffmann's opinion was the "greatest leader of all time."

Just a few weeks after Adolf Hitler, the leader of the NSDAP, was legally appointed Chancellor of the Weimar Republic by Reich President Paul von Hindenburg in 1933, his propaganda minister, Joseph Goebbels, announced: "... We [do not] wish to suppress the creation of trivial amusement, the daily requirement needed to satisfy boredom and sadness. Opinions do not have to be formed 24 hours per day." Goebbels had learned his lessons about the mass media during the Weimar period. The close association of propaganda and entertainment was characteristic of the period that followed the introduction of censorship, but the political orientation of the entertainment was not immediately obvious. This was a phenomenon that was already well established in the Weimar period.

I flew with Udet – Photo essay
Photographer Willi Ruge accompanied Ernst Udet, who shot down a total of 62 enemy aircraft as a fighter pilot in the First World War, on an exhibition flight in the Weimar period. At a time when the German army was radically restricted in terms of personnel and weapons under the Treaty of Versailles, fighter pilots like Udet found a new occupation at the highly popular air shows.

I flew with Udet – Photo essay (continued)

Ruge's photo essay is a classical example of early photo-journalism. Here the photographer makes himself and his camera the topic of his work and thus emphasizes the subjectivity of his photographs. In this way, Ruge expressed not merely a new perspective but the whole new self-image of the "photographer" as a professional.

Willi Ruge described this flight with Udet in his own words in the text that originally accompanied the photos: "I flew with Udet! First, I had a look at things from below – it all began very well, the start was faultless ... then he hit the rudder and I felt a bit queasy ... now we're flying over the city – he sets the twist ... an air pocket pushes us down to 65 feet ... that was all nothing because he now starts to spin ... and with the feeling that the earth is suddenly circling us, we plunge to the depths ... still quite shocked, I see the master standing in front of me, he is not at all bothered, but my wish to take part in an exhibition flight has now been fulfilled for a long time to come."

I WAS RED
IN NOVEMBER

In November 1918, the revolutionary movement spread like wildfire from Kiel through the entire German Reich and encountered little or no resistance from the military and police forces of the old regime. The declaration of the Republic marked the beginning of the dispute as to whether a parliamentary democracy or a republic of workers' and soldiers' councils (*Räterepublik*) should be established in Germany. The fight came to a temporary and bloody climax at the end of January 1919, the scale and brutality of which are merely suggested in this photograph and its original caption: "The Berlin street fights. Alexanderplatz closed off and lined with armored cars." In 1922, Bertolt Brecht summarized the bitterness felt by the radical left whose revolution was quashed by the German army and *Freikorps* (volunteer corps) at the behest of the Social Democratic Party (SPD) as follows: "My brothers are dead /And I hang by a thread/I was red in November /but it's January now."

2

In the Hands of the Generals

During the final two years of the First World War, Germany was under the influence of the Supreme Army Command, headed by Generals Paul von Hindenburg and Erich Ludendorff. Kaiser Wilhelm II had been reduced to a mere representative figure and the truth about the progress of the war was initially withheld from Chancellor von Bethmann Hollweg. The political parties in the Reichstag behaved as though their hands were tied. The military–political power of the Hindenburg–Ludendorff duo was based on the myth of the "Battle of Tannenberg," during which the Russian army had been defeated in East Prussia under Hindenburg and Ludendorff's Supreme Command at the beginning of the war. Hindenburg, a native of East Prussia, was an aristocratic military man of the old school and was called back into service at the age of 67. In the period that followed, he assumed the role of a father figure for the German people and his statues graced the squares in many German towns, placed there as an incentive to donate money to the war effort. His portrait could also be found in the windows of patriotic corner shops and was a symbol of security and trust for the German people. General Erich Ludendorff, an impatient and unpredictable middle-class "strong man" and authoritarian soldier, was also active behind the scenes of power. He was in favor of full mobilization and total war. He later explained that his outlook on life was based on the belief that politics is war whereas peace is the illusion of weak civilians.

War-weariness was widespread in Germany by the spring of 1917. The civilian population had suffered severe hardship during the third winter of the War. But the wheels of the war machine continued to revolve relentlessly, claiming more and more victims. And despite the promises of the Supreme Army Command, there was no hope of victory. Rumors of an imminent invasion by the USA abounded. Political debate in the German Reich was also inflamed by the events of the Russian "February Revolution," which ended in March 1917 with the abdication of Czar Nicholas II.

The Truce Disintegrates

By July 1917, the basis for the approval of applications for new war loans by the Reichstag had changed significantly. Under

Hindenburg (left) and Ludendorff inform Wilhelm II (center) about the war situation.

the terms of the "truce" of 1914, the political parties, including the SPD, had sworn themselves to silence on political and social matters during the War. On 4 August 1914, all of the members of the Reichstag deemed it their patriotic duty to approve the financing of the War: they acted in the belief that Germany was engaged in a war of defense. By 1917, however, the Social Democrats, Catholic Center and liberal left had begun to turn against the ruling doctrine of war. The parties were also demanding the establishment of a parliamentary government constitution, by which the Reich Chancellor would be answerable not only to the Emperor but also to parliament, i.e. the Reichstag. Matthias Erzberger, a left-of-center politician who had hitherto staunchly defended the German war of annexation, was the first to express publicly his opposition to the government and Supreme Army Command.

The Peace Resolution of Summer 1917

On 6 July 1917, Erzberger presented a peace resolution to the Reichstag with the demand that the government publicly distance itself from its plans of annexation and work to achieve negotiated peace before the country was bled completely dry. The Reichstag majority, consisting of Social Democrats, Catholic Center, and liberal left unanimously supported this peace initiative. This marked the laying of

the foundations for the first German democracy, while the First World War was still in full swing, by the parties which would later form the Weimar Coalition.

The Supreme Army Command was unimpressed. Ludendorff mobilized Reichstag opposition against the political leadership. In 1917, Chancellor von Bethmann Hollweg and his hitherto unknown successor Georg Michaelis, the former Prussian state commissioner for food supply, were torn between parliament's demands for peace and Ludendorff's determination to continue fighting. The Supreme Army Command finally gave up its power game on 1 November 1917, when Georg von Hertling was appointed as the new Chancellor. Von Hertling, a 74-year-old half-blind professor of philosophy and former Prime Minister of Bavaria, was in no way equipped to deal with the military–political in-fighting. The war continued in pursuit of the same unrealistic aim, i.e. to subject Europe to German hegemony.

The SPD Split

In 1917, the Social Democratic Party (SPD) also split over the question as to whether or not further war loans should be approved for the government. The "Majority Social Democrats," as members and supporters of the SPD became known from this point, were willing to support loans for the continuation of a defensive war if the annexation plans were dropped. The opposing minority was completely opposed to further loans under any circumstances and eventually split from the mother party to form the "Independent SPD" ("Unabhängige SPD" [USPD]). The new party was a veritable magnet for myriad ideologies which discussed the future of socialism in the German Reich under the influence of the Russian October Revolution. Theorists like Karl Kautsky, who wanted to reconcile the dictatorship of the proletariat with democracy, succeeded in creating consensus among the majority in the party. The Spartacus League, a radical wing led by Karl Liebknecht and Rosa Luxemburg, continued to work for the dictatorship of the proletariat and the fundamental socialist restructuring of German society.

The Army on the Losing Side

There can be no doubt that Ludendorff was fully aware of the serious internal political situation; however, the Supreme Army Command continued to spread its optimistic faith in victory, and he was rewarded with a surge in credibility when the peace agreement with Russia was reached in March 1918. Although Ludendorff knew that the supply situation on the domestic front was catastrophic and morale among the soldiers fighting the positional war on the western front was falling, he put all his eggs in one basket. This last major offensive in the west during the last week of March 1918 finally proved, however, that the German troops on the front had been bled completely dry. In August, the Allies' counterattack imposed severe defeat on the German lines. The German army was in constant retreat after the Battle of Amiens on 8 August 1918.

The alliance of the Central Powers fell apart. On 5 September, Austrian colleagues in Vienna told German Foreign Minister von Hintze "It's over for us!" Austria–Hungary made tentative moves towards peace. Turkey could no longer be relied on for support. Bulgaria signed a ceasefire on 28 September.

The Supreme Army Command allowed no suggestion of doubt about the victory of the German army to creep into its statements until well into September 1918. Thus, civilians and parliamentarians were all the more surprised when the propaganda was finally exposed for what it was. On 29 September, Ludendorff and Hindenburg presented themselves to Wilhelm II in Spa and left the astonished Kaiser and his Chancellor in no doubt that the war was lost: they requested that an attempt be made immediately to establish a ceasefire on the basis of US President Wilson's 14-point plan.

Preparation for the Stab in the Back

The Supreme Army Command indirectly forced the majority parties in the Reichstag to share responsibility for defeat by forcing democratization and allowing the formation of a parliamentary government. This move by Ludendorff, who suffered a nervous breakdown on the same day, was the last resort of a despairing general staff trying to save face and to shift the blame for military defeat onto politics and parliament. Moreover, democratization was one of the Allies' non-negotiable preconditions for their participation in negotiations.

Ludendorff laid the groundwork for the legend of the "stab in the back" as early as 1 October when he made the following statement to the generals of the Supreme Army Command:

"I have requested H.M. (his majesty) to now bring to the government those circles, which are mainly responsible for the fact that we have reached the position we are now in. Thus, we will see these men move into the ministries. They will agree the peace deal which has to be agreed now. They should lie in the bed they have made for us."

This suggestion amounted to the imposition of 14-year sentence on the democratic spirits conjured up by the commander-in-chief. The anti-parliamentary right in the Weimar Republic never tired of repeating that the peace parties of 1917 alone were responsible for the ceasefire and the "shameful peace" of Versailles; because of this, sang the anti-parliamentary song, they had stabbed the German army in the back.

On the Way to Democracy

At Ludendorff's behest, on 4 October the Social Democrats, Catholic Center (*Zentrum*) and German Democratic Party (*Deutsche Demokratische Partei – DDP*) moved into government. The three parties assumed power without agreeing a candidate of their own for the office of Reich Chancellor. Prince Max von Baden, who was not a member of any party, was appointed Chancellor. A request for a ceasefire had already been sent to President Wilson on the previous day. However, the Supreme Army Command had ordered the army to continue fighting without the knowledge of the Kaiser and the Chancellor – an act that bordered on a coup d'état. During a meeting with Wilhelm II, Ludendorff resigned and fled immediately to exile in Sweden. On 28 October the necessary changes were made to the constitution of the German Reich and with a few strokes of the pen Germany became an imperial democracy.

"Don't shoot comrade!" This photograph of a German soldier being taken prisoner was taken from an Allied tank south of Soissons in autumn 1918.

Street scene from the days of the November Revolution 1918.

(Original caption)

THE ABDICATION OF THE KAISER

Revolution Breaks Out

During the ceasefire negotiations, on 29 October 1918 the German fleet on the high seas received an order to set sail and attack the British fleet. The sailors in the ports of Wilhelmshaven and Kiel mutinied against this order, which was doomed to fail. In contrast to the mutinies that had taken place a year earlier in Kronstadt and St. Petersburg during the October Revolution in Russia, naval officers were not attacked. The revolt was short-lived in Wilhelmshaven but Kiel remained in the hands of the rebel sailors, who had been joined by the shipyard workers. On 6 November workers' and soldiers' councils (*Räte*) seized power in five other coastal towns but things were still quiet in Berlin.

On 7 November, mutiny and unrest in Bavaria turned into a full-scale revolt. The first German throne to fall was that of Wittelsbach dynasty. In Munich, Independent Social Democrat Kurt Eisner declared Bavaria as Germany's first socialist republic. The authoritarian monarchist state fell within a few days without any opposition worth mentioning, and the revolutionary workers and soldiers made little use of their guns. People of all social classes throughout the Reich seemed to be united in their desire for three things: peace, democracy, and the abdication of the Kaiser. Wilhelm II vacillated to the bitter end but on 9 November Max von Baden took it upon himself to announce the

Kaiser's abdication and appointed the SPD party leader, Friedrich Ebert, as Reich Chancellor. The Kaiser went into to exile in Holland, a move which many interpreted as flight. Shortly after this, all of the remaining German princes also abdicated. The revolution had run its course with no action taken by the SPD. Ebert and many of his party colleagues saw the establishment of peace as their main civil duty and the Majority Social Democrats' main priority was to avoid a "Russian situation" with economic and political chaos followed by the outbreak of civil war. However, the SPD's visions of social utopia would increasingly come into conflict with their role as parliamentarians.

NOVEMBER 1918

Power to the Councils!

On 9 November 1918 the leader of the Social Democratic Party, Philipp Scheidemann, declared the "German Republic" from a window of the Reichstag building to an enormous crowd which had assembled around the Bismarck monument. Scheidemann did this without consulting Friedrich Ebert, as he knew that the masses could no longer be restrained and were looking for a symbolic break with the old system.

A few hours later, Karl Liebknecht proclaimed "the Free Socialist Republic of Germany" to a jubilant crowd from a balcony of the City Palace. Later that day, Ebert formed a temporary government, the "Council of People's Representatives" (*Rat der Volksbeauftragten*), with three Majority Social Democrats and three Independent Social Democrats.

The Berlin Workers' and Soldiers' Council ratified Ebert's government on 10 November, despite protests from Liebknecht and members of his party. On 11 November, a German delegation headed by Matthias Erzberger signed the ceasefire in Compiègne in the name of the new executive. This marked the official end of the First World War. One of the most bloodless revolutions in history had also taken its course. The event that triggered Germany's November Revolution was the mutiny of the sailors in Wilhelmshaven and Kiel and the soldiers in the local garrisons. The soldiers and workers joined forces in councils which were suddenly established in large numbers throughout the German Reich. But there was no great popular rising. The rest of the German population went about its daily business while the revolution was driven along by the soldiers, sailors, and councils. There was never any question of the mobilization of the masses for the Revolution.

After 9 November 1918, most of the workers' and soldiers' councils did not see themselves as an alternative to a freely elected parliament. The vast majority of them did not identify with the Russian "soviets" and were happy to pursue the conciliatory course of Majority Social Democracy. The aim of this "Black-Red-Gold Revolution," which attempted to represent the legacy of the failed bourgeois revolution of 1848 (whose banner colors had been black, red and gold), was the establishment of a democratic state with the retention of capitalist structures.

In contrast, the supporters of the "Red Revolution" basically rejected parliamentarianism and looked to Russia's October Revolution as their model. They called for the radical overhaul of the political, economic, and social structures, if necessary by means of an armed struggle.

The Kaiser's last journey? The Kaiser on his way into Exile. Wilhelm II (center) at the Dutch border station Rijsden on 9 November 1918. (Original caption)

The SPD's Alliance with the Army

The Coalition Collapses

All in all, the black-red-gold camp seemed to have gained the upper hand in the first weeks of November 1918. However, the new Republic's starting position was weak. Agitation by supporters of the "Red Revolution," for example the Spartacus League, awakened fears of Bolshevist uprisings and civil war in wide sectors of the population. Surprisingly, the bourgeoisie had simply allowed the revolution to happen without making any effort to mobilize the remains of the totalitarian state, army, and administration. Loyalty to the old authorities was simply withdrawn.

But what would happen if the workers' and soldiers' councils actually succeeded in seizing power and establishing a socialist party dictatorship? These may have been the questions uppermost in the Chancellor's mind when Ludendorff's successor in the Supreme Army Command telephoned him at the Reich Chancellery late on the evening of 10 November. General Groener offered Ebert an alliance: the Supreme Army Command would supervise the repatriation of the army and consolidate the new government's position. For his part, Ebert guaranteed government support for the authority of the officers and promised to suppress the soldiers' councils as far as possible. This alliance sealed the common destiny of two basically unequal partners. Defeat in the War gave the military the opportunity to reorganize without having to take political control and at the same time lay the foundation stone for the "state within

a state" later to be established. This agreement enabled the SPD to validate its claim to power in Berlin and the rest of the empire with the help of the old army and voluntary units.

The "Council of People's Representatives" did not pass a law for the formation of a voluntary army until 6 December and, even when passed, it was nothing more than a piece of paper. Although the government recognized the need to establish a republican defense force, the deep ideological split between the Majority SPD and Independent SPD and the basically pacifist mood among the supporters of both parties prevented the implementation of this law. On that same day, however, a demonstration by rebellious armed units in Berlin gave a worrying glimpse of just what counter-revolution would be like. Shooting took place in the working-class neighborhood of Wedding after a meeting of marauding army soldiers in front of the Reich Chancellery and their putsch-like action against the Berlin Executive Council (*Vollzugsrat*), which was the temporary committee for all of the councils. However, Ebert chose to pursue the path of alliance with the Supreme Army Command he had already embarked on. On 10 December, ten divisions of the Guards arrived in Berlin on their return from the War. This demonstration of power by the defeated military had been agreed with Ebert and on the following day he greeted the soldiers with the following words, with their echoes of Ludendorff's stab-in-the-back legend: "No enemy overcame you."

The revolutionary councils responded to Ebert's "security policy" with heavy protests. They failed, however, to hinder the success of the SPD at the First General Congress of the Workers' and Soldiers' Councils, which was held from 16 to 21 December in Berlin. The solid Social Democratic majority ensured that the most important issues were already resolved before the congress even started: the elections to the constituent national assembly were to be held at an early stage on 19 January to curb the revolutionary forces. The supporters of a "pure council system" were denied any opportunity of making their presence felt. The SPD emerged victorious from most of the debates. The vote for the central council, which would appoint and supervise the future government members, went against the Independent SPD representatives. The radical left wing of the party boycotted the vote and thus denied their representatives in the government a working base.

The internal rift within the Independent SPD was a great problem for the government coalition with the SPD, which had been established on 10 November. It was the "Berlin Christmas Fighting," however, that represented the last straw and resulted in the Independent SPD's complete withdrawal of cooperation. This armed conflict was started by the marine division (*Volksmarinedivision*), which was appointed to defend the Reich Chancellery during the second half of November. In the course of December, the marines became more radical in their attitude to the government and they occupied the Berlin City Palace for over two weeks. The "Council of People's Representatives" demanded that the palace be evacuated, but the marines insisted on getting their outstanding pay. On 23 December, the rebel marines imprisoned the government and took the Mayor of Berlin, Social Democrat Otto Wels, hostage. On Christmas Eve, the "Lequis Commando" advanced with artillery against the marines in the City Palace and Royal Stables; however, they refused to obey orders to storm the palace. That same morning a large crowd assembled at

The arrival of the Guards in Berlin on 10 December 1918. The troops move through the enormous crowd of people at the Brandenburg Gate.

the scene of the fight and sided with the marines. The action ended with a defeat for the military and the "Council of People's Representatives," which was forced to allow the marine division to continue to exist in undiminished form. The Independent Social Democrats resigned from the government in protest against the military action. Moreover, the Prussian Prime Minister, Social Democrat Paul Hirsch, dismissed the Berlin Police Chief, Emil Eichhorn, who was on the left wing of the Independent SPD, on 4 January, as Eichhorn had rushed to the aid of the marine division with the Berlin security force, thereby facilitating the insurgents' victory. The leadership of the Independent SPD decided to hold a demonstration in protest against Eichhorn's dismissal on the evening of 4 January with the support of radical working-class forces in Berlin. The German Communist Party (KPD), which had been founded in late December (and in which the Spartacus League played a leading role), did not take an active part in all this. Despite this, the events of the following days became known historically – but incorrectly – as the "Spartacus Revolt."

Down with the Government!

On 5 January, an enormous crowd gathered along the Siegesallee avenue in the Tiergarten park and marched through the Brandenburg Gate to Alexanderplatz, where Eichhorn made a speech from the balcony of the police headquarters. Whilst the strike leaders were holding talks there, armed demonstrators occupied the newspaper quarter where the Social Democratic party organ *Vorwärts* and the major publishing houses Mosse, Scherl, and Ullstein were based. When the leader of the marine division also indicated that the troops stationed in Berlin supported the uprising – a statement which was shortly afterwards revealed as false – the majority of the assembly voted to continue with the occupation of the publishing houses, call a general strike, and oppose the Ebert–Scheidemann government until it finally collapsed.

The next day even larger crowds gathered on the Siegesallee, but it also emerged that the majority of the workers were not prepared to take up arms against Ebert and his government. The militant wing of the KPD and the Independent SPD were quite isolated: the putsch was based on a few thousand activists who had barricaded themselves into the police headquarters and the newspaper quarter. The majority of Berlin workers distanced themselves from the fighting; they were "Majority" Socialists and government supporters.

Ebert and his government colleagues were taken by surprise by the dramatic events that unfolded around the police headquarters. Gustav Noske – the SPD's former naval expert in the Reichstag who had been appointed to the government at New Year – assumed responsibility for the suppression of the revolt. He mobilized troops from the city garrisons, armed workers who supported the government, and brought in volunteer corps (*Freikorps*) led by officers of the former imperial army. With the support of the regular troops, the *Freikorps* instigated a blood bath among the rebels. Most of the rebel leaders were able to flee Berlin, but Karl Liebknecht and Rosa Luxemburg, who had reservations about armed action and had remained in the city, were taken prisoner and murdered by the *Freikorps* on 15 January.

The putsch failed to achieve its aim of preventing the elections to the constituent national assembly and establishing a "dictatorship of the proletariat" in Germany. The constituent assembly was elected by the citizens of the German Republic on 19 January 1919. All those aged 20 and over were entitled to vote and women were also allowed to vote for the first time. The Social Democrats, Catholic Center, and DDP – i.e. the peace coalition of 1917 – were elected with a resounding three-quarters majority.

After the fighting in the newspaper quarter. The headquarters of the Social Democratic newspaper Vorwärts *was occupied by Communists and fired at by the government artillery as a counter move.* (Original caption)

"The day of revolution has come [...] In this hour, we proclaim the Free Socialist Republic of Germany [...] We must now make every effort to build up the government of workers and soldiers and create a new state order of the proletariat, an order of peace, happiness, and freedom for our German brothers, and our brothers throughout the world. We shake hands with you and call upon you to bring about the culmination of the World Revolution."

From Karl Liebknecht's address to the crowd assembled in front of the Berlin City Palace on 9 November 1918

"If the Kaiser does not abdicate, social revolution is unavoidable. But I do not want that, there is nothing I would detest more."

Friedrich Ebert to Max von Baden on 7 November 1918

The Kaiser on the trash heap of history. Photograph taken in Cologne in November 1918.

Left: *People's Representative Friedrich Ebert raises three cheers for the troops arriving in Berlin from the front on 10 December 1918 at the Brandenburg Gate.*
Above: *Revolutionary soldiers and workers march past the Royal Stables in Berlin. November 1918*   *(Original captions)*

In his address "To the German Citizens" of 9 November, the new Reich Chancellor Ebert made the following appeal "Fellow citizens! I bet you: leave the streets! Ensure peace and order!" Revolutionary workers and soldiers were not impressed by this appeal. Ebert saw the returning troops, whose arrival was organized by the re-appointed Supreme Army Council, as a potential source of order.

"Comrades, welcome to the German Republic, welcome back to your home, which has been longing for your return and was constantly concerned for your safety [...] You will not find our country as you left it. New things are happening, German freedom has been created. The German people have shaken off the reins of the old system, which lay heavy on our actions like an evil curse, and have made themselves masters of their own destiny. The hope of German freedom rests first and foremost on you. You are the strongest bearers of the German future [...] We cannot greet you with lavish gifts, comfort, and prosperity; our unhappy country is now poor. The pressure of the victors' stringent requirements is a heavy burden. But we are going to build a new Germany from the ruins."
Friedrich Ebert appeals to the troops returning from the First World War on 10 December 1918

On 24 December the soldiers of the Reichswehr (army) advanced against the insurgent marine division. As a protest against this military attack, the members of the Independent SPD resigned from the "Council of People's Representatives" which was then completely controlled by the Majority SPD.

Above: *Scene from the fighting between the government troops and rebel marines in the Royal Stables and City Palace over Christmas 1918.*
Right: *The 'Council of People's Representatives' at New Year 1918/1919. From the left: Otto Landsberg, Philipp Scheidemann, Gustav Noske, Friedrich Ebert, Rudolf Wissel.* (Original captions)

Above: Rebel marines in the Royal Stables escort the
funeral cortege of their seven comrades who died in the
fighting against government troops on Christmas Eve.
(Original caption)

Left page: *Wilhelm Pieck (KPD) raises three cheers for the revolution on the Siegesallee in Berlin in January.*
Above: *Members of the Spartacus League take cover behind newspaper barricades during fighting in the Berlin newspaper quarter in January 1919.*   (Original captions)

"Workers, Party Comrades!
The Ebert government wants to consolidate its power and ensure the support of the capitalist bourgeoisie, whose unacknowledged representative this government has been from the outset, with the help of the bayonet and its accomplices inthe Prussian Ministry [...]
Party comrades! You cannot, you must not tolerate this! Go out and join the powerful mass demonstrations! [...] Down with the tyranny of Ebert, Scheidemann, Hirsch, and Ernst. Long live international revolutionary socialism!"
Appeal for support by the KPD Spartacus League and the Independent SPD on 5 January 1919

"The Spartacus movement only won small individual victories and did not even have control of Berlin the following morning [Monday 6 January]. During the night, the crowds of workers who had remained loyal to the Majority Social Democracy were alerted, and in the early hours of the morning they marched out of their places of work and descended on Wilhelmstrasse in endless rows from all directions, and physically blocked all of the neighboring access roads, the entire area around the Reich Chancellery [...].
Noske drove around the city recruiting volunteers and showed the extraordinary lack of insight into human nature and vision with which he later facilitated the Kapp Putsch and handed the Republic over to the hands of its enemies."
Theodor Wolff, Der Marsch durch zwei Jahrzehnte, 1936

Above: *Berlin street fights in January 1919. Barricade on Blumenstrasse. A resident of the street returns to her apartment.*
Right: *Troops armed with machine guns during the street fights in Berlin, January 1919.*
Right page: *The government artillery in position. Berlin, January 1919.* (Original captions)

"Workers! Citizens!"
The Fatherland is approaching its downfall.
The threat comes not from outside but from within!
FROM THE SPARTACUS LEAGUE.
KILL ITS LEADERS!
KILL LIEBKNECHT!
Then you will have peace, work, and bread!

The Front Soldiers"

Appeal in Berlin on 1 January 1919

"Our people on the street were calling for weapons.
They were quite excited as time was of the essence
and we were standing around in Ebert's office. I
demanded that a decision be taken. Then someone
said: 'Then go ahead and do it yourself!' To which I
spontaneously replied: 'If you like! Someone will have
to be the bloodhound and I do not shrink from the
responsibility!' Reinhard said that he had been hoping
for this suggestion. An oral resolution was formulated
stating that the government and Central Council
invested total authority in me for the purpose of
restoring order to Berlin."

*Gustav Noske's report of his appointment as Commander in
chief of the troops in Berlin on 6 January 1919*

"This appeal is being made to all those who heroically
protected the German homeland for four years. Please
help now to resolve this extreme crisis. Join the
voluntary groups which the government has set up for
the protection of the borders and maintenance of
safety and order within the borders. [...] The Central
Council of the German Socialist Republic, signed
Cohen. Commander-in-chief of the Government troops
in Berlin, signed Noske."

*Government appeal for formation of voluntary corps
after 6 January 1919*

Above: *Socialist leader Karl Liebknecht making a speech on the Siegesallee in Berlin in December 1918.*
Right: *View from the Reichstag to the Siegessäule (victory column). January 1919.*
Next pages: *A government soldier in the Mosse publishing house, which had been occupied and then surrendered by the Spartacists during the January fighting.*
(Original captions)

"Yes! The revolutionary workers of Berlin were defeated! Almost a hundred of their best were butchered. But there are defeats which are really victories and victories that are more fatal than defeats. The defeated of those bloody weeks in January, they passed with distinction, they fought for great things, the most precious aim of suffering humanity [...] Spartacus – this means fire and spirit, heart and soul, it means the will and act of the revolution of the proletariat [...] Spartacus means socialism and world revolution [...] And whether we still live when it has been achieved – our vision will live on. It will rule the world of liberated humanity. Despite everything!"
"Trotz alledem!" – Karl Liebknecht's last article in the Rote Fahne *journal of 15 January 1919*

The Siegessäule (victory column) was designed by Johann Heinrich Strack in 1864 for the square in front of the Reichstag, and the figure of Victory by Friedrich Drake was added in 1873. It was erected as a memorial to Prussia's victories against Denmark, Austria, and France. In 1938/39, the Siegessäule was moved to the center of the Grosser Stern intersection in the Tiegarten park as part of the "Redesign of the Reich Capital of Germania." As can be seen in this photograph, it still stood on the Platz der Republik in front of the Reichstag during the Weimar period.

"It suddenly became noisy again in the prison. We heard the striking of rifle butts and kicking on the cell doors and cries. A soldier then came to our cell door, kicked it a few times with his boot and shouted: 'Liebknecht and Rosa killed!'"
From the autobiography of Spartacist Karl Retzlaw, who was taken prisoner on 11 January 1919 by government troops in the occupied editorial offices of Vorwärts

GERMANY,
GERMANY...

In the period between the January uprising of 1919 and Hitler's putsch in 1923, there developed strongly opposing political ideas about what "Germany" was, and left-wing coup attempts alternated with plots from the right. The Republic threatened to disintegrate into civil war and social misery. Despite the country's isolation in the diplomatic arena there were many private aid initiatives from abroad. "Reich President Ebert (left) takes tea with American Quakers in 1924 as an expression of thanks for helping Germany's children" ran the original caption for this picture. Within Germany itself, however, this Social Democratic president was considered either a "November criminal" or a "class traitor." He failed in his attempt to steer the "spirit of Weimar" on a democratic course, and even the choice of the national anthem in 1922 – "Deutschland, Deutschland, über alles" – did not have the desired effect. Seven years later German author Kurt Tucholsky wrote mockingly of "... that line from a truly awful poem which a crazy Republic chose to be its national anthem."

3

The Spirit of Weimar

In 1919 Germany continued to be put to the political test; the crushing of the "January rebellion" in that year meant that the "black-red-and-gold revolution" had gained a tenuous victory over the "reds." The bloody actions of the volunteer corps (*Freikorps*) not only opened up deep divisions in the working classes; it radicalized the political climate throughout the Reich. The future core of the "counter-revolution," these troops – recruited from the *Freikorps* and army by the Social Democrats Ebert and Noske – had now achieved their first victory on the home front after a humiliating defeat in the war. The domestic political situation was not nearly as stable and unambiguous as the overwhelming vote for the parties of the Weimar coalition might have indicated. Having gained a total of three-quarters of the vote, the SPD (37.9%), Center (19.7%) and DDP (18.5%) began to build the foundations for the first ever democracy in Germany on a new constitution. The views of the extra-parliamentary and anti-democratic forces clashed with the political aims of the government. In the first half of 1919, the struggle over whether the country should have a "parliamentary Republic or a democracy of workers' and soldiers' councils" escalated. The democratically elected government sent in the *Freikorps* to break up strikes and end armed unrest and worker council experiments; in so doing they strengthened the position of the Republic's enemies.

Germany's first democracy was greatly handicapped by its foreign policy: the severity of the peace terms imposed by the Allies in November 1918 was historically unprecedented. At the beginning of 1919 the Reich still hovered on the brink of war. Until far into the spring Scheidemann's government was hopeful but uncertain about what peace would bring: but the results of the negotiations at Versailles were to exceed the worst fears of the skeptics.

Flight into the Provinces

The constitutional assembly was anything but autonomous when it met on 6 February 1919 in the small town of Weimar. This idyllic princely seat in Thuringia lay under a blanket of snow when the members of the assembly gathered in the National Theater in order to grant the German Republic a new constitution and so secure peace, both foreign and domestic. Situated in the middle of Germany far from troubled Berlin, Weimar seemed the ideal meeting place. In selecting this location Ebert had hoped to reinforce the idea of German unity. In his opening address he also referred to the neo-Classical traditions of Weimar – the city of poets and thinkers, of Goethe and Schiller. But by concluding his speech with quotations from Goethe's *Hermann and Dorothea* and Fichte's *Address to the German Nation* Ebert hoped to do more than inject humanist ideology into the spirit of the new Republic. These reminders of the liberalism of 1848 were also a signal to the nation's former enemies that the new German Reich had broken with the traditions of the old Empire, and now wished to turn its back on what had preceded the November Revolution. There was also a much more prosaic reason: soldiers loyal to the government were able to guarantee the security of parliamentarians in Weimar. The National Assembly conducted its business without interference and on 11 February it elected Ebert as provisional president of the Reich. Two days later, the new head of state called for a coalition government of the SPD, DDP and Center with Philipp Scheidemann (SPD) as the Reich's Prime Minister.

No Glory, No Splendor

From the outset the Weimar coalition was based on compromises reached between the majority SPD and the centrist democratic parties of the Center and the DDP, a political constellation which was quite incapable of creating an independent and self-confident political culture – let alone of sparking any euphoric sense of a new beginning. Even liberal parliamentarians lamented the lack of ceremonial pomp at the opening of the National Assembly, an act of state which seemed to many to be devoid of splendor. It took place in the hall of the National Theater, which was "decorated with flowers as if for a modest middle-class wedding reception" recalled Theodor Wolff, co-founder of the DDP and editor-in-chief of the liberal and internationally renowned *Berliner Tageblatt*. Gustav Stresemann, a conservative monarchist and founding head of the German People's Party, viewed the event with a sense of melancholy. He wrote to his wife from Weimar: "Today was the grand opening of the National Assembly – or it should have been. In my heart I still live in the old days and it pains me to see how everything has changed." Stresemann was later to transform himself into the prototype of a "pragmatic Republican" – a man who made his peace with the new State for lack of any feasible alternative. In foreign policy he took the crucial steps leading to Germany's reintegration into the international community. The anti-parliamentary right wing, on the other hand, continued to gather strength throughout 1919 in order to destroy democracy.

A snow-bedecked Weimar National Theater fronted by the monument to Schiller and Goethe. Johann Wolfgang von Goethe was director of the Weimar Theater from 1791 until 1817.

(Original caption)

The Diktat of Versailles

The harsh peace conditions imposed by the Allies came as a blow to Germany: until the very end they had placed their trust in President Wilson's "Fourteen Points," which provided for a peace treaty based on the right of all nations to self-determination; but the desire for retribution and uncompromising approach of the British leader, Lloyd George, and – especially – the French premier, Georges Clemenceau, dominated proceedings. The entire German press, regardless of their political affiliations, were outraged, and the headlines featured phrases such as "Disgraceful peace" and "Diktat of Versailles." Scheidemann, as head of both the government and one of the coalition parties – the DDP – refused to accept the peace treaty and the government resigned. After just five months of consensus politics the Weimar coalition had exhausted itself under enormous pressure from abroad. A new coalition of the SPD and Center parties headed by Social Democrat Gustav Bauer came to power. The Allies were threatening to resume military operations if the treaty was not signed. With the express approval of the National Assembly, the new Reich government dispatched foreign minister Hermann Müller (SPD) to Versailles, and the peace treaty was signed on 28 June.

Germany lost her colonies along with Alsace–Lorraine, Northern Schleswig, Posen, West Prussia and parts of Pomerania. French and British troops temporarily occupied the Rhineland. The coal fields in the Saar were granted to the French. In Germany the draft was abolished, and the new army of just 100,000 men was not permitted a navy, aircraft, heavy weapons or tanks.

The Allies demanded payment of a reparations bill of 25 trillion dollars, the final sum to be decided by a Reparations Commission. The principle of blame anchored in the final document was historically unprecedented. In order to establish moral legitimacy for the severity of their demands, the victors compelled Germany to admit sole responsibility for the outbreak of the war. It was above all this confession of war guilt that offended the honor of the entire nation. But Germany was not only politically humiliated; it was treated under separate laws, it was militarily weakened and its economy was ruined. In parliament there was no sign of the fighting spirit which had characterized the heated debates over the peace treaty. German politicians from the far left to the extreme right had but one aim – to amend the treaty. Opinions merely differed as to how this should be achieved.

The first unavoidable step was to accept a democratic constitution. Many members saw the vote on the democratic Reich constitution on 11 August 1919 as an act of force – an extension of the peace which had been imposed from the outside. The constitution was passed with 262 votes from the established parties to 75 votes from the nationalist parties, the DNVP and DVP, as well as independent left-wing members. Some 67 members of parliament demonstrated their indifference to this founding act of the state by abstaining.

Despite the overthrow of the state and the revolution of 1918, the Weimar constitution was strongly influenced by bourgeois liberalism. Germany became a federal state with unitary features which granted its citizens far-reaching civic freedoms and fundamental rights. The SPD saw to it that there was far-sighted social legislation, while the Center Party pushed through numerous bills designed to promote school reform, education and the church. Socially and politically, the constitution did not have any systematic concept at its heart. Politically, it also had all the hallmarks of a compromise – it reflected the governing alliance between the moderate sections of the workers and the democratic middle classes. Electoral laws provided for proportional representation and guaranteed voters the greatest possible choice between the various political parties. These parties always gave such priority to their ideologies in the parliamentary decision-making process that even those parties that supported the constitution constantly had to struggle to reach a viable consensus. The electoral laws also favored a large number of splinter groups, which made the formation of long-term majority coalitions difficult. The fathers of the constitution created a democratic "surrogate emperor" – the President – as a counterweight to parliament. Article 48 of the constitution granted the Reich President, who was directly elected for a term of seven years, a great deal of power. Under the terms of this article the President had the right to suspend civic rights and freedoms in case of a "national emergency." Article 48 was the Weimar constitution's answer to the dangers to which the young democracy had already been exposed in its infancy.

On 6 December 1918 the British Army marched into Cologne. Initially a force of 30,000 men, by the end of 1919 it had grown to 55,000. By 1925 the British government had reduced the number to 9,100 and on 31 January 1926 the last British soldiers finally left the city.

A soldier of the British army of occupation on the Rhine patrols along the river in Cologne.

Civil War in the German Reich

An ominous portent of "Bolshevism" occurred in Munich. After Kurt Eisner (SPD), the provisional prime minister, was murdered in the street by a monarchist army officer in February 1919, Bavaria's capital was shaken by general strikes and mass demonstrations. Two successive soviet republics were then formed in April. The "coffee house republic" of communists, anarchists and pacifists led by the writers Ernst Toller, Gustav Landauer and Erich Mühsam was followed by the more soviet-style Bavarian Republic of Workers' and Soldiers' Councils which aimed at establishing a "dictatorship of the proletariat." To protect both soviet democracies from "reactionary attempts at an overthrow" a "Red Army" was founded, which was able to resist the first military attempt of Eisner's successor, Johannes Hoffmann (SPD), to disarm the revolutionaries. The second attack ended in horror, however. On 30 April, Red Guards murdered ten hostages. The *Freikorps* – who were already marching on Munich – were sent into a frenzy at this news and, true to their radical right-wing philosophy, they exacted a terrible revenge. By the time Munich was "liberated" again on 3 May, the death toll had reached 606. Government troops had lost 38 dead; on their opponents' side it was not only "Red" soldiers and their leaders who were the victims – 335 civilians were also among those killed.

The Specter of "Jewish–Bolshevist World Revolution"

Large sections of the German population, as well as the majority of the National Assembly, were shocked that "Bolshevists" had succeeded in establishing their rule – the dictatorship of a minority – over a state capital. In Munich itself the inhabitants greeted the *Freikorps* rapturously and large numbers of people turned a blind eye to their violent excesses. Against this background a political climate developed in which hatred of Marxism and Bolshevism was organized in a united front; indeed, there was hardly another German city in which this phenomenon was manifested as strongly. These right-wing fantasies about a perceived enemy – which the contemporary philosopher and theologian Ernst Troeltsch diagnosed in 1919 as a mood

swing among the educated middle classes – also fed on strong anti-Semitic prejudices from the pre-war years. The fact that many of the leaders of the soviet republics were from Jewish families merely served to rekindle this latent anti-Semitism.

The Counter-Revolution strikes back

The months after the coup proved that the revolution had left the former Imperial power elites intact. Their initial pledges of loyalty were quickly forgotten; on the contrary, their political self-confidence grew in proportion to the hesitancy with which the Social Democrats in particular maneuvered in the political arena. Scheidemann and Ebert became the targets, so to speak, of the right-wing media, who portrayed them in a quite perfidious way as uncultured and power hungry upstarts.

Anyone who agitated against the so-called "November criminals," the "disgraceful peace of Versailles" or the "lie of German war guilt" was protected by the constitutional rights of free speech, but their aims were not just the elimination of the new European peace. The propagandists of the right-wing "counter-revolution" worked themselves into a blind nationalistic frenzy over this issue but at the same time constantly fought against democracy in their own country. Thoughtful democrats such as Matthias Erzberger, who called for moderation and rapprochement with Germany's former enemies, were labeled "traitors" and "appeasers." Allegations such as these went hand in hand with the legend of the "stab in the back," which claimed – contrary to all the facts – that blame for the nation's military defeat lay with the "revolution" and "the socialists and pacifists on the home front" who had betrayed a still undefeated army from within.

The infantry for this counter-revolution had been unleashed by the Treaty of Versailles. While the treaty allowed for an army of just 100,000 men, there were around 400,000 soldiers under arms. All the promises the government had made to veterans, who had formed themselves into the voluntary *Freikorps* and been used against the "Bolsheviks," were now without substance. Despite earlier plans to integrate these troops into the army, they were now left out on the street.

Count Arco Valley, a monarchist officer. On 21 February 1919 Valley assassinated Kurt Eisner, the Bavarian Prime Minister and Independent Socialist, on a Munich street.

The Kapp–Lüttwitz putsch

Counter-revolutionary forces had been forming since October 1919. Under the leadership of the "National Association" established by General Ludendorff, they set about making plans for a putsch and on 13 March 1920 they struck. General Lüttwitz allowed *Freikorps* units from the Baltic, carrying red, white and black Imperial flags, to march into Berlin under the command of Hermann Ehrhardt, a corvette captain. These troops proceeded to occupy government buildings. The putsch leaders set up a government headed by the Pan-Germanic nationalist Wolfgang Kapp from Königsberg as Reich Chancellor, with Lüttwitz as Defense Minister. The Bauer government had fled at the last minute to Dresden and from there to Stuttgart. They replied to the coup with a call for a general strike: "Paralysis of economic life, not a single hand may be lifted, no proletarian may aid this military dictatorship. A general strike right down the line. Proletarians unite!"

The government therefore resorted to a weapon which previously had only been used by the left-wing opposition. The general strike began on a weekend; some 12 million workers joined in and the country was soon threatened with total paralysis. The putsch's chances of success were also severely undermined by the resistance of ministerial bureaucrats in Berlin, who refused to cooperate with the new regime. The army, however, played an infamous role. The much quoted reply – "The army will not fire on the army" – which the chief of staff General von Seeckt is said to have given to a question about his loyalty from Defense Minister Noske is, in fact, highly improbable. Nevertheless, with the exception of their commander, General Reinhardt, the attitude of the general staff was unambiguous: in order not to endanger the future unity of the army and to maintain its importance as an intact element of domestic political life, the military in fact took up a neutral position.

After just two days the putsch was on the verge of collapse, and on 17 March Kapp went into exile in Sweden. This particular manifestation of right-wing conspiracies may have flexed its military muscles but its leaders had proceeded in an aimless and poorly planned manner. The general strike was by no means over once the leaders of the putsch had capitulated. The syndicalists in the Independent Social Democratic Party and the Communist Party now demanded the punishment of all those who had participated in the putsch, as well as the thorough democratization of the government's administration and the socialization of large sections of the major industries. Their undisguised aim was to replace the current SPD-dominated cabinet with a "workers' government."

Wolfgang Kapp. The putsch named after him was a coup d'état led by embittered officers and conservative estate owners.

Divisions in the Labor Movement

An ideological rift opened up in the working classes. The moderate wing was supported by the better educated and more well-off workers, and was organized in the SPD. The radical wing was still able to recruit large numbers of members, mainly from the ranks of unskilled laborers. This left-wing opposition movement still aimed at the complete political and economic overthrow of the Republic. It found the course of reform adopted by its former mother party and its coalition partners deeply offensive. This conflict was irresolvable, particularly as the ruling Social Democrats constantly resorted to the army, the disciplinary tool of the old Empire, to crush proletarian uprisings. After 1918 the SPD directed its suspicions exclusively at the left because it was from that direction that it most feared armed insurrection and coup attempts. In 1920 the general strike once again caused this "internecine socialist war," which had festered since 1917, to erupt violently and a civil war ensued which lasted several weeks. In Saxony and Thuringia armed brigades of workers attacked *Freikorps* units and army troops. In the Ruhr, a "Red Army" was formed by socialist workers of various political leanings; town halls were occupied and vehicles, livestock and foodstuffs were requisitioned.

The Battle of the Ruhr

To put an end to this "Red terror" in the Ruhr, the government called in the troops whose very commanders had so signally failed to prove their loyalty to the parliamentary executive during the Kapp–Lüttwitz putsch. The actions of the army in the Ruhr were marked by violence and brutality; the Red Army lost over 1,000, while the army suffered 208 dead and 123 missing. The "Battle of the Ruhr" was the last in a series of mass movements which had begun with wildcat strikes in the penultimate year of the war. Like all the left-wing revolts of the revolutionary era, it ended in failure and bloodshed. The insurrections of the following years – such as those of March 1921 when there were again workers' uprisings in central Germany and Hamburg which were put down by armed police – were merely Communist coup attempts and were carried out by minority groups.

End of the Majority

From the fall of 1919 the cabinet of the Weimar coalition had clearly lost confidence in the electorate's support and elections to the Reichstag were put off from month to month. The Kapp–Lüttwitz putsch and the fighting in the Ruhr showed, however, that this prevarication did not by any means lead to political consolidation. The election on 6 June 1920 led to a predictable catastrophe for the SPD, Center and DDP, who together only managed to gain 43% of the seats. The ruling coalition's majority had not been able to survive the founding years of the Republic under the pressure of the Treaty of Versailles and internal political struggles: right to the end of the Weimar Republic it was never again to win back a parliamentary majority. From this point on the only possible coalitions were with latent antidemocratic parties, or alternatively minority governments had to be formed which depended on toleration by their political opponents in parliament. Without the backing of parliament or the majority of the people, democracy and the results of the black-red-and-gold revolution were, at the very least, questionable.

Between 1919 and 1930 a total of 16 Reich governments with an average life of eight months attempted to direct the country's fortunes. In 1920 the temporary solution was known as the "citizens' block": the DVP, at heart still a deeply monarchist party, formed a cabinet together with the DDP and Center. On the other hand the SPD – the real founder of the Republic – withdrew from direct participation in national government for several years. It retained its political influence in the Reich however – until 1925 it provided the President in the person of Friedrich Ebert and, until 1932, the SPD ruled the Free State of Prussia, which accounted for three-fifths of the country's territory and more or less served as the bulwark of the Republic. The SPD's room to maneuver was however severely limited in 1922 by its union with the rump USPD party, which had broken away in 1920 over the issue of entry to the Communist Internationale (Comintern, the Moscow-dominated organization of international Communist politics). The SPD now lurched sharply to the left and this made cooperation with the moderate middle-class parties considerably more difficult.

"Appeasers": Targets of Hatred

After the elections of 1920 Germany's domestic political situation began to stabilize. Abroad, however, an ill wind was once again blowing. The implementation of the peace treaty's provisions led continually to heated conflicts with the victorious powers. The crisis reached its first serious impasse when the Reparations Commission presented its demands to Germany at the beginning of 1921: these amounted to 132 billion gold marks to be paid off at an annual interest rate of 6%. The German reaction was similar to that of May and June 1919 – outrage on all sides. To great acclaim from the press and populace at large, the government rejected these demands. Ultimately, however, there was no alternative to a "policy of appeasement"; only by acceding to these demands could Germany undermine claims – especially from its "arch-enemy" France – that it was reneging on the Treaty of Versailles. A reassessment of demands for reparations was only going to be possible if the country first attempted to pay them – and then demonstrated that this would inevitably lead to the young Republic's insolvency.

The divided German nation had no appreciation for this kind of subtle but humiliating foreign diplomacy, however. Defeat after defeat in the international arena had time and again wounded national pride; the country's mood was one of nostalgia which indulged itself in visions of past Imperial glories. From conflict

Finance minister Matthias Erzberger in front of the National Theater in Weimar during the National Assembly in February 1919.

to conflict, governments were seen by the public as weak, and this undermined the legitimacy of the Weimar Republic. This kind of social turmoil encouraged nationalistic fanatics to carry out a series of murders and political assassinations which claimed the lives of Matthias Erzberger – a signatory of the armistice and later finance minister – in 1921, and Walther Rathenau – then the German foreign minister and member of the DDP – in 1922. When Rathenau was killed, the assassin's bullets carried off not just a "political appeaser" but a representative of Jewish liberalism.

"This Enemy is on the Right"

Supporters of democracy were stunned when news of these murders broke. The Protestant newspaper *Christian World* said after Erzberger's murder: "It is outrageous how joyfully countless Protestant Christians have greeted this news. This mood has been expressed openly – on the street, on the train, in families." When news of Rathenau's death on 24 June 1922 spread, hundreds of thousands of workers left their factories and gathered under both national colors and red flags to demonstrate their grief on the streets of Berlin. Terrorist attacks on the state from the political right converted the widespread frus-

tration with the "Weimar System," felt by many people, into an outpouring of heartfelt public sympathy.

After Rathenau's murder Chancellor Josef Wirth (Center) concluded a fiery speech in the Reichstag with the words: "There is the enemy [turning to the right], who pours his poison into the wounds of our people. There is the enemy – and let there be no doubt: this enemy is on the right." This situation called for strong words and tough measures in parliament. In July the "Law for the Safeguarding of the Republic" was passed, which gave the judiciary the effective means to mete out severe sentences for lynch-law killings and to outlaw extremist organizations. But the Republic's judiciary had never made any secret of its aversion to democracy and of its sympathy with the political right. In practice, therefore, everything remained as it had been: left-wing offenders were severely punished while rightist opponents of the Republic could continue to count on receiving mild sentences. There is justification for the historical truism coined at the time and still current today: "Justice in the Weimar Republic was blind in the right eye."

In the Reichstag Reich Chancellor Joseph Wirth (Center Party) announced: "This enemy sits on the right."

The "Rathenau Oak" on the Königsallee in Berlin-Grunewald. It was here that Walther Rathenau was murdered.

Democracy is Put to the Test

On the fringes of a European conference on the post-war economic order held in Genoa in April 1922, German foreign minister Rathenau signed a treaty with the Soviet Union in the neighboring town of Rapallo. This document called for both countries to drop claims for war compensation and to boost their trading contacts. In an era of never-ending defeats for German foreign policy, the Rapallo treaty was a psychological success. But the Allies, in particular France, regarded the Russo–German rapprochement with suspicion.

Germany's economic problems were attributable to its defeat in the war. The pre-war economy had been healthy, and Germany had been one of the leading industrial nations in Europe. In order to finance the war, the German state took out loans which were intended to be covered later by its defeated enemies. After Germany's own defeat this house of cards collapsed under the sheer weight of the demands for reparations. Post-war governments did not dare to plug the gaps in the national finances by raising taxes, and therefore burdening their voters still further. In order to pay back these war debts, the Reichs-bank simply kept printing new banknotes – a policy which led to galloping inflation.

Passive Resistance in the Ruhr

On the assumption that Germany wanted to renege on its reparations obligations, France occupied the Ruhr at the beginning of 1923. In a counter-move, the government of Josef Wirth called for a policy of "passive resistance." The entire economy, including heavy industry and the coal mines, was brought to a standstill. This, in turn, set off inflation which rocketed ever upwards to reach astronomical figures.

The young Weimar Republic faced imminent collapse. On 13 August 1923 a "Grand Coalition" of DVP, Center, DDP and SPD was formed. Remarkably, it was Reich Chancellor Gustav Stresemann – leader of the decidedly nationalist right-wing party, the DVP – who called for an end to passive resistance in the Ruhr as it threatened to ruin Germany completely. His decision, which was made on 26 September, was nothing less than an unconditional surrender, but it ended an international stand-off and paved the way for a policy strategy which was oriented to European realities. The currency was stabilized on 15 November 1923 with the introduction of a new *Rentenmark* (= 1 trillion inflation marks), security being provided by the entire wealth of the Reich.

By ending passive resistance, Stresemann had made an unpopular decision and the nationalist press as well as papers close to the Center Party made him a scapegoat for what they saw as the defeat in the Ruhr. On the day of the "capitulation," 26 September 1923, the Reich government declared a state of emergency for the entire country.

The German October

Both the left- and right-wing opposition simultaneously opened up several fronts against the Grand Coalition. In the Rhineland and in the Palatinate separatist groups attempted to found "autonomous republics" with the aid of France, the occupying power. This separatist episode in the Rhineland failed, however, due to the resistance of the population. In Saxony and Thuringia popular front governments were formed from the SPD and Communist Party, which set up their own armies in the shape of "Proletarian Hundreds." These attempts by the Communists and Comintern to set the scene for a "German October Revolution" were ended by the Stresemann cabinet when it sent in the army.

Bavaria prepared for the first blow against the Reich on 26 September. The state government declared its "own" state of emergency on the basis of Article 48 and named the aristocratic Gustav von Kahr "General State Commissar." Von Kahr intended to spread order throughout the Reich – especially to the "Marxist swamp" of Berlin – from the "seedbed of order" that was Bavaria. In Bavaria, there was a danger of a dictatorship which would be able to rely on the locally stationed army units. On 1 October the Bavarian supreme commander, General Otto von Lossow, rejected an order from Berlin to shut down the NSDAP newspaper, the *Völkischer Beobachter*. In the face of this insubordination, the Reich government was, to all intents and purposes, impotent.

Von Kahr's plans were clearly inspired by loyalty to the Wittelsbach monarchy and they were not national, but Bavarian in nature. His sometime ally, Adolf Hitler, was however interested in the bigger picture and wanted nothing less than a "national revolution." As head of the National Socialist German Workers' Party (NSDAP) Hitler had succeeded in uniting the numerous small nationalist parties in Bavaria under his leadership. In addition, the heavily armed paramilitary troops of the "Fatherland Associations" were at his command. Inspired by the Italian Fascist leader Benito Mussolini, Hitler wanted to stage a "march on Berlin" to topple the Reich government.

The March on Berlin

Adolf Hitler's dreams of dictatorship faded in the space of just a few hours. The "Hitler putsch" began on the evening of 8 November 1923 with the shots Hitler fired in a Munich beer hall to interrupt a political gathering of von Kahr's supporters. Waving his gun he called for a "national revolution" with the "support" of von Kahr and von Lossow. Overnight, however, these two men declared the proclamation invalid; and the Bavarian army division again placed itself at the command of the chief of staff, von Seeckt, who in the meantime had taken over executive power in Germany in the name of the Reich government. The coup ended at midday the next day. A demonstration headed by Hitler and Ludendorff – who was present at all the "counter-revolution" scenarios – was scattered by the bullets of the Bavarian police as they marched past the Generals' Hall (Feldherrnhalle). Hitler and his followers were quickly arrested. With the failure of the Hitler's putsch the worst of Germany's internal crises were over. The NSDAP and other right-wing extremist organizations, as well as the Communist Party, were banned throughout the Reich. Hitler was sentenced to five years imprisonment in 1924 but was released just nine months later. He used his time in prison to compose *Mein Kampf* ("My Struggle"), a book later to become the "creed" of the National Socialist movement.

"The German Reich is a Republic. The power of the state rests with the people." (Article 1)
"If public security and order are seriously threatened or disturbed, the Reich President may take all measures necessary to restore that public security and order including the use of armed force if necessary. To this end he may, either wholly or in part, temporarily suspend the basic rights contained in articles 114, 115, 117, 118." (Article 48)

From the Weimar Constitution of 1919

"The achievements of our people during the four years of the war were enormous; they are eloquent testimony to our inherent strengths, which have today been dissipated by the revolution. A nation which has attained such things has the right to life [...] may it find the men who, like their leaders in the field, are happy to take on the responsibility and direct it with steadfast purpose and an iron will, bestowing a fresh and powerful spirit on the troubled life of the nation – men who, by their actions and with loyal followers drawn from the best of our people, will unite our creative national forces."

Erich Ludendorff in My memories of the war, *1915–1918*

The last photograph of Reich President Ebert, taken at his writing desk a fortnight ago on 15 February 1925.
(Original caption for Friedrich Ebert's obituary)

The first phase of the revolution focused on democratization, a demand which large numbers of Germans were able to support. In the second phase, from January 1919 onwards, many members of the industrial proletariat were no longer satisfied with what they had achieved the previous November. The soviet movement in the Ruhr and in Central Germany was characterized by calls for the nationalization of key industries and greater participation of workers in the decisions of industry. Scheidemann's government reacted to the resulting unrest and strikes by sending in the *Freikorps*. Both of the soviet republics in Munich were also ended by the use of force. The Munich debacle only signaled a provisional end to left-wing coup attempts, however; it was followed by the "Battle of the Ruhr" in 1920 and the "German October" in Central Germany.

"Anyone caught fighting against government troops with a weapon in their hands is to be shot on sight."
Order of the Social Democratic supreme commander Gustav Noske during the March uprising in Berlin in 1919, in force from 9–16 March

Above: *Citizens fighting in Central Germany. Red Guards being led away with their wounded leader in Mansfeld, 26 March 1921.*
Right page: *March 1919. State of emergency in Hamburg. Arrest of a ringleader at wire entanglements.*

(Original captions)

As well as depriving it of significant portions of its territory, the Treaty of Versailles imposed stringent military cuts on the German Reich: the former general staff was to be dissolved; the army reduced to 100,000 men, and the navy to 15,000; all heavy war material such as airplanes, submarines or tanks were forbidden; almost the entire high seas fleet was to be handed over. This last requirement was, however, circumvented by the navy when they scuttled the battle fleet at Scapa Flow on 21 June 1919. Later, too, the army constantly tried to evade the Treaty's disarmament clauses; after the Rapallo Treaty of 1922 with the Soviet Union a secret agreement was reached with the Red Army which provided for a uniform weapons training.

Top: *How Germany is being disarmed. These planes are waiting to be scrapped.*
Left: *An unusual picture: high-ranking Russian officers at German army maneuvers in the fall of 1927. The head of the Russian deployment section and three Soviet divisional commanders as participants in this year's fall maneuvers by the 5 army division.*

(Original captions)

Above: *The mass grave of the German fleet in the scrapyard at Kiel. According to the Treaty of Versailles the remains of the fleet which was not destroyed at Scapa Flow is to be scrapped here. The once proud* Lothringen *is reduced to this.*

Right: *The army maneuvers near Frankfurt/Oder. Reich President Hindenburg was present at the exercises. Attack with dummy tanks.*

(Original captions)

After the Treaty of Versailles came into effect on 10 January 1920, there were still over 250,000 men in the German army, including all the *Freikorps* units. The final date for the reduction of the army to the agreed levels was 10 July 1920. Signs of conflict between the Bauer government and those sections of the army still to be demobilized were misinterpreted by the Defense Minister, Gustav Noske, and culminated in the Kapp–Lüttwitz putsch. On 13 March 1920 *Freikorps* units under the command of General Lüttwitz marched into Berlin and Wolfgang Kapp declared himself Reich Chancellor. The counter-revolution went awry after just a few days. The general strike sparked by the coup throughout the country led however to the "Battle of the Ruhr." The Ruhr uprising was once again brought to an end by the newly installed Müller government using precisely those elements of the army and *Freikorps* who themselves had sympathized with rebels just a few weeks before.

Above: *Berlin during the Kapp putsch. Captain Hermann Ehrhardt, whose troops were the first to advance into Berlin, on 13 March 1920.*
Below: *The Berlin Pleasure Garden during the Kapp putsch of 1920.* (Original captions)

After the Allies' Reparation Commission declared in January 1923 that Germany had deliberately failed to fulfill its reparations obligations, French and Belgian soldiers acting on the orders of their governments seized the Ruhr – with its iron, steel and mining industries – as security. The next day the German government called for passive resistance in the Ruhr. In March and April former members of the *Freikorps* went over from passive to active resistance and carried out bomb attacks on railway stations in the occupied zone. One of their leaders, Leo Schlageter, was arrested by French military police and executed on 26 May. This unleashed a storm of protest throughout Germany and even the German expert of the Communist Internationale, Karl Radek, called the "fascist" Schlageter a "martyr of German nationalism" and a "courageous soldier of the counter-revolution."

"We will do everything to ensure that men like Schlageter, who were prepared to die for a common cause, did not die in vain but gave their lives for a better future for all mankind."
Karl Radek in a speech to an expanded executive committee of the Comintern in Moscow on 20 June 1923

Left: *Reich President Friedrich Ebert leaving the Museum.*
Right page, above: *Reich Foreign Minister Walther Rathenau in his car, in which he was fatally wounded by a gunman on 24 June 1922.*
(Original captions)

Right page, below: Matthias Erzberger.

The murders of Matthias Erzberger in 1921 and Walther Rathenau in 1922 were not isolated incidents. Every politician and person in public life who was on the side of the Republic, who supported the "appeasement policies" of the government and put them into action, was at risk. Those responsible for the violence came from a scene fueled by nationalistic and anti-Semitic ideology. The anti-Semitism of the Weimar era had its roots in the racist movements of the second half of the 19th century which equated hatred of Jews with opposition to Modernity. Depending on the political views of the individuals in question, Jews in Imperial Germany – who had just been guaranteed full civil rights – were either Capitalists or Liberals, Socialists or Marxists, Freemasons or Pacifists. After many Jews fought alongside their compatriots in the First World War, right-wing anti-Semitic propaganda began again with the revolution of 1918. Lynch-law killings became a politically justifiable means of combating what was seen as a "Jewish–Bolshevist world enemy." In his "Account of the German Jews" in 1934, Arnold Zweig listed the prominent Jewish victims of the early Weimar Republic, whose murderers all came from the same racist and nationalistic scene: " – that corner which has sent fewer poets than murderers out into the world: the murderers of peaceful Erzberger; of Rathenau, the man of Rapallo (they were satisfied with merely making death threats against Stresemann); those who reconquered Munich and whose victims included Kurt Eisner, Gustav Landauer, Eugen Leviné – and all those 'forces for reconstruction' who set out in the Kapp and Hitler coups to smash the Republic."

Right: *Clothes Week at the Berlin Emergency Aid organization in 1923. Due to the desperate conditions in Germany, poor people are not able to buy new clothes. For this reason the German Red Cross, supported by the army, organized a collection of old clothes and shoes. Our picture shows a room at a collection point flooded with donations.*
Below: *Norwegian donations for needy Berlin schoolchildren are here being distributed under the gaze of the president of the Norwegian Emergency Aid Fund, Mr. Ellef Rignes. 15 wagonloads of foodstuffs have arrived and every child is to receive 5 pounds of butter, 2 pounds of cocoa, 2 pounds of sugar, 2 tins of sardines, 5 tins of milk, 4 herrings, 1 pound of sausage and a piece of soap. The picture shows Berlin schoolchildren receiving their generous gifts from Norway, Berlin 1924.*

(Original captions)

Inflation had risen continually since the end of the war and this had helped the state to demonstrate its insolvency to its Allied creditors. After the passive resistance in the Ruhr, which began in January 1923 and consumed vast sums of public money, the depreciation of the currency spiraled out of control. The printing presses worked ceaselessly to produce money, and the suffering of the masses increased from day to day.

"Poverty is gradually crowding out every sense of order, cleanliness and morality, leaving only room for thoughts about how to combat the hunger and cold."
From an official brochure of the city of Berlin, 1923

Right: *Inflation in Berlin, 1922. A crowd gathers to buy butter at a municipal stall.*
Bottom: *Clothes Week run by the Berlin Emergency Aid 1923 [...] The collections by apartment building concierges provide German Emergency Aid with clothes which are no longer needed.*

(Original captions)

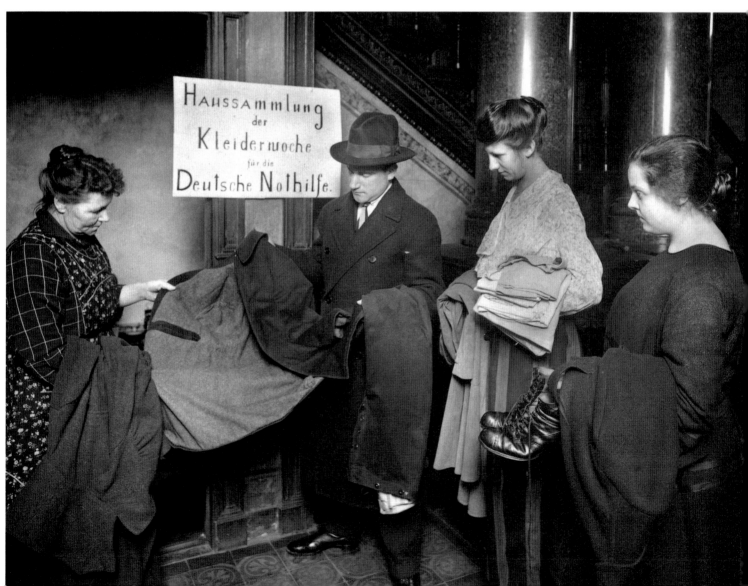

"Proclamation to the German people. The government of the November criminals in Berlin has today been declared null and void. A provisional national German government has been formed. This consists of General Ludendorff, Adolf Hitler, General von Lossow, Colonel von Seisser."

Proclamation from 8 November 1923

On the evening of 8 November 1923 in a Munich beerhall, Hitler forced von Kahr, Lossow and Seisser to join his planned "national revolution" at the point of a gun. These men then recanted their position overnight and made arrangements to suppress the uprising. Hitler's putsch fell apart in just a few hours the next day. He and other participants in the attempted coup were sentenced to prison terms in the Landsberg fortress on 1 April 1924, although the sentences were suspended at the end of the year. The danger of a putsch from the right was banished but agitation by nationalist parties and paramilitaries on the streets of the Republic continued unabated.

Top: *Judgment in the Hitler–Ludendorff trial. General Ludendorff, who was acquitted (left), with the main defendant, Hitler, and Dr. Weber. Taken on the day of sentencing in Munich, 1 April 1924.*
Above: *Ludendorff's car is greeted with jubilation as it passes through the streets of Munich.*
Right: *Followers of the Extreme Nationalists wearing Hitler uniforms drive through the Brandenburg Gate, distributing leaflets. May 1924.*
(Original captions)

The Weimar Republic was characterized by the militarization of political life. After the war many veterans continued their armed struggle in the *Freikorps* – this time against the internal enemy of "Bolshevism." Paramilitary units were also formed: the Stahlhelm (Steel Helmet) was founded at the end of 1918 and openly opposed the Republic and the Left.

Left page: *'German Day' in Halle on 11 May 1924. View of the host of national delegations gathered on the racetrack.*
Right: *General Hans von Seeckt and his wife in conversation with Christmas guests of the army.*
Below: *The 'Junior and Senior Steel Helmet' organization with their flags remembering those killed in the First World War, 1 March 1925.* (Original captions)

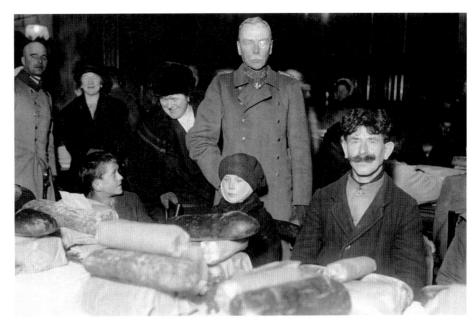

The workers' movement saw no alternative but to use paramilitary means to counter the militarization of society; they founded the "Reich Banners Black-Red-Gold" and the "Red Front Fighters' Alliance."

Top: *The "Reich Banners Black-Red-Gold" organized its first national rally on 22 February 1925 in its founding city of Magdeburg. This alliance of Republican war veterans was formed a year ago today and in its first year has a membership of 4 million. Over 150,000 Reich Banner members holding their flags took part in the celebrations along with a large number of Magdeburg's inhabitants. Our picture shows Reich Chancellor (retd) Hermann Müller during his speech on the cathedral square.*
Right: *The "Black-Red-Gold" Reich Banners Rally in Magdeburg. The old battle flags of 1848 are flown during the gathering on the cathedral square, 22 February 1925.*
(Original captions)

Left: *When night comes! Picture taken in the municipal refuge for the homeless. View of one of the dormitories which can house up to 100 people.*
Above: *Hugo Stinnes.*   (Original captions)

The depreciation of the currency hit the middle classes particularly hard; they lost most of their savings because all capital investments tied to the mark were wiped out. The magnates of finance and industry were however able to pay off their debts and successfully used the inflationary era to buy up other companies to form large concerns. An example of this practice was set by Hugo Stinnes, who built up a gargantuan conglomerate by purchasing large numbers of companies in different sectors of the economy. After his death in 1924 his empire disintegrated, however.

The nation's printing presses, which for years had constantly churned out floods of paper money, were brought to a standstill on 15 October 1923 by the establishment of the *Rentenbank*. Along with the creation of the *Rentenmark*, which was fixed at a value of 1 billion paper marks and a parity of 4.20 marks to the dollar, the Reichstag passed a law, accepted by all parties in parliament, which prohibited the state from unnecessarily expanding the money supply. Both measures enabled confidence to be restored in the German currency and economy.

The money destroyer – at the right is the slit where blades and steam are used to shred the money completely.
(Original caption)

THOSE WERE
THE DAYS

The German foreign minister, Gustav Stresemann, received little
gratitude at home for his conciliatory approach to the victorious powers
after the First World War. Instead, right-wing nationalists turned him
into an object of hate and thought nothing of making death threats
against him. Even the public demonstration of domestic bliss pictured
here could not gloss over such hostility. "Reich Foreign Minister Dr.
Stresemann and his wife celebrate their silver wedding anniversary in
Wiesbaden. Our picture shows Dr. Stresemann and his wife in the garden
of their home." But few of those who lived through the charmed years
between 1924 and 1929 were able to perceive that the apparent stability
of the age was only an illusion. Leonhard Frank described this mirage of
tranquility in an autobiographical sketch: "Those were the days. The
after effects from the war we had lost were no longer to be felt [...] Every
day Michael and his friends became aware of a present which was full of
beauty, and they said to each other: "We're doing all right!"

4

Germany Emerges From Isolation

In the history of the Weimar Republic, the "golden twenties" have become a synonym for the heyday of art and culture between 1924 and 1929. During 1924 there were increasing signs that parliamentary democracy had overcome the challenges from both the right and the left, and that there had been a consolidation in the domestic political arena. From his prison cell, Adolf Hitler was forced to watch as the NSDAP he had built up was banned, and the party structure – which had been tailored to serve him as leader – collapsed. The failed "Hitler putsch" not only nullified the "national revolution" he had called for, it also compromised the main right-wing forces in the mind of the public for years afterwards. There was no denying the fact however that solid anti-democratic and anti-republican sentiment continued in large sections of the population, as well as in the economic and bureaucratic elites. The extreme left, on the other hand, had effectively been crippled by the events of 1923. After the failure of the "German October," a Communist coup attempt was no longer seen as an immediate threat.

After fighting for its political and economic life for four years, the Weimar Republic was left with a vast number of the socially dispossessed. Inflation had wiped out people's savings, particularly those of the middle classes: these so-called "losers of the war" never went on to develop a basic confidence in the Republic. The economic upturn after the currency reform of 1923 did not significantly change this state of affairs. It was not until 1927 that wages once again reached their 1923 levels, and full employment was never achieved, though with the help of foreign credit the Germans experienced an illusory economic boom.

The successes of Gustav Stresemann's foreign policy are undeniable if looked at from a modern perspective. From November 1923 until his death in October 1929 he held the office of foreign minister in all the coalition governments. His long-term foreign policy strategy showed him to be the political beacon of the Republic, and he entered the history books as one of Europe's greatest statesmen. He saw a continuation of Rathenau's "politics of appeasement" – the revision of the Treaty of Versailles by peaceful means – as the only feasible way of re-establishing Germany's position among the international great powers. The solution of the reparations problem; reconciliation with France; the lobbying for support from Great Britain and the United States; the reform of the eastern border with Poland and co-operation with the Soviet Union – these were the fundamental aims of Stresemann's policies and they were based on Bismarck's foreign policy model of maintaining a power balance between East and West.

Tension in Europe Eases

A change in the political climate of western Europe favored the realization of Stresemann's goals. In 1924 a Labor government was elected in Great Britain which was more interested than its conservative predecessors in achieving a pan-European balance of power, and was increasingly critical of French efforts to gain hegemony in central Europe. In the same year, the "National Block" in France, which had been responsible for the aggressive actions in the Rhine and Ruhr, lost its parliamentary majority to a coalition of left-wing parties. In this combination of factors Stresemann saw "for the first time, a glimmer of light on an otherwise dark horizon."

A fundamental precondition for this easing of tension in Europe was created using the solutions proposed by an independent commission of experts under the chairmanship of the American banker, Charles G. Dawes, on the issue of reparations. The Dawes Commission calculated the sums to be compensated according to the principle of economic viability, and the overhaul which the German economy underwent at the end of 1923 favored this new approach. In the summer of 1924 the plan was finally adopted by the Allies and the Germans at the London conference.

The Locarno Pact

In the late summer and fall of 1925 the Swiss resort of Locarno on Lake Maggiore became the political focus of the great European powers. Gustav Stresemann met with his colleagues Aristide Briand, from France, and Austen Chamberlain, from Great Britain, to hammer out a common European security treaty. On 12 October Germany, France, Belgium, Great Britain, Italy, Poland, and Czechoslovakia signed the Pact of Locarno, which confirmed the western borders that had been laid down in the Treaty of Versailles. The Rhineland, which was still occupied by France, was to be demilitarized at an unspecified future point, and all the parties to the treaty agreed to put all future conflicts to arbitration. The guarantors of the treaty were Great Britain and Italy. The treaty affirmed Germany's western border and secured its relationship with France while the question of the eastern border with Poland remained open.

The Locarno Pact was essentially the work of Aristide Briand and Gustav Stresemann; on 10 December 1926 both men were awarded the Nobel Peace Prize for their joint efforts. The conclusion of the treaty seemed finally to signal a new Europe and the beginning of the end for Versailles. It was not until many years later that Briand developed his bold vision of a united Europe; while in the short time that remained to him, Stresemann continued to base his actions on the realities of European politics and was a proponent of the sovereign nation state.

The pathos of his speech on the occasion of the signing of the Locarno Pact was an exception to this rule:

"We have a right to talk about a common European idea [...] This, and the devastation wreaked by the First World War, has resulted

Foreign Minister Gustav Stresemann leaving the conference on reparations in The Hague on 6 August 1929.

The British (Sir Austen Chamberlain), German (Gustav Stresemann) and French (Aristide Briand) foreign ministers debating over coffee in the Hotel Splendide in Lugano on 17 December 1928.

in us being bound together in a common community of fate. If we go down, we go down together; if we wish to attain great heights we cannot do so by fighting with one another, only by working together."

The End of Isolation

In order to emphasize the end of its international isolation – and to be better able to control its development in the future – Germany was given a permanent seat at the League of Nations in September 1926. Now that it was integrated into an international power structure the Weimar Republic was obliged to keep to the League's statutes. The first sitting in the Reformation Hall in Geneva was undoubtedly a personal triumph for Gustav Stresemann when Briand announced: "Today is a sign that there is peace for Germany and for France."

Germany Opens Up to the East

In order to spare Moscow the nightmare of an Anglo–French attack on the Soviet Union via German territory – now that the Weimar Republic was allied to the Western Powers – Stresemann concluded the Treaty of Berlin with his Russian counterpart in 1926. As well as being a non-binding friendship and neutra-

lity pact in case of war with a third state, the treaty provided for secret agreements of mutual assistance between the German and Red armies. The Russians were dependent on German skills and technology to build up a modern army. The two countries not only produced weapons forbidden in Germany under the Treaty of Versailles, they collaborated in training their general staff. Ultimately this illegal form of cooperation could not be kept secret and it soured relations between Germany and France as well as on the domestic political scene. In 1926 the former Chancellor, Philipp Scheidemann, made sensational revelations about this military liaison which placed great pressure on the government, army and Communist Party to justify their actions.

Stresemann's balancing act in foreign policy was a work of art in itself. His obvious successes, however, were neither recognized nor acknowledged as such by many Germans. Like his French counterpart, Briand, the German foreign minister encountered violent resistance to his negotiation of a new European strategy. In conservative and nationalist circles the Dawes Plan and Locarno Pact whipped up a storm of hatred and bitterness against Stresemann. These groups were particularly exercised over the thought that Alsace–Lorraine would forever

remain in the hands of the "arch-enemy" France. In the nationalist press of the wealthy and ultra-conservative media mogul Alfred Hugenberg – who became leader of the DNVP in 1928 – Stresemann was vilified as a "thief and murderer," a "traitor" and "treacherous dog," and was accused of drunkenness and corruption. In the course of this campaign of slander, plans to assassinate Stresemann were uncovered; throughout the Reich nationalist units were marching to the battle song *In victory shall we crush France*. The pressure from the street became too great for the DNVP and in 1925 it resigned from the government.

Without Regard to Losses

Since coming into office the German foreign minister, Gustav Stresemann, had found himself engaged in an exhausting form of trench warfare within his own party – the DVP – which he had to win if he was to ensure the success of his foreign policy on the domestic political stage. The Dawes Plan of 1924 guaranteed Stresemann an economic base from which further steps could be taken to ensure Germany's economic recovery. The agreement had led to Germany's first big loan from Wall Street, with which the country was then able to attract additional foreign capital; a financial cycle began which ultimately developed into the powerhouse of the transatlantic economy. Germany was now in a position to repay its reparation debts to the Entente nations who, in turn, were able to pay back their debts to the USA; the American banks for their part once again supplied the German economy with credit.

From the Dawes to the Young Plan

Nevertheless, it was clear to all those involved that the Dawes Plan was only a temporary economic measure. In the long term the maximum yearly installments of reparations payments were unworkable: from 1928 Germany was scheduled to repay 2.5 billion Reichsmarks a year. In addition the plan was based on a system of control which inhibited economic growth. The German railways and central bank were under foreign supervision and no longer accountable to the German government. Main responsibility for maintaining the plan lay with Parker Gilbert, the Allied reparations agent in Berlin, who criticized the extravagance of local authorities and states throughout the German Reich. In view of the reckless expenditure of public money, Stresemann shared this opinion: "When the Prussian State spends 14 million marks on the rebuilding of the Berlin opera house, and will perhaps spend over 20 million, the whole world comes to the conclusion that we are swamped with money. None of the victor states has been able to afford anything similar. When Herr Adenauer [Mayor of Cologne] builds a magnificent exhibition center and boasts of having installed in it the largest organ in the world, it has the same effect […] Please be so kind as to inform me what I should say to the representatives of foreign powers when they tell me that all these things give them the impression that Germany had won rather than lost the war." (Letter to the Mayor of Duisburg, Karl Jarres, 24 November 1927.)

It was, therefore, yet another foreign policy success for the Germans when they achieved a second review of the reparation regulations after long and arduous negotiations in 1929. The Young Plan, drawn up by the American economic expert Owen D. Young and ratified in 1930, returned financial and economic sovereignty to the Weimar Republic. This modified payment plan covered an almost unimaginably long period – final payments were to be made in 1988 – but it considerably reduced the annual burden on the German economy and nation.

The End of an Era

While negotiations over the Young Plan continued, Stresemann's health deteriorated and he succumbed to a heart attack on 3 October 1929. As with that of Rathenau, the foreign minister's funeral became a state occasion during which, for a brief moment, the Republic forgot its differences. Despite all the criticism to which he had been subjected during his lifetime, Stresemann became a mythical figure after his death, even though he had failed to achieve his great goal; after a period of apparent peace and harmony, by the end of the 1920s Europe had once again slipped into an era of mutual antagonism in which nations eyed one other with distrust.

In the presence of large sections of Berlin's population, Gustav Stresemann was laid to rest on 6 October 1929.

(Original caption)

"I Cannot Bear It Any More!"

It was with these words that the 54-year-old Friedrich Ebert appealed to his party colleague, Otto Braun, not to nominate him for re-election as Reich President in 1924. Just a few weeks later, on 25 February 1925, the first president of the Weimar Republic died after six turbulent years in office.

Above: *Luise Ebert, wife of the Reich President, with Defense Minister Groener in the VIP box at the Berlin Press Ball, 1931.*
Right: *The birthplace of the deceased Reich President decked in mourning. The house in the Pfarrgasse in Heidelberg where Ebert was born, festooned with flags and pine branches.* (Original captions)

In 1918/19 Ebert, as provisional prime minister, had guided the tumultuous events of the revolution into the gentler waters of parliamentary democracy with the assistance of troops from the army. He managed to keep the parties of the Weimar coalition united after the founding of the Republic in 1919 because he recognized that only a "compromise between the classes" would ensure its survival. The radical left denounced his policies as those of a "class traitor" and vilified him utterly. When the Weimar Republic threatened to disintegrate under the opposing pressures of right and left, the President worked behind the scenes – and without regard to his own party affiliation – to forge parliamentary majorities and governments capable of sustaining coalitions. Nor did he shrink from criticizing the reluctance of the SPD to enter coalitions. At moments of danger, such as in the fall of 1923, he made use of Article 48 of the constitution in order to take quick and effective action. Nevertheless, influenced by his military and bureaucratic advisers, he ruled for a total of two and a half years between 1920 and 1925 with the help of special powers, an approach that may well have established a political precedent which would later become an everyday phenomenon during the presidential governments from 1930 to 1933.

Ebert is not considered one of the foremost German statesmen, but he was a committed democrat and a German patriot whose greatest achievement lay in being able to unite the Republic's democratic forces and formulate a consensus. It was not only the Communists who hated him for this; because he personified the Republic's new political elite the contempt of the conservative establishment for this former saddler was limitless. Both Ebert and his wife Luise – who, as the Reich's "First Lady," was a constant target of the tabloid press for her inability to adapt to the rigid etiquette of the upper classes – were frequently the victims of slander and libel. In order to redeem his personal honor, the president went to court 173 times during his term of office. A particularly infamous and offensive charge was that of treason, an accusation against which Ebert was forced to defend himself in a libel action brought by the right in the last days of his life. It was because of this trial that he postponed an urgently needed appendix operation, a decision which was to have fatal consequences. The judges in the trial affirmed that, during a strike by metal workers in Berlin in the last year of the war, he had indeed been guilty of treason. The Reich President a criminal? The prejudices of the right-wing, who thought of the Social Democrats as "unpatriotic rogues," now became part of the official record as a result of this astonishing judgment; the legal decision in the Ebert case was yet further proof that the judiciary was overwhelmingly anti-Republican.

Hindenburg by the Grace of Thälmann!

Historian Hagen Schulze described Ebert's premature death as "a murder with words and paragraphs," and the full significance of the Weimar Republic's loss was demonstrated just a few weeks later in elections for a new Reich President in March and April 1925. Instead of having a Republican at the helm, the nation now had a monarchist fossil: von Hindenburg, the alleged "victor of Tannenberg" and self-proclaimed victim of the "Republican stab in the back." By deciding in favor of Hindenburg, the conservative camp had expressed its desire for a strong state – on the familiar Imperial model – which knew how to put parliament and the political parties in their place.

The crowd singing the German national anthem as von Hindenburg, the newly elected Reich President, arrives in front of the Reich Chancellery in Berlin.

Black-red-and-white versus Black-red-and-gold

This election took on the significance of a plebiscite on the Weimar Republic. Until the second round of voting, however, the result was undecided. After votes had been cast in the first round on 29 March 1925 the right-wing candidate Karl Jarres (DVP) had achieved a relative, but not absolute, majority followed by the Social Democrat, Otto Braun. A carousel of candidates was now put forward from both sides of the main political divide, which was defined by the colors of the opposing camps – black, red and white for the conservatives, and black, red and gold for the Republicans. In the second round on 26 April the conservative block (DVP, BVP, DNVP, and the German People's Freedom Party) put forward 77-year-old Field-Marshal Hindenburg as their common candidate. Hindenburg won with 14.7 million votes to 13.8 million for the former Chancellor, Wilhelm Marx (Center), who had represented the parties of the Weimar coalition. Marx failed to garner the votes of the BVP – the Bavarian sister organization of his Center Party – for the decisive victory. The 1.9 million votes cast for the Communist Party leader, Ernst Thälmann, were only useful to the Republicans for making speculative calculations after the event by pointing to the fact that Hindenburg had not been able to unite a majority of voters behind him. In their election propaganda, however, the Communists had left no doubt as to their anti-Republican feelings: "It is not the task of the proletariat to look for the most able representative of bourgeois interests. This would be to choose the lesser of two evils: either the civil dictator, Marx, or the military dictator, Hindenburg." The Social Democratic newspaper, *Vorwärts*, responded on 27 April with the headline "Hindenburg by the grace of Thälmann!" Although just over half of all voters were opposed to Hindenburg, this slim majority was divided and incapable of acting in concert.

A Defeat for Democracy

Republicans reacted with shock to this blow against democracy. The day after the election Theodor Wolff wrote the following comments in the liberal newspaper *Berliner Tageblatt*:

"The Republicans have lost a battle; the former monarchist, Field-Marshal Hindenburg, is to be President of the German Republic. The officer and landowning classes are today popping champagne corks just as they did after Rathenau's murder [...] What is one to do with a people which does not learn from its misfortunes, and which time and again – even for the tenth or twelfth time – allows itself to be led around on a halter by the same people?"

Foreign Minister Stresemann had opposed the candidacy of Hindenburg – though it was supported by his party – because he feared that France, especially, would see his election as an affront. On 9 June 1925 he noted in his diary:

"It is extraordinarily difficult to discuss complex issues of foreign policy with the Reich President because he quite naturally clings to definite and one-sided ideas. There seem to be forces hard at work steering the President."

Hindenburg – the Great Right Hope

The "forces" which Wolff and Stresemann vaguely hinted at were in fact well-known and could be found in Hindenburg's closest circles – a clique from the old general staff, East Prussian estate owners and – not least – Oskar von Hindenburg, who was mockingly known as "the son not provided for in the constitution." Right from the outset, therefore, the army and large landowners had access to the President in order to be able to overturn any parliamentary decisions which displeased them.

Hindenburg did not fulfill any of the grandiose visions dreamt up by his most ardent admirers, but neither did he trigger any of the apocalyptic scenarios which had been predicted by his most committed opponents. The prevailing conditions in both foreign and domestic policy gave him and his "advisers" little opportunity to intervene. In true Prussian fashion, he remained loyal to the Republican constitution, a fact which initially surprised his political friends and served to mollify some of the more outspoken opponents of the Republic. More than anything, however, the new President satisfied the wishes of his voters for a strong leader and national greatness. The result of the plebiscite showed that such political sentiments influenced the voting patterns of large sections of the population.

Timidity in the Face of Power

In foreign policy the Weimar Republic followed a clear strategy, but on the domestic political scene there were constant tensions and structural problems. The search for coalition partners was wearisome because parties were unwilling to make political compromises and lacked the courage to reach the necessary decisions. After the SPD toppled Reich Chancellor Stresemann in 1923, the middle-class parties, particularly the DVP, felt little desire to cooperate with the Social Democrats. In addition there were conflicts between the Catholic parties of the BVP in Bavaria and the Center in the rest of the Reich. On the other hand, after the failure of the "Citizens' Block Government" in 1925, the liberal left party of the DDP was utterly incapable of entering into a coalition with a strengthened DNVP – a party whose heightened anti-Republican chauvinism thereafter also became intolerable for the other bourgeois parties.

The Burden of Compromise

The SPD played a unique role in these events. According to its own conception it was the "real party of state" without whose initiative the Weimar Republic would not have taken the shape it did. Most of the time its members formed the strongest grouping in the Reichstag until mid-1932. Of the 16 Reich governments of the Republic between February 1919 and March 1930, four were led by Social Democratic chancellors and SPD ministers were represented in four further cabinets. In the period between 1923 and 1928, however, the SPD withdrew into oppo-

sition; in the four previous years its members had seen the gap between the party's ideological claims and political reality yawn ever wider. The Republic had become a bourgeois–liberal constitutional state which abstained from making any far-reaching social changes. This timidity in the face of power had its roots within the party itself because, ever since the party had reunited with the rump Independent Social Democrats, its readiness to enter coalitions with moderate parties at national level had declined. Moreover, whenever political mistakes were made and crises occurred, public opprobrium tended to rain down mercilessly – and often viciously – on the SPD alone. By sitting it out on the opposition benches the party continued to hope that it might recover from the political blows of its opponents on both the left and the right.

The SPD – a Party of State

Even if the Social Democrats did not directly participate in national government for long periods of time, they were in actual fact a party of state. They represented a large section of the workers who accounted for almost 50% of the population. Until 1925 the Reich President was a member of the SPD. In several federal states Social Democrats occupied key positions in the administration, for example as mayor or chief of police. Prussia, the largest state with three-fifths of the country's land area, developed into a political and administrative bastion of the Republic. Here the Republicans found a particularly loyal political companion in the Catholic Center Party. An alliance between Social

Democrats and a party with religious affiliations might at first sight seem surprising, but in fact both groups represented sectors of society who had been oppressed by the state during the Bismarck era. While the Center Party was drawn more and more into the conservative camp at a national level and cooperated with the parties of the right, in the Prussian parliament it remained true to the "Weimar Coalition" of 1919 and its senior partner, the SPD. Out of consideration for the many Catholic voters in the Rhine provinces, the party did not wish to hand over power in Prussia – the largest state in Germany – to the German People's Party and German Nationalists, who drew their support largely from Protestant voters. The "Weimar Coalition" ruled Prussia until Franz von Papen's coup of 20 July 1932, and was a guarantor during this time of the continued existence of the Weimar Republic.

Weak Parliamentarianism

As an opposition party, too, the SPD often played a crucial role. During the period of apparent internal stability from 1924 to 1928, the parties within the center–right spectrum from the DDP to the DNVP participated in a series of ever-changing coalitions under chancellors Wilhelm Marx and Hans Luther. Government policies were thus never able to build on permanent majorities in the Reichstag. The SPD supported all of Stresemann's foreign policy measures in order to prevent his strategy from foundering on the opposition of the DNVP. On the domestic political scene, however, their votes brought down the Flag Bill of 1926 and the Center Party's draft legislation on confessional schools in 1927. In the same year Social Democrat members of parliament made a major contribution in transforming welfare for the jobless into an unemployment insurance scheme.

In the legislative period from 1924 to 1928 parliament saw five different governments; their members, however, remained largely unchanged. Under these circumstances there could be no really stable parliamentary culture in the Weimar Republic. Instead, these constant rearrangements played into the hands of anti-Republican propagandists, who derisively referred to events in the Reichstag as a "talking shop."

Elections to the Reichstag imminent. View of the Platz der Republik in Berlin with the Bismarck memorial and the Reichstag.
(Original caption)

"In the evening I waited for the election result at the Democratic Party Headquarters. Shortly after one the outcome was definite: Hindenburg has been elected. This sequel is likely to prove one of the darkest chapters in German history."

Count Harry Kessler,
Diary entry from 26 April 1925

"It will not be classes nor parties nor mutually exclusive and conflicting groups, but a feeling of community and a spirit of serving and self-sacrificing love of our fatherland that alone will be the basis on which we can build a better future."

Reich President von Hindenburg in a speech during a visit
to Stuttgart, 11 November 1925

The first official photographs of President von Hindenburg after taking office. The President is standing in the cross-fire of the photographers. Berlin 1925. (Original caption)

The first President, Friedrich Ebert, shaped and gave voice to political reality in the Weimar Republic. His death on 25 February 1925 came as a massive blow. After two rounds of elections Field-Marshal von Hindenburg was elected as Ebert's successor. In spite of the nation's defeat in the war and the changed political system, Hindenburg knew how to preserve and build on the reputation he had as a "people's Emperor."

Right: *Berlin coach drivers reading the news of Friedrich Ebert's death on 25 February 1925 in the Social Democratic party newspaper,* Vorwärts.
Below: *The funeral of President Friedrich Ebert took place on 4 March 1925, attended by large numbers of people. The coffin was set up on an ornate catafalque in front of Potsdam Station.* (Original captions)

Top: *The President visiting the Leipzig Trade Fair. Our picture shows President Hindenburg greeting the cheering crowds in front of the court buildings after his arrival in Leipzig 1925.*
Left: *Hindenburg ill. Concern for the health of the President. Our picture shows President Hindenburg being enthusiastically greeted by his grandchildren as he takes a walk in the gardens of the Presidential Palace.*
Above: *President von Hindenburg attends the army's maneuvers near Frankfurt an der Oder, 1932. The President with his son Major Oskar von Hindenburg (right). The chief of general staff, General von Hammerstein (left), reports.* (Original captions)

Left: *Gustav Stresemann in conversation with the Rumanian Foreign Minister Titulesco at the Lugano conference, December 1928. Seated at the table on the right is the French Foreign Minster, Aristide Briand.*
Below: *A huge demonstration of German Nationalists against the Locarno Pact took place in the Berliner Lustgarten [Berlin Pleasure Garden] on 15 November 1925. The national delegations lower their flags as the national anthem is sung.*
Right page: *March by patriotic organizations. Demonstration against the Locarno Pact in the Berliner Lustgarten, 15 November 1925.*

(Original captions)

Although the SPD was the strongest party in parliament until 1932, after the electoral defeat of 1920 it never again achieved the political prominence it had during the Weimar Republic's founding era. In the middle period of the Republic it supported all the important foreign policy decisions of the coalition governments. In the domestic political arena it collaborated from time to time with the Communist Party – for example over a planned referendum on the confiscation of royal property – in order to play to the anti-bourgeois sentiments of its voters. This meandering course at national level prevented the party from assuming the role it had set itself in 1921 of becoming a left-wing people's party. It was only in Prussia – where it was in a clearly defined and consistent coalition with the Center and DDP – that the SPD successfully pursued the politics of government. Until 1932 this coalition in the largest state in the country formed a kind of bulwark against the rise of fascism.

Above: *The Social Democratic Party conference in Magdeburg. On Sunday afternoon this year's Social Democratic Party conference opened in Magdeburg with the usual formal sitting. It began with a procession which took three hours to file past. Our picture shows the Prussian prime minister, Otto Braun, speaking in the courtyard of the exhibition center in front of a massed gathering. Because of the unusually high temperatures the Prime Minister took his jacket off during his speech and spoke in his shirt sleeves.* (Original caption)

Above: *Social Democrat May celebrations in Berlin. The Social Democratic Party held its traditional march on 1 May in the Berliner Lustgarten, during which Member of Parliament Künstler delivered a speech.*
Left: *Propaganda parade of furniture vans bearing posters designed to win people over to a policy of dispossessing the country's princely families. A referendum moved by the Social Democrats and Communists for 20 June 1926 was unsuccessful as it failed to achieve the required majority of 20 million votes.* (Original captions)

Top: *The party leader of the German nationalists, Dr. Hugenberg, during his speech from the VIP stand of the German Stadium.*
Above: *The great Stahlhelm march in Munich, June 1929. Provisions being distributed at the Stahlhelm camp.*
(Original captions)

"The Stahlhelm demands the recognition of the black, white and red colors. The German Empire experienced the age of its greatest honor under this flag, and it led the German people in its incomparably heroic fight against a world of enemies [...] Stahlhelm does not want the German people, who have been driven into poverty and desperation, to become the prey and breeding ground of Bolshevism."
Demonstration of the Stahlhelm paramilitary organization on 8 May 1927

The German Nationalists were members of the Republic's bourgeois governments between 1924 and 1927. After Alfred Hugenberg, spokesman for the radical wing of the party, became chairman of the DNVP in 1928, he led the party on a strict anti-parliamentary course with the aim of uniting right-wing opponents of the Weimar Republic under his leadership.

Above: *German brothers in need! National Socialist student demonstration in front of
Berlin University. National Socialist students held an extraordinary gathering in front of the
university at the same time as a demonstration by the General German Students' Union.
Here, the leader of National Socialist Youth is seen addressing the students.*
(Original caption)

Above: *The liberation of the Second Zone. Liberation celebrations in the Rhineland in 1929. After the withdrawal of the 151st French infantry regiment and the lowering of the French tricolor at Ehrenbreitstein, the fortress was occupied by the German police. View from Ehrenbreitstein to the flag-lined Deutsches Eck where the Rhine and Mosel rivers join.*

Left page: *The great British evacuation of the Rhineland territory began on Saturday when advance parties from the 2nd battalion of the Leicester Regiment and the 2nd battalion of the Dorset Regiment left for England. For nearly 11 years the British Army has been in occupation of the Rhine, the headquarters being first in Cologne and then in Wiesbaden. General Sir William Thwaites held his final inspection of the British soldiers on Friday last. They had a great send-off from the inhabitants of Wiesbaden and from their comrades who are following them to England during the next few weeks. The photo here shows a fond farewell salute from a British soldier to his wife as he leaves for England.* (Original captions)

"Germany's burden has been reduced by the Young Plan. All our opportunities for the future lie open to us. The supervision of our economy and our finances is going. We are once again masters of our own house. In a few months the Rhineland will be free, no further controls will remain."

*Gustav Stresemann in conversation
with Theodor Wolff, 1929*

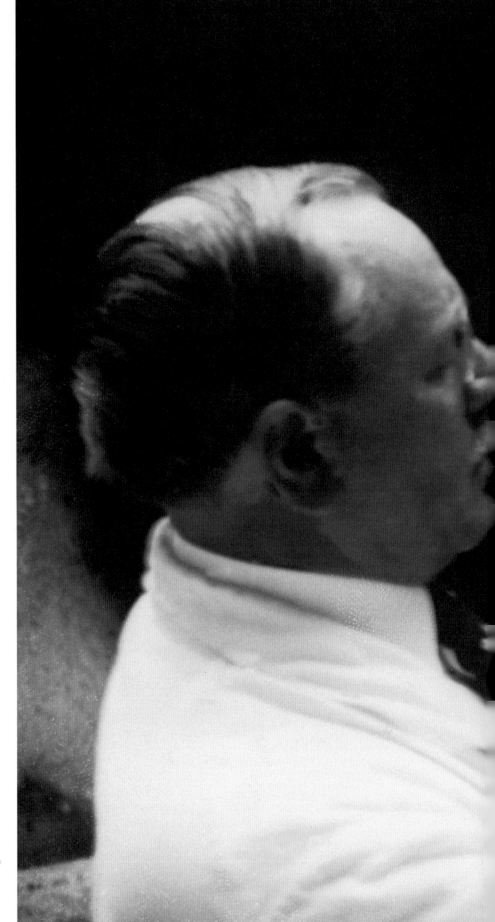

"I was sitting in the barber's chair when I overheard 'Stresemann is dead'; I went numb. The *Paris-Midi* carried the official announcement. he died of a stroke at half past five this morning. It is an irreparable loss whose consequences cannot be foreseen. That too is the way people feel here. Everyone talks about it. Barbers, waiters, drivers, newspaper sellers."

Count Harry Kessler's diary entry during a stay in Paris
on 3 October 1929

The death mask of Reich Foreign Minister Dr. Gustav Stresemann. Our picture shows Prof. Dr. Lederer working on the death mask. (Original caption)

WE ARE A POOR COUNTRY!

The German public keenly followed the exploits of the *Bremen* when it won the Blue Riband for the fastest crossing of the Atlantic; when Fritz von Opel's rocket car tore around the Berlin Grand Prix race track; and when the largest flying boat in the world, the DO-X, landed in New York. German self-confidence had its greatest triumphs when technical innovation was combined with luxury. The original caption for this picture announced proudly: "Sleeping berths in the DO-X. One cabin provides enough space for two people." However, in 1929 journalist Kurt Tucholsky warned people not to equate such technological and economic success with general prosperity: "We are a poor country! In Prussia alone we have 28,807,988 marks for horse-breeding [...] and 2,164,000 marks for relocating our ambassadors and envoys [...] And I, the bookkeeper, draw a yearly salary of 3,600 marks and my wife spends 40 marks a week. I would have to work for 433 weeks to earn the amount that Herr Tirpitz, who botched the organization of the German fleet, gets as a pension."

5

The German Economy Takes Off

From 1923/24 the currency reform, the Dawes Plan and foreign credit – particularly from America – sparked an upturn in the German economy. Production, consumption and national income grew constantly in the period between 1924 and 1929. Dramatic growth was achieved by the electrical, chemical and optical industries. New branches of industry such as automobile and aircraft manufacture and the production of brass, aluminum and synthetic fabrics expanded at the same rate. Film and radio not only became mass media but resulted in the creation of countless jobs. There was tougher competition in the market for coal as well as iron and steel, which could not compete without state subsidies – though here, too, there were increases in production. Agriculture, on the other hand, was largely inefficient; from 1927 it entered a period of prolonged crisis and would not have survived without state support. The general climate for investment was optimistic and was bolstered by large-scale technological projects which were greatly admired by the general public.

The airship *Graf Zeppelin*, the long-range Dornier DO-X flying boat and the passenger ship *Bremen* became international symbols of the efficiency of the German economy. Investment doubled, and workers as well as employers benefited from the profits.

While the economic upturn was undeniable, industrial production and wages did not reach their pre-war levels again until 1928/29, the difference being that the working week was now significantly shorter. The export industry expanded much more quickly, already reaching its 1913 level by 1926. State finances also showed a positive result for the five years from 1924 to 1929, and the budget was almost balanced in spite of the enormous burden of reparation payments.

The Transatlantic Economic Cycle

In the first half of the 20th century the global economy was defined by the USA, Britain, France and Germany. Even before the First World War, however, the United States had begun to leave its European competitors far behind. In the 1920s the continental European economy was dominated by the three great regional economies, supported by American capital. Britain, France and Germany accounted for half of Europe's population and together they produced around three-quarters of Europe's industrial goods.

At the beginning of the 20th century Germany had taken the lead over its European competitors and, after surviving the various crises of 1919 to 1923, it was able to do so again – even if this aroused the suspicions of Britain and France who were little interested in a politically and economically strong German Reich.

With the Dawes Plan, however, a transatlantic economic cycle began which benefited all four leading global economies. After the war American investors were anything but isolationist and actively sought out suitable investment opportunities abroad. Germany, a highly indebted and politically isolated great power with a colossal industrial capacity, offered them the ideal market. Money either flowed directly into individual companies and industries, or entered the coffers of the municipalities and local authorities in the form of public investment. To many people, Germany seemed like "a colony of the New York stock exchange."

Imbalances

In order to remain competitive on the world market, German industry was forced to restructure. Since the beginning of the war other industrial nations had established themselves on the international market as providers of the classic German export products – steel and semi-finished products. Heavy industry lost the key position in the economy which it had previously enjoyed in the Empire, not least because of its dependence on the production of weapons. The restrictions the Treaty of Versailles placed on armaments finally ended the dominance of heavy industry, and other branches of the manufacturing sector, such as machinery, chemicals, precision instruments, and optical and electrical goods went on to flourish.

The bankrupting of countless small and medium-sized enterprises during the inflationary era led to an unprecedented concentration of economic power. The heavy industrialist Hugo Stinnes, for example, invested in durable material assets such as banks, hotels, factories and newspapers while his debts more or less eliminated themselves in the wake of the currency reform. In the left-wing press Stinnes became the symbol of a pathological form of unscrupulous capitalism which profited from others' misery. Stinnes did not live to see the collapse of his Babylonian empire – he died in 1924 – but other concerns had more long-term success. A dynamic export industry – including the newly established concerns I.G. Farbenindustrie AG (1925) and Europe's largest coal and steel conglomerate, Vereinigte Stahlwerke (1926) – developed on the back of dollar credits. Well-established electrical companies like AEG, Siemens & Halske and Bosch also became world market leaders.

Concentration and Rationalization of the Economy

Despite relatively high wages, factories were forced to rationalize their production methods in order to stay internationally competitive. The 1920s was the era of the conveyor belt and the philosophy of Taylorism, which applied new engineering and scientific principles to manufacturing. Work became easier but more monotonous. Although large sections of industry flourished, workers could no longer be sure of their jobs. In 1926/27 the so-called "rationalization crisis" led to countless workers being laid off and the numbers of German unemployed climbed to over 2 million.

Large companies started to make an appearance in the commercial sector as well. Great department store chains like Tietz, Wertheim and Karstadt used innovative methods of advertising and selling. Although they barely made inroads into the traditional markets of the retail trade, the department stores were held responsible for low profit margins. There was discontent among tradesmen who blamed industrial modernization for their misery, and unrest spread in the agricultural sector. After 1924 agricultural products from the USA, South America and Australia flooded the German market and brought down prices.

Political Difficulties

The economic boom of the 1920s had feet of clay. Although the export industry experienced a rapid upswing, the domestic market made only slow progress and even stagnated in many areas. Discontent and insecurity were widespread in all branches of the economy, amongst employers as well as workers. It is still a matter for debate whether misjudged economic and social policies led to the downfall of the Weimar Republic. Today the notion that the forces of capital were to blame for the rise of Hitler and the National Socialists by giving them "a foot up" is no longer convincing – even if large sections of industry and the employers did have nationalistic, anti-republican and "anti-Bolshevist" tendencies.

Left page: *The airship* Graf Zeppelin *returning home to an enthusiastic reception from the public.*
Above: *The vast reserves of coke at the 'Robert-Mülser' mine in Bochum-Werne. Around 100,000 tons of coke which have not found a buyer are stored here.* (Original captions)

"The chief characteristic of this new German corruption of the press, this corruption by industrial magnates, is [...] that they do not operate their publishing business as an end in itself according to commercial methods, but as a sideline to their other business interests without regard to its profitability. Newspapers are no longer a source of income to them but an advertising cost: they are an economic and political propaganda machine, the last link in a vertical trust."

Fritz Wolter in Die Weltbühne, *24 May 1923*

"If you wish to gaze into the abyss of the exploiter Capitalism in all its brutality, you need to go down to the haulage level of a mine shaft [...] broken bones, crushed limbs, torn-off fingers have no power to turn its greed for profit into any other feeling even for a moment. Keep going, keep going; every 45 minutes the cage shoots up and down the shaft. There are no interruptions here [...] Somewhere in a shining hotel, well-dressed, well-fed men – the owners of gold watches, elegant cars, sophisticated women – have determined this pace."

Ludwig Turek, Ein Prolet erzählt
(A proletarian speaks), 1930

Bochum Association – photo essay
This report was a photo-journalist's ode to the decline of heavy industry. The play of light around the furnaces of the steelworks had long been a source of fascination for photographers. The original caption read:
The steelworks silhouette.

Bochum Association – photo essay (continued)
Above left: *In the steelworks.*
Above right: *Battle of light against dark.*
Right page: *Tapping a sample of steel.*

(Original captions)

"There are three factors which above all have served to drive down the hourly rate of production: firstly, the appalling diet of the workers which has continued to exhaust them now for seven years. Secondly, the poor state of much of the equipment. And thirdly, the use of poor quality raw material as well as lack of it."

From the commentary on the production statistics of a blast furnace and steel refinery, 1922

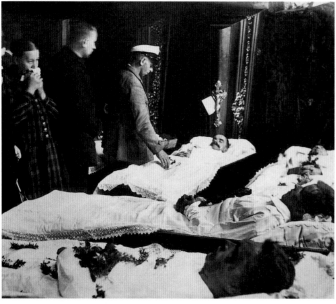

Left page, above: *Horrifying mining disaster in Hausdorf near Neurode (Silesia). The first stage of the rescue.*
Left page, below left: *Farewell to the victims. The dead are laid out in their coffins prior to their burial at the cemetery in Hausdorf.*
Left page, below right: *151 coffins on their way to the hospital of the Mine Workers' Guild, where the dead will be housed prior to burial.*
Above: *Rescue of a seriously injured miner.*
Right: *Three of the small group of miners who survived the terrible catastrophe.* (Original captions)

"In the afternoon of 9 July 1930 there was a serious accident at the Kurt Mine in Hausdorf near Neurode which claimed the lives of 152 victims. 60 miners are still trapped underground and it is hoped that some of them may be rescued, although the worst is feared."

The New York Times, *11 July 1930*

Left page: *A so-called fast train which, in a journey lasting almost three-quarters of an hour, transports miners to the most distant tunnels of the mine at a depth of 820 feet (250 m).*
Above: *Even today there are still some miners who keep to the tradition of making their devotions to the patron saint of miners, St. Barbara, before they descend into the mine. This picture is particularly interesting because it shows a view of the modern mine building in the background.*
Above right: *Modern fluorescent signs give miners the best safety advice: 'Think of your wives and children!' and are read by all those descending into the mine.   (Original captions)*

The Bleicharley Pit – photo essay
The traditional mining areas in the Ruhr and Upper Silesia entered a deep depression after the war, not least because of the repressive measures resulting from the Treaty of Versailles. The original text of this photo essay from Upper Silesia emphasizes this fact: "*The Bleicharley pit is the only lead mine still left in Germany after the Treaty of Versailles.*"

Chassis off the conveyor belt – photo essay

In the 1920s German industry introduced modern, rationalized production methods in order to be able to maintain its position in the world market with products which were value for money. At the Rüsselsheim plant of Adam Opel AG, the conveyor belt and timed production processes dominated the workshops as of 1924. Opel was the first European automobile manufacturer to have rationalized its production in this way, and this article reported on these innovative practices. The original text grumbled that "Modern methods in the automobile industry in Germany are often borrowed from America." Just how dynamic the global market had become was shown when the American manufacturer General Motors bought into Adam Opel AG in 1929.

Left: *View of the production line. Prefabricated steel parts can be seen piled up in the center. They will then be finished and mounted on the chassis.*
Below: *The chassis is carefully inspected before it is sent off to distribution.*
Right page: *A conveyor belt carries the chassis into the paint room for finishing. High-power mercury lamps are used in this work, which depends on precision and an even application of paint.*

(Original captions)

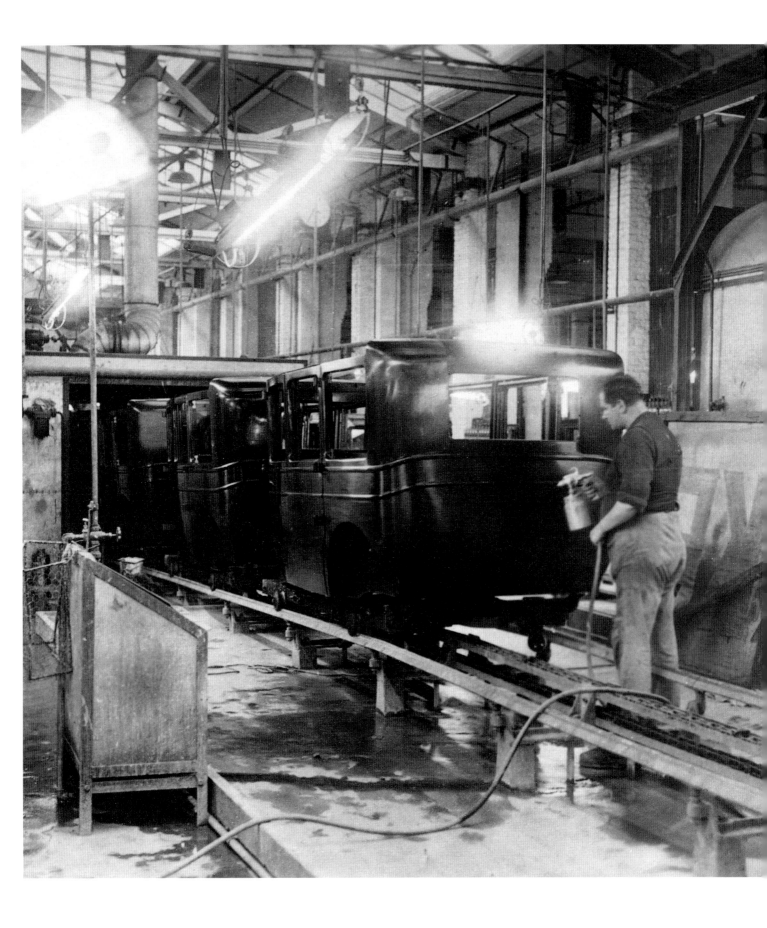

WE ARE A POOR COUNTRY!

Left page, above left: *'Catch, mate!' A workman lifts a beam.*
Left page, below left: *Scaffolders carry an entire arsenal of tools around their waist.*
Left page, right: *Now that's a head for heights! High above the water, workers without safety ropes balance on the rungs of a ladder.*
Above: *For these men, getting to work involves a climbing trip.*

(Original captions)

A bridge gets a new coat – photo essay
One of photo-journalism's merits was that it opened up work environments to people who would normally be denied access. In this report, Walter Süssmann accompanied a brigade of Berlin bridge workers:
"The arch of the iron bridge stretches over the river. It is to be given a new coat of paint because the old one has become rusty and is a threat to safety. A difficult 'measuring-up' process takes place: the bridge is completely encased in a suspended scaffold from which its new coat is painted directly onto its body."

The German ship *Bremen* crossed the Atlantic from Cherbourg to New York in just four days, 12 hours and 17 minutes to win the Blue Riband for the fastest ocean passage. This trophy was celebrated in Germany as a national victory and in the press reports and newsreels of the day it symbolized the country's seemingly unstoppable economic rise. Two years later the award went to the *Bremen's* sister ship *Europa*.

Above: *The battle for the Blue Riband! The maiden voyage of the giant ship* Bremen *on 25 June 1929. The Lloyds' vessel* Bremen *today left the wharves at Bremen to sail to Bremerhaven where she will receive her finishing touches. From Bremerhaven she will begin her first journey.*
Right page: *Launch of the North German Lloyds' ship,* Bremen. *The gigantic 46,000 ton steamer was built at the 'Weser Ship and Machinery Company' in Bremen and was christened and launched on 16 August 1928 in the presence of Reich President von Hindenburg and other prominent figures. Our picture shows the enormous braking chain from this leviathan.* (Original captions)

WE ARE A POOR COUNTRY!

The gigantic new bridge at Cologne-Mülheim; the largest suspension bridge in Europe and the 32nd bridge over the Rhine, was officially opened in a ceremony on 13 October 1929.

Left: *The first stunning view from the new bridge down to the Rhine, whose banks were lined with hundreds of thousands of people attending the dedication.*
Above: *Two masterpieces of German technology: the airship* Graf Zeppelin *flying over the Rhine to greet the new bridge and the assembled crowds.* (Original captions)

Critics at home and abroad continued to attack the extravagance of German local authorities, including this prestige project – the Mülheim cable suspension bridge – supported by the mayor of Cologne, Konrad Adenauer. After the competition jury in 1927 favored a more cost-effective proposal, Adenauer threw his weight behind this more prestigious – and expensive – design.

"The suspension bridge is there because the mayor of Cologne wanted it: and today we are glad that it is there."
The Prussian Welfare Minister Hiertsiefer on the occasion of the bridge's opening, 13 October 1929

The 1920s was the era of the airship, and the leader in the field was the German Zeppelin plant in Friedrichshafen, on the shores of Lake Constance. The international flights undertaken by the firm's owner, Dr. Hugo Eckener – the first was to New York in 1924 – reached their peak with the *Graf Zeppelin's* circumnavigation of the globe between 15 August and 5 September 1929. This airship became a national symbol, but the age of the Zeppelins came to an end after several serious fires in the 1930s. Commercial aviation then concentrated exclusively on the building of fleets of aircraft which were able to transport passengers more quickly and cheaply – and in greater safety.

Right: *The* Graf Zeppelin *starts on its first trial flight. The new airship* Graf Zeppelin, *which was built with money from the Zeppelin-Eckener Fund, yesterday took off on its first trial flight. Our picture shows the* Graf Zeppelin *in its hangar shortly before the flight.*
Below: *The construction of the world's greatest airship in Germany. Work on the new transatlantic Zeppelin cruiser, the L.Z. 127, the largest airship in the world, is making great progress. The atmosphere is feverish in the gigantic hangar of the Zeppelin airship factory at Friedrichshafen on Lake Constance. Our picture shows the walkway in the lower keel of the ship.*
Right page: *One of the side engine gondolas is mounted onto the frame.*

(Original captions)

Left page: *The* Graf Zeppelin *started on its voyage round the world on 15 August 1929. It flew over the Reich capital, Berlin, in bright morning sunshine, to the jubilant cries of the crowd which had gathered in the streets and on the roofs of buildings. Here, people wave at the airship as it flies over the Brandenburg Gate.*

Above: Graf Zeppelin's *visit to England. The famous German airship* Graf Zeppelin *reached Hanworth Aerodrome on the evening of 18 August 1931, its first stop on a pleasure tour through England. Our picture shows a rear-view of the airship during its majestic landing at Hanworth.*

Right: *At Friedrichshafen new direction finding trials were carried out recently by the airship* Graf Zeppelin. *Our picture shows a new type of bearing ring used by the Zeppelin. Friedrichshafen, 30 November 1928.*

(Original captions)

"The second American flight of the *Graf Zeppelin.* Pictures from our special photographer on board the airship."
Above left: *A stunning view from the window of the passenger gondola: sunrise over the Atlantic.*
Above right: *Looking out of the window.*
Left: *Work and pleasure during the flight. In the foreground two passengers in the ship's lounge are pictured having breakfast. In the background is a journalist writing his report on a typewriter. This is the sort of scene which can be witnessed every day in the lounge of the* Graf Zeppelin *during its voyage around the globe.*   (Original captions)

"The *Graf Zeppelin's* round-the-world flight – exclusive snapshots of life on board." The importance of the *Graf Zeppelin's* flights for the German public was illustrated by the battle over exclusive rights to the photographs of its first flight to the USA in 1928. Two large Berlin publishing companies had secured exclusive German rights to pictures of the transatlantic crossing, which had been proclaimed as an event of national importance. This inevitably led to protests by the Association of German Newspaper Publishers. Their formal objections could not however prevent further exclusive rights to photographs being sold in the battle to boost the readership of newspapers and magazines. Even during the 1929 flight, there were exclusive reporters on board the craft.

"We are of the opinion that the German people have a right to be informed as accurately as possible about an event in which they are participating not only with their hearts and minds, but also with their wallets."
Protest note from the Association of German Newspaper
Publishers dated 3 November 1928

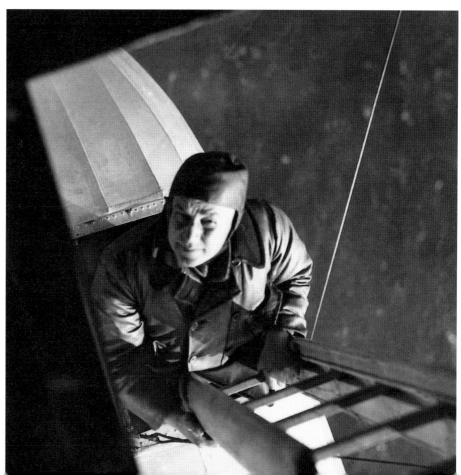

Above left: *At the helm of the* Graf Zeppelin.
Above right: *On the bridge of the* Graf Zeppelin *with Dr. Eckener, who has performed a tremendous, new feat with this flight.*
Right: *Descent from the engine gondola.*

(Original captions)

WE ARE A POOR COUNTRY!

Top: *The giant German flying boat, the Dornier DO-X, arrived in New York on 6 September 1931, carrying 60 passengers, and landed on the water near the Battery in New York harbor after flying over the city. The plane left Lake Constance in Germany nearly a year ago.*

Above: *A triumph of German technology. The gigantic flying boat DO-X, which was launched yesterday and has already completed its first test flight to the complete satisfaction of experts, is a triumph of German technology and of the greatest economic significance to the aeronautics industry. Our picture shows the great moment – the launch of the craft on 13 July 1929.*

Right: *An unusual shot showing how the tail of the giant DO-X compares in size with rowboats manned by sightseers.*

(Original captions)

The flying boat DO-X, built in the Dornier plant in Friedrichshafen, took off on its first flight in 1929. Weighing 50 tons and equipped with 12 engines, it was the largest airplane of its day. The craft had a crew of 12 and could accommodate as many as 100 passengers on three decks; special sleeping cabins for guests were also provided. The flying boat had a wing span of 1,575 feet (48 m) and could reach a speed of 150 miles (240 km) per hour. The prototype took two and a half years to produce.

Towing ten tons – photo essay
These pictures reflect the everyday lives of Frisian herring fishermen. During the crises of the Weimar Republic fishing assumed an important role in providing the population with food.

"The only product of mass consumption of any significance which showed no decline in 1922 and 1923 compared with the pre-war period is sugar. All other food and semi-luxury goods show appalling declines in consumption (with the exception of herrings in 1920 and 1923 – herrings are well-known as the 'poor man's meat' – and rice between May and December 1921.)"
Commentary on statistics on foodstuffs and semi-luxury goods between 1920–23

Above: *Mending nets on board.*
Top right: *Hosing down the decks after the catch.*
Right: *Ready to haul the catch on board.*
(Original captions)

Top left: *Washing the fish in tubs on board.*
Left: *Sorting the catch.*
Above: *The wife of an 80 year old fisherman – herself a typical representative of the Frisian fishing people.*
(Original captions)

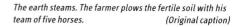

The earth steams. The farmer plows the fertile soil with his team of five horses. (Original caption)

"The maximum amount of work recorded for a female farmer was 4,396 hours or almost 15 hours a day spread over 300 working days. The maximum amount of work for a male farmer was 3,961 hours or more than 13 hours a day in the course of 300 working days. In reality working hours are much less favorable, because during the slack season it is not possible to work 13 hours, so that in times of high demand it is not 13 but rather 15 and more hours that are required."

Adolf Münzinger, Der Arbeitsertag der bäuerlichen
Familienwirtschaft
(The workload of farming families), 1929

SO YOU WANT TO BE RICH?

The benefits brought about by the Weimar welfare state – such as the eight-hour day – were an attempt to enlist the political support of the socially disadvantaged section of the population. The state also attempted to care for disturbed and difficult young people, many of whom had become criminalized due to their parents' poverty. "The spirit of the Ulmenhof [children's home] is 'Care without punishment.' Cheerful, berry-brown children illustrate how sound the motto of the home is." This caption to a photograph from a home for problem children illustrates the trend among magazines to idealize social relations. Despite this, the middle-class press was unable to dispel the fact that the Weimar Republic was deeply divided by yawning social divisions. During the Depression in particular, social conflicts frequently erupted, with many people feeling isolated and abandoned in their poverty: It was a widespread sentiment, summarized by Ringelnatz with his characteristic wry humor in the following lines: "Come tell me your troubles/So you want to be rich? – Why aren't you then?"

6

A Divided Society

Imperial Germany's legacy to Republican democracy was a vastly divided, hierarchical class-based society. The Weimar coalition parties attempted to smooth out the huge social differences of the Empire, but for many people to the right of the political center the changes were too radical, while for many unprivileged people social change was not happening fast enough. By the middle of the "roaring twenties" the social topology of the Republic was characterized not just by a huge rift between rich and poor, but also politically by two conflicting viewpoints, one of which wanted to put an end to the "Weimar system," the other aiming to realize its Utopian dreams and ideals.

Ideological Divisions

A major feature of the social make-up of the Weimar Republic was the religious rift in society. Under Bismarck, the Protestants had relegated the Catholics to the level of second-class citizens in the fight for cultural superiority. After the 1919 revolution, the Catholics tended to be more supportive of the state, while the Protestants supported those parties that were most vigorously opposed to the new Republic. However, the growing secularization of society eroded the politically active Catholic circles, who to begin with were politically homogeneous, and who saw themselves represented by the Center Party.

The most distinct ideological dividing line in society ran between the class-conscious workers and non-Marxist Germany. According to statistics, 45% of the employed population were workers, of which about one-third voted for the two Marxist parties. Although split uncompromisingly into social democratic and Communist circles, the working class projected to the outside world an identity that cemented the dividing line between "socialism" and the "bourgeois world." However, the bulk of the working class was ideologically by no means as entrenched as party activists would have liked, and as their political opponents assumed. An integrated socialist way of life was practiced primarily by the elites in the SPD (Socialist Party) and KPD (Communist Party).

New and Old Middle Classes

While working-class numbers stagnated during the 1920s, the dynamic modern service industry during the Weimar Republic gave rise to a huge army of white-collar workers. Their ultimately heterogeneous political mentality was based on the need to distinguish themselves from blue-collar workers. The white-collar workers, however, were the most insecure group of all. This was perhaps due to the group's unusual need for an ideology: while left-wing white collar workers often behaved like the vanguard of the proletariat, those on the right settled into markedly nationalist and anti-Semitic attitudes. The majority of white-collar workers saw themselves as the "new middle class" and as the dynamic representatives of a social breakthrough.

The "old middle class" was set apart from this new group by its – at least ostensible – financial independence. Just as it had in Imperial times, its core group, made up of craftsmen and small traders, mainly held conservative and clearly anti-social-democratic views, because they felt themselves crushed between the interests of the big corporations and the working class. After the period of runaway inflation, many of them turned from the liberal parties to the nationalists. Similar trends could be observed among smallholders in the west of the country, while the big landowners east of the Elbe were traditionally monarchist and nationalist. There was, however, one point on which the farmers of the mid-1920s were united: Germany had to be protected by customs against cheap overseas imports and saved from further industrialization.

Landowners and Industrialists

The protectionist views of farmers were shared by the coal and steel industry, which under the Kaiser had been accustomed to receiving defense contracts; these of course had to cease after the Treaty of Versailles. For industrial magnates such as Hugo Stinnes, "national stature" also meant a re-armed German nation. It is therefore not surprising that such circles, having survived the threat of their industries being nationalized, rejected a partnership with the employers and toyed recurrently with the idea of a "national dictatorship."

Racing fever. On the racetrack with a camera. The facial expressions and posture of these four gentlemen tell the story of the race. The decision has been made – you guess who placed a winning bet and who has lost! (Original caption)

The export industries were more liberal, i.e. less anti-trade union and less obsessed with authority. The growth industries, such as chemicals and electrical engineering, needed qualified, highly motivated staff, and therefore developed a cooperative climate. In this way they also managed to persuade the trade unions that it was in the common interest to encourage rationalization. Furthermore, being international concerns, they had a stake in promoting the German government abroad. The foreign minister Gustav Stresemann and his DVP were therefore respected in these business circles.

Civil Servants and Academics

The majority of civil servants and academics remained aloof from the Republic and from democracy. The majority of civil servants retained the attitudes they had held in Imperial times. Their sense of class remained rooted in Kaiser Wilhelm's time. In most cases they fulfilled their duty to their "new masters" with Prussian obedience. However, many of this class of "pragmatic republicans" were alienated by their low salaries and redundancies in the early stages of stabilization.

In particular academics on the government payroll, but also private practitioners such as solicitors and doctors, seemed to view the new social order as social degradation. The social historian Arthur Rosenberg described the

The Lustgarten in Berlin was the scene of a massive workers' demonstration against the compensation agreement for aristocratic families dispossessed of their lands.
(Original caption)

typical academician as nationalist and anti-Semitic, hostile to the Republic, and to taking part in democratic government, or in any politics of appeasement and compromise towards foreign powers. As the Jews improved their position in society, anti-Semitism became socially acceptable. Since 1920 it had not been unusual for Jews to be forbidden membership to student organizations, and after the Rathenau murder many students expressed

sympathy for the "killers of Jewish filth." In this environment of conservatism tainted with chauvinism and anti-Semitism, the National Socialists were in the 1920s just one of many small groups of radical academics: it was not until after the economic depression in the early 1920s that more and more members of these circles rallied under the swastika.

The political and social attitude of the army was typified by General Hans von Seeckt's maxim, "The Army serves the state, only the state; for it is the state." After his promotion to Army Chief of Staff in 1920 he was responsible for reducing the Reichswehr to 100,000 men. The proportion of officers from the old Prussian pre-war army remained high. Only members of the old top brass and those who carried the whiff of the old monarchical stables were spared by Seeckt. Henceforth the Reichswehr existed in isolation as a conservative elite apart from the Republic.

Celebrities at the Berlin Press Ball. Seated on the right, Lilian Deyers and Liane Haid. Seated on the left, Konrad Veidt and Gertrud Molo.
(Original caption)

The Social Heritage of the Empire

The drastic treatment meted out to the army after 1920 illustrated an important aspect of the social structure of the Weimar years. The old social classes of the Imperial era became entrenched in their positions, while at the same time fragmenting even further within the old boundaries and becoming increasingly radicalized – yet the careers of these generations continued to follow the political, economic and social tracks that had been laid in the old Reich. A demographic breakdown of the 1925 census showed a predominance of women over men in the 30s and 40s, while there was a corresponding preponderance of males in the younger and older generations. When projected onto the social reality of the post-war period, this meant that after the lost war ex-soldiers returned to their old jobs, pushing the women who had kept the wartime economy on its feet out of the job market; for a variety of reasons this market had no room for the younger generation.

The generals of the Reichswehr for their part could cite the Treaty of Versailles and throw young volunteers and officers from the front, many of them traumatized in the trenches, out onto the street. The experience of the war, and also the state of the economy, prevented them from returning to a normal way of life, which led to thousands of embittered former soldiers continuing the struggle against internal enemies. They joined the *Freikorps* (voluntary corps) and their populist and nationalist supporters' movements, and were soon to join the National Socialists' Stormtrooper Units, to be known as the SA.

To oppose the right-wing militants by paramilitary means, their political opponents, mainly working-class, joined the "Black-Red-Gold Reich Banner" or the communist "Red Front Fighter Association." The militarization of political life during the 1920s was relatively far advanced, and led ultimately to a degradation of social behavior in politically extreme environments.

Equally important for the socialization of the younger generation was the fact that they grew up in a time when spiraling inflation meant money was just slipping away through their fingers. In addition, even during the economic upswing there were by no means sufficient jobs to offer all of them a chance for training or earning a living. This financial insecurity often gave younger people, particularly among the urban poor, the sense of being a lost generation. Their protest was expressed in big cities like Berlin in the formation of unorthodox groups or "wild cliques" (*wilde Cliquen*), which countered the modest aims of the workers' movement with crass materialism and hedonism, and often lived out their feelings of disillusionment in illegal ways.

The problems of middle-class youth were no less real, as after 1919 they also fell into an abyss of uncertainty. With the breakdown of the monarchical social order, the family authority of the upper middle class, the mainstay of the Imperial era, faltered. Such "new" political trends that did develop were vague and uncertain. Many young people sought refuge in clubs and societies, particularly those involved in hiking and other outdoor activities. This romantic form of middle-class youth movement was not new, but it reached its height during the 1920s. The societies were a rebellion against both the hollow rituals of their members' middle-class parents and the "Americanization" of society. However, it was not only middle-class hikers who preached a return to nature and the cult of communal living; young social democrats also went on hikes and sang songs from the *Zupfgeigenhansel* (a popular book of folk and folk-style songs) to the sound of guitars.

Even before the world economic crisis of 1929, youth unemployment was a huge social problem with no solution in sight. But this was not the only reason why young people flocked to the radical parties. It was also related to the aging of the conventional parties.

The joys of the countryside! The hiking season has begun with the first warm days of spring. Hikers can be heard everywhere, singing as they move through the countryside. Here these hikers are studying their map.   (Original caption)

A Society in Crisis

Society in the Weimar Republic was separated by many lines of division, both cultural and political: the isolation of the Jews, the conflict between the nationalistic "Capital of the Movement" Munich and the cultural "Babylon" of Berlin, or the cultural pessimism of the intellectual right in opposition to the unbounded belief in progress of the bohemian left were all illustrations of this. The class structure of the Wilhelmine era was in a state of constant flux. While initially only the political fringes were radicalized, during the 1920s the traditional social environments were continuously eroded.

However, in the wake of the 1919 revolution, the Republic initially drew its support from the moderate forces in the middle and working classes. The government built a social welfare state which, when compared with other countries, ensured an exceptionally high level of social provision, and above all high wages. A "Central Workers' Association" of employers and unions was set up and to a certain extent succeeded in realizing long-cherished dreams of the workers' movement, such as introducing an eight-hour day, wage agreements in all professions, and the recognition of trade unions.

Against this background a state emerged where much was subsidized and redistributed, and the effective policy on working hours and wages further encouraged welfare provision and led to large-scale social housing construction. However, as early as 1927, critics such as the allied reparations agent Parker Gilbert warned of the consequences of a fiscal and social policy that was too profligate with state finances. Public money was invested in the construction of modern residential areas, schools, hospitals, theaters and sports facilities, which was beneficial from the viewpoint of social policy, but extravagant and potentially disastrous from the financial viewpoint.

The intentions of the German welfare state were clear. It was trying to buy the loyalty of social and economic groups by means of subsidies and generous social policies. However, even during the "economic miracle" of 1924 to 1928 the traditional antagonisms between the economy and the welfare state again came to a head. Social achievements such as the eight-hour day were criticized and were revised piecemeal, as the high levels of social security were considered harmful to the competitiveness

Above: *Massive clothes collection campaign for Winter Aid in Berlin, 1931. Donated items are loaded onto trucks by soldiers of the Reichswehr. Below: 50 poor children get a square meal. The Winter Aid Service feeds poor children as guests of the wealthy of the city in the new market hall.* (Original captions)

of the German economy. Monopolization and reduction in social provision in the second half of the 1920s gave rise to growing dissatisfaction and insecurity among wide sections of the population. However, there was also a psychological aspect that should not be underestimated: if the initially high social standards of the Republic were directly linked to the economic optimism that abounded among economists and politicians up until 1929, the demanding mentality of broad sections of the population is not surprising.

When the repercussions of Black Friday, the Great Crash of 25 October 1929, had fully hit the economy of the Weimar Republic, the welfare state was faced with bills that it was no longer able to pay. The Weimar Republic, after the USA, was the country most strongly affected by the world economic crisis. The German economy had already been weakened for the reasons mentioned above: to this were added the unfortunate economic situation and high levels of unemployment even before the outbreak of the crisis, the debts run up by the state, industry and agriculture, the consequences of inflation and the psychological and political repercussions of reparations.

"As we enter the inner circle we finally see the pond, the center, around which the rising, horseshoe-shaped banks are crowned with a circle of houses. The houses have a neat row of attic windows, small and large windows and colorfully inset balconies. [...]This is one of the many new residential areas that represent the greatest advance into the chaos of the limbo between town and country. A housing crisis, combined with a thirst for beauty, today's tendency towards the communal and the enthusiasm of the young generation of architects have been at work here, as they were in Lichtenberg, Zehlendorf and other parts of the city, to create residential areas with a human face. It is work which is continually being developed further, and is probably the most important thing that is currently happening to Berlin. This new, rising Berlin is something beyond description, I can only praise it."

Franz Hessel describing the Britz residential area, from
Spazieren in Berlin *(Walks in Berlin)*, 1929

"If of all the people looking for accommodation in Hamburg 34% want a two room flat, and 50% want a three-roomed flat, but 68% say they can only pay up to 50 marks rent, the result is a sharp contrast between what people want and what they can afford, which is something that needs to be said publicly: What people want must comply with what they can afford, and arrangements should be made accordingly."

Director of the Hamburg Housing Office, 1927

Minimum living space is the order of the day. New housing construction methods are needed since emergency housing regulations have made the minimal apartment a priority for our time. Areas of 42 to a maximum of 72 square yards require skillful and economical ground planning. The Hufeisensiedlung in Berlin-Britz by the architects Bruno Taut and Martin Wagner. Photographed 11 November 1927.
(Original caption)

The Weimar generation of architects was driven by the idea of "building for a better world;" their ambition was to put into practice the reformist ideas of the pre-1914 era and improve the circumstances of the socially deprived population. Supported by the Reich, the provinces and the municipalities, the first phase of public housing construction began. Even though between 1927 and 1930 up to 300,000 new apartments a year were made available either through new construction or refurbishment, demand still far outstripped supply. It was usually the more highly paid craftsmen, civil servants and government workers who were able to afford the new housing. The world economic crisis and mass unemployment made the housing situation even more precarious, with the threat of eviction hanging like a sword of Damocles over many families, even better off ones.

Left page, above: *A new construction method: A seven-room house for 16,000 marks. The Berlin architect Emanuel Joseph Margold has made a notable contribution to the topical problem of building cheap, good quality housing. Using his new method, he has built a house with seven rooms, kitchen, bathroom, built-in furniture, running water and warm air central heating, ready to move in for only 16,000 marks. 13 April 1931.*

Left page, below: *A model development on Bruchfeldstrasse in Frankfurt am Main designed by the city architectural adviser Ernst May in 1928. An idyll on the roof gardens.*

Above: *'How should or how will we live?' Deutscher Werkbund (German Craft Federation) home exhibition in Berlin, 1931. A view of the combined dining and living room, with the sleeping couch front right also replacing a bedroom (Two-room apartment by the Dessau Bauhaus, designer Ludwig Mies van der Rohe)*

Left: *A Berlin house for singles. The Berlin sexologist Lewy-Lenz and the architect Franz Salomon have built a model building for single people at Soorstrasse 6 to house approximately 20 unmarried writers and actors. Each apartment consists of two rooms (living room and study), a hall with cooking facilities, a very well equipped bathroom and a balcony. The picture shows the view onto the balcony from the living room.*

(Original captions)

"Nobody went hungry in Wahlhausen, although the food was simple. With military precision at 12:00 sharp, we children had to stand behind our chairs and to wait for the adults to say grace. [...]Politics and the world at large were far away, and as a farmer it was even easy to take inflation in one's stride. The barley crop, the price of beechwood, Schweizer's (the cowhand's) twins and the foal that was expected were all immeasurably more important than everything that was happening out there in the country at large."

Fritz Huschke von Hanstein,
Eine Jugend auf dem Lande (A Country Youth)

Left page: *A rural idyll. Old fishermen's houses in Holstein.*
Left: *The Black Forest and its inhabitants. An autumn walk through one of the most scenic regions in south-western Germany. Our photograph shows a Black Forest farmhouse parlor.*
Below: *Lock-keeper's family saying grace.*

(Original captions)

Above: *Wash day. Despite the poverty of their homes, the people of the cave village keep everything extremely clean.*
Left: *Only when right up close do you notice this unique settlement.*
Right page: *View of an underground dwelling. Almost level with the ground, and protected against the wind and the weather.*

(Original captions)

The Subterranean Village – photo essay
On the edges of almost all the larger cities in unemployed Europe and in America you would come across emergency shelters and shanty towns for thousands upon thousands of destitute families no longer able to afford their rents. In America they were called Hoovertowns, after the US president Herbert Clark Hoover. In Germany Bertolt Brecht, in his controversial film *Kuhle Wampe* (1931/32), turned his attention to a huge emergency shelter outside Berlin. On a piece of waste land, homeless families had made their own dwellings by digging holes in the ground.

A report by the photographer Willi Ruge describes life in this "subterranean village" as follows:
"Just over 30 miles from Berlin, the capital of the Reich, the city of world commerce – and the city of vacant apartments – lies this sorry settlement [...] In this village, which lies in the vicinity of the beautiful Lake Werbellin, despite the abject poverty, the greatest harmony reigns among all those living there. They have been bonded together by their poverty, and have regained the will to survive. Again and again, you have to shake your head at these mad times, which condemn strong, healthy human beings to idleness and families to live in holes in the ground."

The Subterranean Village – photo essay (continued)
Left page, above: *Young cave-dwellers. They are not yet aware of the wretched times we live in. To them, happiness is a slice of bread.*
Left page, below left: *A mother's love overcomes all.*
Left page, below right: *The village's oldest residents*
Above: *Bedtime.*
Left: *A document for our times – mother love is strong even in a hut.*   (Original captions)

Above: *Midwifery course for medical students. At the obstetrics clinic of Berlin University students are given the opportunity to learn about all aspects of childbirth. First they train using a doll, while later on they assist with patients in the obstetrics clinic. Our photograph shows a midwifery lesson using a model and doll.*

Left: *New mothers wanted. In the Adoption Bureau of the Berlin Provincial Welfare and Youth Department. The adoption office of a children's home: Tending to the children.*

Right page: *A modern children's hospital in Berlin-Lichterfelde. The German Red Cross child sanitarium is one of the most up-to-date of its kind in Europe from the medical and pedagogic points of view. Note the beds of those convalescing have been placed in the open air on the verandah in order to speed up the recovery process. Our picture shows a scene from the sanitarium verandah. Berlin, 1 April 1931.* (Original captions)

"The current adverse social conditions of the population of Berlin find their expression in: 1. The high number of unemployed and people in temporary work among patients' parents [...]This can also be explained by the fact that unemployed parents are often not in a situation to provide sufficient nourishment and clothing for their children, particularly those infants who are not being breastfed. For this reason they are also often loath to take their children from the hospital."

Dr. S. Buttenwieser in a report on the situation in the child wards of the Friedrichshain Hospital in 1930

Above left: *One of the little children in the care of the city of Berlin with a nurse.*
Center left: *Under the sun-lamp.*
Below left: *In the play-pen. Here the smallest inmates can play to their hearts' content until they are tired or hungry.*
Above: *There is no risk of infection. All children have their own cup, washcloth and towel.* (Original captions)

Nanny Berlin. A paradise for orphans – photo essay
The achievements of the Weimar welfare system were drops in the ocean. Before 1923 and after 1929 in particular, social deprivation was part of everyday life for a large section of the German population. The caption to this report on a Berlin orphanage at the end of the 1920s shows the charitable and patriarchal approach of middle-class magazines: "Social deprivation finds its most poignant expression in the reception offices of orphanages. Thousands of tiny human beings live there, cared for by doctors and nurses. Not only babies, but also children of school age are brought to Mama Berlin because large numbers of parents are simply unable to provide for their own children. Each year thousands of children cross the threshold of the orphanage."

"Family M. 2 attic rooms and kitchen, 10 people. The flat is crowded and damp, but clean. A 15-year-old girl and an 11-year-old boy share the same bed. The same is repeated for two more girls and two more boys. Only one baby and a small child have their own sleeping facilities. Many of the children are undergoing treatment for tuberculosis and so have to stay away from school. Family A. 1 room and a kitchen, 9 people: Two parents and 7 children aged from 12 to 1 year. 2 beds, 1 cot and 1 cradle."

Soziale Praxis *(Social Practice), Berlin, 1923*

Light, Air and Sunshine – photo essay
On 9 July 1922 the Youth Welfare Law was adopted, coming into force in February 1924. However, the financial situation of the Reich, the Provinces and the municipalities prevented youth welfare from meeting its expectations. Often working mothers had to place their children in the care of unregistered, so-called "wild" kindergartens. The photographer Robert Sennecke, for his 1930 report, visited the model kindergarten in the Berlin suburb of Köpenick, "situated in the idyllic district of Mittelheide."

Berlin's newest home for children in Köpenick. It was opened at the end of April. The home has been built in accordance with the latest principles and includes a kindergarten (for children who have not yet reached school age) and day care (for children over the age of 6). It accommodates 70 to 90 children. Shown in the photographs are the games room [left], the garden [top] and relaxation in the rest room [above].   (Original text from photo essay)

Above left: *The slide.*
Left: *Lunch time.*
Above: *Adam's ale is a favorite drink on days like this.*
(Original captions)

SO YOU WANT TO BE RICH?

What Berlin is doing for its rising generation – photo essay
A number of years ago public and private corporations undertook to send schoolchildren to vacation homes during the summer vacation; however, a large number remained, unable to participate for financial reasons. The Wilmersdorf district youth office has built a day camp in the forest of Grunewald, where schoolchildren from Berlin, who have to spend the vacations in the city, are given the opportunity to enjoy themselves in the open air. Some 700 children travel daily to the Grunewald forest, some by underground, others by tram, where they can spend the hot summer days playing under supervision in the fresh woodland air. The schoolchildren are of both sexes, aged from 6 to 15. Boys and girls are divided into four groups, depending on their age. Each group is led by teachers, assisted by young helpers.

(Original text from photo essay)

Left page, above left: *The first day at school. There is less to smile about afterwards!*
Left page, above right: *Preparing for school. Dot, dash, comma.*
Left page, below: *The end of the primer? The "reading-box" of the future. Children arranging blocks.*
Right: *Hooray for the Easter Holidays! – but it's also report time. Pupils scrutinize their school report cards.*
(Original captions)

"In the spring of 1922, school ended with the valediction. The headmaster, Herr Bottermann, delivered a fiery farewell speech in the presence of the parents, including my own, a speech which could well have been delivered under the Kaiser: he made no mention at all of the new republican and democratic Germany. With hindsight, I can merely repeat that the so-called November Revolution in proclaiming the Republic may have brought about a democratic constitution which was almost too extreme, but the cohort of teachers and civil servants, which was one of the bulwarks of the middle class, barely changed its basic views. The majority of young people, and in particular students, displayed anything but revolutionary fervor."

Wolfgang Stresemann, son of the Foreign Minister

Hooray, it's recess! – photo essay
The Weimar Constitution tried to breathe a new liberal spirit into the Imperial school system. However, the conditions of "mass education" were such that the government only succeeded in scratching the surface of the authoritarian structures of teaching and learning. Corporal punishment was banned only in the province of Saxony. In addition to the three-tier state school system, with grade, middle and high schools, there were numerous religious and private schools. Compulsory schooling lasted eight years.

"Moral education, a civic outlook and personal and professional diligence in the spirit of German citizenship and national reconciliation shall be aimed for. Teaching in public schools shall make provisions to avoid infringing the sensitivities of people with differing viewpoints. Citizenship and labor instruction shall be taught at schools. All pupils shall receive a copy of the Constitution on completion of school."
Constitution of the German Reich 1919 (Article 148)

Left page, above left: *Mother's sandwich is delicious.*
Left page, above right: *Children in the playground during recess.*
Left page, below: *First graders at the water fountain.*
Top: *Elli has something interesting to say.*
Left: *One of many practical jokes: A schoolboy pushes a sheet of paper with a cheeky comment under a classmate's collar.*
Above: *The chalkboard invites jokes and comments about the teacher that few dare to express aloud.*
(Original captions)

Pupils' tribunal in a modern Berlin school – photo essay
Educational reforms during the early 20th century aimed to
build up pupil independence and responsibility. However,
they were only widely introduced in private schools whose
educational methods radically questioned the general
system of education. This is shown in the text to this
photo essay:
*In the Berthold Otto School, one of the most radical of the
reforming schools, self-determination of the pupils has
been applied in every activity. The teacher is entirely a
background figure. The pupils themselves devise the
syllabus. The final principle of the right to self-
determination is of course to uphold discipline, to
accommodate the demands of the majority and also to
punish infringements against the community. The children
have their own 'judicial system,' and teachers are not
involved in any way other than giving advice when asked in
difficult and complicated cases. Verdict and punishment are
decided by an elected tribunal.*
*Our photographs give a spontaneous view of the children's
court, with the passionate election of the judge, the
indictment, and then the trial.*

Left page, top: *Hans for deputy judge! He is fair! Noisy
electioneering in the school yard.*
Left page, below left and right: *Scenes during the trial.*
Right: *The new teaching method at the Hellerau
Experimental Primary School in Dresden.*
*The children in this school are taught not by conventional
methods, but with the aid of pictures and models. Children
are encouraged to use their own initiative and work out
their own method. In our photograph: Children learn by
themselves how to handle a microscope. Photo from 1928.*
(Original captions)

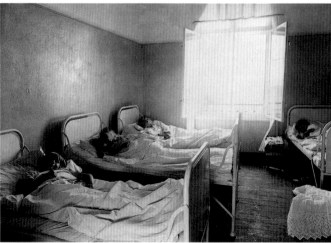

Berlin children on vacation by the North Sea – photo essay
For most working class households, family vacations were out of the question. Only members of the "worker aristocracy" could afford the holidays on offer. A fortnight's holiday by the Mediterranean cost 22.585 Reichsmarks per day, while according to the Reich Statistics Bureau, the average daily expenditure of one worker in 1927/28 was 12 Reichsmarks for an individual, and 32 Reichsmarks per household. There were, however, alternatives to the middle-class type of vacation for working-class families and their children. They went on hikes or day trips, went camping or visited the new holiday hostels that were being built in many places.

Above: *Vacationing students at the seaside.*
Left: *Girls' dormitory, with a view of the sea from the window.*

(Original captions)

The German North Sea island of Helgoland has become a summer camp! Each year thousands of German children from all parts of the Reich are sent for lengthy holidays in Helgoland, paid for by the state and the municipalities. There they are accommodated in the former naval arsenals, which have been fully fitted out as vacation hostels. With good food and constant walks, the children can really enjoy themselves. *(Original text from photo essay)*

Above: *Children waiting to embark for Helgoland at Cuxhaven Quay.*
Left: *Enjoying a vacation by the North Sea. Front view of the Wittdün holiday hostel with its view of the sea.*
(Original captions)

The Bellboy Code – photo essay
The big Berlin hotels were frequented by the stars and moneyed classes of the Weimar Republic. This photo essay gives an insight into the bellboys' drill at the Hotel Excelsior.

Left page: *A bellboy whose shoes are not considered clean is sent back to polish them again.*
Above: *Shoes make the man (or boy). Like hands, shoes are also inspected for cleanliness.*
Right: *Hands and fingernails must be spotless.*
Bottom: *Buttons are always tricky.*

(Original captions)

When you see a young bellboy, you can't help smiling and thinking, 'How charming!' But take a look behind the scenes, and you will see that the life behind the closely fitting uniform is one of great discipline. These young bellboys, barely out of school, lead a hard life. They are trained in manners, punctuality and above all unquestioning obedience. Anyone who sees them changing shifts in the hotel foyer between three and four o'clock could hardly suspect that these youngsters, not yet out of childhood, are on duty for hours that would be demanding even for an adult. For eight hours they stand at their post, or run errands from table to table and from story to story. One shift is from the early morning to past midday, while the other lasts from the afternoon to midnight.

(Original text from photo essay)

The first duty of a bellboy is cleanliness. He must keep himself and everything he has to deal with in good order. Every day on starting work, he is checked by his superiors to see that his hands are clean, that he is washed and combed, that his shoes shine and his ears are spotless. Every bellboy has to ensure that his uniform is in order and that loose buttons are immediately sewn on again. But the young boys often find ways of circumventing the rules. If one of them doesn't want to make the trip to the tailor's all he needs to do is to push a matchstick through the eyelet of the loose button, thus effecting a makeshift repair.

(Original text from photo essay)

"Further education colleges are there to provide the intellectual base for democracy, to awaken national awareness, to satisfy the intellectual hunger of the worker, to renew German idealism, to win ground for the Protestant church among the people, and to keep the unemployed away from the pubs; they should also assist in caring for infants, maintaining the culture of the past and laying the foundations for a culture of the future."

Ironic commentary by Werner Picht on the excessive demands made of further education, 1919

The sixty-year-old college student – photo essay
A major critic of the boom in further education colleges
after 1918 was the workers' movement, which ran its own
educational institutions. It regarded the colleges as deeply
bourgeois, doing nothing to raise class consciousness, and
instead imbued by the educational concept of a "united,
ordinary, hard-working people." This photo essay describes
adult education at a Berlin evening college anecdotally:
*It is not rare to see among the scholars those of a mature
age, including a not inconsiderable number that have
already completed their sixth decade [...]Depending on the
social position of the students, lessons are either free of
charge or charged at the low fee of 10 marks per semester.*

Left page, above: *Old and young side by side at the desk.*
Left page, below left: *The youngest woman in the class.*
Left page, below right: *A final year student.*
Above: *English lesson in a senior class. The teacher helps
with pronunciation.*
Right: *Supper during the break.*

(Original captions)

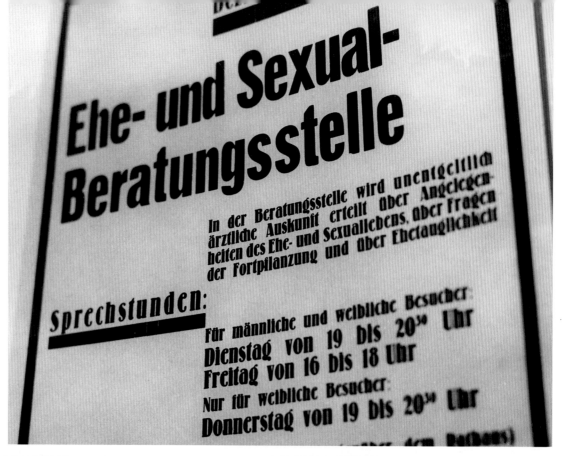

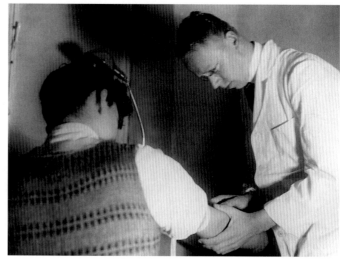

State support for matrimonial happiness – photo essay
On 6 June 1919 Magnus Hirschfeld opened the "Institute of Sexual Science," which also offered a sexual advice bureau – the first establishment of its kind in the Weimar Republic. In its first year of existence it was visited by 3,000 people seeking advice. Over the next 14 years almost 400 such advice bureaus came into being, although the majority were maintained by voluntary organizations such as the Mutterschutzbund (League for the Protection of Mothers) and International Workers' Aid. However, this article emphasizes the work done by government organizations: "One of the most important achievements for the people's well-being in modern times is public advice for people

wishing to marry. The aim of this institution, at present based on private initiative, is to elucidate all the questions of importance to public health before embarking on matrimony. The advice given therefore is not on economic matters, but on health and the discussion of psychological conditions, lack of consideration for which can lead to complications in marriage. The most important issue is and remains that of maintaining and fostering public health. The institution is thus primarily active in the city and subject to the control of the health authorities.
(Original text from photo essay)

Top: *The poster for the Matrimonial Advice Bureau.*
Above left: *Young couple in the waiting room.*
Above right: *A doctor takes a blood sample to check the man's health.*
Right page, above left: *Filling in a questionnaire.*
Right page, above right: *The doctor in charge prescribes treatment.*
Right page, below: *This view of the waiting room proves that all classes use the Matrimonial Advice Bureau.*
(Original captions)

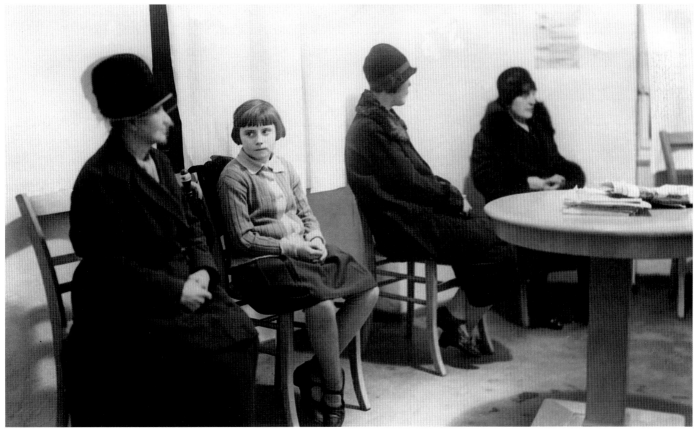

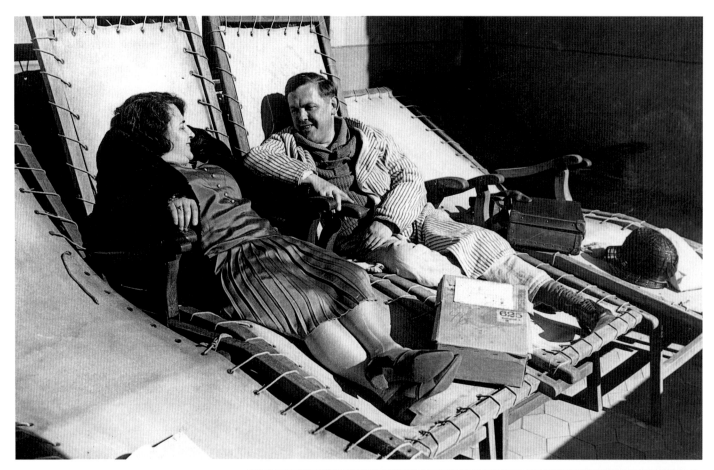

Visitors' day at the hospital – photo essay
From a purely statistical point of view, under the Weimar
government general health care improved considerably
compared with the Wilhelmine era. In 1930 there were 7.4
doctors for every 10,000 people. This compared with 4.8 in
1910; and in comparison with 68.1 during the pre-war
period, there were 90.9 hospital beds per 10,000 people.
While respiratory diseases were on the decline, child
mortality continued to be high, and the numbers of patients
with cancer and cardio-vascular diseases grew. The state of
public health generally mirrored the economic situation.
This photo essay from 1930 follows a group of visitors and
their relatives in hospital:
*Three times a week , on Wednesday, Saturday afternoon
and mainly on Sundays, the hospital gates are opened to
the hordes of visitors.*

Above: *A wife visits her sick husband.*
Right: *Grandpa is taken to see his loved ones.*

(Original captions)

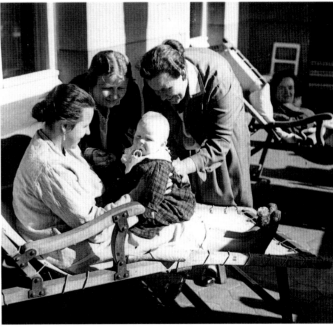

Above left: *The first outing of spring with the visitors.*
Above: *A baby visits its sick mother.*
Left: *Go on, take a few flowers!*

(Original captions)

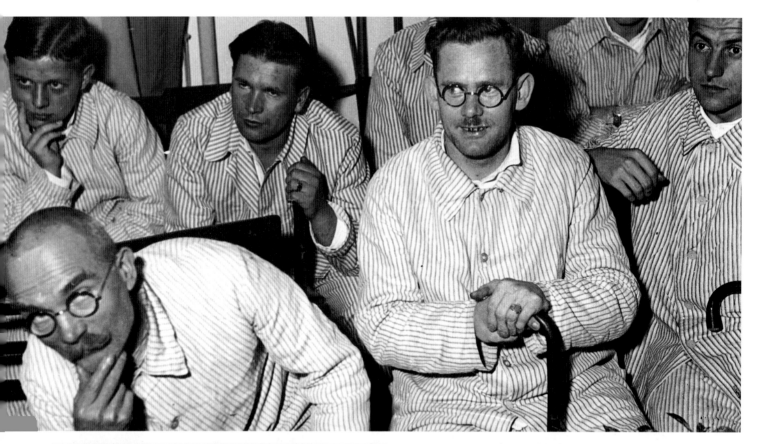

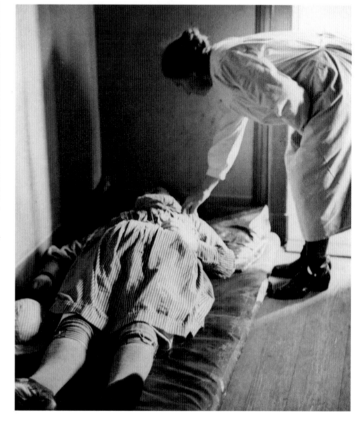

Entertaining the Sick – photo essay
This photo essay gives a typical example of a private charitable initiative. The photographer accompanies a theater group on its tour of Berlin hospitals: *The Thespians visit the sick and the burdened. The Homann dramatic troupe has undertaken to perform exclusively in hospitals, hospices and reformatories.*

Top: *Spandau Hospital. A group of invalid patients watches the performance with fascination.*
Above: *Society scene from a production at the Rehbrücke Home for the Blind.*
Right: *The Wuhlgarten Home (Mental Asylum). One of the patients at the home has suffered a sudden collapse and has been lain down on the mattresses which are there at the ready. Her protective hat lies beside her. Candid photograph with the Ermanox.*
Right page: *The Wuhlgarten Home (Mental Asylum). Patients with less serious conditions are taken from the houses where they are accommodated to the theater performance.*

(Original captions)

"In 1927 more than 280,000 people were accommodated in Prussian penal institutions and prisons. On an average day there were 36,000 prisoners in 20 penitentiaries and 935 jails. Some 6,300 officials and 920 auxiliary staff and clerks work in the penal administration system."

Dr. Schmidt, Prussian Minister of State and Justice, Berlin, 5 September 1928

"Today's prison officials need to know how to deal with difficult psychopaths; they need to be prepared and able to treat the prisoners individually, to know the underlying cause of the offense (unwillingness to work, obsessive acquisitiveness, alcoholism, sensuality, etc.), and to explain these to the prisoners to prevent them re-offending."

Secretary of State Hölscher, The Purpose and Course of Punishment, 1928

Far left: Modern-day punishment at the Fühlsbüttel Penitentiary in Hamburg. Securing the education of prisoners: a class in the prison yard.
Above: The prison bank, staffed by prisoners, where pay for labor is calculated, as well as expenditure for food and drink or tobacco, savings and the payment of the balance on release. Every prisoner has his own account.
Left: 'Two Years in the Workhouse.' Our photograph shows an old street sweeper. (Original captions)

Women in prison – photo essay

According to Prussian statistics for 1927/28, about seven per cent of the inmates of penal institutions were women. Half of the cases were property offenses: "It is a moving fact that the next highest group of offenses is murder, the majority of victims being the women's own husbands. And how much wretchedness and despair must lie behind the number of child murders," the Reichstag deputy Agnes Neuhaus concluded in 1928. A photo essay from 1930 shows the prison conditions at Barnimstrasse women's prison, the only jail in Prussia that was run by women, and comments: "In its entire structure and organization the jail shows the direction taken by penal institutions today, which aims to place less emphasis on punishment than on improvement."

Top: *Everything changes with time, even penal institutions. In accordance with modern thinking, things are gradually improving and becoming more humane day by day. This picture [...] shows women prisoners doing gymnastics. Gymnastics has been taught at the women's prison since 1919. All healthy women under the age of 30 must participate.*
Above right: *Bleaching linen on the lawn in the fall.*
Above: *Prison life in Germany today. Barnimstrasse Women's Prison. The largest and most modern women's prison is situated in Berlin's Barnimstrasse. Our photograph shows a mother and child in an individual cell.*
Right: *The prison school. Modern languages can also be studied on request.*
Right page: *Returning from exercise.*   (Original captions)

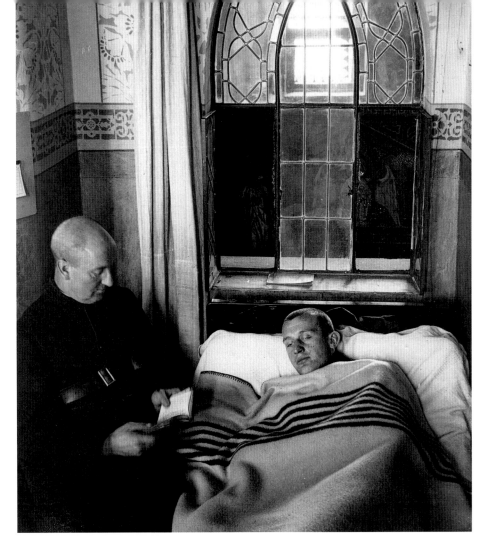

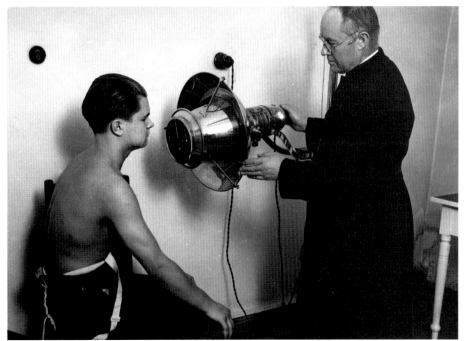

Behind the monastery walls: a clinic for drug addicts –
photo essay

Contemporaries called 1920s Berlin the cocaine capital of
the world. In his autobiography, Carl Zuckmayer wrote:
"Taking 'coke' was at the time highly fashionable in
Schwabing as well as in various Berlin circles on the
periphery of the art world. The vice was considered
interesting or a sign of genius." The poet himself succeeded
in resisting the drug, although during the inflationary
period of 1922 he tried his hand at dealing, with little
success. Sigmund Freud, on the other hand, carried out
"experiments" on himself, and Johannes R. Becher,
Gottfried Benn and Ernst Jünger were not averse to cocaine.
The "nude dancer" Anita Berber fell victim to cocaine
addiction, when she died in 1928 at the age of 29 as a
consequence of her extreme lifestyle. The Berlin police
dealt with an average of three or four "narcotics offenses" a
day in the mid-1920s. This photo essay follows the history of
those who were convicted:

"Outside the gates of Berlin, where the lake of Weissensee
lies, is St. Joseph's Sanitarium, a monastery behind whose
walls patients with nervous disorders and addicts find a
cure [...] It was Alexians, disciples of St. Alexius from the
monastery in Neuss, who set up a sanctuary for treatment
and peace here in Weissensee. [...] Here a lengthy course of
treatment is applied, which aims to gradually wean patients
off the drugs. Such treatment lasts several months, and only
a small percentage find the strength to break their
addiction for life."

Left page: *As everywhere in the institution, the seriously ill
are separated from the less serious cases, and accompanied
by several monks even during exercise.*
Above: *The Suicide Room: Anyone using this room has at
some stage attempted suicide, so a priest is always in
attendance.*
Right: *A patient is given sun-lamp treatment by a doctor.*
(Original captions)

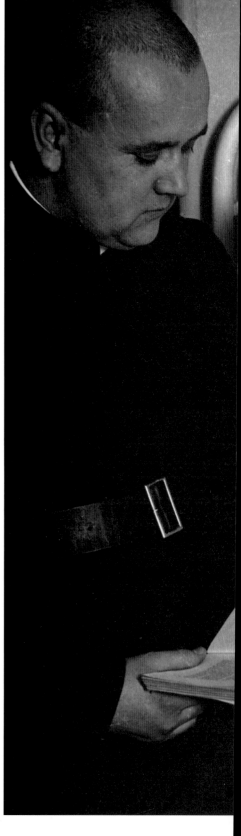

Behind the monastery walls: a clinic for drug addicts –
photo essay (continued)

Above: *The patients can relax by playing billiards and
other games, although a monk always keeps a discreet
eye on them.*
Below: *Occupational therapy: where possible, the monks
involve their patients in farm work.*
Right: *One of the oldest inmates even succeeded in building
a primitive radio.*

(Original captions)

SO YOU WANT TO BE RICH?

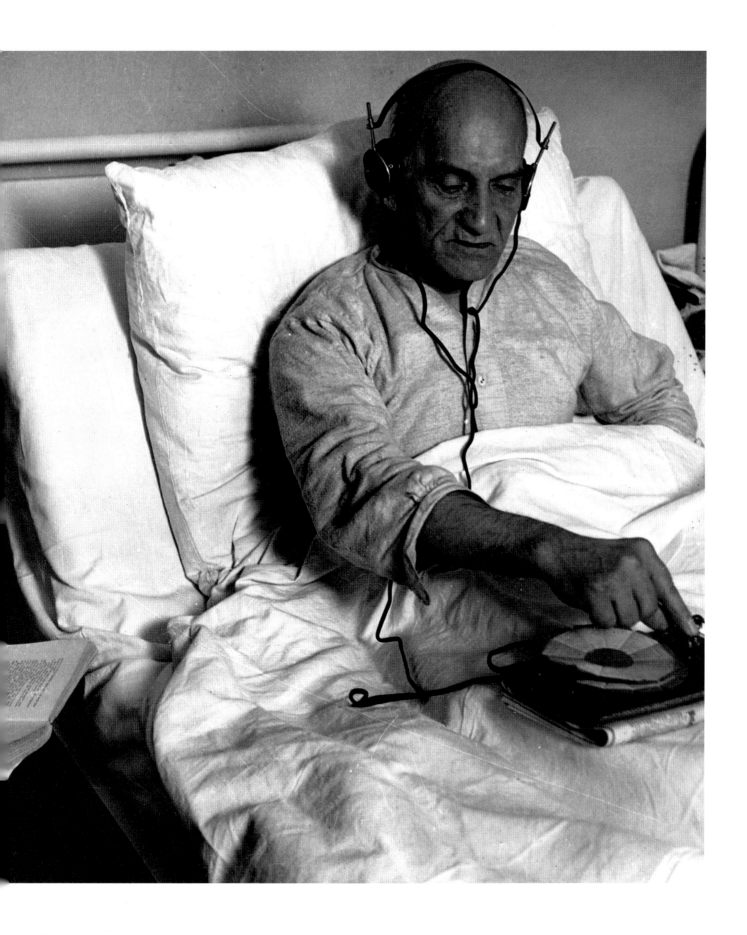

Five marks a suit – photo essay
When the Brüning government introduced its deflationary policy in 1930, the system of social security began to founder. The reduction in state social provision combined with mass unemployment triggered poverty on such a large scale that private and church welfare societies, the social democratic *Arbeiterwohlfahrt* or the communist International Workers' Aid were unable to do much to relieve it. This report highlights the private contribution of women working voluntarily in a Berlin clothes repair shop: "When looking at the inhabitants on the outskirts of Berlin, you immediately notice how down-at-heel and ragged the people look. This poverty is due to the large scale of unemployment, and buying clothes, even in second-hand shops, is beyond the means of the majority of the jobless. For this reason the city, together with charitable organizations, tries to ensure that the poor do not have to go about in rags. For a small sum, or even free against a note from the social welfare organization, the so-called 'clothes repair shops' give people the chance to wear clothes fit for a human being. The Schöneberg clothes repair shop has of necessity been housed in the old bath-house. A group of charitable women got together and gave unstintingly of their time to collect old clothes, underwear, shoes, etc., and repair them after disinfection. Some sample prices: hats 60 pfennig, ladies' summer dresses 50 pfennig, pair of shoes 1 mark, a frock coat with white waistcoat 8.50 marks, etc."

Left page: *The shower room of the old bath-house is now used for ironing clothes.*
Above: *View of the repair hall of the welfare office.*
(Original captions)

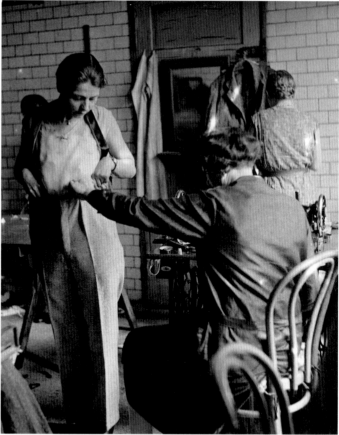

Five marks a suit – photo essay (continued)
Top: *Old clothes are repaired under showers and beside bathtubs.*
Above right: *The final fitting.*
Above: *The new suit costs only five marks.*
Right: *Girls' dresses can be obtained for as little as 50 pfennig.*
Right page: *The store room.* (Original captions)

Above: *The big winter clothes collection campaign in Berlin, 1931. Male and female volunteers hurry from one apartment to another to collect clothes from individual residents.*

Right: *Breakfast at a Berlin experimental school. The City Magistrate of Berlin has set up an experimental school in the sheds of Elementary School 308. The reason for this was the mistrust of school shown by working-class children. Attempts are being made to overcome this problem by giving the children, 90% of whom come to school on an empty stomach, free milk or cocoa at 10:00 a.m. The milk and cocoa is prepared and distributed by the children's mothers. Our picture shows breakfast being distributed to the pupils.* (Original captions)

"The recently introduced Winter Assistance Campaign is particularly characteristic of the current role played by private welfare. Further social deductions from workers and the middle class is something the government considers difficult to implement, and for this reason they have appealed to the populace to make 'voluntary' sacrifices to alleviate the burden on public social welfare."

Berliner Tageblatt, *4 October 1931*

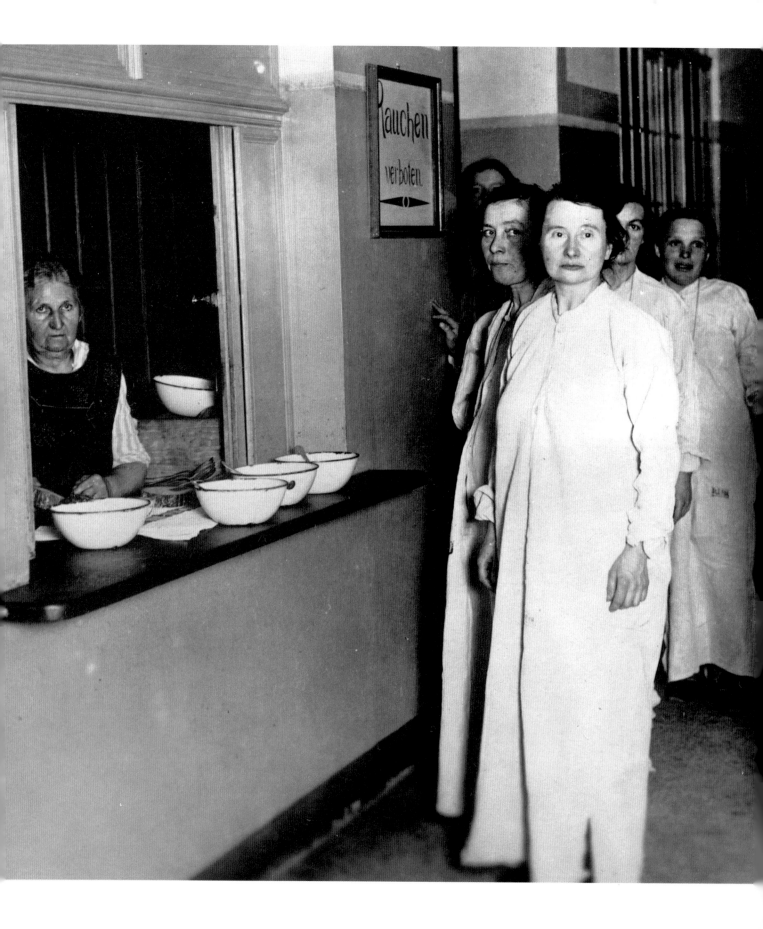

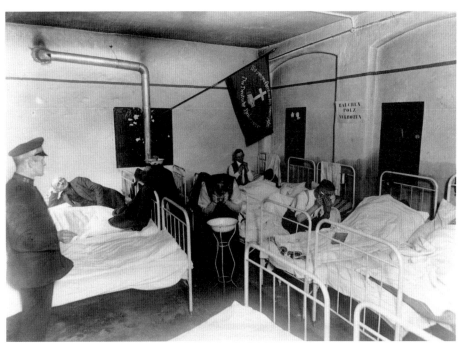

Left: *A refuge for homeless women. After the women have put on their long gowns, which are the refuge's uniform, they are given soup and bread for supper.*
Top: *A German Salvation Army. For technical and financial reasons, the German Salvation Army has split off from the main Salvation Army in order to make all its proceeds available to the German poor, instead of 30% as was originally the case. In a disused factory building at 138c Müllerstrasse in Berlin they have set up accommodation* *and under the dedicated guidance of Commander Harfensteller they help anyone who knocks at their door. This picture shows the Salvation Army dormitory.*
Above: *Berlin's 'Supermarket for the Poor.' For their work, day laborers are paid in kind and also given a meal.*
(Original captions)

Money on the street. Since war and inflation have destroyed the livelihoods of many Berlin shopkeepers, there is a new opening for them: street trade. Stalls and carts, previously seen only on market days, are now to be found on all street corners. The rent and rates for a shop are too high, and so they have to try and earn a few pennies by trading on the street. In a loud voice, the seller draws his customers to his goods and sings their praises. It is surprising what you can acquire on the street: rubber collars, cigarettes, chocolate, braces which last 'forever,' 'genuine' gold plated brooches and necklaces, books and handbags, all 'ridiculously cheap', and a once-in-a-lifetime opportunity. But a street trader's life is not easy, and he often has to pack up his goods in the evening without having made a single penny. On the other hand, by skillfully advertising their goods, others succeed in getting a decent turnover. In any case, it is not an easy business, and it will not make you rich.   (Original caption)

SO THAT'S THE WAY THE WORLD IS...

7

"The band of the 'Katakombe' cabaret on the Kurfürstendamm in Berlin" ran the original caption for this photo, which was taken before the group split up. "How political can or should art be?" was a question which dominated the "roaring twenties," and the 'Katakombe' cabaret – which was founded in 1929 – was not the only group of artists to fall out over the issue. Ernst Busch and Hanns Eisler, the most committed and politically aggressive members of the group, left in December 1930 to establish themselves in the Bellevuestrasse away from the bright lights of the Kurfürstendamm. Like Busch and Eisler, Bertolt Brecht also thought that it was the duty of art to criticize the status quo. In *The Rise and Fall of the City of Mahagonny* Brecht's protagonist, the lumberjack Paul, functioned more or less as a mouthpiece for Brecht's own views: "So that's the way the world is: peace and harmony, they don't exist/but hurricanes – they do/and typhoons where hurricanes aren't enough/and that's how we are:/we have to destroy whatever's there."

The Shock of the New

Countless retrospectives have conjured up an image of the second decade of the 20th century as the "roaring twenties." As far as the Weimar Republic is concerned, however, this rather broad term really only indicates that art and culture in this era were detached from the unpleasant realities of a society plagued by economic and political crises. New social opportunities were created, and nowhere were discussions more controversial and heated than in the artists' circles and literary cafés of the capital. But this upheaval was not confined to Berlin – the entire Republic underwent a kind of culture shock. To the artists and performers of the interwar period, the revolution of 1918/19 came as a welcome release from the official culture of the Imperial era, which had stifled the cultural avant-garde. Now, though, the experiences of the First World War had shaken the very foundations of social life. Cultural life and thought were characterized by a neurotic sense of insecurity, a situation which was intellectually volatile: it was not only on the political "stage" that proletarian and revolutionary ideas clashed with nationalist ideologies.

The cultural elites of the Weimar Republic came from remarkably different social and ideological backgrounds; whether from the right or left, however, they all had one thing in common – they all claimed to occupy sound intellectual standpoints and defensible ideological territory. With unflagging energy they all strove to establish absolute truths, paying little or no regard in the process to the achievements of the Republic's constitutional fathers. Culture and politics during the "roaring twenties" were like fire and water: extravagant ideas on one side, and on the other a dreary and depressing reality. An essential characteristic of "Weimar culture" was its fierce criticism of conditions as they actually existed in the country, something to which the authorities responded with increasing censorship – especially when this criticism was expressed by the left. There were a few "pragmatic Republicans," such as Gerhart Hauptmann and Thomas Mann, but their support for the Republic was more a matter of the head than the heart. Even those who do not subscribe to the idea that art is simply the playground of the emotions might today ask the question whether it really was the task of culture to give unconditional support to the drab reality of life in the Republic after the repressive years of the Empire. The free play of the spirit permitted under the new Republic was too much of a temptation – and the achievements of the country's parliamentary representatives were too undistinguished – to have inspired a cultural response. In this age of "isms" the arts and sciences in Germany were free as they had never been before, and this was especially true in terms of their relationship with the state. The rules governing democracy meant that people's ideas and convictions could be taken to extremes – a phenomenon which could be observed at another crucial place in public life where opinions were formed: the Reichstag. The fatal difference between these two spheres however lay in the fact that it has always been the duty of the parliamentarian – rather than the artist – to produce a democratic consensus.

To the modern historical mind the "culture of Weimar" means "classic Modernism." In his autobiography Stephen Spender described the contemporary cultural elite: "Almost all the German intellectuals whom we knew accepted and practiced a kind of orthodoxy of the Left. This attitude influenced the theater, the novel, the cinema, and even music and painting." It was in fact Erich Maria Remarque, Fritz Lang, Paul Hindemith and Georg Grosz who – along with many others – provided the essential cultural momentum of the Republic and whose works dominated the feature pages of the newspapers. "Modernist" works enjoyed international recognition – and even resonate to this day – though they were neither popular nor generally accepted by audiences of the day.

Cultural Conservatism

Along with "classical" Weimar artists and the emergence of a new mass culture, traditional styles of art and patterns of thought continued to linger. These older cultural elements gave rise to a critique of civilization and a powerful sense of cultural pessimism which were manifested in works such as Oswald Spengler's popular book *Decline of the West*. The opinions of the lyric poet Gottfried Benn were of a piece with Spengler's: "Since 1918 German literature has been written on the basis of catchwords like speed, jazz, cinema, the exotic, and technology and has expressly rejected all spiritual problems […] Personally I am against Americanism. I am of the opinion that a philosophy of purely utilitarian thought […] is not suited to Western man and his history." Critics like Spengler or Benn attacked Western art as either "Americanism" or "cultural Bolshevism." This strongly pessimistic cultural mood went hand in hand with a marked anti-Semitic approach which was directed against the supposed domination of the nation's culture by Jews. One of the main targets of such criticism was the central role which many Jews undeniably did play in journalism, publishing, theater and film.

The Veidt dance troupe: Alfred Döblin's Marriage at the Volksbühne in Berlin.
(Original caption)

This drama by Döblin was inspired by a working group whose members included Bertolt Brecht, Erwin Piscator and Fritz von Sternberg. *Marriage* had its premiere on 25 November 1930 at the Studio Theater in Munich. After two weeks the production was closed because of allegations of Communist propaganda.

A new member of the writers' academy: Alfred Döblin. (Original caption)

Döblin, a doctor by profession, was possessed of an enormous creative drive. He reflected on life in Berlin in countless essays, plays, and prose works. His novel *Berlin Alexanderplatz* is considered one of the central works of modern German literature.

This conservative intellectual movement may not have given birth to any exceptional works of art, but it was able to draw on the support of large sections of the population.

The Age of Isms

Expressionism, Dadaism, Surrealism, Verism, Constructivism ... The roots of Weimar culture can be found in the era of the German Empire. In the first decade of the 20th century the Expressionists were the first in the field of fine art to turn against the academic culture of the Empire. This anti-bourgeois movement was widely influential in painting, poetry and drama and affected other producers of culture who were not themselves Expressionists: Arnold Schoenberg's atonal music, Max Reinhardt's stage productions, Walter Gropius's functionalism, Albert Einstein's and Max Planck's scientific theories, Gerhart Hauptmann's dramas and the great novels of the Mann brothers – such as Heinrich's *Professor Unrat* or Thomas's *The Buddenbrooks* – were all children of the pre-1914 era. The literary cabaret – the focus of intellectual Weimar culture – also experienced its heyday in the Berlin of Wilhelm II, when texts by Frank Wedekind and Walter Mehring were performed.

During the first years of the Republic it was Expressionism that continued to set the tone. Radical opposition to the world of the bourgeoisie; revolutionary unrest; and the sheer joy of experimentation inspired yet more avant-garde movements. Dadaism represented a still greater intensification of these attitudes in its fundamental rejection of all previous concepts of art. The avant-garde movement essentially came to an end around the years 1922/23 and it was followed by a rejection of the utopian claims of Expressionism.

"Weimar culture" subsequently developed a greater interest in the realities of modern life. Modern society and its associated manifestations such as technology were no longer demonized but were interpreted as new challenges which had to be modified. *Neue Sachlichkeit* ("New Objectivity") now became the real artistic doctrine of the Republic. It too had its roots in the years before 1914 – though the term was first coined in 1923 – and it became a collective concept for a series of different genres whose common feature was an artistic examination of modern industrial society which was cooler and more analytical in nature. The works of the "New Objectivity" movement are many and varied and include: novels by Alfred Döblin, Hans Fallada and Erich Maria Remarque; Erich Kästner's poems and Egon Erwin Kisch's journalism; the films of G.W. Pabst and Walter Ruttmann; August Sander's photography; Gropius's and Mies van der Rohe's "new buildings;" the Bauhaus with its experimental design ideology; and the social satire of artists like Otto Dix and Georg Grosz.

Cultural War

Artistic creativity slackened after 1929/30 and ideological positions became polarized. More and more artists turned away from "New Objectivity," with the extreme left regarding art as just another political weapon. At the same time forces on the right intensified their attacks on "Modernism," and this led to an unbridgeable gap opening up right through German society. The nation was not only politically divided: now, hostile and irreconcilable cultural camps also confronted each other. The political stages of the Republic therefore also have their counterparts in "Weimar culture." The early years of the Republic were dominated by Expressionism, which opposed the realities of the new social situation from a utopian standpoint; the phase of stabilization from 1924 to 1929 was the age of "New Objectivity" which itself took a greater interest in social realities. Politics and culture were also marching side by side at the end of the Republic: from 1930, political polarization and increasingly authoritarian forms of government were reflected in proletarian and revolutionary art on the one side and nationalistic – and, frequently, National Socialist – themes on the other. Virtually no limits were placed on radical thought in the Weimar Republic. While the judiciary did hand down prison sentences for the expression of anti-Republic views, they did this generally only to left-wing thinkers and writers such as Carl von Ossietzky.

"Weimar culture" was no myth invented by its protagonists, exiled after 1933. There is no doubt that it was elitist – the avant-garde art of the day held no attraction for the masses – yet names such as "Bauhaus," or expressions which seem to define the era, such as "the 1920s novel," do represent the period's uninhibited pleasure in experimentation and its radical break with tradition. In the 1920s the influence of German artists extended beyond the boundaries of the Republic and, indeed, it can still be felt at the beginning of the 21st century. Weimar culture struck audiences as particularly modern and unusual because the left-wing avant-garde integrated new media and techniques of production into their work – partly with the purpose of conveying their message to the anonymous masses. Bertolt Brecht and Erwin Piscator staged their agit-prop theater in working class districts and at the gates of factories, and "agit groups" staged events in the streets. Often praised by liberal and socialist critics, their artistic strategies soon ran up against the limits of public comprehension in the class society of the Republic. Exceptions only served to prove the rule: by 1933 Alfred Döblin had sold a respectable 55,000 copies of his experimental novel *Berlin Alexanderplatz*, and it was translated into numerous languages.

From 1933 any critical voice was crushed under the jackboots of the SA (*Sturmabteilung* or Nazi militia). Germany's cinemas, art galleries and bookshelves were dominated by nationalist ideology, supplemented with banal entertainment. The National Socialists left Döblin and his colleagues no choice but to leave the country in droves.

"it is not the aim of the Bauhaus to have a 'style'. no system, dogma or canon, no recipe and no fashion! it will be alive so long as it does not hanker after form but rather seeks the fluid nature of life itself behind changeable forms!"

Walter Gropius, Bauhausbauten Dessau, *1930*

"Every German has the right to express his opinions freely in word, print, image or otherwise within the general framework of the law. [...] There will be no censorship."

Article 118 of the Weimar Constitution

Bauhaus Dessau – the most modern art school in the world!
– photo essay
The Bauhaus in Dessau was ceremoniously opened by Walter Gropius on 4 December 1929.

The 'Bauhaus' Design School was founded by the German architect Walter Gropius in 1919. It is now situated in Dessau where it is under the direction of Johannes Meyer [director 1928/30]. Broadly speaking his workshops and classes cover all aspects of the artistic design of buildings in the broadest sense, as well as practical work. This includes painting, sculpture, stage design, murals, weaving, metal working and much more. Teaching is based on the most up-to-date ideas and many of the teachers are themselves renowned artists. This picture shows a view of the canteen with the building's characteristic transparent walls, whose large windows are divided into a regular grid.
(Original caption)

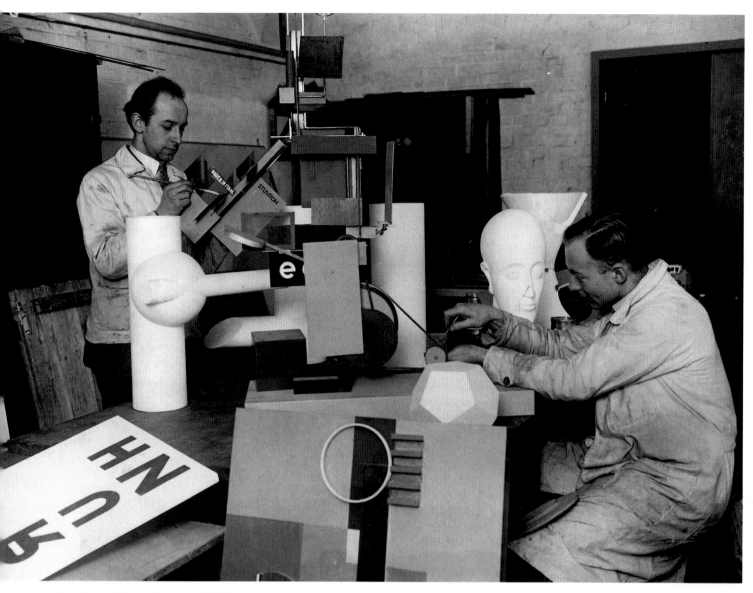

Above: *Bauhaus designers at work in the sculpture workshop at the Bauhaus Design School in Dessau, 4 December 1929.*

Right: *Professor Walter Gropius has taken over artistic direction of the German Craft Federation Exhibition, which will take place this year in Paris.*

(Original captions)

The development of the Bauhaus paralleled the history of the first German republic. In 1919 Walter Gropius founded the first reformist art school in Weimar – where the constituent National Assembly had sat – with the support of the SPD-dominated state government of Thuringia. Ludwig Mies van der Rohe wound up the school in Berlin in 1933 under massive pressure from the National Socialists, who had seized power just a few months earlier. The period between these dates was marked by financial problems and debates within the school on the direction it should take. In 1924 the existence of the Bauhaus was threatened by the victory of right-wing parties in the Thuringian parliament: the new state government fired Gropius and drastically cut the budget. "The Bauhaus was slowly but surely throttled to

death," said the former SPD Minister of Education Max Greil, who himself had been a supporter of the Bauhaus. From the outset, modern art and design – whose development in the rest of Germany was decisively influenced by Bauhaus – were seen by conservative parties as "Bolshevist" and "left-wing." Gropius always denied that the Bauhaus style had a political character. In the meantime, however, the "New Objectivity" movement had been politically appropriated to become a symbol of Modernism and of a new age. In 1925 the Bauhaus found a new home in Dessau, where it remained until 1932.

SO THAT'S THE WAY THE WORLD IS...

Bauhaus Dessau – the most modern art school in the world!
– photo essay (continued)
Right: *Our picture shows the Bauhaus designed by Gropius in Dessau. It is constructed entirely of concrete, glass and iron. For a small tuition fee, anyone may register here to study a wide range of arts such as architecture, painting, commercial art and printing.*
Below: *Bauhaus pupils at their looms producing craft textiles in the "Bauhaus Design School" in Dessau.*
(Original captions)

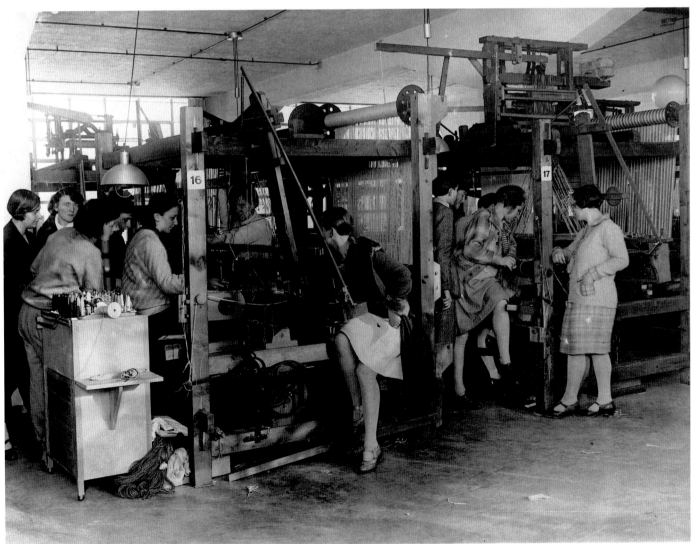

The attic dwellers – artists' lives – photo essay
In the mid-19th century the short stories of the French
writer Murger gave rise to the archetypal bohemian, and
since then the real counterparts of his literary creations
have haunted the artistic circles of the world's great cities.
They all have in common an anti-bourgeois attitude –
everything else is a matter for individual interpretation,
as this report from a 1920s Berlin garret shows.

Top: *Happiness in the corner. A neglected windowsill
in the studio.*
Above: *Laundry day.*
Right: *Potatoes à la Michelangelo.*

(*Original captions*)

The attic dwellers – *artists' lives* – photo essay (continued)
Left: *Getting ready to visit Mr. and Mrs. Bourgeois.*
Top: *Stuck at home.*
Right: *Her, his muse.* (Original captions)

"'Oh', said Carola, you don't get it. I'm just not cut out to be a Communist. I am and always will be an eternal revolutionary, even against parties or revolutions. I fight against the morality of good and evil, I despise convention, I defend myself from my own nature which is rooted in tradition, and am at the same time hopelessly susceptible to the animal in me. There are moments in which I would love to wipe myself out in order to liberate myself."
Tilla Durieux, Eine Tür fällt ins Schloss *(A door slams), 1927*

SO THAT'S THE WAY THE WORLD IS...

The attic dwellers – artists' lives – photo essay (continued)
Left: *Any luck this morning? Ever hopeful of finding a check in the post.*
Right: *A regular visitor – from the bailiff's office.*
(Original captions)

In view of the characters who populated the night life of Berlin and Munich, it irritated the writer Erich Mühsam to read of his name constantly being connected with the word "bohemian":

"Perfumed boys decked out in gigantic ties, their Napoleonic curls dripping with hair-oil, chirrup their way through the literary cafés at night with their castrati voices, deluding themselves into believing that their complete lack of activity, which is brought about by intellectual impotence, marks them out as bohemians. Others flatter themselves with the same lunacy: out-of-work artists occupying shabby studios with their girlfriends and who, having once read Murger, splash out on a bottle of Moselle when they have a couple of coins to spare – while their real desires and aspirations are of being overwhelmed by commissions, and of living in an elegant villa in a park surrounded by their loving family."
Erich Mühsam, Unpolitische Erinnerungen

The target of Dadaism was the petit bourgeois conformist. Provocation and scandal were important weapons of the Dada movement, which was formed in Zurich in 1916. At the end of the war the major actors in the movement attempted to persuade the German public that a world which had fallen apart could not be cured by the traditional methods of fine art. In June 1920 the first International Dada Fair was held in the Galerie Burchard in Berlin. It was attended by international artists such as Francis Picabia, Hans Arp and Max Ernst as well as the Berlin Dadaists Georg Grosz, Raoul Hausmann, John Heartfield, Hannah Höch, Wieland Herzfelde and Johannes Baader. By this time, however, the movement had already passed its peak.

"We joyfully welcome the fact that in galleries and palaces bullets are ripping into the masterpieces of artists like Rubens."
Dadaists John Heartfield and Georg Grosz in Der Gegner
(The Opponent), 1920

"The worker himself, the new breed of humanity, will one day have to decide which of the collected works of history is worthy of preservation. Are Rembrandt, Rubens, Michelangelo, Beethoven, van Gogh responsible for their works being nothing more than objects of speculation for the bourgeois classes? [...] Herr Heartfield and Herr Grosz, do you really want to win the trust of the working classes by damning every aspect of 'bourgeois culture' and destroying treasures which – let us not forget – were purchased with the sweat of the working man, the proletariat? Should not their sons at least be finally able to enjoy them?"
Reply of the Rote Fahne *(Red Flag) on 9 June 1920 to Heartfield and Grosz's article in* Der Gegner

"Piscator, we can say here without hesitation, has nevertheless and in spite of everything created something extraordinary. Yet again! He has brought in Georg Grosz and achieved grandiose, biting satire; in the background there are pictures of quite extraordinary effect. As a director, Piscator has come up with something new – the production line on stage! – which gives the lie to all those who predicted his creative imagination would run into a blind alley."
Piscator's The Good Soldier Schweik, *an article in the* Rote Fahne *dated 25 January 1928*

Left: The painter Georg Grosz stands in front of his painting *The Agitator* in his Berlin studio; the work was intended as a reference to Adolf Hitler. The photo was taken on 17 September 1928 and the following original captions read: "Georg Grosz accused of 'blasphemy': the Berlin district attorney has confiscated several of Georg Grosz's sketches for the stage set for *The Good Soldier Schweik* and has now instituted proceedings against him for blasphemy."

Above: *Modern theater in Germany. On Saturday 13 April 1929 the unusually successful premiere of the opera* Machinist Hopkins *by Viennese composer Max Brand took place in the Duisburg City Theater. In both its staging and direction this 'machine opera' was the absolute epitome of modern theater. Our picture shows "The Machine Hall," a scene from the premiere of the opera* Machinist Hopkins *in Duisburg.*

(Original caption)

"That the term 'technology' derived originally from the word for 'art' is proved by its mature creations with their austere yet sincere forms. To establish a connection between this art and the art of the stage requires artists who have schooled their eyes as much in the modern romance of machines as they have in the splendors of medieval architecture. A sense of what is natural and the correct use of symbols are conditions for the appropriate representation of forms and goals."

Karl Deutsch, Die Maschine als Bühnenelement
(The machine as an element of drama)

"And there are people who don't see this. And there are people who have forgotten it. In the war they suffered and hated their masters and obeyed and murdered! Everything forgotten [...] They will suffer again and they will hate their masters again and they will obey again [...] and they will murder [...] again. And they could be different if they wanted. But they didn't want that. They stone the spirit and mock it, they violate life, they crucify it [...] again and again and again."

Ernst Toller in the anti-war play Hinkemann, *1923*

Left page: *Communist demonstration against war. On the occasion of the 15th anniversary of the outbreak of the World War a large Communist anti-war demonstration took place in Berlin's Pleasure Garden. Our picture shows a group demonstrating against gas warfare.*
Left: Hinkemann, *Ernst Toller's tragedy about a war invalid. Heinrich George as the crippled Hinkemann (final scene).*
Above: *The writer Ernst Toller.*

(Original captions)

"I think of my early childhood days, of the pain of the boy whom the others taunted with the word 'Jew,' of my childish conversations with the image of the Savior, of the dreadful pleasure I felt when I was not recognized as a Jew, of the first days of the war, of my passionate desire to prove that I was a German, nothing but a German, by putting my life on the line [...] The German language – is it not my language, the one in which I think and feel, speak and act, a part of my being, the home which nourished me and in which I grew up? But am I not also a Jew?"

Ernst Toller, Eine Jugend in Deutschland
(A youth in Germany), 1933

"My basic idea was that theater should once again become a celebration as it was in antiquity and in the Middle Ages under the leadership of the church. In large cities it has mainly become a source of entertainment and amusement [...] The first active attempt at such an approach was a performance of *Everyman*, held with the approval of the archbishop on the cathedral square and with the best actors from throughout Germany and Austria. A temporary stage was built in front of the cathedral entrance. Heralds signaled the start of the play. The actors entered from neighboring squares. All the church bells were rung. There were mysterious calls from the towers of the church, from the heights of the fortress and from the distance calling Everyman to death. A devil jumped up onto the podium from amongst the audience. Faith and the Angel came out of the cathedral at the end. The broad squares of the city were thronged with spectators. Monks and priests at the windows of the neighboring monastery, the archbishop and the cathedral chapter seated in the first row. Traffic came to a complete standstill and the entire city listened and watched breathlessly. A wonderful play of light: daylight gave way to sunset and finally torches were lit."

Max Reinhardt, Auf der Suche nach dem lebendigen Theater *(On the search for a living theater), 1924*

"EVERYMAN. A play about the death of a rich man."

Advertising slogan for the drama Everyman *by Hugo von Hofmannsthal. Premiere directed by Max Reinhardt in 1911 in Berlin (Schumann Circus). Produced again by Reinhardt at the Salzburg Festival on 22 August 1920, it went on to become a permanent part of the festival repertoire.*

Three giants of the Weimar theatrical world: the director Max Reinhardt founded a theater empire in Berlin and at the Salzburg Festival. He rejected political drama and after 1914 increasingly resorted to productions of classical works. The playwright Carl Zuckmayer wrote critical comedies and has been immortalized in the literature of the German theater for his attack on Prussian militarism, *The Captain of Köpenick* (1931). In her day, Maria Orska was one of the most prominent German stage actresses and her permanent repertoire included Grillparzer, Ibsen and Strindberg. She committed suicide in 1930.

Above: *The annual drama festival in the picturesque city of Salzburg was opened on Sunday 31 July under the direction of world famous impresario Max Reinhardt and was attended by prominent theater critics and patrons from around the world. The opening play was Hugo von Hofmannsthal's* Everyman. *Musical by Einar Nilson. Our picture shows Helene Thimig as 'Faith'.*

(Original caption)

SO THAT'S THE WAY THE WORLD IS...

Above: *The writer of* The Merry
Vineyard *and* Schinderhannes, *Carl
Zuckmayer, deals with the story of a
circus family in his latest play*
Katharina Knie, *whose premiere
took place recently in Berlin. Scene
from the Berlin production with
(from left) Hedwig Wangel, Frau
Lennartz, Albert Bassermann and
Karl Ettlinger. Berlin 1929.*
Left: *Photo study of Maria Orska in
various roles.*
Right: *The actress Maria Orska, who
only returned to her apartment two
days ago from the clinic in which she
has been recuperating for some
time, was found yesterday
afternoon suffering from an acute
overdose of Veronal. There had
obviously been a suicide attempt.
Frau Orska was taken to hospital
where she had still not regained
consciousness last night despite
the best efforts of her doctors.
Berlin, 15 May 1930.*

(Original captions)

UNWAHRSCHEINLICHE BEGEBENHEIT

In 1921 an American court found Nicola Sacco and Bartolomeo Vanzetti, two immigrant Italian workers, guilty of murder and robbery and sentenced them to death. They were executed on 23 August 1927. In the months prior to their deaths their cause was taken up by an international protest movement and the case of "Sacco and Vanzetti" dominated international headlines for many months. Suspicions grew that the American judicial system, though lacking conclusive evidence in the case, had wanted to make an example of two Italian workers who were anarchists and who had fought for improvements in wages. In Germany at the end of August hundreds of thousands marched in the streets carrying banners which read "Revenge for Sacco and Vanzetti." Erich Mühsam turned the story into a play which was premiered at the "Theater in der Stadt" in 1929 under the direction of Leopold Lindtberg. Mühsam's *Sacco and Vanzetti* was one of a series of "topical plays" which, especially in the period from 1928 to 1930, attacked the judiciary and its standards. Faithful mirrors of the "unpopular Republic," dramas such as *Das Urteil* (The Judgment), *Die Verbrecher* (The Criminals), or *Die Nacht vor dem Beil* (The Night before Execution) set out to mirror faithfully the prevailing conditions in the "unloved Republic." Though these works depicted the wretched state of affairs in Germany, they were not able to offer any solutions.

Left page: *Interior decoration in a café. Regular customers at the Romanisches Café have decorated the walls of the establishment.*
Above: Sacco and Vanzetti *on stage. The play's plot is taken straight from American newspaper reports and official documents. Our picture shows a scene from* Sacco and Vanzetti. *From left to right Sacco (Friedrich Gnas), Governor Fuller (Hans Leibelt) and Vanzetti (Ernst Busch). Berlin 26 April 1929.*
Below: *Maximilian Harden has died. The world famous German writer, publicist and editor of the magazine* Zukunft *died yesterday, 30 October 1927, aged 66.*
(Original captions)

Berlin was the focus of activity of actors and artists, the literary community and journalists. Maximilian Harden had been one of the most influential conservative journalists at the turn of the century. The First World War turned him into a pacifist and he became a committed opponent of National Socialism. After suffering serious injuries in a right-wing radical attack in 1922, he turned his back on his home town and settled in Switzerland. Another native of Berlin, Alfred Döblin, gave a unique description of the "Moloch metropolis" of Berlin in his novel *Berlin Alexanderplatz* (1929), now a classic of 20th-century literature. A visit to the Romanisches Café near the Gedächtniskirche was essential for local intellectuals as well as those from outside the city if they wished to climb the ladder of Berlin's "Kurfürstendamm society". In the second volume of his autobiography *Fackel im Ohr* (The torch in my ear) Elias Canetti wrote of the peer pressure of the day: "Visits to the Romanisches Café [...], while a pleasure, were not undertaken solely for this purpose. They were done out of the necessity of showing oneself, and no one was immune to this pressure. Anyone who did not want to slip into obscurity had to be seen there."

"Great cities are remarkable and powerful machines. In the streets one can almost feel the energy from the people's drives and tensions rising like a vortex that has them in its power. According to observations, birds prefer flying in groups because a uniform movement of their wings supports each of the neighboring birds and thus eases the act of flying. This observation has given rise to a certain mechanical principle, and the same observation provides the explanation for something else: it indicates the economic rationale behind imitation, which is that of saving energy. It explains the human tendency to mimic and the tendency of crowds to move uniformly. In this way people in great cities are induced to adopt the same metropolitan tempo."
Alfred Döblin, Der Geist des naturalistischen Zeitalters (The Spirit of the Naturalistic Age), December 1924

"The political apathy of people in peaceful times means that they are more easily led off to the slaughterhouse. Because today they are too lazy to sign a piece of paper indicating their willingness to disarm, they will have to shed blood tomorrow."

Albert Einstein in the periodical Menschenrechte *(Human Rights) dated 11 November 1928, on the occasion of the tenth anniversary of the armistice.*

"We want our Republic, which until now has been the fortunate gift of our defeat in the war, to have its own Republicans. And we see these Republicans as neither socialists nor as the bourgeoisie. Those are irrelevant definitions when it is higher things that should count. We call Republicans those people who are concerned with ideas instead of utility, and with people instead of power."

Heinrich Mann, Sinn und Idee der Revolution *(The meaning and idea of the revolution), a speech in the Political Council of Intellectual Workers in November 1918*

Right: Einstein's speech is made into a gramophone record. On 10 November 1930 Professor Albert Einstein gave a talk on his scientific theories in front of a microphone in the Schwechte Hall in Berlin. This speech was transferred to a gramophone record.
Below: Heinrich Mann addresses detectives. At a conference of detectives from the Federation of Prussian Police held near Berlin on 22 January, Heinrich Mann spoke on "What the public needs from the criminal investigation department." Our picture shows the author during his speech.
Right page: The German talkie. Thomas Mann – at the right in front of the microphone – speaks to the camera.
(Original captions)

"The Republic and democracy are today such inherent facts for every one of us, every individual, that to deny it would be tantamount to a lie. Until recently we were ruled over by historically ordained powers furnished with the imposing authority of inherited glory and mystery. It was simply human to preserve them and allow them to go on existing even when their degeneration into banal theatricality had long since turned any allegiance towards them into an embarrassment [...] But all that is over. Those powers no longer exist. Fate has – let us not cry out in triumph: 'swept them away'; let us rather say, objectively, that fate has eliminated them. They are no longer placed over us and, after all that has happened, they never will be again. Whether we wanted it or not, the State has been granted to us. It has been placed in our hands, those of every one of us. The State has become our affair and it is up to us to handle it well. That – and nothing else – is the Republic."

Thomas Mann, Von deutscher Republik *(On the German Republic), lecture on 13 October 1922 to celebrate Gerhart Hauptmann's 60th birthday in the Beethoven Hall in Berlin*

"After the collapse of the Empire Thomas Mann espoused a conservative philosophy – in the generic rather than in the party political sense of the word – and seemed to be little inclined towards democracy and the Republic [...] As Thomas Mann is undeniably one of the nation's leading intellectual lights it is extraordinarily pleasurable to see him join those who urge understanding, love and sincere cooperation with respect to the new state."

The Berliner Tageblatt *commenting on Thomas Mann's speech, on 17 October 1922*

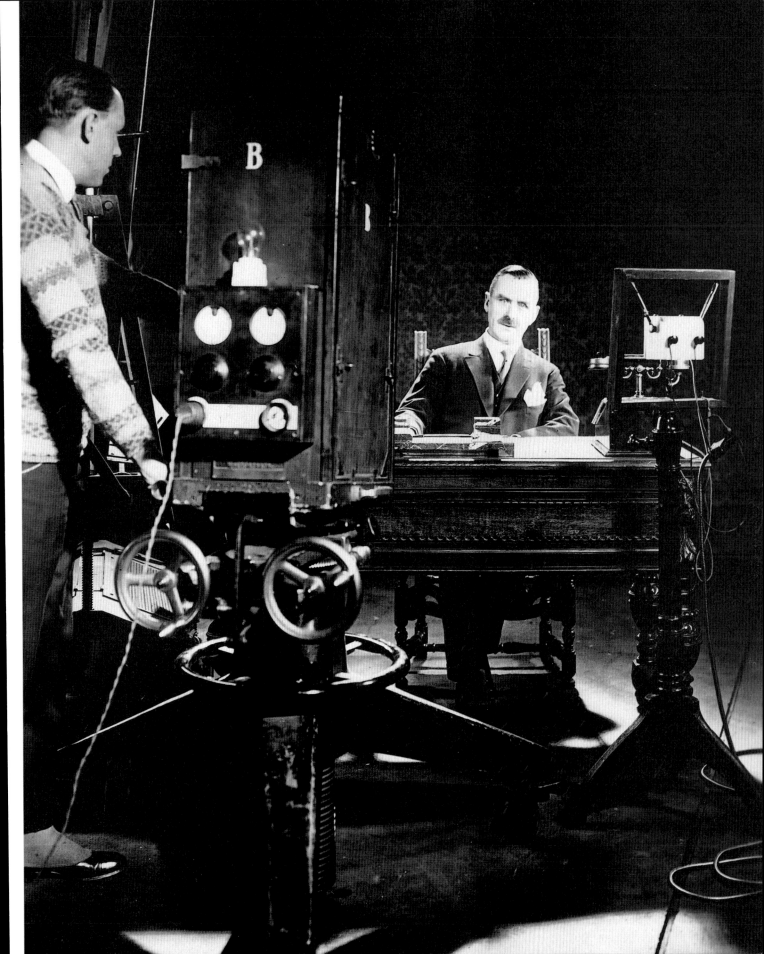

"I believe in the immortality of the theater [...] Theater is a liberation from the conventional theater of life for it is not the task of the actor to disguise but to reveal. Today we can see, hear and fly across the ocean, but the road from ourselves to those closest to us is unimaginably long. The actor is on this road. With the light of the poet he descends into the still unfathomed depths of the human soul, his own soul, in order to transform himself and, his hands, eyes and mouth full of miracles, to return to the surface."

Max Reinhardt, speech at Columbia University, New York 1928

Left: *The most recent photo of Gerhart Hauptmann, who celebrated his 65th birthday on 15 November 1927.*
Below: *On 16 February 1932 Gerhart Hauptmann's most recent play* Before Sunset *will be premiered under the direction of Max Reinhardt. The main roles will be taken by some of the country's best actors, including Werner Krauss and Helene Thimig. Our picture shows Gerhart Hauptmann (center) and Max Reinhardt during a discussion about the play's direction.* (Original captions)

Above: *Gerhart Hauptmann turns 70. Memories from the Riviera in 1909. From the left, Gerhart Hauptmann, Frau Eva Chamberlain, Frau Gerhart Hauptmann, Frau Küchler and Siegfried Wagner.* (Original caption)

"In view of the Hauptmann celebrations which are taking place at the moment all over Germany, there will be some who will ask themselves whether we have the right to indulge in such celebrations today; whether it is appropriate in times of the most terrible economic distress, days in which chaos threatens to overwhelm us [...] But one may – indeed one should – celebrate at this of all times! Man does not live by bread alone, and if all the troubles and cares of these unhappy hours had no other meaning than to secure a pitiful little piece of our naked material existence, then they would essentially have no meaning at all and life would not be worth living. It is at times like these that we must lift our eyes up to those who are our leaders and guides in the land of the spirit and the soul. This year's Hauptmann celebrations have been called a cult of personality; it has been said they are unworthy of a people's state and especially of socialist workers. It is certainly true that the culture of a people, or even of mankind, is never the work of individuals no matter how highly they may be placed. It results from the cooperation of unnumbered and unknown millions of industrious workers applying their minds and their hands; and no one has more happily and gratefully acknowledged the dependence of the genius on his people than Gerhart Hauptmann."

Konrad Haenisch, Social Democratic politician and editor, "Why we are celebrating Gerhart Hauptmann," in Die Volksbühne *(The People's Theater), 1922*

The old master of modern painting – photo essay

During the Empire, Liebermann made his reputation with adaptations of French Impressionism – though this earned him considerable criticism at the time. As Arnold Zweig emphasized in his *Bilanz der deutschen Judenheit* (Account of the German Jews), the Jewish visual artist was an exception in Germany: "This was one of the remarkable occasions when German Jews seemed to confirm the prejudice that Jews in general had only a limited talent for the fine arts. And indeed, compared with the wealth of important literary and musical contributions they made, Jews played only a subordinate role in the painting and sculpture of Germany and even of Europe." The Weimar Republic appointed Liebermann President of the Prussian Academy of the Arts in 1920. Liebermann radiated energy and creativity until an advanced age; he painted an unforgettable portrait of Ferdinand Sauerbruch as late as 1932. In that year he celebrated his 85th birthday, which provided the occasion for a magazine to honor him with this photo essay. In 1933 he was stripped of all his offices by the Nazis, and he died two years later in Berlin. The original text of the article ran as follows: "We visited the great painter at his idyllic country house on the Wannsee near Berlin. To our joy we were able to establish that Professor Liebermann was perfectly prepared to help with our report, and placed himself entirely at our disposal. With great pride he showed us around his property, introduced us to his dachshund, explained the sundial in his garden and led us to an excellent fishing spot on the Wannsee (which he had still not used because, as he explained, he was not old enough) [...] At the end of our session we asked Professor Liebermann if he had a particular birthday request. The following conversation unfolded: 'Yes! Listen, my dear man, if you want to do me great favor for my birthday, then try to take a picture of my wife ... she won't do it!' he added in his unmistakable Berlin dialect. With camera at the ready we lay in wait as Professor Liebermann conveyed his wishes to his wife. She immediately jumped up saying 'No, I'm not letting myself be photographed!' – but it was already too late."

Left page: *The first woman to take charge of a class of men in an academy: Frau Käthe Kollwitz, the famous Berlin artist, has become director of the master studio for graphic arts at the Prussian Academy of Art. She is the first woman to direct an academic master class. Our picture shows Käthe Kollwitz at her Berlin home. 1927.*
Above: *The world famous pianist Arthur Schnabel on his way to Leningrad [today St. Petersburg] to participate in concerts marking the 100th anniversary of Beethoven's death. Berlin 1927.* (Original captions)

"13 February 1927
Another concert by Schnabel. Calm and solemn rendition of the sonata in E-flat major, opus 7. Then I became tired and couldn't follow the music. After the interval he played the sonata in B major, opus 106, one of the very late sonatas. I was alert and able to listen, and was utterly moved as I hadn't been for a long time. I cannot imagine that there is another art which is so able to penetrate into the inner being of a person like music. The fine arts are so concrete, one is always confronted with the tangible. But in this adagio the soul is laid bare. Just what I always imagined when I thought of making a figure of a woman 'who sees the song of the world.' And looks. Wordlessly. Goethe – he was able to find the words. Expressions like 'labyrinth of the heart' or 'blessed desire' and many more. He found words which could take their place beside the music of Beethoven [...]
26 February 1927
Today the last Schnabel concert. His final piece was Beethoven's sonata in C minor, opus 111. As with opus 106 I was able to follow it closely. The peculiar flickering tones became flames – I was transported to other spheres, and the heavens opened almost as they do in the Ninth. Then a return to oneself. But a return after one has seen heaven. Lucid – comforted – this music good. Thank you, Schnabel!"

Käthe Kollwitz, Diaries and Letters

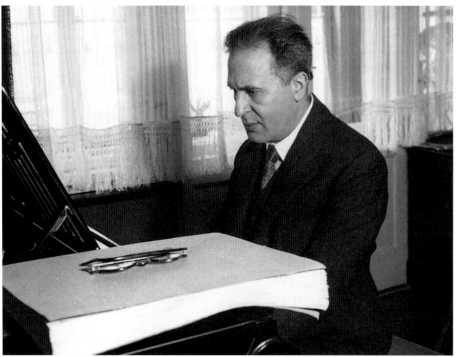

Top: *Erich Kleiber as a proud father. Our picture shows the General Director of Music, Erich Kleiber, on the balcony of his Berlin apartment with his little daughter Veronika, who was born on 28 March. Kleiber's wife, whose maiden name was Goodrich, is from California.*
Above: *General Director of Music Bruno Walter.*

Above: *Premiere of Karol Rathaus's opera* Fremde Erde *in Berlin. The premiere of Karol Rathaus's four act opera* Fremde Erde *will take place in the State Opera 'Unter den Linden' on 10 December 1930. This completely modern opera is set in America and its set features New York, skyscrapers and the world of the 20th century. Erich Kleiber, who has just returned from a concert tour to America, is to direct. Hörth is in charge of the production, and the set design is in the hands of Emil Pirchau. Our picture shows a scene from the third act. New York, 8 December 1930.* (Original captions)

SO THAT'S THE WAY THE WORLD IS...

"In terms of music Berlin was still a bastion of traditionalism," as Yehudi Menuhin later recalled of the 1920s. Contemporary feature articles in the Berlin press enthused over Wilhelm Furtwängler's rousing Beethoven interpretations with the city's Symphony Orchestra. Journalists were equally taken by Bruno Walter's sensual version of Mozart at the German Opera or productions like Otto Klemperer's *Flying Dutchman* at the Kroll Opera House in which the singers appeared in modern costumes — which caused Wagner's son, Siegfried, to denounce the production

as "cultural Bolshevism." Berlin's concert halls and opera houses were however open to new influences. Arnold Schoenberg, the creator of 12-tone music, taught at the Prussian Academy of the Arts from 1925. One of his pupils, Alban Berg, was able to arouse the interest of the young director at the State Opera, Erich Kleiber, in his *Wozzeck* libretto, which he had adapted from the play by Georg Büchner. And it was Kleiber who premiered the "neo-objective" opera *Fremde Erde* in 1930. Karol Rathaus's opera debut was a homage to life in big American cities

and it was a paean to progress. Berlin's critics clashed over the new music and themes of such operas, but the works themselves were essentially "revolutionary" echoes. The musical Big Bang had been Alban Berg's *Wozzeck*: "When the great, dignified figure of the composer appeared in front of the curtain there were cries of bravo, as well as boos, and waves of enthusiastic support and utter hostility erupted."

Above: *The Zoppot Vacation Opera Society. Some of the participating artists pictured on the beach at Zoppot. From the left: Karl Jöken with his wife Käte König (Berlin State Opera), Hermann Karowski (City Theater Hamburg), Eric Enderlein, Genia Guszalewicz, Herbert Janssen (all from the Berlin State Opera), Elly Glawitsch.*

Far left: *Otto Klemperer becomes conductor of the Philharmonic Choir.*

Left: *Paul Hindemith at the height of his fame as a viola soloist.*

Right page: *This morning Arturo Toscanini arrived at the Anhalter Railway Station in Berlin to direct a concert by the New York Philharmonic Orchestra as part of the Berlin Art Week. Berlin, 27 May 1930.*

(Original captions)

During the First World War the Hungarian choreographer Rudolf von Laban worked in Switzerland. It was at this time that he began to produce the first elements in his dance theory which regarded "the inner drive for movement" and the "activity of the body" as existing in an almost mathematical relationship. The dancer represented the perfect harmony of body, soul and spirit and was confronted with three-dimensional space to which he responded with a system of 12 different types of movement; these Laban formulated in a symbolic language of his own devising, the "Labanotation." Laban was in the vanguard of new German dance, a form which had its roots in eurhythmics and gymnastics as well as in Expressionist art. Expressive dance sought to anticipate in bodily movement the "new mankind" on its way "back to nature." Throughout his life Laban regarded it as his goal to "promote the freedom and spontaneity of the individual through movement."

Left page: *Rudolf von Laban has been entrusted by the General Director of State Theaters with overall choreographic direction. Herr von Laban will take up his post after the Bayreuth Festival, for which he is director of dance. Our picture shows Herr Rudolf von Laban with the dance notation he invented himself.*
Above: *The Laban Choreographic Institute in Berlin-Grunewald. "Striving together."*
Right: *Rehearsal of the State Opera Ballet. Rudolf von Laban surrounded by young dancers.*   (Original captions)

In 1920 Mary Wigman founded the school in Dresden bearing her name. A pupil of Laban, Wigman soon achieved an international reputation for her guest performances at German and international dance venues. As a soloist and teacher she embodied the German Expressionist dance of the 1920s. Her pupils included Hayna Holm, Yvette Georgi and Gret Palucca. She also formed the Mary Wigman Dance Group in 1921, with which she toured both in Germany and abroad. The dynamic images of this photo essay provide an insight into study with her pupils.

The Mary Wigman School – photo essay
Above left: *Group dance in the open air.*
Above right: *Improvisational jumps.*
Below: *Mary Wigman, one of Germany's greatest classical dancers. She has created a new style of classical dance and is accompanied by a percussion group marking only the rhythm. Our picture shows the dancer and choreographer Mary Wigman in one of her poses.*
Opposite page: *Pirouette practice outdoors.*　　　　　　　*(Original captions)*

Berthe Trümpy, a dancer from Switzerland, was an assistant at the Mary Wigman School in Dresden from 1920 to 1924. In 1926 she founded the Berthe Trümpy School together with the talented young 20-year-old Vera Skoronel, who had made her debut at the age of 12, and had been teaching dance since she was 14. The Trümpy School was famous not only for training dancers, but for encouraging and supporting non-professionals. The expressive dance movement developed a sense of mission which was typical of the times, and based its concept of dance on "the natural movement of the human organism" as described by Mary Wigman in *German Dance*: "True, physical movement is not dance as such, but it does provide an elementary and indispensable foundation without which dance would not exist."

The new temple of dance in Halensee. In December 1927 the dancer Berthe Trümpy, a pupil of Mary Wigman's, built a dance school in Berlin-Halensee, based on designs by the architect Gellhorn; it is to be dedicated soon. Our picture shows 'Silhouettes at the window' (Berthe Trümpy School).
(Original caption)

Left page, above: *The dancer Valeska Gert. As a dancer Valeska Gert founded the modern satirical dance pantomime. She was also a successful actress and cabaret performer.*
Left page, below: *The variety troupe "The Sisters S..."*
Above: "*That's you!," the new review at the Kurfürstendamm Theater in Berlin by Friedrich Hollaender. Première on 21 July 1927. Our picture shows the first scene 'The Wild Tribe [i.e. the Saxons. H.N.]. From the left: Marion Ralfi, Hugo Fischer-Köppe, Annemarie Hase, "Schafheitlein" [Franz Schafheitlein. H.N.], Martin Emil Koslek, Frau Blandine Ebinger.*

(Original captions)

Even before the First World War the great reviews in Berlin's theaters caused a sensation with their combination of music, sex, and lavish sets. They went on to become one of the city's main tourist attractions. This tradition of big budget reviews continued into the 1920s. Directors such as Eric Charell, Herman Haller and James Klein staged productions with lavish costumes and illusionist effects. The "chorus girls" were not only noted for their perfect dance performances: as a rule they showed a lot of bare leg – and often a bit more. During the heyday of the reviews between 1924 and 1929 there were times when as many as 13 different productions ran at the same time. Friedrich Hollaender, who had contributed to the success of cabaret with many hit scores and scripts, was inspired by the format of the review. Cabaret performances were typically a jumble of various themes and styles and he began to provide them with a framing device, calling his productions "Hollaender Reviews." In *Das bist du!* (That's you!) the "plot" concerned animals that break out of the zoo to build a menagerie for humans: "Roll on up! We'll show you our trained beasts let loose for the first time – so don't get too close! You'll see 'The Big Boss,' 'The Hysterical Old Nanny,' 'The Chameleon' (which playfully changes its colors)!" Hollaender spiced up his productions with acerbic, critical references to current events but he never really went beyond the typical review format which provided its audiences with an undemanding and amusing evening's entertainment. One critic remarked: "A mirror of our times? Just a bit. Not so mercilessly radical that it could get on the nerves of a well-dressed audience, but just enough so that they come away with a couple of scratches."

The largest German film company, UFA, was founded in November 1917 with studios in Berlin-Neubabelsberg and Tempelhof. In the early 1920s the company made several successful films which were also sold outside Germany, but it entered a period of crisis at the end of the inflationary era. The explanation lay partly in competition from America, which was starting to force its way onto the German market, but the studio had also produced the big-budget production *Metropolis* in 1927. Against all expectations it failed at the box office and became a financial disaster. The right-wing industrialist Alfred Hugenberg purchased the crisis-ridden company in 1927 for 15 million marks and in so doing put the finishing touches to his media empire. UFA had been bailed out but in the coming years the direction of the company was to be heavily influenced by Hugenberg, who was able to exploit film's economic and political potential.

Left page: *Filming in the UFA studios in Berlin-Babelsberg.*
Above left: *Director Fritz Lang during filming of* Dr. Mabuse the Gambler *1922.*
Above right: *Elisabeth Bergner and Rudolf Forster in Paul Czinner's film* Ariane *1931.*
Left: *Lilian Harvey in the UFA film* Du sollst nicht stehlen *(Thou shalt not steal), 1928.*   (Original captions)

The Austrian actress Elisabeth Bergner had been very successful in films like *Fräulein Else* (1929), *Ariane* (1931) and *As you like it* (1936). *Ariane* was her first talkie, and it was directed by her future husband Paul Czinner. In her memoirs, Elisabeth Bergner relates an anecdote about Rudolf Forster, the film's male lead, who embodied the ideal of a "superior man of the world." But, wrote Berger: " [...] he could not dance a step. And there were dance scenes in a night club for which a dancing instructor had to be hired for Rudi. He practiced and he practiced and he swore and he swore – it was hilarious to watch and listen to."

Above: *Faust (Gösta Ekman) and Mephistopheles (Emil Jannings) in F.W. Murnau's film* Faust, *1926.*
Right page: *Emil Jannings, whose successful film career in American is known to all, is paying another visit to his homeland with his wife, the former actress Gussy Holl. Gussy Holl and Emil Jannings shortly before their arrival in Berlin on 15 May 1929.*

(Original captions)

"He too ended his days in madness, although it was described as the Thousand Year Reich of Adolf Hitler: instead of being classed as the inmate of an asylum he bore the title of 'Cultural Senator' [...] In his early days Jannings was closely involved with the rise of German film, he was a great admirer of the medium and placed his talents at the disposal of many capable directors. But he always made sure that he was directed by those with the most distinctive personal style and the most unshakable control of their performers. He was a real mountain of a man and his massive body was filled to overflowing with all the qualities of an actor at the peak of his profession. He was a master of make-up, not only on the outside of his head but on the inside as well. The mirror was his other half. [...] Day and night, he and his followers were on the look-out for sausages and for stories worthy of his talent."

Josef von Sternberg in his memoirs Ich, Josef von Sternberg, *1967*

When the director Fritz Lang described the "history of great film in Germany" in 1926, he also praised his own ability to combine form and content at a high artistic level in silent movies like *Metropolis*. Lang denied that American film was capable of achieving similar quality, yet at the same time he seemed to sense what innovations were yet to come from America: "The speed with which film has developed in the last five years makes it dangerous to make any prophecies because the medium is likely to outstrip them. Film does not stand still." Three years later the first talkies were screened in German cinemas: Robert Land's *Ich küsse Ihre Hand, Madame* with Marlene Dietrich in the lead role, and Walter Ruttmann's *Melodie der Welt*.

The talkie is on the march in Germany as well. Our picture shows the famous actress Anny Ondra in front of the recording equipment while the director listens to her voice through headphones. The sound equipment is shielded from the camera by a pane of glass.

(Original caption)

HAPPY DAYS ARE HERE AGAIN

Life in the Weimar Republic was dominated by work and was hence the very antithesis of the leisure-dominated years of the late 20th century. However, the introduction of legislation for an eight-hour day and six-day week meant that those who were actually in gainful employment had more leisure time than they ever had in Kaiser Wilhelm's Germany. Because it was relatively limited, this freedom was all the more precious to the citizens of the Weimar era. This phenomenon is reflected in the original caption of the opposite photograph: "Sport and dance in the sunshine. There is nothing more enjoyable or healthy than exposing your body to sunshine and moving around in the fresh open air." The emerging mass media, particularly the magazines, latched gratefully onto this trend and songs such as "Happy days are here again ..." by the Comedian Harmonists were major hits:
"Happy days are here again/The skies above are clear again
Let us sing a song of cheer again/Happy days are here again."

Fun and Games

Reading the autobiographies of artists and intellectuals from the Weimar period, it is easy to get the impression that "modern mass culture" swept over the Republic like a wave and spread like an epidemic. This wave also encompassed "high" culture, yet few succeeded in riding its crest. Both Erich Kästner's *Emil und die Detektive* (*Emil and the Detectives*) and Thomas Mann's *The Buddenbrooks*, which was published in 1901, sold over half a million copies. The literary bestsellers also included Erich Maria Remarque's *All Quiet on the Western Front*. This anti-war novel also exploited the options offered by the mass media: it was published as a radio play and made into a talking movie in 1930. Major commercial successes in serious culture were, however, the exception.

The new media – radio and film, paperbacks, magazines, and gramophone records – tended to be rather lightweight and frivolous. Their success was, however, astounding; it was as if the Germans had been eagerly waiting the advent of these lighter forms of diversion. Secretaries and their bosses both hummed the latest hits, and people of all classes poured into the movie theaters.

Couples in both Berlin and the provinces danced the Charleston and shimmy, foxtrot and tango. People enjoyed light entertainment as a distraction from everyday life. Everyone was touched by the new consumer and leisure-oriented entertainment industry, which took off with a bang and was an integral part of the "roaring twenties."

Society in Transformation

Everyday life in the Weimar Republic did not necessarily become any easier for large sectors of the population. It is worth remembering a characteristic crisis indicator: even in the reputedly "good times," unemployment figures sometimes approached two million. But many things had changed. The introduction of the eight-hour day and legal holiday provisions gave those in gainful employment previously unheard-of freedom. Attitudes and habits changed, albeit gradually, in response to this newly gained freedom and the wide variety of leisure activities on offer. Numerous taboos were broken, ranging from obligatory church attendance on Sundays to wide-scale alcohol consumption. More and more people became physically active, taking up hiking, boxing, and swimming. With the emergence of the new lifestyle, liberal adults now accepted children and youths as individuals in their own right, although the traditional educational ideals of the Wilhelmine era had not disappeared altogether. People also began to discover their sexuality, although the inhibited bourgeois formality of the Imperial era could not be abandoned overnight. More and more Germans tried to expand their individual horizons and free themselves from the traditional restraints.

Mass Media Message Versus Reality

The gradual conversion of broad sectors of the population to new ways of life had not yet reached the level of a revolution, as social conditions remained difficult. As Herbert Marcuse remarked in 1937: "The demand for happiness sounds rather dangerous in an order which, for most people, means poverty, shortages, and problems." Correspondingly, the anti-modernist nationalistic camp reacted strongly against the "democratization" of culture, which in their opinion promoted excessively libertine behavior in the German people: the much-maligned state was once again held responsible. Elements of the cultural heritage which had previously reinforced the status of the upper classes were now produced on a mass scale and made popular by the new media. Similarly, entertainment products, such as musical hits, also penetrated the elevated circles of the "educated." Mass culture started to break down the boundaries of the class society. It was as impossible to insulate the "traditional" from the "vulgar" as it was to forcibly withhold access for the socialist working class to the products of the capitalist leisure industry, such as the films produced in the studios of Hollywood and UFA in Babelsberg near Potsdam.

Left page: *Hot – Hot – Hot – and all Berlin heads to Wannsee Lakeside to cool off. Our photo shows: Sliding into the water. 21 July 1929.*
Above: *Berlin's 'highest' bar. A garden has been built on the roof of the Hotel Eden, six stories above street level. There is a function room with a dance floor and a bar. Our photo shows the function room of the newly opened roof garden of the Eden Hotel. The vast windows offer a panoramic view of the city.*   (Original captions)

"Some boring old nosy parkers peek sleepily from behind their curtains as we head off on Sundays singing and shouting [...] Suddenly, we've reached the water. We are in a place where we can escape from the real world for the entire day. Off with our dresses and we're free. We play ball and throw the javelin. We just do this and that. One of us braves the water and the next follows soon after. The splashing starts when everyone is in. The sun is good to us. The evening comes far too quickly and we have to leave. We shorten the journey back to the train station by singing our songs."

Two young female textile workers describe
their Sunday outings, 1928

"We were very popular, for example at the six-day bicycle races. That was quite a party. Oskar, the other guys and I were up on the platform as guests. Then they recognized us. And Oskar presented a prize to the guy who did the tour and he invited him to a posh supper in the 'Hotel Eden' where we were also playing. That kind of thing makes you very popular. Or on New Year's Eve I was driving along the Kurfürstendamm in my little Mercedes. As I drove past the corner where the police officer was standing, I gave him a bottle of champagne. They recognized us. 'Oh, Oskar!'"

From an interview with Albert Joost,
who played in his brother Oskar's famous
Berlin dance orchestra from the late 1920s

Tea dance in the Hotel Esplanade in Berlin.

Left page: *A new UFA movie theater opens on the Kurfürstendamm in Berlin on 15 September. It has a very modern design and a particularly innovative lighting system. Our photo shows the exterior of the 'Universum' theater.*
Above: *Photographs from the film ball at Berlin Zoo. On Saturday, 16 November 1929, the film ball was held in the function rooms of the Berlin Zoological Gardens. In addition to the world of film, politics and the police were also well represented. Our photo shows: actor Hans Albers (center) with friends. Photograph Alfred Eisenstaedt.*
(Original captions)

"We Berliners are passionate moviegoers. The weekly news report keeps us up-to-date on world events. The most beautiful women of two continents are ours every day with alternating pictures of their tears and laughter. We have our big movie theaters around the Gedächtniskirche church on the Kurfürstendamm, near Potsdamer Platz, in the suburbs, and also the thousands of small movie theaters – bright, attractive lights shining out in the dim streets in all the neighborhoods. There are even morning movie theaters, veritable centers of warmth for body and soul."
Franz Hessel, Spazieren in Berlin *(Strolling in Berlin), 1929*

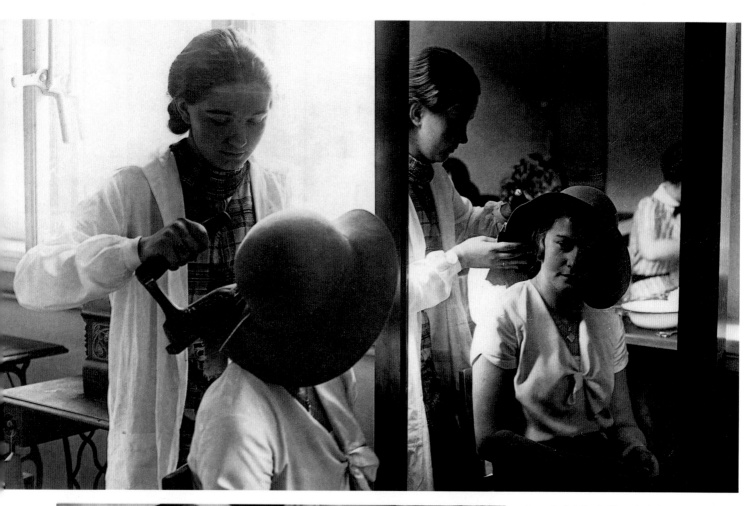

Above: *Berlin's first fashion school. The latest fashion accessory is ironed into shape.*
Left: *German School of Fashion. The actual fabric to be used for the final design is stuck down on the sketch.*
Right page: *Interesting photograph of the production of wax mannequins, which has became a new industry. This type of detailed decoration was once considered unimportant, but today the figures are given the final touch by artists. Our picture shows: Manicure for the "mannequins" – polishing the fingernails.*

(Original captions)

The Berlin clothing industry was established in the mid-19th century and by the mid-1920s it employed approximately 100,000 people. The clothing manufacturers around Hausvogteiplatz square created "Berliner Chic" – versatile clothes based on the latest Parisian designs. Knee-length dresses and skirts, stockings made from synthetic materials, saucy little hats and conspicuous make-up were the hallmarks of the woman of the "New Objectivity," who increasingly set the tone in the streets, offices and factories of Berlin.

HAPPY DAYS ARE HERE AGAIN

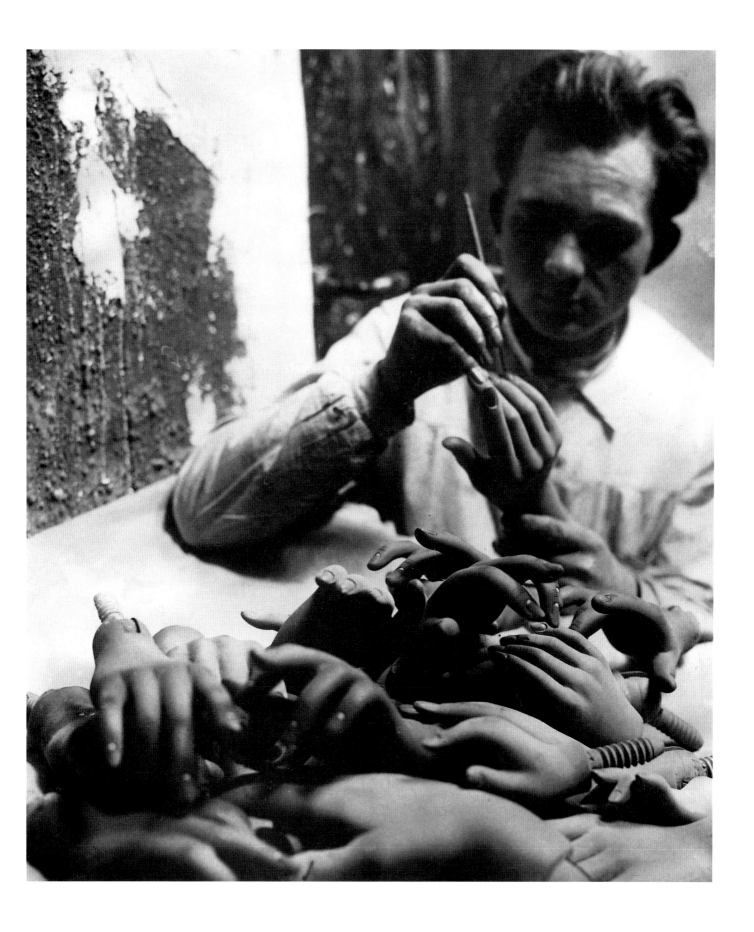

Left: *Miss Germany 1929. The selected candidates came to Berlin yesterday from every corner of Germany to meet the jury at Kroll's, which organized the competition as part of a ball. Our photograph shows the Berlin candidate who was voted Miss Germany: Miss Elisabeth Rodziel, who will go to America next year to participate in the international beauty pageant.*

Above: *Massary Premiere in the 'Metropole Theater.' The 'Metropole Theater' opened for the 1932/33 season on 1 September with Fritzi Massary. A production of the operetta* Eine Frau, die weiß, was sie will *(A woman who knows what she wants). Our photo shows Fritzi Massary surrounded by her suitors in a scene from the production.*
(Original captions)

The Metropole Theater at 56/58 Behren Street was Berlin's most popular musical theater. Fritzi Massary, who was born in Vienna, enjoyed major success here with revues such as *Eine Frau, die weiß, was sie will* and rose to become the "revue star." Tilla Durieux, an equally famous actress who was famous for her work in Piscator's theater, provides an insight into the ups and downs of life on the stage, the center of the universe, in her novel *Eine Tür fällt ins Schloß (A door slams)*, in which the main character Carola goes through a creative crisis.

"She allowed herself to be persuaded, put the dress back on, went onstage, blinked into the lights like a bull before the fight, was able to hear the prompt's first words and wanted to throw herself into her role but couldn't! She fell into a kind of fainting fit [...] There was tremendous confusion. Fortunately, a courageous understudy, who had followed the rehearsals in the hope that her great colleague would be struck by an illness, was waiting in the wings."
Tilla Durieux, Eine Tür fällt ins Schloß *(A Door Slams)*, 1927

Above: *Charlie Chaplin – guest of the British ambassador – Visit to the Berlin Metropol Theater!* Charlie Chaplin, who arrived in Berlin for a week on 9 March 1931, was the guest of the British ambassador, Sir Horace Rumbold, who held a dinner in his honor on 10 March. After the meal, Chaplin, Sir and Lady Rumbold and the ladies and gentlemen of the British embassy went to see Kálmán's operetta Veilchen von Montmartre (Violet of Montmartre) in the Metropol Theater. From the left: Karl Jöken, Gitta Alpar, Charlie Chaplin, Annie Ahlers, and Sir Horace Rumbold.

Right page, above: *Tea at five with Josephine Baker.* Josephine Baker has now opened her own bar in the former 'Pavillon Mascotte' in Berlin where she receives the guests and does the honors herself.

Right page, below: *The green and blue – an unusual friendship.* As everyone knows, some 400 American naval cadets and sailors are currently staying in Berlin. Their visit will last two days and they aim to enjoy Berlin as much as possible in this short time. Our photo shows two bluejackets from the USA who have made friends with a Berlin cop. Berlin, 7 July 1930.　　　*(Original captions)*

"Trusts, skyscrapers, traffic police, film, technological miracles, jazz band, boxing, magazine, and direction. Is that America? Maybe. As I haven't actually been there, I can't say. But I know that the ideas for all these things came to us from America. But is this – Americanism? Are they not instead the external and obvious symptoms of a more secret, intellectual, spiritual being? Isn't Americanism just a new attitude that has grown out of and emerged from our European fate?"

Rudolf Kayser, Amerikanismus *(Americanism), 1925*

"The rapid pace of life in our time, the more intensive ways of working, the change to living in tenements, further and further removed from nature – all this creates this agitated atmosphere which is constantly seeking change and stimulation and can offer no resistance to the increasing attractions [of the amusement industry]."

Eduard Bernstein,
Die Geschichte der Berliner Arbeiter-Bewegung
(The history of the Berlin workers' movement), 1910

HAPPY DAYS ARE HERE AGAIN

Left: 'Café am Zoo' on the Kurfürstendamm in Berlin.
Below: *Moissi to become a director in a New York Theater.
A new German theater is to open in New York. Like the
Irving Place Theater, which was very successful before the
First World War, it will stage a range of German theater
productions. The theater will be run by Americans with
Alexander Moissi as artistic director. Our photo shows: the
great actor Alexander Moissi.*

Above: *The Press Ball in the Zoo. The Berlin Press
Association Ball, the high point of the social season, was
held in the Zoo function rooms on 28 January 1933. The ball
also provided a glimpse of the latest fashion creations. Our
photo shows VIPs from stage and film. From the left: Lien
Deyers, Liane Haid, and director Josef von Sternberg.*
(Original captions)

Familiar traditions from the Empire disappeared at the end
of the First World War. The new Republic had problems
providing political and moral support for its citizens,
particularly in the anonymous metropolis of Berlin with its
3.8 million inhabitants. In the winter of 1918/1919, Georg
Grosz saw the capital city as drowning in "sin, pornography,
prostitution, violence on the streets and cocaine pushers."
During the hyperinflation of 1923, Berlin finally became the
"Babylon" which the German nationalist supporters of the
"conservative revolution" wanted it to be. During the
"roaring twenties," a new social mix emerged in Berlin that
included aristocrats and old elite, nouveau-riche and those
who had profited from inflation: the artistic avant-garde,
the demimonde and underworld, which Carl Zuckmeyer
referred to in his memoirs as "the new Kurfürstendamm
society." Promiscuity was the order of the day: "Who,
Moissi? I slept with him. Old school," a dialogue between
two young women at a dance in 1924 about the sexual
habits of one of the most celebrated actors of the time,
recorded by Carl Zuckmayer in his memoirs.

"Quite right miss, two monocles and one idea."

"I can't understand what he said but he has an attractive voice."

"Yes, I'm also alone."

"Please, please dearest miss, I would be absolutely delighted ... "

"What? I said that it is very damp outside."

"All right, if you promise not to get too fresh, come to Table 3!"

"Fresh? But I am very shy!"

"The telephone has done its job ..."

Flirting on the phone – photo essay

In the 1920s, the Berlin ballrooms advertised a wide variety of promising features and services: "magnificence," "artistic attractions," "intimacy" in the atmosphere of the "most cultivated luxury venue in the world" near the "high life bars" and "exquisite restaurants." The photographs and text of this essay are suitably frivolous and give the magazine reader an impression of how quickly "young Berliners" were able to get close in the ballrooms: "Table telephones, the best fun in the ballroom." After his visit to one of the most famous of these establishments, Franz Hessel senses little "social or moral purpose:"

"The invention of the table telephone is psychologically very astute: the average Berliner is not actually as self-confident as he would like to seem. On the telephone, he summons up his courage [...] and his resolve is strengthened by the verse which he reads in the interesting program: *Don't be shy, just give her a call/Then you'll find out if she likes you at all.*"

Franz Hessel, Spazieren in Berlin
(Strolling in Berlin), 1929

"Bellboy, our coats please!"

(Original captions)

Five minutes after the tea dance – photo essay

This photo essay reflects the typical photojournalistic perspective of the late 1920s in Germany: a view behind the scenes in a factory or backstage in a theater. Yet even the events "five minutes after the tea dance," which might seem somewhat banal at a first glance, can suddenly be made interesting. The focus is always on people, even if the text and captions once again betray the "social-romanticism" typical of the bourgeois magazines:

"Just a short time ago, the tango orchestra created that indefinable and fascinating mood with the melting tones of a new hit tune, the spiritual aroma of the modern tea dance, the atmosphere in which the chic ladies and gentlemen get to know each other over tea. At this stage, it is impossible to imagine the social life of the capital without the tea dance and, taking into account the current economic climate, its impresarios have reduced prices so much that even the humblest shorthand-typist can feel like a great lady for two delectable hours in this most elegant setting. Our photos show what happens when the music ends and the tea dance is over. The venue has undergone a remarkable change in just five minutes and the photographer conscientiously portrays the poignant aftermath of the dance."

Above: *The waiter will smile when he sees that a lady has left her lipstick behind.*
Left: *The waiters clear away the last cups.*
(Original captions)

Top: *His colleagues start polishing the floor as it starts all over again in one hour's time.*
Above: *A bellboy keeps up his strength with a substantial sandwich.*
Left: *The toilet attendant also checks the afternoon's profits.*

(Original captions)

From Adrian Wettach to Grock – photo essay

Grock, the clown, grew up in the circus arenas of the 1920s. A master of his art, he got by with very few props – a broken chair, a trumpet – and was very economical in his movements. His performances were finely tuned productions which did not need to rely on silly pranks or personal vanity: "My gags simply come to me. A gambler would call it luck, a writer inspiration," he said. Critics described him as "a big child in the body of a wise man," who was able to transform peals of laughter into tears.

He was always remembered by contemporaries for entering the ring with a garden gate under his arm. He placed it in front of him, glanced at the audience, opened it, carefully closed it again and then put it back under his arm: "Our reportage shows the incredible talent for mimicry and the versatility of the world-famous clown Grock, whose real name is Adrian Wettach. Grock is currently appearing in the Busch Circus in Berlin."

(Original text from the photo essay)

Left: *He is still Adrian Wettach. Only the tip of his nose and corners of his mouth betray the fact that in a few minutes Adrian Wettach will become Grock the clown.*
Below left: *The artist's rubber face can show any expression, in this case anger!*
Below: *'—immmpossible!'*
Right page: *Grock in the ring.*

(Original captions)

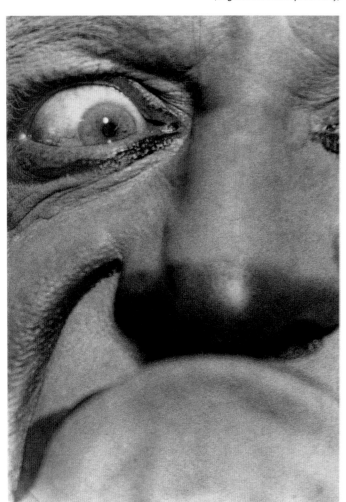

Above: 'Gold Rush.' Masked ball of the International Association of Vaudeville Theater and Circus Directors in the Berlin Sportpalast. Original costumes: negro, lampshade, political ape, painter's palette.
Left: The circus is coming! A turn that never fails: the fake zebra. *(Original captions)*

Above: *The circus is coming to town! Afternoon tea with the circus people. The lion tamer, dressage rider, clown, and trapeze artist enjoy a cup of tea together.*

(Original captions)

As forms of amusement, vaudeville and circus acts had already passed their peak in the 1920s. As early as January 1914, a vaudeville fan identified the cause of this crisis: "The cinema sits like a god on a monumental pedestal and folds its hands over its bulging stomach: Veni, vidi, vici. It has triumphed." Film stole the audiences of vaudeville theaters, which were previously the haunts of the petit-bourgeoisie and working classes. More and more vaudeville venues were converted into movie theaters. The Bosch circus's permanent venue in Berlin was increasingly used for sport and political events. In 1919, however, a long-awaited dream of the artists was fulfilled: in these eventful times they managed to squeeze a country-wide wage agreement out of their directors. In response, the latter also formed an association in the late 1920s with the illustrious title of *"International Varieté-Theater- und Circus-Direktoren-Verband"* ("International Association of Vaudeville Theater and Circus Directors").

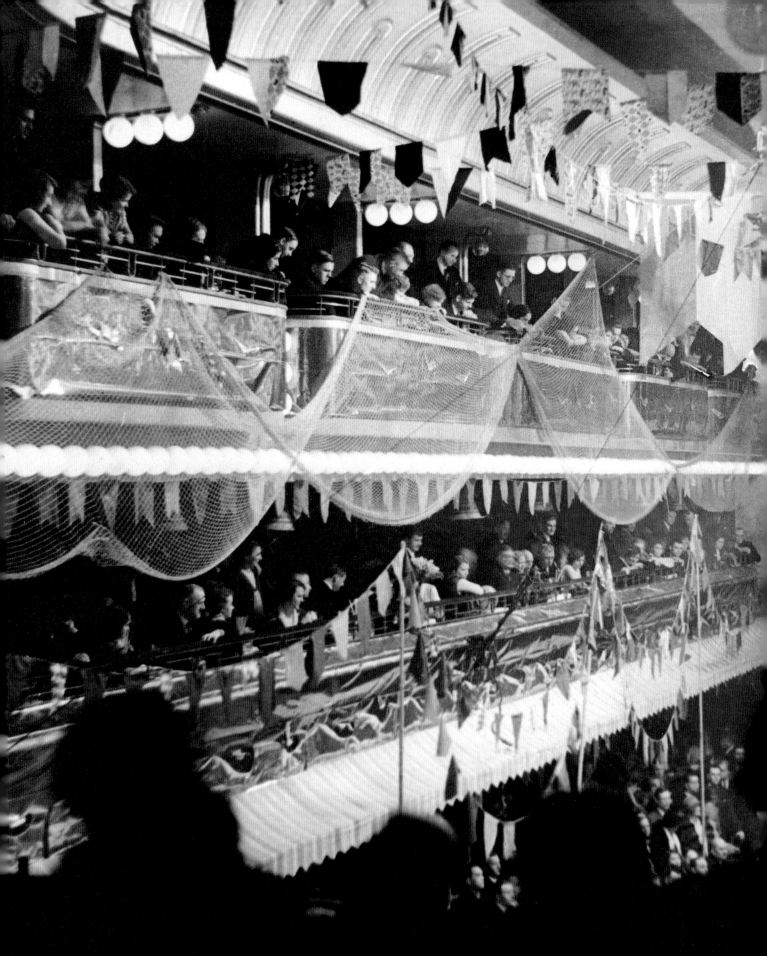

Left: *Entertainment for fifteen hundred people.*
(Original caption)
Above: *The dance floor disappears and the vaudeville show begins.*

Non-stop fun – photo essay
The photographer visited the "Alcazar" on the Reeperbahn in Hamburg, the infamous red-light district in the port's St. Pauli neighborhood. Following the extensive conversion of the "Gross-Ballhaus-Varietés" vaudeville theater, the building was reopened on 3 March 1930. The photo essay gives readers an impressive account of the efforts made at the time to impress the spoilt audiences.

"St. Pauli! What does it have in common with Yoshiwara, Whitechapel, Montmartre, Sin-Sing and – last but not least – Hollywood: it is a name known throughout the world. All over the world, anyone who says, hears or reads this name will have the same colorful images: ports, traveling people, honky-tonk night clubs, distant sounds and – girls, oh yes, the girls of St. Pauli [...] and the flashing colors, longing for euphoria, freedom, distance, joie de vivre."
Ludwig Jürgens, Sankt Pauli, *1930*

Non-stop fun – photo essay (continued)
Top: *Work continues on the new decor late into the night.*
Above: *The dance floor disappears at the flick of a switch.*
Left: *The show as seen from the control room.*
Right page: *The magical world of the vaudeville show.*

(Original captions)

Cupid on horseback – photo essay
Egon Erwin Kisch, whose work as "the racing reporter" became the embodiment of "social documentary" in the print journalism of the Weimar Republic, described the atmosphere in a hippodrome [equestrian circus] in the Hamburg red-light district of St. Pauli in the early 1930s as follows:

"Times are hard in St. Pauli. Of the twelve ponies that adorn the hippodrome near the Grosse Freiheit, nine are standing around looking miserable. The girls who once only had to show their garters while riding now have to strip up to their hips and even that's not enough. Before paying for the rider's drink, the gentleman from other parts demands that she take off her panties. Times are hard in St. Pauli."
Egon Erwin Kisch, Mein Leben für die Zeitung
(My life for the Newspaper), 1926–1947

Left page, above left: *Frolics on horseback.*
Left page, above right: *The hippodrome's main attractions: horses' heads and ladies' legs.*
Opposite page, below: *St. Pauli stable.*
Top: *Musicians display placards showing their fees.*
Right: *Cowboys and Indians drink up some courage.*
(Original captions)

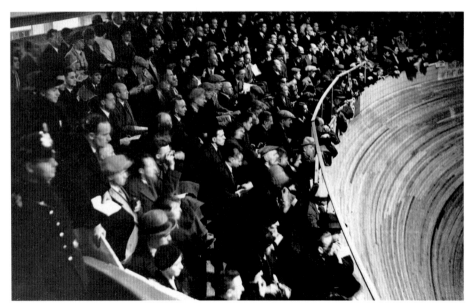

Left: *The six-day-race is on again in Berlin. The 24th six-day race, the annual highlight for cycling enthusiasts, got underway last night at the Berlin Sportpalast. Our photo shows: When the action on the track starts to pall, it is more interesting to watch the spectators. They are the experts, the 'ones in the know,' who are familiar with each rider and give an expert critique of each phase of the race.*
Below: *The six-day-race is on again in the Berlin Sportpalast. The 24th six-day event started in the Berlin Sportpalast in front of an enormous crowd on 7 November 1930. 15 pairs of cyclists lined up at the start. Our photo shows the start of the six-day race.*
Right page: *A view of the six-day race in the Berlin Sportpalast.* (Original captions)

"If you want to see the people of Berlin work up a sweat, be sure to catch part of the 144-hour event, which takes place in a vast hall. You can see the cream of society in the center area and stalls: prominent people, well-known faces, beautiful shoulders in sable and fox. However, if you want to sit among the true connoisseurs, those who participate in the most immediate and typically Berlin way, you will have to mix with the sweaters and windcheaters in the gallery. Nothing goes unnoticed there: the criticism is strongest and the clapping loudest. Cards are played if there is no action. Then the first names of the favorites, well known to everyone here, ring out loud and clear and nobody needs to figure out the number and color of the jersey on the backs of the riders racing through the smoke."

Franz Hessel, Spazieren in Berlin *(Strolling in Berlin), 1929*

"To the Avus races. Two hundred thousand people are reported to have been present. What was interesting to watch was how a totally unknown young man suddenly becomes the darling of a gigantic crowd. It happened to young Brauchitsch when, in a German Mercedes car, he won over Caracciola, who has been the German favorite so far. Suddenly Brauchitsch's name was on everyone's lips. The closer the race between him and Caracciola became, the more he was cheered. And when, at the last moment, he streaked ahead and won, the crowd went mad. The reasons were that he was driving a German car, but still more that he is a youngster, a handsome one at that, and an outsider. So the surprise factor entered into it too."

Harry Graf Kessler in a note in his diary
for Sunday 22 May 1932

Berlin's six-mile (9.8 km) long Avus racetrack was opened in 1921. The track, which runs between the Grunewald forest and Nikolaussee in Berlin, is still acknowledged as the prototype for all highways.

The big international car race on the Avus on 22 May 1932. Europe's best drivers on the Avus. Starting line for small class, cars up to 1500 cc.

(Original caption)

THE SYSTEM
IS COLLAPSING!

From 1929 onwards, the global economic crisis threw a dark shadow over
Germany. It had devastating political and social consequences, as well as
economic ones. When the Darmstadt & National Bank was declared
insolvent in July 1931, Joseph Goebbels triumphantly announced in his
National Socialist newspaper *Der Angriff* (The Attack): "The system is
collapsing!" The National Socialists had experienced a meteoric rise in
support in the Reichstag elections of 1930 and were now hoping to seize
power in the near future. However, their election triumph of July 1932
still denied them their repeated objective of an absolute majority. The
"brownshirts" marched through Berlin before the first session of
parliament after the elections. This picture was originally titled
"National Socialist Reichstag representatives on the way to a conference
in Hitler's headquarters in the Hotel Kaiserhof in Berlin before the
opening of the Reichstag in 1932."

Governments Without Backing

After the harsh struggles of its early days the Weimar Republic managed to attain a degree of stability from 1923/24 on. After that, however, a process of decline, which spread slowly and insidiously over the next five years, set in. With the appointment of Hindenburg after Ebert's death, the German democratic state assumed a basically conservative direction. And even the bourgeois cabinet in place from 1924 to 1928 failed to win the enduring trust of voters in German parliamentary democracy. Socio-political tensions meant large coalitions were out of the question, while right-wing coalitions split sooner or later over differences on foreign and cultural policy. Without exception, the Weimar government parties tended to give priority to individual issues and hence neglect their actual mandate to create policies that would be capable of winning the support of a majority by means of compromise, and to formulate resolutions which could be generally accepted and applied. Following the downfall of the Marx cabinet over a classical matter of ideology, i.e. education policy, Stresemann's foreign policy stood out from all the rows and squabbles of the Reichstag election campaign of 1928. His party, the DVP, wooed the voters with the following slogan: "What do you care about the others – *you* vote for Gustav Stresemann!" Behind the scenes, foreign minister Stresemann was actively promoting the idea that following

the fall of the Marx cabinet in spring 1928, for the foreseeable future, there could be no realistic alternative to a major coalition with the Social Democrats.

Food for Children, not Armored Cruisers

In the aftermath of its party conference of 1927 in Kiel, the SPD was ready, after a long period of abstention, to resume a role in government. The party announced a new "Will to Power" which was aimed at blocking further conservative alliance cabinets, and based its optimism on the positive developments in the Prussian Weimar coalition. The SPD went into the election campaign with the slogan "Food for Children, not Armored Cruisers" and joined the KPD in a demand for the abandonment of what they saw as the pointless project of building the "Armored Cruiser A." They wished to use the money to provide free food at the country's elementary schools instead. Following the counting of votes in the Reichstag elections on 20 May 1928, there was great jubilation among Social Democrats, who had increased their vote by over 4% and were thus guaranteed over one third of the Reichstag mandate.

At the same time however, alarm bells were ringing: the bourgeois liberal center was weakened by the election result and there

were also signs of splits among middle-class and agricultural interest groups. At the same time there were initial indications of increased radicalization as the KPD increased its vote to 10.6%, although the NSDAP only managed to increase its vote in certain agricultural regions, for example Dithmarschen in the Holstein region.

Cabinet without Majority

The "Great Coalition" did, however, come into being. Five weeks passed before the new Reich Chancellor, Hermann Müller (SPD), who in 1919 had taken the difficult step of signing the peace treaty in Versailles, was able to present his "Cabinet of Personalities" to the public. However, behind this promising concept lay little more than a parliamentary farce. The leaders of the DVP, Catholic Center, DDP, and SPD parties may have been united in government but the cabinet was ultimately unable to rely on the support of a parliamentary majority, as its various factions did not feel included in the decisions taken by this cabinet.

This problem soon came to light with the first crisis of government in the fall of 1928 when the SPD stepped into a fatal trap which had been set during the election campaign. Along with Chancellor Müller, the Social Democratic ministers Severing, Wissell, and Hilferding were unable and unwilling to uphold the party's vehement opposition to the "Armored Cruiser A," whose compact structure offered a way of circumventing the Versailles ban against the construction of large warships, against the bourgeois cabinet majority. However, the SPD Reichstag faction stuck to its fundamentally pacifist stance and pleaded for immediate cancelation of the construction of the warship. Thus, the leading government party's faction duped its ministers and the Chancellor and exposed them to public ridicule by adhering to strict faction voting – they themselves expressed the vote of no confidence, while the government resolution was carried by the parliamentary majority of parties from the DDP down to the NSDAP. Having just assumed greater responsibility in government, the SPD undermined its credibility in the first important vote.

The masses were not particularly interested in events unfolding in the Reichstag. In contrast, Berlin city dwellers showed considerable enthusiasm when the *Graf Zeppelin* arrived in the city on 5 November 1928. This photograph shows a crowd gathered in front of the Reich President's Palace.

Bloody May

1 May in Berlin. The notorious Scheunenviertel neighborhood saw heavy clashes on 1 May and there was shooting. Our photo shows demonstrators fleeing from the police. (Original caption)

The Reichstag elections of 1928 revealed the initial signs of radicalization which led to a series of bloody clashes between Communists and National Socialists, and also between Social Democrats and Communists, in December in Berlin. The capital city's chief of police, Karl Friedrich Zörgiebel, responded to these outbursts by placing a ban on all open-air assemblies and demonstrations. This edict was still in force on 1 May 1929, the traditional labor day when the KPD had called for mass demonstrations. An eye-witness recalled: "I found myself in Ziethen Street, almost at the corner of Hermann Street, and wanted to go down Hermann Street when suddenly there was shooting. Everyone was running. The cops jumped out of the house entrances and immediately opened fire but I was unable to figure out what they were shooting at. I was pushed into a bar on the corner of Ziethen and Hermann. There was an armored car outside the pub in Hermann, which repeatedly fired salvos with its machine gun in the direction of Hermannplatz square [...] The following statement says it all about the mood among the police: 'We would like to smoke out the whole lot of them. We would like to use quite different methods but we're not allowed to.'"

The street battles in the "red" neighborhoods of Neukölln and Wedding, described above, lasted three days. The heavy-handed reaction of the Prussian police claimed over 30 lives, including several housewives on their way to do their shopping. In addition 194 people were injured and 1,228 arrested. The obvious question was: how could such a bloodbath happen after so many years of peace?

Futile Search for the Class Compromise

From 9 November 1918, the Social Democrats had left no doubt as to the fact that there was no alternative to their policy of "class compromise" in a parliamentary democracy. This party represented mainly well situated and employed members of the working class who, in contrast to the words of Marx and Engels, had more to lose than their chains. Ironically, in order to enforce its opposition to revolutionary violence as a party concerned with the well-being of the state, the SPD never shied away from the use of repressive methods. One need only recall its repeated use of volunteer *Freikorps* and soldiers against the action of the far left. This strategy against their "socialist brothers" may have seemed arrogant and callous, but the opposition between the Social Democrats and the Communists was never merely tactical, but fundamental in nature from the outset.

Violence played a central role in the KPD's fundamental opposition, and particularly in its agitation activities. From 1920, this initially disorganized and ideologically divided group professed a single aim: the suppression of the Weimar democracy and establishment of a "Soviet Germany." In 1928 the Communists, who primarily represented the underprivileged and needy sectors of the working classes, were back in the ascendant following the decrease in party membership from 380,000 to 180,000 during the party ban of 1924. Ernst Thälmann had built up a tightly organized party apparatus that was ideologically dominated by the Communist International (Comintern) and took its instructions from Moscow. At the Sixth World Congress of the Comintern, the "World Revolution" was re-evaluated for Germany in the form of the so-called "social-fascism theory." A time of economic and political crisis had followed a phase of the relative stabilization of capitalism. In this situation, which was deemed a positive one for the "revolution," it was a question of attacking the international pillars of capitalism. In Germany these were seen to be the Social Democrats, who were, moreover, seen to be moving closer to fascism in their policies. The "social fascists" were the new face of the German bourgeoisie.

Growing Rift Between The Workers' Parties

By spring 1929 unemployment had risen to almost three million. The Social Democrats were in government again. The economic forecasts of the KPD had proved well-founded, while the SPD seemed to fulfill its opponents' prophecies with its adoption of an unrelenting "orders are orders" line on 1 May. It is doubtful that the KPD wanted to start a civil war by breaching the demonstration ban; it simply wanted to consciously provoke the authority of the state. The relationship between the workers' parties had – at least at leadership level – reached a low point: they were ideologically torn, bitter, and full of hate. After the events of "Bloody May," an even deeper rift ran through the working classes: while one group upbraided their opponents as "social fascists," the other retorted with the crass accusation "commies" and lumped their opponents together with the enemies of freedom, the National Socialists. The NSDAP and Adolf Hitler were able to capitalize on this conflict. Hitler created a mass party based on the socialist model which, however, operated outside all of the boundaries of social conflict in Weimar society.

The NSDAP – A New Kind of Party

The Hitler putsch in 1923 had failed miserably in its revolutionary strategy. While imprisoned, Adolf Hitler decided to exploit the legal scope offered by democracy as party leader. The infantry should not only be present throughout the Reich, but should also cause terror from below in street fights and brawls. This dual strategy actually took the following form: the SA (*Sturmabteilung* or Nazi Storm Troopers) committed numerous acts of violence and murder and thus created an atmosphere of terror and violence on the streets. This stirred up the longing for a "strong man" among anxious and order-loving citizens. Meanwhile, from parliament, Hitler pilloried the inadequacies of his political opponents and the weaknesses of the despised Republic, and promised to help.

As soon as he was out of prison, Adolf Hitler made himself mobile by buying a multi-cylinder Mercedes. From the outset, the NSDAP made use of the very latest technology and media, and by 1928/29 had built up a party apparatus which differed from all other parties in its broad mass effect. Even before its major electoral successes from 1930 on, the NSDAP knew how to build a country-wide network of support bases and local groups. If there were no active party members in remote locations, they were shipped in trucks, cars, and boats to lend support, as propaganda events were organized with military precision and always accompanied by the appearance of uniformed SA. Many people in the German provinces had never previously experienced this kind of party demonstration of pseudo-military power. And Hitler knew just how to use the most modern methods to convey his propaganda formula of "one people, one Reich, one leader" in a way that was highly effective in terms of mass psychology. By doing this, he focused the political, economic, and religious desires of many voters during the last crisis of the Weimar Republic on the person of the "Führer."

This kind of propaganda and ongoing street-fighting campaign was expensive. The NSDAP financed its activities through membership fees and contributions: it was the only party that charged an entry fee for its propaganda events. However, it is unlikely that these resources were sufficient to pay for such extravagant displays of power. It is an undisputed fact that money was donated to the NSDAP from certain business circles. However, many academics now reject the theory that National Socialism was solely financed and controlled by major capitalist interests. They also refute the contradictory theory that there were no structural links between capitalism and the rise of national socialism. As is often the case, the historical truth lies somewhere between these extremes. Long before Hitler's political breakthrough, there was a readiness among the industrial elite to sacrifice parliamentary democracy in favor of an authoritarian solution which would rigorously curtail the welfare state and make it possible to develop the ailing economy on the backs of the working classes. In the 1920s these circles, dominated by the magnates Fritz Thyssen and Hugo Stinnes, were a minority. In the early 1930s the world economic crisis and the self-surrender of German parliamentary democracy created a climate of acceptance for a political solution involving Hitler in an authoritarian presidential cabinet, even among businesses that had previously been vehemently opposed to the National Socialists. It was hoped that such a political solution would make it possible to create the conditions that would allow the German economy to recover.

Above right: *National Socialist election meeting in the Berlin Pleasure Garden [Lustgarten] on 4 April 1932. Führer Adolf Hitler is greeted enthusiastically on his arrival in the Lustgarten.*
Above: *Mass demonstration by National Socialists in the Lustgarten in Berlin for the forthcoming presidential election. 4 April 1932.* (Original captions)

Black Friday

The alarm bells were ringing loud and clear, and not only in America. On Thursday 24 October 1929, shares collapsed at close of trading on Wall Street in New York. The next day, "Black Friday," the newspapers informed the world about the stock-market crash. This date seemed like the end of the world for people at the time, and to this day it is acknowledged as the beginning of the global economic crisis. After many years of excessive investment, there was a surplus of goods available far in excess of demand. Global over-production was, however, only one of the many contributory factors that had been amassing and were obvious by the end of 1929. The immediate consequence of the crash was the collapse of the transatlantic financial economy. In order to remain solvent, the US banks called in their short-term loans to Europe. Because of its effects on international finance and economic interdependence of nations, what initially seemed to be a severe but temporary economic crisis extended to 1931 and became the most serious economic crisis of the 20th century.

The vicious circle of bank insolvency, liquidations, mass unemployment, and social poverty set in, sooner or later, in all Western industrialized nations. In the traditional democracies of Great Britain and France, the depression severely affected all social classes, but faith in the parliamentary system was never really shaken. In the USA and the Weimar Republic reaction developed in completely opposing directions. Thanks to the policy of the "New Deal" initiated by Franklin D. Roosevelt, American democracy assumed a high level of socio-political responsibility and enjoyed a growth in the trust and support of its citizens. However, the young German Republic wandered into a labyrinth lined with a series of grave difficulties: the crisis in the economy, high unemployment even before this crisis, extensive state, industrial, and agricultural debts, the consequences of inflation, and the psychological and political burden of reparations.

The Great Coalition Under Fire

The most urgent task facing German domestic politics in 1928/29 was to solve an equation of rising unemployment, increasing welfare spending, and shrinking tax revenue. As already mentioned, however, Reich Chancellor Müller's "Cabinet of Personalities" had had the worst possible start. The crisis over "Armored Cruiser A" was not quite over in October 1928 when the coal and steel industry made its uncompromising position on wage policy all too clear. During the "Ruhr iron dispute," 230,000 employees were locked out for over a month in what became the biggest strike in German industrial history. The right wing of the employers' camp was looking for open confrontation, as it wanted to replace mandatory state arbitration with individual company agreements. This conflict represented the unspoken breakdown of socio-political consensus between industry and the Weimar welfare state. With the increasing deterioration in the economy, the demands from industrial, agricultural, and commercial groups for the abolition of the system which favored workers over employers, i.e. parliamentary democracy, grew ever louder.

Radicalization of the Parties

It would have taken a very strong government to withstand such attacks. Unfortunately, Germany's coalition government was anything but strong. Differing views on the Ruhr strikes within the SPD weakened the party. The radicalization of the constitutional DDP party, which responded to its gradual demise with German nationalistic and anti-Semitic attitudes, took a less conspicuous course. Yet another mainstay of the "Weimar Coalition," the Catholic Center, shifted to the right. The election of the prelate Ludwig Kaas as party leader in December 1928 resulted in growing support for anti-parliamentary and authoritarian ideas in this Catholic party. In August 1929, Kaas tried to halt the ongoing erosion of the Catholic community in the following speech: "The need for a leader of great style has never been more urgently and impatiently desired by the German soul than in these days, during which the patriotic and cultural crisis weighs on us all."

This kind of authoritarian tone, coming from an established party, undermined the political culture of the Weimar Republic and made it increasingly difficult for the SPD to defend the "Great Coalition" under the leadership of a Social Democratic chancellor both outside and within. When Prussian policemen began shooting at Communists, as happened for example during the "Bloody May" unrest of 1929, the abstract theory of "social fascism" began to ring true for supporters of the KPD. The economic crisis was accompanied by angry protests from the radical workers against the Social-Democratic "bigwigs" in Müller's government.

Violence Hinders Political Action

The streets of Berlin were not the only place where loud blasts were heard in spring 1929. Bombs exploded in front of official buildings in northern Germany. The *Landvolkbewegung* (Rural People's Movement) owned up to the attacks. This movement was formed by many indebted farmers from Schleswig-Holstein to protest against the compulsory auctions of their farms. During an organized tax strike, there was commotion at cattle markets and violent attacks on policemen and bailiffs. There were farmers who preferred to set fire to their own farms rather than hand them over to the treasury. This spontaneous farmers' revolt was an expression of the dissatisfaction of those who felt neglected by the "social democracy" of the Weimar "system." In their eyes, the blame lay firmly with "Müllerism," named after the man who had signed the peace treaty and was now on the point of signing an Allied reparations program.

A New Versailles

Everything pointed to the continuing disintegration of the democratic consensus of the "black-red-gold coalition" and the increasing radicalization of all parties and interest groups. The cabinet's foreign policy successes did little to change this. Stresemann's life's work was completely ignored by the German right. The previously mentioned "Young Plan," which was supposed to return to Germany its economic and financial policy sovereignty, encouraged party political polarization and ultimately rendered the National Socialists politically acceptable.

Hugenberg's Campaign

In the fall of 1929, the German right organized a mass press campaign which was unprecedented in the Weimar period. The driving force behind the campaign was Alfred Hugenberg, who had taken over the leadership of the DNVP in 1928. In his countrywide, mass circulation common newspapers and magazines, Hugenberg had anti-Young-Plan tirades printed every day as well as frequent benevolent comments about a new "ally" which had hitherto refused to work with the monarchists – the NSDAP. The press tycoon also financed a "Reich committee" comprising the National Socialists, the paramilitary *Stahlhelm* (literally "steel helmet"), and the DNVP as "national opposition," whose purpose was to make the people's opposition to the "new Versailles" felt by referendum. People were asked to vote in favor of a "law against the enslavement of the German people" which demanded the removal of the war guilt clause from the Versailles Treaty and the imprisonment of all those who had signed the Young Plan. The nationalists' campaign to stage the plebiscite barely cleared the constitutional hurdle – 10.02% of all those entitled to vote supported it – but the decisive vote of 22 December 1929 ended with a failure. Instead of the required 21 million, only 5.8 million Germans voted in favor of the proposed law. Of the members of the "Reich committee," the DNVP emerged as clear loser, having been worn down by its leader's style. The clear winners, in contrast, were the National Socialists, who had been able to promote themselves nationwide as a new force in the national opposition in a mass propaganda campaign financed by another party. They had now been accepted as partners by the established right-wing parties. As the Reichstag elections of 1930 showed, the NSDAP was winning more and more support among right-wing voters.

DNVP Reichstag representative D. Doehring spoke along with party leader Dr. Hugenberg at a meeting organized by the Greater Berlin Regional Associations of the DNVP on the evening of 27 January 1931 in the Berlin Sportpalast. The topic for the meeting was Germany past, present and future.

(Original caption)

Wait and See!

After Hindenburg's election as Reich President in 1925, the Weimar Republic became more conservative. This did not have a great deal to do with Hindenburg himself, as he remained largely inactive and up to the late 1920s had a rather stultifying effect on German domestic politics. In economic circles, however, he was respected and received substantial donations. Thus, in 1927, the President of the Reich was able to repurchase his family estate Neudeck in East Prussia. He always had a sympathetic ear for his landowning neighbors who, unlike the industrial employers and workers, were not represented in the Great Coalition. In future, this circle would only support a right-wing government, and this was not altered by the subsidies and customs policies of Müller's administration.

Influential advisers who were close to Hindenburg worked on realigning the government to the right from spring 1929. These included Major-General Kurt von Schleicher, who had been appointed head of the ministerial department in the Reichswehr ministry, State Secretary Otto Meissner, Hindenburg's civilian ally, and Oskar Hindenburg, who as the son of the president and an army officer was used to formulating his own policies. They were all pushing for the removal of the Social Democrats from government. Their candidate for chancellor of a "Hindenburg Cabinet" was Heinrich Brüning, who had been elected as the new leader of the Catholic Center Party in December 1929. His nationalist and conservative politics, financial policy experience, and not least his experience on the front as an officer in the First World War qualified him in the eyes of the right, who also saw potential in his socio-political leanings for possible recognition from the Social Democrats. Hindenburg supported the plans for a presidential government and let Brüning know late that year that he would have full powers in accordance with Emergency Article 48. Furthermore, the President indicated that he did not wish to send the Social Democrats into opposition until after the ratification of the Young Plan, so that the new government would not be burdened with the heavy baggage of an additional reparations agreement – the right's invective on the subject of the "New Versailles" was still in the air.

The End of Parliamentary Democracy

Soup kitchens in Berlin! Together with commerce and industry, the government has organized further aid to help relieve the misery of Berlin's unemployed and poor for the coming winter.

(Original caption)

One thing is true of the political situation at New Year 1929/30: no Weimar government ever had to face more opposition from extra-parliamentary political and economic interests. Parliamentary democracy's most dangerous opponents could be found in the corporate centers of heavy industry, on their estates east of the Elbe, and in top army positions. With a total of 66 out of 491 seats in the Reichstag, the Communists and National Socialists did not yet pose a serious threat in parliament, but the scale of the street fighting and agitation they were involved in should not have been underestimated. The situation in the Reichstag had also been deteriorating steadily since the formation of the Great Coalition. The "Cabinet of Personalities" had no support among the parliamentary factions. Moreover, with Stresemann's death in October 1929, the government had lost its only charismatic member, who as a former monarchist reformed as a "pragmatic Republican" had developed an iron will for political compromise. Above all, the Social Democrats

must have felt completely isolated as advocates of "democracy" when their former alliance partners the DDP and Catholic Center withdrew from the "black-red-gold" consensus and when they were held responsible in both the radical right and left-wing press for all of the Republic's failures and mistakes. However, all was not lost – not yet, at any rate.

Unyielding to the Last

In early 1930, an already divided and not very determined SPD faced the last battle to save parliamentary democracy. In fact, the will of all the participants to sustain the current government alliance was put to a particularly severe test. Once the Reichstag had passed the legislation for the implementation of the Young Plan on 12 March 1930, the capacity of the four coalition parties to reach a consensus had reached its limits. Against the background pressure of national debt and high unemployment, the DVP and SPD had been arguing

about the financing of unemployment benefit for months. It was none other than Brüning, Hindenburg's candidate for the chancellorship, who finally presented a proposal for a compromise on 27 March, suggesting that benefits would temporarily remain at present levels with the prospect of an increase in the near future. The DVP also agreed to the proposal, if unwillingly. With the exception of labor minister Wissell, the SPD government members also pleaded for its acceptance. Along with the majority of the SPD members of the Reichstag, Wissell continued to demand an increase. They were acting in the firm belief that the inviolability of the Weimar welfare state could only be proven by a refusal to give in, otherwise everything that had been achieved since November 1918 would collapse. Hence, they believed that the immediate breakdown of the coalition was a justifiable price to pay.

First Presidential Cabinet Takes Office

The resignation of the Great Coalition was followed by the formation of an authoritarian government run by presidential decree. As early as 29 March 1930, Brüning formed a government from the bourgeois Catholic Center and right-wing parties. Brüning's policies were based initially on collaboration with the Reichstag, with the support of the President of the Reich and the emergency legislation passed by him. The Reichstag could reject the emergency legislation, but in this event the president had the option of dissolving parliament and calling an election. This "presidential decree system" made Brüning independent of the Reichstag and effectively abolished parliamentary democracy. The introduction of this form of government marked the end of parliamentary democracy in the Weimar Republic.

The Hunger Chancellor

Brüning tried to resolve the economic crisis by introducing drastic economic measures: his "deflation policy" meant increased taxes, reduced state spending on welfare, import restrictions, pay reductions, and reductions in the prices of basic foodstuffs. This economic policy had two objectives: firstly, it was imperative that inflation, as experienced in the early 1920s, be avoided, and, secondly, Brüning wanted to show the Allies that Germany could not afford any more reparation payments and that they should, therefore, cancel their demands. Both aims were achieved, but at an excessive price. The brunt of the suffering was borne by the German people, who were given little or no help from the government. From one month to the next, the social situation deteriorated dramatically and the German economy slumped deeper into depression.

Chancellor Brüning passed emergency laws on the basis of Article 48 for the first time when a Reichstag majority rejected unpopular measures for budgetary rehabilitation. This system continued to prove effective for a short time for the immediate implementation of new budgetary and finance policy measures, and as a way of cracking down on the increasing street violence and criminality that was being organized by both extreme right and left-wing parties. However, such political action could not be popular. The opposition Social Democrats remained quietly

On 23 June 1931 Reich Chancellor Brüning broadcast an address on the political situation on German radio.
(Original caption)

in the background in the Reichstag and tolerated Brüning's economic measures, not least as a way of maintaining their coalition with the Catholic Center Party in Prussia, which the SPD saw as the stronghold against fascism. However, the KPD and NSDAP protested loudly. The English poet Stephen Spender, who was visiting his friend Christopher Isherwood in Berlin at the time, described the situation as follows: "Brüning had abandoned the attempt to govern through the yelling mob of members of twenty-nine different political parties, which was the Reichstag [...] and, using emergency powers under the Constitution, governed by decree. Every decree [was] accompanied by dissenting cries of 'dictatorship' from the extreme Right and the extreme Left [...]. The Brüning regime was neither democracy or dictatorship, socialism or conservatism, it represented no group nor class, only a common fear of the overwhelming disorder, which formed a kind of rallying place of frightened people. It was the Weimardämmerung."

Not surprisingly, the Reichstag elections of 14 September 1930 became a protest vote with 82% of the electorate going to the polls, making it the highest turnout in any Reichstag

election during the Weimar period. The Social Democrats lost 10 seats, the German People's Party (DVP) lost 15, and the German National People's Party (DNVP) lost 32. The winners were the KPD, with a gain of 23 seats, and the National Socialists who achieved a sensational landslide, increasing their number of representatives in parliament from 12 to 107 in one fell swoop. 6.4 million people voted for the Nazis and made them into the second strongest party in the Reichstag, behind the SPD and ahead of the KPD. Hitler's party had attracted a large number of previous abstainers and had successfully exploited the "panic of the middle classes," as observed by sociologist Theodor Geiger in the fall of 1930. In contrast, the white- and blue-collar workers and the unemployed actually contributed little to the rise of National Socialism. The NSDAP was now firmly on its way to becoming a *Volkspartei* (national party) with support across the social classes, and it started attacking the bases of the traditional parties, which were securely rooted in their individual power bases.

The SA and SS Ban

There were more than six million people unemployed in Germany in early 1932. Marching music and calls to join in the fighting rang out all over German towns and cities and the songs of the activists could be heard in the courtyards of the city tenements. Demonstrators carrying red flags with hammers and sickles or black swastikas passed through the streets. "Red guards" and supporters of the *Reichsbanner* Social Democrat paramilitary organization wearing windcheaters and peaked caps clashed with the SA brownshirts in bloody street battles which claimed the lives not only of some of the fighters but also of innocent bystanders. The latent civil war between the "reds" and the "browns" tended to flare up at weekends in particular.

During the elections, the Nazi militia continued to stage violent protests on German streets. Their brutality prompted Brüning to ban the SA and SS on 13 April, just a few days after Hindenburg's re-election as Reich President.

Hindenburg Overthrows Brüning

Brüning's economic policy was basically an integral part of his foreign policy. After the Darmstädter & National Bank, known as Danat for short, and other major German banks temporarily stopped making payments, the queues of people in front of banks joined the images of crowds in labor exchanges and soup kitchens as potent symbols of the crisis in capitalism. By the end of the year, an Allied committee had no option but to acknowledge the insolvency of the German Reich and hence signal the end of reparations. Chancellor Brüning was not in office to experience this single policy success as he had been dismissed by his former mentor Hindenburg on 30 May.

Intrigues against the "Agricultural Bolshevist"

The reasons for Brüning's dismissal were numerous. From summer 1931, the consensus among the major forces in German society, from entrepreneurs to the leaders of the Social Democrats, most of whom had previously supported Brüning's economic policies, collapsed. The President began to have more and more doubts about the popularity of his

Termination of payments at the Danat bank. Concerned depositors gather at the bank.   (Original caption)

The uniforms of the SA cavalry troop commanders.
Left: *Two Stars.* Right: *Rider Insignia.*

(Original caption)

Chancellor. Hindenburg was already deeply disturbed by the fact that it had been the votes of Social Democrats and Catholics that had ensured his re-election in spring 1932: Hitler had won the votes of the right. Moreover, the army chief General von Schleicher had been plotting closely with the National Socialists for the downfall of the Center Chancellor, as the SA ban had thwarted his plans to integrate the parliamentary groups into the army. The big landowners were not well disposed to the government, as they would no longer benefit from the planned *Ostsiedlung* ("Eastern settlement") agricultural reform which was to involve the settlement of unemployed people on plots and unprofitable holdings in the east of the country and in this way provide them with an agricultural livelihood. Hindenburg had listened carefully to the outraged landowners when they described Brüning as an "agricultural Bolshevist." In general, Hindenburg's clique believed that in order to prevent even further radicalization, Brüning's cabinet

would have to be overthrown and Hitler and his party apparatus integrated into the existing system.

Brüning's fall represented yet another massive shock for the Weimar Republic. The moderate phase of the "presidential decree system," which had been tolerated by the Social Democrats, had now come to an end. In order to prevent the formation of an even more right-wing government, the SPD, which remained the Republic's largest party, opted to tolerate this basically anti-democratic cabinet; this support of the Catholic Center Chancellor in turn ensured the continued existence of the "Weimar Coalition" in Prussia, which the SPD viewed as an important bastion of anti-fascism in the German Reich.

The Cabinet of the Barons

Brüning was succeeded as Chancellor of the German Reich by Franz von Papen, an unknown Westphalian aristocrat, former career officer, and diplomat. Von Papen, a vain, scheming, and politically insignificant "stuffed shirt," was an ideal puppet for Schleicher's plan to bring down democracy. He was a member of the Catholic Center, but his political thinking had been strongly influenced by his democracy-hating peers in the elite conservative Berlin "Herrenklub" ("Gentlemen's Club"), a haunt of prominent representatives of high finance, industry, and the landowning aristocracy. Just a few months earlier, von Papen had proposed to his party colleague Brüning a plan to establish a "national dictatorship" based on the nationalist right and National Socialists. Hitler tolerated the appointment of von Papen when the latter reassured him that the Reichstag would soon be dissolved and new elections held. A promise to lift the ban on the SA clinched the deal.

Von Papen formed a "Cabinet of Barons" which was independent in party political terms. Its members were East Prussian estate owners and members of the top echelons of the military, and it represented an extremely narrow social basis for government. One of the first of von Papen's actions as Chancellor was to fulfill his promises to Hitler. On 4 June the Reichstag was dissolved and ten days later the ban on the SA and SS was lifted. This immediately revived the bloody street clashes with the Communists. In terms of foreign policy, von Papen reaped the benefit of his predecessor's efforts when Germany's reparation obligations were finally canceled at a conference in Lausanne, Switzerland.

The Prussian Coup

Prussia's special place in the German Reich as the last bastion of the Weimar Coalition of the SPD and Catholic Center had long been a thorn in the flesh of the conservatives. The Braun–Severing cabinet may have been a minority cabinet, but it remained in office because the Communist and National Socialist majority in the regional parliament were unable to work together. With the help of two emergency decrees, which earned the quiet applause of von Schleicher and the declaration of a military emergency, von Papen deposed the Braun government without explanation and appointed himself Reich Commissar for Prussia. This was without doubt an illegal coup which revealed that the Weimar constitution was now defunct. The deposed ministers protested but did not call for violent resistance.

Elections in a Climate of Civil War

In the elections of 31 July 1932, the NSDAP emerged as the strongest group in the Reichstag with a total of 230 seats. Hermann Göring took over as Reichstag President from the Communist Clara Zetkin. The newly elected Reichstag assembled in September, only to disband immediately when an emergency decree was defeated. In the elections of 6 November – the fifth of that year – the Nazis lost 34 seats but remained the majority party in the Reichstag. Both elections were accompanied by heavy street fighting and violent clashes between the National Socialists and the left. The country seemed to be on the brink of a civil war and tumultuous scenes were also played out in the Reichstag.

No Room to Maneuver

Von Papen's authoritarian "Cabinet of Barons" was skating on thin ice – just one tenth of the Reichstag supported the government. Thanks to his "Prussian Coup," he had ruined any chance of cooperation with the Social Democrats and on the right Hitler vehemently refused to comply with von Papen's authoritarian government. At the same time, Communist and National Socialist workers had joined forces in a transport strike in Berlin. Von Papen's only option would have been the declaration of a state of emergency combined with the dissolving of the Reichstag and outlawing of extremist parties. However, this was rejected by von Schleicher: the army was not ready for a fight with the National Socialists and Communists.

Von Papen's government, which had lost the little public support it still enjoyed, resigned on 17 November.

Soldiers on the Templehof parade ground in Berlin on 4 September 1931. Von Papen raises his hat to greet the members of the Stahlhelm.
(Original caption)

Hitler on the Threshold of Power

Following unproductive negotiations with the Catholic Center and Hitler, Hindenburg appointed General von Schleicher as Reich Chancellor. The General had a strong army behind him but no support in the Reichstag. In a radio announcement to the German people on 15 December 1932, von Schleicher presented himself as a "all-party administrator representing the interests of all," neither capitalist nor socialist, right nor left but with the single task of creating employment for all. He outlined a political program which included Brüning's earlier idea of agrarian reform: it was intended to allocate up to 600,000 hectares of land in East Prussia, Pomerania and Mecklenburg for "internal colonization," a major resettlement project for the urban unemployed and homeless. This move placed him in an isolated position within the Hindenburg clique: the East Prussian landed elite now saw their former friend as a deadly enemy. Moreover, vague reassurances about the nationalization of the coal and steel industries made industry sit up and listen in alarm.

Like his predecessors, von Schleicher was faced with the problem of creating a sufficiently broad base for action in a Reichstag which was incapable of reaching any kind of consensus. The main obstacle here was Hitler, who categorically refused to enter any kind of cooperation agreement except on his own terms.

Von Schleicher tried to cause a split in the NSDAP. He wanted to persuade its left wing around Gregor Strasser – Hitler's rival within the party – to join forces with the Christian and Socialist trade unions to form a "trade union front" as a basis for a non-parliamentary government. However, this plan failed when, thanks to the intervention of Hitler and Goebbels, Strasser was stripped of his position in the party and the Social Democrats rejected all of the "gray General's" requests out of hand.

Hitler Boxed In

Gregor Strasser's fall revealed a split in the ranks of the National Socialists. At the same time, the party's vote was declining while its debts to major industrial sponsors were increasing. The party was in a serious crisis and Hitler, who needed to present his voters with tangible political results, began to show signs

First photograph of the new Hitler cabinet. From the left standing: Secretary of State Meissner, Gereke, Reichstag President Göring, Count Schwerin-Krosigk. Seated: Reich Chancellor Hitler, von Papen; Standing: Dr. Frick, General von Blomberg, Hugenberg.
(Original caption)

of a willingness to negotiate. Von Papen, who privately retained the President's trust, saw in von Schleicher's difficulties and Hitler's willingness to compromise an opportunity to form a broad-based government of "national concentration." Von Papen and Hitler met for discussions in Cologne with a banker acting as mediator. Oskar von Hindenburg, State Secretary Meissner, Hugenberg as the representative of the DNVP, and the Stahlhelm were involved in the secret wheeling and dealing that went on behind the back of the Reich President. An agreement was reached on a "shadow cabinet," with Hitler as Reich Chancellor, von Papen as Vice-Chancellor and just a few other National Socialists. Hence, Hitler seemed to have been "contained" by the DNVP and the Stahlhelm.

The Reich President Nods his Head

When agreement had been reached on the distribution of ministerial posts, the result of the negotiations was presented to Hindenburg. The confused and elderly man was told that this was the only way of thwarting von Schleicher's plan to declare a state of emergency and establish a military dictatorship as a means of avoiding a seizure of power by Hitler. Hindenburg resolutely refused to appoint the "Bohemian private" as Reich Chancellor but was subject to further intensive canvassing from his confidants, members of his class, and industrial leaders. Von

Schleicher was painted as a "Socialist" and it was rumored that he intended to lead the Potsdam garrison in a march into Berlin to remove the President from office. Attention was drawn to the need to include Hitler's mass party in the rebuilding of the Reich. Hindenburg finally relented. Like that of Brüning, von Schleicher's fall was due to the refusal of the President to dissolve the Reichstag after the rejection of an emergency decree.

On 30 January 1933, Hindenburg appointed Adolf Hitler, the leader of the National Socialist Party, as Reich Chancellor of a government of "national concentration" consisting of National Socialists, German Nationalists, Stahlhelm, and representatives of the conservative establishment. The day ended with a massive torch-lit parade through the Brandenburg Gate organized by the National Socialists and Stahlhelm supporters.

The next day, Theodor von Wolff made the following bitter comment in the *Berliner Tageblatt*: "*It's over.* Hitler is Reich Chancellor, Papen Vice-Chancellor, Hugenberg economic dictator. The jobs have been distributed exactly the way the gentlemen of the 'Harzburg Front' wanted."

"The Social Democrats' fight against social reaction is no longer just a fight for people's rights. The National Socialists, the open supporters of dictatorship, want to destroy this right of the people. They want to raise brutal violence with the knife and revolver to a state sanctioned system. The Communists are doing them a valuable service with their methods of fighting and by splitting the workers."

SPD Election Appeal of 20 July 1930

"The National Socialist movement will seek to attain its aim in this state by constitutional means. The constitution shows us only the methods, not the goal. In this constitutional way, we will try to gain decisive majorities in the legislative bodies in order, in the moment this is successful, to pour the state into the mold that matches our ideas."

Hitler addressing the Reich Court 1930

Unemployed men in Berlin.   *(Original caption)*

Left: *National Socialist Party Conference in Nuremberg 1927. The National Socialists march past Adolf Hitler and guests of honor on the old market square in Nuremberg in front of a massive crowd.*
Top: *Big meeting of German nationalist party in Nuremberg. On Sunday August 21st 1927 the meeting of the National Socialist Party of Germany took place in Nuremberg. Photo shows a group of nationalist leaders at Nuremberg. In the center is Adolf Hitler.*
Above: *Photo shows the SA troops with their flags marching through Nuremberg.*

(Original captions)

"Whoever controls the streets, controls the masses. Whoever controls the masses, controls the state."
Joseph Goebbels 1926

After its re-establishment on 26 February 1925, the NSDAP worked assiduously on the promotion of its public image. Party conferences were just one of the events they exploited to this end. Unlike the annual meetings of democratic parties, whose purpose was the exchange of opinions and development of informed political opinion, at NSDAP party conferences, the party, the SA and the SS paid homage to their leader Adolf Hitler in order to present themselves to their rivals as a highly organized and resolute alternative that needed to be taken seriously. From 1927, the party conferences were held in the old Free Reich city of Nuremberg, whose medieval backdrop was consciously selected to associate these demonstrations of power with distant memories of late medieval German glory. After the fourth party conference in 1929, the NSDAP dropped the spectacle until 1933. After the "seizure of power," the shows of party strength in Nuremberg assumed a quasi-state character.

The Social Democratic Head of the Berlin Police Force, Karl Friedrich Zörgiebel, reacted to a series of bloody clashes between the Communists and National Socialists in December 1928 with a ban on all outdoor meetings and demonstrations. Weeks before 1 May 1929, he decided to maintain the ban for the traditional labor day. However, the KPD called for mass demonstrations in defiance of the ban. With the full support of his party, Zörgiebel cracked down in a campaign of repression that resulted in over 30 deaths, 194 injured and 1,228 arrests. These events ultimately confirmed the Communists' "social fascism theory."

"Intensive agitation must now begin against the fact that this social–fascist dictatorship will be merely a dictatorship of the bourgeoisie against the working classes for the purpose of the extreme economic and political suppression of the working masses. Under the social–fascist dictatorship, Wels and Social Democracy will represent the interests of the bourgeoisie just as under bourgeois democracy, which is nothing more than the veiled dictatorship of the bourgeoisie."

Ernst Thälmann at the KPD party conference, 10 June 1929

Above: *State of emergency in Neukölln and Wedding in Berlin. Pedestrians being searched for weapons and papers in the Wedding area on 3 May 1929.*
Left: *Remarkable pictures of May Day scenes in Berlin: Fighting all night in the streets. Fierce fighting has been in progress between the Communists and the Berlin police following less serious riots during May Day yesterday. Firing has been frequent during the night, bombs have been thrown, and at least ten have been killed (including policemen) and about 100 injured. Our photo shows a Communist under arrest in Berlin yesterday.*

(Original captions)

Right: To avoid clashes, the police authorities had prohibited public demonstrations in Berlin on 1 May. Despite the ban, the Berlin Communists held their usual May demonstrations in the working-class neighborhoods of Neukölln and Wedding. On the order of the Social Democratic chief of police Zörgiebel, the crowd was dispersed by armed policemen and a number of people were killed. This photo shows a police attack on a crowd gathered on Hermannplatz square in Neukölln.

THE SYSTEM IS COLLAPSING!

Left: *The municipal authorities provide games tables for the unemployed. The Kreuzberg local authority office in Berlin has set up tables and benches on Hohenstauffenplatz square to give the numerous card players who constantly hang around on the square the opportunity to play a few rounds. The players who now crowd around the tables are mainly unemployed. Berlin 21 August 1931.*
(Original caption)

THE SYSTEM IS COLLAPSING!

Notice at museum entrance in Parochialstrasse in Berlin (1931):

"For people 30 pfennigs. For unemployed and children 15 pfennigs."

B. Nelissen Haken, Stempelchronik, *Hamburg 1932*

Top: *Sign of the times! – The crisis in the retail business. Due to the severe economic crisis, the number of formerly prosperous stores being forced to close their doors for business is increasing, as they can no longer afford to pay rent from their meager turnover. The shop here is in the most popular part of Friedrichstrasse and is a striking example of the catastrophic state of business in Berlin and probably also throughout Germany.*

Above: *A bus for the unemployed. A Berlin company has set up a private bus for unemployed people who have to travel from distant suburbs to have their cards stamped. The journey costs ten pfennigs. The first bus for the unemployed commutes between Johannisthal and the labor exchange on Sonnenallee in Neukölln. Our photo shows: a group of unemployed people waiting for the bus at the bus stop in Johannisthal.*

Left: *Emergency accommodation in the hallway. In Ruppiner Strasse 29 in Berlin, the Sprembergs have moved into the hallway after the old lady with whom they previously shared a one-room apartment evicted them. The couple, who have one child, were unable to find anywhere else to live. Berlin 1930.* (Original captions)

Above: *Due to disagreements over the wage reduction policy in the Ruhr mining industry, there have been strikes and riots at many pits in the west German coal mines, some of which have escalated to bloody conflicts. On several occasions, miners who are still working were prevented from entering their workplace by acts of sabotage. Demonstrations and meetings of Communist miners are taking place everywhere. Our photo was taken during the conference of shaft delegates of the R.G.O. (Revolutionary Trade Union Opposition) in Schützenhof near Bochum, at which demands were made for the continuation of the strike in the Ruhr area. Bochum 1 May 1931.*
Right: *IAH (International Workers Aid) soup kitchen for striking metal workers. Carts go from shop to shop collecting food for the soup kitchens for striking Berlin metal workers. Berlin, 25 October 1930.*

(Original captions)

Having decided to tolerate Brüning's presidential cabinet in 1930, the Social Democrats faced a very difficult situation. Not only did they severely try the patience of their supporters, they also offered their opponents some very welcome scope for attack. The Communists blamed the SPD for helping to promote the growth of fascism in Germany. The SPD's policy of silence gave the National Socialists an opportunity to present themselves as the only realistic alternative to the KPD, in the absence of any truly democratic option. The Reichstag was basically disempowered after Brüning's appointment by Hindenburg, and the fact that with its 143 seats the SPD was the strongest party, ahead of the NSDAP with 107, carried little weight. The protest against the policies of "Hunger Chancellor" Brüning shifted increasingly to the streets. Extra-parliamentary sympathies could not be won by tolerating Brüning. By 1930/31, parliamentary democracy was well on its way to self-destruction, as the leader of the SPD party organ indicated on 13 December 1930 in a comment on the adjournment of the Reichstag until February of the following year: the unanimous opinion seemed to be that "this Reichstag is a monster and we'll only be happy when we get shot of it."

"The great central idea of International Workers Aid was to record, form and use in an organized way the solidarity of the proletariat ..."
Willi Münzenberg, Address on Solidarity Day, *1931*

THE SYSTEM IS COLLAPSING!

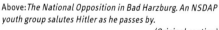
Above: *The National Opposition in Bad Harzburg. An NSDAP youth group salutes Hitler as he passes by.*
(Original caption)

Right: Adolf Hitler speaks in the Berlin Pleasure Garden during the elections for Reich President on 10 April 1932. Behind him Joseph Goebbels and (in the foreground) Gregor Strasser.

"He [Adolf Hitler] is a marvelous orator, and possesses an extraordinary gift for hypnotizing his audience and gaining adherents. Even though his policy is a negative one, his personal magnetism is such as to win over quite reasonable people to his standard…"
Colonel Kühlenthal in the defense ministry, to the British Military Attaché in May 1930

"All propaganda must have the common touch and its intellectual content should be pitched at the level of the most limited of those at whom it is aimed."
Adolf Hitler, Mein Kampf, *1925*

Left: *The election campaign reaches its climax. Goebbels speaks to the National Socialist crowds in the Berlin Pleasure Garden on 9 March 1932.* (Original caption)

Below: The leaders of the Stahlhelm – Seldte and Duesterberg (from left) – with Alfred Hugenberg (in civilian dress) in Bad Harzburg.

"The National Socialist street publicity campaign led some people to completely overestimate this circus of a party," confirmed internationally renowned editor Theodor Wolff in a comment on the expected success of the NSDAP in the *Berliner Tageblatt* of 14 September 1930, the day of the Reichstag elections. Even if this very perceptive political commentator, like many others, underestimated the danger of fascism, he predicted difficult times ahead for parliamentary democracy: "The Reichstag, incessantly disturbed by the noisy breakdown of its spirit, will have problems in reasonably discussing the difficult tasks for which the country expects solutions to be found, and then the gun runners who wanted this result and the parroting bourgeoisie who elected this howling band will indignantly cry that 'parliamentary democracy' is responsible for the mess." Wolff's pessimistic predictions were far exceeded by the reality that followed. Hitler's party succeeded in obtaining 18.3% of the vote and in one fell swoop increased its number of seats by 95. During the Reichstag sessions of the following years, the 107 NSDAP representatives staged riots in their brown SA uniforms which the party Reich propaganda director acknowledged with surprise in his diaries as follows: "It's pandemonium (!), but in the end it's all great propaganda for us." Outside parliament, the SA, the party's infantry, increasingly gained in significance, not least as a result of the rapid growth in its membership from 88,000 to 260,000 in the course of 1931. The terror caused

by the SA increased in this period to an extent which prompted the police to see them as a massive threat to public safety. The same year also saw the formation of the "Harzburg Front," which was named after the conference and the parliamentary march of the "National Opposition" on 11 October 1931 in Bad Harzburg. Alfred Hugenberg's attempt to unite the NSDAP, Stahlhelm, parts of the DVP and a series of nationalistic groups through a vote of no confidence in Brüning's government misfired. The coup ultimately failed on account of the leadership rivalry between Hugenberg and Hitler. The increasingly aggressive leadership claims of the NSDAP and its "Führer" caused the Harzburg Front to collapse finally in spring 1932, when it proved impossible to reach an agreement on a candidate for the upcoming Reich President election. Stahlhelm nominated its vice-president Theodor Duesterberg, who also had the support of the DNVP, while Goebbels declared on 22 February in the Berlin Sportpalast : "Hitler will be our Reich President!"

Above: *Preparing for the election for German Reich President on 13 March 1932. Election posters on Potsdamer Platz in Berlin for Reich President Hindenburg and for Hitler, the leader of the National Socialists.*

(Original caption)

Hindenburg hesitated to declare himself willing to stand for re-election in spring 1932. He deeply resented the fact that, in contrast to 1925, this time it would be the votes of Social Democrats that would help elect him. The SPD's election slogan was: "Hitler not Hindenburg means chaos and panic in Germany and all over Europe [...] Free the German people from the threat of fascism with a single act! Beat Hitler! Vote Hindenburg!" Reich Chancellor Brüning made more effort than others to ensure the re-election of his political foster-father Hindenburg. Although the Chancellor was fully aware of the elderly Hindenburg's senility, he praised him in his last speech of the election campaign on 11 March as a politically aware spirit and as a "symbol of power and unity in the whole world." He ended his speech with the following appeal: "Hindenburg must win because Germany must live." The first ballot on 13 March showed that there was no other candidate who could have held up against Hitler.

However, the final result was not known until the second ballot on 10 April: 53% of votes for Hindenburg, 36.8% for Hitler and 10.2% for Thälmann. Brüning, the most active campaigner for the old and new president, was made to feel the wrath of Hindenburg on 15 April when he raged against the fact that he had been re-elected with the help of the Social Democrats and the Catholics. As a matter of form, Brüning offered the government's resignation and the President opted to reserve judgment and come back to it at a later date. The old man was upset for other reasons, as he feared that the recent action of his Chancellor would finally compromise him in German nationalist circles. Brüning's cabinet had banned all National Socialist electoral groups on 13 April by means of the "Emergency Decree to Secure State Authority," as a search of the Prussian Ministry of the Interior had brought to light clear proof of concrete plans for SA mobilization and a putsch.

THE SYSTEM IS COLLAPSING!

Far left: *Canvassers in Berlin working for the National Socialists on the first day of the Reich Presidential election on 13 March 1932.*
Left: *Reich Chancellor Dr. Brüning – during his last election address in support of Hindenburg in the Berlin Sportpalast.*
Below: *The face of Berlin on election day. On 10 April 1932, when Berliners went to the polls for the second time to elect a Reich president, the city made a very lively impression. The streets were livened up with leaflet distributors from all the parties trying to persuade the doubters and undecided voters on their way to the polls to support their candidate. Our photo shows: Communist leaflet distributors in front of one of their bars.*

(Original captions)

Left: *The National Socialist Reichstag representatives present themselves in their brown uniforms for the opening of the new Reichstag in August 1932.*
Above: *The Grand Berlin Prize. The race for the Grand Berlin Prize was held at the Grunewald track. The race attracted many prominent personalities. Jockey Sajdik on* Wolkenpflug *snatched victory from Printen on* Aventin. *Our photo shows Reich Chancellor von Papen (left) and Reich Army Minister General von Schleicher on the VIP rostrum.*
(Original captions)

14 June 1932

"François-Poncet thinks there may be more to be got out of the von Papen cabinet than out of Brüning's government, [...] being a cabinet of the Right, any concessions wrung from it would be accepted by the Right, whereas Brüning always had to count on their opposition. His view may be right but I cannot help feeling that the change of government has caused the Nationalist and jingo element in the Foreign Office here to throw off the mask ..."

Sir Horace Rumbold, British Ambassador in Berlin,
in a letter to Sir Rober Vansittart, 14 June 1932

"... von Papen and his friends do not consider that they are by any means done with. I should very much doubt, however, whether, in the event of [...] the President deciding to renew the experiment of a presidential cabinet, von Papen would be at the head of it. There are strong personal objections to him on all sides, and I think I remember writing to you some little time ago to say that I found it difficult to take him seriously. He is, in fact, a 'light weight,' and was, I am told, a light weight gentleman rider when he was in the army."

Sir Horace Rumbold in a letter to Sir Clive Wigram,
22 November 1932

The Westphalian Catholic Center representative Franz von Papen was a completely unknown quantity. He attracted attention for the first time in early 1932 when he made a speech recommending "a dictatorship on a national basis" to Reich Chancellor Brüning. Von Papen's aims reflected those of the clique that surrounded Hindenburg. On 1 June the time was ripe, and the long-desired restoration of a non-democratic Germany took off at quite a pace. Hindenburg appointed von Papen as Reich Chancellor, who formed the "Cabinet of the Barons." The new government felt its most urgent priority was to fulfill the promises Adolf Hitler had wrung from General von Schleicher as a price for his toleration of the new government. The Reichstag was dissolved on 4 June and the ban on the SA was lifted on 16 June. Von Papen then succeeded in crediting himself with the final cancellation of Germany's reparations obligations under the Treaty of Versailles. This was, in fact, the hard-won outcome of Brüning's foreign policy. On the domestic front, the "Cabinet of National Concentration" started the so-called "Prussian Coup." The Prussian regional government continued its opposition to National Socialist and Communist street terror. The street battles of the "Altona Bloody Sunday," which resulted in 17 deaths and over 100 people injured, gave the government the argument it needed – but by no means the legal basis to take action. The deposition of the Braun–Severing Prussian government on 20 July was, therefore, nothing short of an illegal coup.

Below: Shop windows smashed again in Berlin. A large number of windows in the Tietz department store on Alexanderplatz were broken during stone-throwing on 3 June 1931.
Right: Hand to hand fighting in German streets. Fighting between Nazis and Communists and police has been taking place daily in the streets of many of the German cities, including Berlin where there have been many casualties. Photo shows hand to hand fighting as police intervene in a fight between Nazis and Communists in a street on the outskirts of Berlin.
(Original captions)

"Germany awake!
Death to the Jews,
People to the guns!
People to the guns!"

SA song

"The fascists standing threatening
Over there on the horizon!
Workers, you must take arms!
Red Front! Red Front!"
Song of the "Red Wedding" Communist Group, 1929

The Reichstag election campaign of summer 1932 took place against a background of civil war in Germany. People dreaded the weekends in particular, as life in the streets was taken over by demonstrations, calls for fighting, brawls, and riots. From mid-June until 20 July, the Prussian police force alone recorded 99 deaths and 1,125 injured as a result of the escalating street terror, mostly involving members of the SA or the Red Front alliance, but also including Reichsbanner (SPD paramilitary) supporters, policemen, and innocent civilians. In Berlin, the SA had made a "sport" of beating up Jewish pedestrians on the Kurfürstendamm and breaking the windows of Jewish stores long before 1933. After the election of 31 July 1932, a new phase of terror started. The NSDAP had doubled its number of seats to 230, but with only 37.3 % of the total mandate, Hitler was still a long way away from the absolute majority he dreamed of. The party leader had continuously promised his supporters that victory was just around the corner in the form of a single-party National Socialist government. The frustration at the failure of this promise to materialize unleashed a wave of terror by the SA, whose revolt in Königsberg on 1 August marked the beginning of a series of bomb attacks and assassinations throughout the entire country. The government tried to stem the terror by introducing emergency legislation on 10 August.

THE SYSTEM IS COLLAPSING!

The KPD made an attempt to unite the workers' movement against National Socialism by launching an appeal to "all German workers" on 25 April 1932. Around the same time, it also started the "Anti-Fascist Action," which was aimed at coordinating the resistance of all Social-Democratic and Communist organizations and groups. The KPD's resolve soon evaporated, however, and on 14 July 1932 a memo was sent to the leaders of all party divisions stating: "Any neglect of our struggle against the leaders of Social Fascism, any blurring of the differences of principle between us and the SPD [...] is a threat to the implementation of our revolutionary mass policy." This was a clear message which completely rejected any effort by the KPD and SPD to take combined action against the Papen government's "Prussian Coup" on 20 July. The Social Democrats had hitherto viewed Prussia's Social Democratic government as a "bastion against fascism." The fortress fell with no resistance worthy of mention. The SPD leader feared that an organized violent response would lead to the outbreak of civil war and that the "Iron Front" and parts of the Prussian police would become involved in a futile battle against the SA and Red Front.

Above: The unrest in Berlin has been concentrated in the past few days around Communist Headquarters, Liebknecht House on Bülowplatz. The entire building was cleared by the police. The photo shows the arrested persons being led to police trucks to be transported to the nearest police stations. Berlin 1931.
Right page: The "Anti-Fascist Action" marches on. On 3 July, the campaign began for the Reichstag elections to be held on 31 July 1932 and demonstrations, calling for the parties to continue fighting, were organized for 2 July. An anti-fascist demonstration was held by the Communist Party in the Pleasure Garden in Berlin. For the first time, this event was attended not only by the KPD members but also members of the Social Democratic Party and the Reichsbanner – i.e. all groups coming under the heading of "anti-fascist." Our photo shows a shot of the demonstration with Berlin Cathedral in the background.

(Original captions)

"What happened to the resistance? What came of the big words shouted at the meetings? 'Reichsbanner,' 'Schufo,' 'Eiserne Front,' 'Hammerschaften' – we were waiting impatiently, and we young ones, particularly so. The groups of one hundred had been told to be ready, we were hoping for the go-ahead – until the telephone call came from Berlin: we have telephoned the Reich court! [...] During the night I buried my Parabellum pistol in my parent's allotment. It was all over!"
Social Democrat Heinz Kühn in his memoirs. Kühn, who was born in 1912, was youth leader of the Reichsbanner in Cologne on 20 July 1932; from 1966 to 1978 he was Prime Minister of North-Rhine Westphalia

"Their practical aim was not so much to obstruct an unparliamentary system of government but to obstruct the civil war."
The left-wing Social Democrat Arkadij Gurland in the Marxistische Tribüne of 15 June 1932, looking back on the SPD's approach during the Weimar period

Number 34/35 Köpenicker Street became a focal point during the Berlin tenants' strike, which started in late 1932 in the dark damp tenements of Swinemünder Street and by the end of the year had spread as far as the newly constructed areas of the city. The tenants, who were for the most part unemployed, protested initially against the intolerable condition of their apartments. However, their protest soon grew into a general social movement whose motto was: "For us food comes first." This unofficial strike was not defined by party interests and represented a unified front of the lower classes. The Social Democratic journal *Vorwärts* and the National Socialist *Angriff* printed only sporadic accounts of the strike, but daily reports appeared in the Communist *Rote Fahne*.

Left page: *Tenants' strike in 34/35 Köpenicker Street. The tenants in 34/35 Köpenicker Street in Berlin went on strike on 23 September 1932 in protest against the high rents and miserable condition of their building. Their strike motto is 'First food! – And then rent.' Our photo shows a view of the backyard of the building. Their slogan is painted on the house wall. Some tenants have Communist flags and others have swastikas hanging from their windows.*
Above: *On the occasion of the Reich Presidential election in Berlin of 10 April 1932. A Communist children's group going from one backyard to the next singing workers' anthems urging people to vote.*   (Original captions)

"The business people who live here have special contracts. Of the 110 families who live here, 80 are on strike. Even the five Nazi families in the building have joined the strike. And the SPD supporters have also joined in!"
Comment of a tenants' council from the "Wanzenburg" (Bedbug Castle) building at 1 Molkenmarkt to a reporter from the Rote Fahne; *edition of 7 September 1932*

"The biggest group participating in the increasingly widespread tenants' strikes is the unemployed. This reveals something about the cause of the strike. The argument began a few months ago when officials started doing more thorough means testing, a move which has lowered the amounts of support […] The Wedding district authority pays the lowest contribution, exactly two pfennigs for each person in receipt of support per month."
Welt am Abend, 17 October 1932

Left: *Adolf Hitler briefs new members of the Reichstag 6 December 1932.* (Original caption)

Following the dissolution of the newly elected Reichstag by the Papen government in August 1932, it was necessary to hold the fifth election that year. The poll of 6 November was overshadowed, however, by the strike by the Berlin transport companies. The strike was concerned primarily with wage agreements, but the Communists and National Socialists used it to further agitate an already tense public mood. When the Communist trade union "RGO" called the strike on 2 November, despite a failed ballot, the National Socialist unions joined in. In the next few days, the SA and Red Front fighters' alliance marched together. Social Democratic trade unionists were beaten up and streetcar tracks destroyed. Policemen who tried to protect those prepared to work were attacked. The "red–brown" chaos on the streets prompted the majority of the strikers to call off the strike on 7 November. The Reichstag elections of the previous day were not influenced by these events. The NSDAP lost almost two million votes, while the KPD increased its vote by over two percent.

Above: *Transport strike in Berlin. Following the planned further wage cuts, the employees of the Berlin Transport Company went on strike this morning. This has led to a complete standstill of all streetcar, subway and car transport. Our picture shows women bringing food to their menfolk on picket lines at the entrance to a tram depot. 3 November 1932.*

Right page: *Berlin public transport on strike. On 3 November 1932, the employees of the Berlin Transport Company (omnibus, streetcar and subway trains) went on strike. As rail was the only other means of transport available, everyone headed to the train stations. Our photo shows the enormous crowd at the ticket counter at Berlin Wannsee station.* (Original captions)

"I beg you to see in me not just a soldier but a cross-party representative of the interests of every class, whose time in office will hopefully turn out to be a short one, who has not come to bring the sword but to bring peace [...] The point of a bayonet is not a comfortable place to sit; in other words, it is not possible to govern permanently without the broad support of the population."

Reich Chancellor von Schleicher in a radio address to the German people on 15 December 1932

Schleicher visits Hindenburg. Reich Chancellor von Schleicher went to the Reich President this morning for discussions about appointments to the cabinet posts that remain open. Reich Chancellor von Schleicher and former Reich Labor Minister Schaeffer setting off for the Reich Chancellery from the Reich Defense Ministry. 4 December 1932. (Original caption)

Above: *Home again for Christmas. The first prisoners released under the amnesty leaving Tegel prison in Berlin are greeted by their friends (this shot was not posed).*
(Original caption)

Right: Carl von Ossietzky (right) at the beginning of his sentence in Tegel prison in Berlin in November 1931.

The repeated unsilenced calls of a Communist visitor from the gallery gave rise to a very heated mood in the Reichstag chamber on 7 December 1932, and things deteriorated into a brawl between NSDAP and KPD representatives. The first session of the Reichstag under the new government of General von Schleicher was constructive in one area at least: the parties agreed on a general amnesty for political crime, with the exception of murder and betrayal of military secrets. The latter vote was aimed primarily at pacifist Carl von Ossietzky, who was sentenced to prison in 1931 for an article about German re-armament plans, published in the *Weltbühne*.

"To have been to prison is an important experience which no political person can erase from his existence. It is contact with a separate world that remains locked up within us and about which we know less than we do about Tibet or Easter Island. Prison, which should no longer punish in Germany today but improve and educate, has, so to speak, become the sick bay of bourgeois order [...] Guilt? This is not a word ever spoken in this house. Here there are only victims."
Carl von Ossietzky in Weltbühne *1932, after his release from Tegel prison in Berlin*

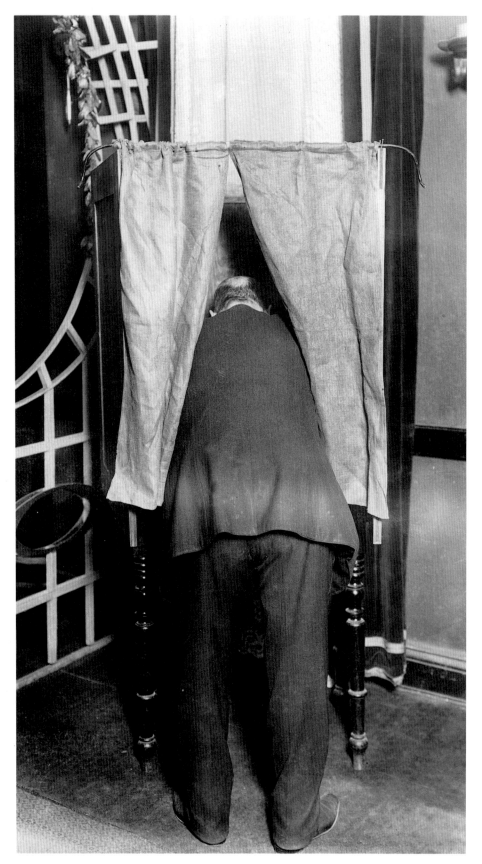

Left: *The election of the Reich President on Sunday,
13 March 1932. The vote is secret. John Doe puts his crossed
voting slip into an envelope behind drawn curtains in the
voting booth.* (Original caption)
Right page: Reich President von Hindenburg greets his new
Reich Chancellor Adolf Hitler.

"What is John Doe doing? He's facing the coming
elections with a strong sense of perplexity. [...] But
there is something he can do. The Democrat and
Republican John Doe can hold tight to his conviction
that just like all periods in human history, this is
merely a period of transition and that as sure as the
sun rises gain, the progressive spirit must dominate
again [...] However, the voter John Doe will probably
answer that this advice is of little use to him now and –
to use a Berlin turn of phrase – his Aunt Fanny could
do a better job of ruling."
Theodor Wolff in the Berliner Tageblatt *of
18 September 1932*

"Hitler reported to me. Papen totally against
Schleicher, wants to overthrow him and get rid of him
completely. Still has the old guy's [Hindenburg] ear.
Even lives with him. Arrangement prepared with us.
Either chancellorship or power ministries – defense
and interior. That sounds all right."
Joseph Goebbels, diary entry of 10 January 1933

"And now gentlemen, may God be with you!"
*Reich President Hindenburg after swearing in the new
government under Reich Chancellor Hitler in his office on
30 January 1933*

"If Hitler starts by sticking to the constitution, and
even if it is the utmost hypocrisy, it would be wrong if
we give him the chance to breach the constitution. [...]
If Hitler takes the constitutional road then he is at the
head of a right-wing government which we can and
must fight, even more than the earlier governments,
but it is a constitutional government."
*Ernst Breitscheid to SPD party committee
on 31 January 1933*

THE SYSTEM IS COLLAPSING!

STROLLING IN BERLIN

Like 68-year-old coachman Gustav Hartmann, pictured here, the ordinary man on the streets of Berlin may not have cared less whether the capital city of the Weimar Republic was cursed as a "den of Marxist iniquity" or feted as a dazzling center of entertainment and the arts. For people like Hartmann, it was just a question of day-to-day survival. Modernity in the form of the automobile was a very real threat to him and his trade. Hartmann's final epic coach-trip, which started on 1 April 1928 and won him the nickname of "Iron Gustav," attracted enormous interest in the newspapers and magazines. The original caption to this photograph was: "Wannsee—Paris—Berlin. The oldest driver from Wannsee makes the last trip with his horse-drawn cab." The middle-class media, in general, were beginning to express an interest in the lives of the "ordinary people." *Flaneur* scribes like Franz Hessel wanted to discover the city beyond the boulevards: "These were a few modest attempts to stroll through Berlin, all around and up and down, and now, my dear fellow citizens, do not hold it against me if I missed some important and remarkable events [...]"

10

The Back Streets and the Boulevards

The saying goes that if the cosmopolitan spirit was not exactly at home in Berlin between 1919 and 1933, it was certainly a permanent guest there. The city was a magnet for those who saw themselves as young and modern, progressive and, perhaps, somewhat frivolous. Conservative opponents of the capital dismissed it as a hotbed of vice, violence and pretension: "Chicago on the banks of the Spree" and "Parvenupolis," and this view was indeed substantiated by the goings-on in the city at the time. The young Republic's political struggles were played out here. At the same time Berlin became a symbol of the modern age. Indeed, much of the character of modern Berlin dates from that period of flourishing museums, literature, theater, and music. In our mind's eye, the "roaring twenties" unfold as we stroll along the great Berlin boulevards, Unter den Linden and the Kurfürstendamm, around which metropolitan life was enjoyed to the full in the movie theaters and nightclubs. The newspaper offices in the press quarter and film studios in Babelsberg were the center of the universe. In the midst of all these other worlds, the politically charged capital with its seat of government in Wilhelmstrasse appeared rather marginal.

If, however, we were to trace the paths and read the accounts of contemporaries, a completely different picture would emerge: "We want to try to do it, we want to learn a little indolence and enjoyment and look at this thing Berlin in all its chaos and confusion of things precious and nasty, true and false, funny and respectable, learn to love it, and find beauty in it until it is beautiful," wrote Franz Hessel in 1929 in his "Epilogue to Berliners" in *Spazieren in Berlin (Strolling in Berlin)*. Hessel, the urban stroller or *flâneur*, found soul mates in the photographers and photo-journalists whose work illustrates his literary impressions so well. They too took time to "stroll" through the city with their cameras, where they discovered not just the glamour of the big boulevards but also life in the backyards of the working-class neighborhoods.

The photo-journalists dug deeper into the "other" Berlin than would ever have been possible for a bourgeois literary *flâneur* like Hessel. With the intention of creating a photographic document of social reality, they followed in the footsteps of their kindred spirit, writer and journalist Egon Erwin Kisch. In his article

Above: *A Berlin advertising company has come up with the idea of erecting small pedestals with advertising slogans in the middle of crossroads. The platforms, which are heated in winter, provide a place for policemen to stand. This ingenious idea is very welcome as it helps the traffic warden 'to keep a cool head with his warm feet,' as the old saying goes.*
Right page: *Shadows in Love.*

(Original captions)

"Berlin at Work" the "racing reporter" established that behind all the city's glamour and luxury lay the work of people who themselves would never partake of the luxury which they help to create. Kisch was here commenting on the fate of "those who for the sake of a subsistence wage allowed themselves to be rushed here and there, day and night, whose names are not even known to those who pressurize them in this way."

"Down the Linden! Clippety clop!"
On foot, on horseback, two by two!
With a watch in your hand, a hat on top,
No time! No time! No time!
We smooch, we kiss, we box, we scuffle,
A tire bursts, the taxi bustles!
All at once the meter ticks!
[...]
Make money! My God! The city cries:
No time! No time! No time!"

Walter Mehring, Das Ketzerbrevier
(The Heretic's Prayerbook), 1921

"Metropolitan *Berlin*, the capital city of Prussia and
the German Empire, is with 3,804,000 inhabitants the
third biggest city in Europe, after London and Paris,
and lies [...] on the river Spree, 34–39 m [111–126 feet]
above sea level. According to the census of December
1919, the city of Berlin has a population of 2,071,257, of
which 81.6% is Protestant, 11.7 % Catholic, 5.3%
Jewish; 44% were born in Berlin and 31,000 were
native speakers of Polish. In October 1919, the
population decreased to 1,902,509 [...] As regards the
overall visual image of the city, Berlin, as is well
known, gets by without any great variety of scenery,
and despite being more than three-quarters modern, it
also has a real historical side."

Karl Baedeker, Berlin und Umgebung, Handbuch für
Reisende *(Berlin and surroundings; a guide book for
travelers)*, 1921

Unter den Linden viewed from the Brandenburg Gate.
(Original caption)

Left page: *Berlin in the mist. A picturesque bridge in the Museum quarter.*
Above: *This is Berlin! It may look like the park in a spa town but it is actually Schinkelplatz square in Berlin.*
Right: *Scenes from street life in Berlin – shoe-shiner, 'Unter den Linden.'*   (Original captions)

Unter den Linden – "The heart and soul of the capital": this is how contemporaries liked to describe the magnificent boulevard. The young lovers strolled on Sundays under the trees planted by the Great Elector in the 18th century that line the avenue, while the rich and powerful drove along in their chauffeur-driven cars. The monumental architecture lining this great boulevard was the work of architects like Carl Gotthard Langhans and Friedrich Schinkel. The latter also created the Ionic colonnade on the Museum Island – "This wonderful island" which *flâneur* Franz Hessel described as "the young Berliner's grove of Academe." The picture galleries of the Old Museum, the New Museum, the National Gallery and the Boden Museum provided the city's residents with real places of learning in uncertain times. The Pergamon Museum, another treasure-trove of art from past times, was opened in 1930. In the face of all these awe-inspiring buildings, the protagonist of Erich Kästner's novel *Fabian* (1931), wandering aimlessly around Berlin, complains: "This city, its life, and its culture were quiescent. The panorama was like an expensive funeral."

Above: *Nocturnal images, Potsdamer Platz.*
(*Original caption*)

Right: Potsdamer Platz square; in the background "Haus Vaterland" and the Potsdamer Bahnhof railway station.

Berliners were very proud of the first traffic tower on Potsdamer Platz, which was the busiest intersection in Europe during the 1920s and 30s. This early version of the traffic light was built in an effort to control the permanent jam of trucks, trams, bicycles, and horse-drawn carriages on the square. However, it attracted even more traffic as everyone wanted to get a look at the new innovation. The traffic congestion was really the result of serious planning errors. The road network was missing two north-west-running streets which could have relieved the strain on Leipziger Strasse and Potsdamer Strasse. 50,000 automobiles would hardly have been noticed on the wide streets. Motorization levels in Paris and New York were significantly higher than in Berlin.

Above: Unter den Linden as seen from Friedrichstrasse.

"As long as 'Unter den Linden'
The old trees are bloomin'
Nothing can overcome us,
Berlin is always Berlin!"
Marching song from the 1923 revue Drunter und Drüber
(Topsy-Turvy), music by Walter Kollo

Left page, below: *A new way to make a name for yourself: a young poetess takes to the streets. Erna Thaler, a young poetess, found a novel way to make herself known to the masses. With police authorization, she distributed her poetry in the middle of Potsdamer Platz in Berlin while reading from her work to the people gathered around.*
Above: *News stand on Potsdamer Platz.*

(Original captions)

"[...] Streets. For they are the home of the eternally restless, roving spirit which experiences, discovers, and invents as much outside the walls of the houses as the individual within the sanctity of his four walls. For the masses — and the *flâneur* lives with them — the shiny enamel company nameplates make an equally good if not better decoration than an oil-painting in a bourgeois drawing room. The fire walls are their desks, newspaper kiosks their libraries, letter boxes their sculptures, benches their boudoirs, and the café terrace the bay window from which they look down on their household."

Walter Benjamin, "Die Wiederkehr des Flâneurs" (The return of the flâneur*), review of Franz Hessel's book* Spazieren in Berlin, *1929*

"When I am confronted with an opposing view expressed in a tone of honest indignation, it is my wont to take another look at my opinion. But I now ask myself: Is it calumny that after one-and-a-half years not one single Kapp criminal has been sentenced? (Absolutely right!) Is it calumny that the 'Kappist-in-chief,' Captain Ehrhardt, was able to go in and out of the defense ministry without a warrant being issued for his arrest? Is it calumny that, in contrast, excessively heavy punishment was meted out to the Communists of the March putsch, that in numerous judgments, in the current situation, Communist activity was defined as devoid of honor and hence worthy of imprisonment?"

Social Democratic Justice Minister Gustav Radbruch at the 1921 Party Conference

Left page, above: *The notice board on which the barristers indicate their room numbers in case someone needs to speak to them.*
Left page, below: *Lawyers at their books.*
Above: *The satisfied expression no doubt reflects a lucrative settlement.*   *(Original captions)*

The law troops – photo essay
During the 1920s, on average 2,000 criminal cases a year ended with a judgment passed by the judges at the criminal court and approximately 80 were dealt with by jury trials at the three Berlin regional courts. The capital's press latched onto any case with potential for sensation. In addition to numerous political trials, there were cases involving corruption, fraud, and bribery. One high-profile case involved the Sklarek brothers, who duped the banks with fake orders and caused a local authority scandal by bribing city councilors from all parties. This case ended with the resignation of the Mayor of Berlin, Böss. Iwan Kutisker swindled the Preussische Bank of 12 million marks by giving the directors presents in the form of geese. Max Klante devised a dubious betting system and cheated

thousands of racing fans out of their stakes. The photo essay about the "Berlin Lawyers' Association" at the Berlin Mitte district court takes a respectful look at the working world of the men who represented the accused: "Every morning you see clever-looking men sitting on the trains, trams, and buses who do not read the newspapers as they travel to the city center but pull documents out of their briefcases which they study with impressive speed and complete concentration. If you see them getting off around Alexanderplatz, you'll immediately know that they are lawyers from the Berlin Mitte district court or from the regional court, 'Germany's biggest court of justice'."

Left page: *The Berlin bock beer season has started. The delicious 'nectar' became available again at the beginning of the New Year. The first barrel of bock beer is rolled up. (Bock beer, in German literally 'buck' beer, is a type of dark beer brewed near the city of Hanover.)*
Above: *Black cargo.*
Right: *Berlin flower seller. Women work – men are unemployed! Here it's the husband who carries the flowers.* (Original captions)

"Mama, the man with the coal is here!
Child, be quiet, I can see him clear.
I have no dough, you have no dough,
Who sent for the man with the coal?"
Berlin skit on a song from the operetta Gasparone

Right: *Punting heavy barges along the canal seems like hard work to city dwellers.*
Below: *Sunday morning. Time for beauty treatments.*
Below right: *A grocer supplies food to the bargemen from his primitive motor boat.*
Right page, above: *There's nothing like a chat when the work is done.*
Right page, below: *Playing cards is the favorite way of passing time on the boats when things are quiet.*
(Original captions)

Life on the barge – photo essay

This photo essay also betrays the typical romanticization by bourgeois magazines of working-class life. There is no reference to the "Problems of the New City Berlin," published in a collection in 1926. Despite enormous investment in the development of the ports and the well developed network of waterways which extended from Danzig (now Gdansk) to Duisburg, attempts to increase internal shipping in Berlin had failed. Up to that time, only one quarter of the capital's freight was transported by water, whereas an annual 15 million tons of goods were transported by rail. This photo essay from the late 1920s focused entirely on depicting the 'atmosphere' of the bargemen's lives.

"The large freight barges on the Havel and Spree and the interlinked network of canals made Berlin into the most important internal shipping center in Northern Germany. The life of these romantic characters of the waterways takes such a different form to that of the 'land lubbers' that it is really worth spending a day on these ships. The only romantic things about the heavy work, which starts early in the morning at sunrise and normally lasts for 12 hours, are the small changes in landscape and surroundings."

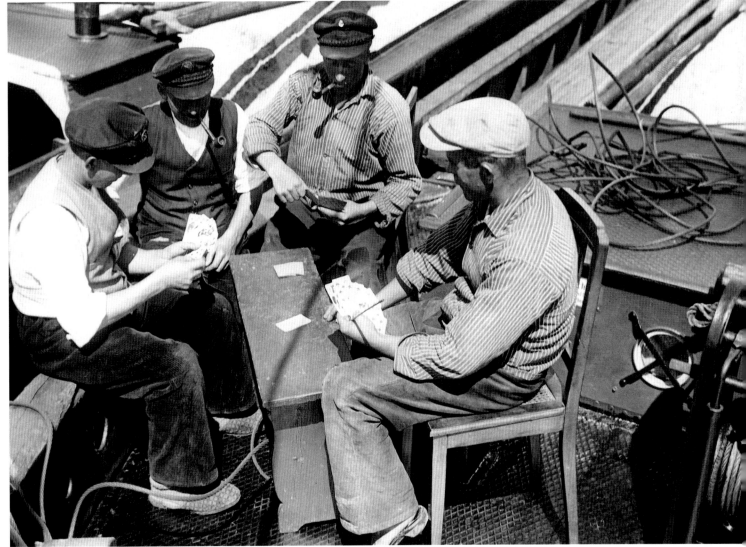

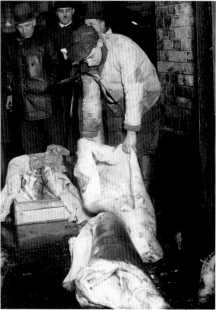

Fish Auction – photo essay

The central market hall at Alexanderplatz was officially opened in 1886 and was steadily expanded in subsequent years. Most food landed in this "belly of Berlin" through direct connections with the rail network. In the mid-1920s, the hall director complained that the market was threatening to burst at the seams: "Wholesale fish trading is being carried out in unsuitable premises around the central market halls, sometimes even on the street." It was business as usual while the city planned the construction of new market halls:

"Due to its high nutritional value and relatively low price, fish is one of the most important foodstuffs. For this reason, the Berlin municipal authorities have devoted all their attention to this source of nutrition for the population over the past decade and promoted this trade in every possible way, particularly in recent years. Berlin needs 5,500 carloads of fish of every kind every year. The daily supply runs to approximately 18 carloads. The city sales agent for fish sells the supply at auction. The accompanying photos give a clear impression of how this business operates. Individual shopkeepers and market traders buy their weekly stock of fish at these auctions."

Right: *Auctioneer and clerk during the fish auction in the central market.*
Below: *Store room for live fish at the city sales agent's auction rooms.*
Left page, above: *Auctioning of live fish in the central market.*
Left page, below: *Unpacking mackerel shark.*
(Original captions)

Used car sales in Berlin – photo essay
In the 1920s, in contrast with later years, the advertising industry ignored adventurous upper-class men and focused instead on the woman at the wheel. She became the symbol of Weimar motoring culture. In fact, this close association of women and the car was behind the wider acceptance of motoring in Weimar society. The enthusiasm of Berliners for motoring was unbounded, as noted by Carl von Ossietzky in the *Weltbühne*:
"A IIIB driving license is now more valuable as a qualification than a Ph.D., and almost as valuable as the lieutenant's commission once was." Even if the text tries to suggest otherwise, for most people, ownership of a "Maybach" or "Adler" was just a dream: "Used cars are offered for sale at low prices in the yard of a former barracks in Berlin. The car sale attracts a lot of visitors and many deals are done."

Above: *A future car owner behind the wheel of her new car.*
Left: *The engine of one of the cars for sale is shown to eager potential buyers.*
Right page: *An Opel can be bought for as little as 350 marks.*
(*Original captions*)

"It's not very nice to speak of the delights of driving – if we are not talking about the bus or at best a taxi – as long as those who are unable to afford a car significantly outnumber those who can. But I hope that soon the car will no longer be the privilege of the affluent and that it will be no more luxurious than, say, the bathroom."
Revue star Fritzi Massary in the magazine Die Dame – Ein deutsches Journal für den verwöhntem Geschmack *(The Lady – A German journal for extravagant tastes)*

"Another flat tire?
– Just beyond Halle. It wasn't too bad. A man helped me.
– Darling, you mustn't approach men on the road.
– What are you thinking! I don't approach them. I just wave at them.
– And they stop?
– Always.
– And then?
– Depends.
– But darling, you can't ...
– Oh, don't worry about me. Cars are so complicated."

Friedrich Kroner,
Das Auto meiner Frau
(My wife's car)

The puncture. Photo Walter Süssmann.
(Original caption)

Beneath the streets of the metropolis – photo essay
With his social essay "Four hours in underground Vienna," (1902) Viennese journalist Max Winter created a classic of social documentation. He accompanied a so-called *Strotter*, who collected flotsam and jetsam that landed in drains, salvaged and then resold it. Winter's essay formulated the basic questions of city research: What goes on behind the façades, how do people live, who are the insiders and outsiders in this society, how do they eke out their existence? This photographer follows Winter's tracks in the 1920s and discovers the "light effects of underground Berlin." However, this photo essay has nothing of the expressive power of the original.

Left page: *The steps leading down to the underground drains at Nollendorf Square.*
Right: *Into the manhole.*
Below: *The drains fork below Martin Luther-Street.*
(Original captions)

Right: *The Berlin city authorities set up an enormous kitchen in the covered market in Treskow Street in which 200 women prepare meals for 16,000 people each day. The meals were distributed at 20 different distribution points: Eighty women – 100 hundredweight of potatoes. Our photo shows: Doing the same work for thirty years.*

(Original caption)

Above: *Unemployed men seek shelter in freezing temperatures. Berlin: In the middle of what has up to now been a relatively mild winter, a cold spell has hit Germany and Europe! Temperatures dropped to 7 °F in Berlin and the lakes and rivers look like something out of the Arctic with their thick covering of ice. This weather affects the unemployed worst of all – many of whom are also homeless and have no coal to produce a bit of warmth and comfort. The city of Berlin has 'heating halls' in many neighborhoods where a cup of hot coffee and a warm stove are provided for these unfortunates. Our photo was taken in the heating hall in Neue Königstrasse in Berlin on 11 February 1932.*

(Original caption)

Above: *Flowers in the snow: After the first snowfall in Berlin. The flower seller on Potsdamer Platz under her enormous snow umbrella.*

Right: *Freezing cold in Berlin. A new cold spell from the north has hit Berlin and is making its presence felt even more acutely as it is accompanied by a sharp north-east wind. In the early hours of Wednesday, the temperature in Berlin was 5 degrees. Meteorologists predict a sharpening of the frost. This animal lover uses big covers to protect the workhorses from the cold.*

(Original captions)

Left: *A summer day in Berlin's working-class neighborhood on the banks of the Spree river.*
Above: *Little musicians.* (Original captions)

"'Comrades!' said the third member of the 'Kanter' youth group finally, 'I do not like preaching to my friends but you must listen to me now: Robinson Crusoe could not set sail until he had a seaworthy vessel, not a rudderless, leaky wreck like the one we are on at the moment. The proletariat cannot be freed until the economic situation has changed, when the bell tolls for capitalistic production. And it will toll, Franz, despite your lack of hope up there on your abandoned rock!'"

Paul Michaelis, Der Robinson der Robinsons, Ein humoristische und sozialistische Erzählung für die Arbeiter- und Fortbildungsschul-Jugend *(The Crusoe of Crusoes. A humorous and socialist tale for working-class and evening school students)*, 1921

"Sometimes I get the urge to go into the backyards. In the older parts of Berlin, life becomes more intense and intimate around the back of the houses and the courtyard buildings. This makes the backyards rich, the poor backyards with a little patch of green in a corner, the poles for carpet-beating, the dustbins, and the wells left over from the time before running water was installed. The only time I can do it is in the mornings when singers and violinists appear, or the barrel-organ man, who whistles away with two fingers in his mouth, or the one-man band [...] Then I can stand beside the old porter woman [...] She takes no offense at my presence and I can look up to the windows facing the courtyard at which the typists and seamstresses from the offices and factories gather. Overcome with joy, they stop until some annoying boss comes along and they have to return to their work. The windows are all bare. Only one on the top floor where a bird-cage is hanging has curtains, and when the violin cries from the heart and the barrel organ drones and moans, a canary starts to sing; it is the only voice from the silent rows of staring windows. It is beautiful. But I would also like to have my share of these backyards in the evening, the last games of the children who are called to come home again and again, and see the young girls coming home and wanting to go out again. Alone, I can find neither the courage nor an excuse to intrude, my trespassing is too obvious."

Franz Hessel, Spazieren in Berlin, *1929*

Above: *A dance in the backyard. A traveling one-man band performs in the courtyard of a Berlin tenement. He does not practice his art in vain.*
Opposite: *A Berlin working-class tenement.*

(Original captions)

Left page: *Courtyard music. Photo Walter Süssmann.*
Right: *Heinrich Zille, who died on 9 August 1929. The artist at the last Zille festival in the Sportpalast in Berlin.*
(Original captions)

"What I saw and experienced in my childhood probably helped me in the composition of some of my pictures. Sometimes it's the other way around. The poor young artists painting affluence and big ham sandwiches while the rich people portray the poor in their words and images. I stayed in my own milieu – if not in the way that a rich young artist described to me. Once by chance he had two children as models, who I often drew, and when he complained to their mother that they were so dirty, the indignant woman replied: 'They're never dirty enough for Zille.'"

Heinrich Zille, excerpt from the description of his life and work presented in 1924 on the occasion of his admission to the Prussian Academy

"Heinrich Zille, you once said you looked like a cab driver. Leave it. When you get to heaven, God will stick wings onto your back, put a little trumpet in your hand and press a crown on your hair. And then you'll be hallelujahing up and down. And when the people ask: 'Who is that singing so off-key up there?' – I want to answer: 'Shh. He's flying up there. Berlin's Very Best.'"

Kurt Tucholsky in Weltbühne *20 January 1925*

As the son of a tradesman, artist Heinrich Zille grew up face to face with the Berlin working-class milieu. His vicious caricatures in the *Simplicissimus* mainly bemoaned the social indifference and brutality of the German Empire. His photographs, which later became very famous as social documents, represent only part of his creative output. During the Weimar period, Zille remained loyal to his subject in his drawings but shifted his focus to harmless and ribald depiction of Berlin types. His customers – the magazines of the 1920s – were only interested in social romanticism. The former tireless barfly, who carried out his social studies at beer tables, had aged and was forced to give up alcohol due to diabetes. He had many friends in the cultural and entertainment world, for example Max Liebermann and singer Claire Waldoff. The Prussian Academy of the Arts acknowledged Zille's contribution to the arts and made him a member of the Academy on 1 February 1924. The leisure industry erected a memorial to him during his lifetime. From 1925, during carnival time, impressive costume festivals were held at the Berlin Sportpalast, in which Zille was financially involved, and his appearance was the highlight of the event. Up to his death in 1929, he may have cried into his bottle of mineral water at the "Zille-Ball" over the fact that the wrong people were in the right costumes. In the words of a song later composed about these costume balls: "Even the judge's wife Mrs. Booker is running around as a hooker."

Like the history of the pub, that of the *Stammtisch*, i.e. table reserved for regulars, is closely linked with political developments in Germany. The "bourgeois" revolutionaries of 1848 had reserved tables in almost all of the major towns and cities and were popularly known as "bar-room republicans." The intellectuals of the time looked down on the numerous reserved tables for the petit bourgeoisie and politicoes: "They form alliances, launch fleets, send armies on the march, kill potentates etc. And the more lively the discussions, the better the beer tastes." For the workers' movement, the pubs of the Wilhelmine era were not just places for social encounters, but assumed increasing importance as centers of political discussion and organization. It is no wonder, therefore, that the "Red Berlin" of the Weimar period could boast the most pubs of any German city. In the working-class neighborhoods, most of the pubs and reserved tables were under the firm control of the Social Democrats and Communists. During the unrest of the early 1930s in the capital, the "red" pubs became an increasing target for National Socialist SA troops, who tried to spread their terror in these social bastions of the working class. Following its rise to power in January 1933, the NSDAP, which itself had originated in the beer halls of Munich, had the working-class pubs identified by informers, prohibited "left-wing" publicans from trading, or sent them to concentration camps. The "left-wing pub nests" were later converted to SA or SS group headquarters.

Spellbound by the newspaper. At the Stammtisch *we know better, especially when it comes to politics.*

(Original caption)

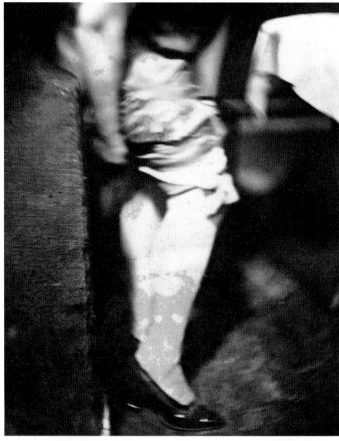

Above: *Poster for the Widows' Ball*
Above right: *The slipped "garter."*
Right: *Hand in hand, the symbol of true love.*
(*Original captions*)

"The people fall on their long-withheld pleasure like a pack of hungry wolves. Never have we danced so much and so quickly in Berlin."
Berliner Tageblatt *dated 1 January 1919,*
after the lifting of the ban on dancing

"Walter, the gold-hearted 'consoler,' the most famous life and soul of the party in Berlin [...] Once again, the place for all the lonely people to meet [...] Widows' Ball for those past the first flush of youth in the magnificent ballroom in Ackerstrasse [...] An old-style German ball, for middle-aged people only, lively ball music [...] Clare's refined Widows' Ball, the talk of the town. Only the elite can be found in Auguststrasse."
Advertising slogans for "Widows' Balls," 1929

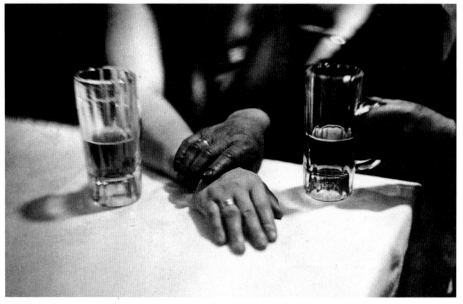

Top: *It's looking good, a delightful widow at the cash desk.*
Above right: *Isn't he irresistible? A lounge lizard at the Widows' Ball.*
Above: *For the girl, the hot evening meal consists of two sausages with potato salad.*

(Original captions)

With Berlin's Merry Widows – photo essay
While the new jazz dances like the "shimmy" had youthful bodies in a frenzy in the dance halls and bars in the area around the Kurfürstendamm, the more mature met locally for what was known as "ice-skate dancing" or "the dance lesson shuffle" at the "widows' balls": "No entry for men under 25 years." These events were not only attended by women who had lost their young men in action; there was, indeed, a shortage of men after the First World War. Those returning from the front were greeted by the new wind of emancipation. Not only could women now vote, but they were often quite assertive as well, even "cutting in" on dancing couples in the way that only men had done in the past. This photo essay from the late 1920s was less interested, however, in behavior at social dances than in the "intimate" goings-on "on the sidelines": "An expedition with the camera through the nocturnal paradise of the merry widows. Widows' ball – does such a thing still exist, we ask, looking at the pictures. Before the War, the widows' ball was thought of as a place for loners; nowadays, however, the crowd is much more congenial."

"Men have sure proof of love in the devotion of women. But what proof do women have of men's love? Where is the test of the declared love of a man? [...] Something more than this obvious service, which ninety-nine men are willing to provide and of which sixty are capable, has to be provided. This 'more' is now the bank account, if one thinks how far men will go in their efforts to get as far as the bank account."
Franz Blei, Beweise für die Liebe, (Proof of Love) *1928*

"That can only happen
once, it won't happen
again. That is too good to
be true!
[...]
Just once in a lifetime
Can this be mine.
For every spring
Has just one May!"
From the UFA Film Der
Kongress tanzt *(Congress
Dances), 1931. Music by
Werner Richard Heymann*

"And just because she
has nothing to do at the
moment, she thinks of
Olga's brother. Nice boy.
What was his name
again? She doesn't
know. He kissed her last
night in the car. Today
he's leaving. Shame? Not
really. But it was fun
with him yesterday. She
hadn't kissed anyone for
a long time. You don't
often go for someone
like him. The years of no
choice from seventeen to
nineteen are gone. The
boy was nice. The kiss
was nice. Nothing more.
It doesn't linger. That's
good."
Irmgard Keun,
Gilgi, eine von uns
(Gilgi, one of us), 1931

Left page: *Two late arrivals
who haven't missed their
connection after all. Photo
Walter Süssmann.*
Right: *What price youthful
bliss? 5 pfennigs per head
per hour. Photo Walter
Süssmann.*
(Original captions)

Left: *Saison! (The Season)* Photo Walter Süssmann.
Below: *Berlin weekend in the summer of 1927. A snapshot of Berliners enjoying their weekend in Potsdam.*
Right page: *Enjoying a cup of coffee.* Photo Walter Süssmann.

(Original captions)

"The sexual needs of today's youth are the sexual needs of today's parents, who, when they remember their own youth, are dumbfounded at their children's lives and cannot cope with the fact that their seventeen-year-old daughter Ilse has a friend and bedfellow in eighteen-year-old Fritz. They look to the right for guidance, where they hear: discipline, strictness, beating, prayers, long skirts, long hair in plaits. They look to the left and are told: let them live, it's good for the health, sport, progress, do away with the consequences, let them use birth control. These parents of today have no real trust in the guidance from the right or the guidance from the left, because they cannot base their recommendations or orders on the security of their own marriage, for this marriage does not usually have any examples for how life should be lived now. [...] The mother of 1928, who will soon be fifty, carries herself like her eighteen-year-old daughter but thinks tired sterile thoughts about the alleged freedom of this daughter and the narrow cage of her own life back then, when the relations added up her dowry and his income and decided it would be a happy marriage."

Franz Blei, Sexuelle Not der Eltern
(The sexual needs of parents), 1928

Above: *Berlin's beach: Wannsee. An unemployed dance band has the visitors spellbound. These modest chaps are happy to exchange the parquet floor for a sand stage. The audience's applause is spontaneous and heartfelt.*
Right: *Wannsee beach now has a real city feel. On these warm days, the people of Berlin seek recreation during their free time on the delightful beach at Wannsee. A lively beach culture is developing there. Our photo shows: family coffee at Wannsee beach.*
        (Original captions)

Above: *Bathing fashions on the Juvena house boat. A house boat belonging to the Juvena company is anchored in front of the beach at Wannsee. Guests are shown the latest swimwear creations accompanied by coffee, cake, and music. Gymnastic displays show the freedom of movement allowed by the comfortable modern beachwear.*
17 May 1932.
Right: *An unusual couple at Wannsee beach. Photo Walter Süssmann.*
Overleaf: *High season at Wannsee beach. Photo Walter Süssmann. Berlin: The long-awaited hot summer weather has finally arrived. One could almost say, it's too much of a good thing. – But the inhabitants of the big city know what to do because they usually have their "Lido" nearby and, as everyone knows, water all over the world is refreshing and – wet. Our photo shows the beach at Wannsee near Berlin on the day when a record 70,000 people visited.*

(Original captions)

FROM ADENAUER
TO ZUCKMAYER

ADENAUER, KONRAD

Politician

born: 5 January 1876 Cologne, died: 19 April 1967 Röhndorf

A., a lawyer, was appointed lord mayor of his native city of Cologne in 1917 by →Kaiser Wilhelm II and called to the Upper Chamber of the Prussian Parliament. A. cooperated with the Allies, who occupied Cologne for seven years from the end of 1918. Beyond Cologne, the Catholic Center politician gained his reputation as the leader of the Prussian Staatsrat (central organ representing the Diets of the Prussian provinces) from 1921 to 1933, and he was an influential figure within his party. A. lost all his offices when the Nazis came to power and was imprisoned for several months in 1944. He was restored as lord mayor of Cologne after the Second World War, and as Federal Chancellor (1949–63) and leader of the Christian Democratic Union (CDU) (1950–66), he played a key role in the formative years of the Federal German Republic.

ALBERS, HANS

Actor

born: 22 September 1891 Hamburg, died: 24 July 1960 Kempfenhausen near Munich

After the First World War, A. returned seriously injured from the front to the Berlin stage where he played in the Theater des Westens and the Deutsches Theater. His biggest popular success in the theater was in the role of Mackie Messer (Mack the Knife) in the *Threepenny Opera*; he was also well known as an actor in both silent and talking films (*The Blue Angel*, 1930). A.'s career suffered no interruption during Nazi rule.

BAKER, JOSEPHINE

Singer and Dancer

born: 3 June 1906 Saint Louis, died: 11 April 1975 Paris

B. (Freda Josephine McDonald) made her debut on Broadway in 1921. Her show *Revue Nègre* was initially unsuccessful in Paris, but she subsequently made a name for herself as a jazz singer and entertainer. In Germany her fame depended mainly on her extravagant

costumes, whereas in France her artistic potential was recognized and she was feted as a major star for decades. She became a French citizen in 1937 as part of a protest about discrimination against Afro-American artists in US society.

BASSERMANN, ALBERT

Actor

born: 7 September 1867 Mannheim, died: 15 May 1952 Zurich

B. started his career at the Meininger Hof Theater; from 1900, he worked in Berlin at the Lessing Theater and Deutsches Theater and also for some years under →Max Reinhardt. He became popular in the 1920s for his work in other theaters and also for his film appearances. In 1934, he was forced to emigrate to the USA with his Jewish wife. He moved to Switzerland in 1946 and made occasional appearances in Germany.

BAUER, GUSTAV

Politician

born: 6 January 1870 Darkehnen (East Prussia), died: 16 September 1944 Berlin

Originally an office clerk, B. founded his own trade union – the Office Employees Association – at the age of 25. As an SPD Reichstag representative (from 1912), he supported the peace of Brest-Litovsk. He was undersecretary in the cabinet of Prince → Max v. Baden, labor minister under → Scheidemann, and succeeded the latter as chancellor. In his inaugural speech of 22 June 1919, B. expressed his opposition to the Treaty of Versailles but ensured that its conditions were fulfilled. In 1920, he rejected the Allies' request for the handover of war criminals for sentencing. He also deployed the voluntary corps (*Freikorps*) to deal with domestic unrest. This resulted in a split in the workers' movement, despite the fact that the latter had saved B.'s government by holding a general strike during the Kapp putsch. B.'s cabinet resigned in March 1920 due to pressure from the trade unions. B. was vice-chancellor, finance and transport minister in the →Müller and →Wirth governments.

BECKMANN, MAX

Artist

born: 12 February 1884 Leipzig, died: 27 December 1950 New York

As a young artist, B. was close to the Berlin Sezession impressionists, who were strongly influenced by the Expressionists. As a medical orderly in the First World War, he had a nervous breakdown, an event which had far-reaching implications for his general outlook and artistic style. B. became one of the main representatives of Expressionism and thematically his work focused on the psychological suffering of urban man (*Hell*, 1919). His work was widely appreciated in the Weimar period but also attacked by the Right. He left Germany in 1937 and taught in the USA in the 1940s. His late work is dominated by large, abstract contemporary metaphors executed in triptychs.

BENJAMIN, WALTER

Writer and Philosopher

born: 15 July 1892 Berlin, died: 27 September 1940 Port Bou (Spain)

A literature critic, translator, and philosopher, B., a friend of →Brecht and Theodor W. Adorno, was forced to emigrate in 1933. As a Jew, Communist, and intellectual, he simultaneously embodied the three arch-enemies of the Nazis. In Paris, he worked on the book which he intended to become his main opus: *Paris, die Hauptstadt des XIX. Jahrhunderts* (Paris, the capital city of the 19th century). He published very little in exile, mostly in the journal *Zeitschrift für Sozialforschung* (Journal of Social Research), including in 1936 his cultural–political essay *Das Kunstwerk im Zeitalter seiner technischen Reproduzierbarkeit* (The Work of Art in the Age of Mechanical Reproduction). Under constant threat of being captured by the Nazis, B. committed suicide. B.'s importance as a social critic was not acknowledged until the 1960s.

BENN, GOTTFRIED

Writer

born: 2 May 1886 Mansfeld/Westprignitz,
died: 7 July 1956 Berlin

A dermatologist, B. published his first poems about morgues and dissecting rooms in 1912. His blunt and remote style divided audiences but he became the leading poet of Expressionism. In 1931, he wrote the libretto for →Hindemith's *Das Unaufhörliche*. In 1932 he became a member of the Prussian Academy of the Arts. As an opponent of Modernism, he initially welcomed the rise of the Nazis but later opposed the regime. B.'s work was banned in 1938. He served in the army during the Second World War as he had done in the First. His later work is concerned with overcoming materialism and nihilism through art.

BERGNER, ELISABETH

Actress

born: 22 August 1897 Drogobytsch (Galicia),
died: 12 May 1986 London

Following her studies and early work under the Austrian monarchy, B. (Ella Ettl) made her acting breakthrough in 1922 in the role of Strindberg's Queen Christina in Berlin. Following further stage and screen successes, she became an idol of the Weimar era. She successfully embodied both types of the ideal woman, the feminine and the emancipated *gamine* with tie and cigarette. After the Nazis came to power, she lived in exile in Great Britain and in the USA. She was able to resume her career after the war and was a recipient of several honors in Germany.

BRAUN, (CARL) OTTO

Politician

born: 28 January 1872 Königsberg (now Kaliningrad),
died: 15 December 1955 Ascona (Switzerland)

From 1888, the lithographer B. was one of the SPD *Jungen Wilden* ("young wild ones") when the party was still illegal. He worked his way up from post to post until he was appointed to the SPD party executive in 1911. In 1913 he became a member of the Prussian House of Representatives. B. was a founder member of the Association of German Agricultural Workers and a member of its executive from 1909 to 1920. B. was Prussian agricultural

minister in 1918–21 and Prussian Prime Minister with two months' interruption from 1920 to 1933. As PM he reformed the Prussian regional administration to make it one of the democratic pillars of the Weimar Republic. Despite his popularity and his widespread influence, he was unsuccessful in his candidature as →Ebert's successor as Reich President. Deposed by →von Papen's "Prussian coup" in 1932, B. left office and fled to exile in Switzerland the following year. While in exile, he developed plans for the re-establishment of democracy in Germany, but was never active in politics again.

BRECHT, BERTOLT

Writer

born: 10 February 1898 Augsburg,
died: 14 August 1956 Berlin

His first Expressionist dramas *Baal* and *Trommeln in der Nacht* not only brought instant fame to the young Brecht in 1922, but also gained him the Kleist literature prize and contact with left-wing artists and publishers. Just two years later, he was producing his own plays in the Deutsches Theater. His opera *The Rise and Fall of the City of Mahagonny (1927–30)* was one of the most controversial shows of the era, and his *Threepenny Opera* (Music: Kurt Weill) of 1928 was one of the great stage successes of the Weimar period. B.'s work focused on the social and economic contradictions and injustices of his time and his belief in his ability to overcome them. B. (Eugen Berthold Friedrich B.) was a supporter of the revolutionary aims of Communism but was never a member of the KPD. From the late 1920s, he warned of the dangers of National Socialism. After the Reichstag fire, he fled Germany with his family. The Nazis stripped him of his German citizenship in 1935. Important elements of B.'s poetical work were written in exile, particularly those concerned with anti-fascism. *The Good Woman of Sichuan* (1939–41) became the model play for "epic theater." In 1948, B. returned to Berlin, where he attained world fame for the productions of his plays by the Berliner Ensemble. Disappointed by the development of the official state in the GDR, B. withdrew increasingly from public life from 1953. Literary criticism acknowledges B.'s importance as a writer, particularly for his plays and socialist didactic dramas (*Mother Courage and her Children*, 1941, *The Caucasian Chalk Circle*, 1947). However, his work also includes short stories, theoretical writings and some 2,800 poems.

Otto Braun

BREUER, MARCEL LAJOS

Architect
born: 22 May 1902 Fünfkirchen (Pécs/Hungary),
died: 1 July 1981 New York

B. worked as both an architect and furniture designer. From 1925, he was director of the furniture workshop at the Weimar Bauhaus. During this time he designed the first tubular metal chair which went into mass production. He was also director of architecture and interior design at the Dessau Bauhaus. His most famous buildings include the Folkwang Museum in Essen and the UNESCO building in Paris. B. managed to continue working in Europe until 1936 before emigrating to the USA, where he taught architecture at Harvard.

BRIAND, ARISTIDE

Politician
born: 28 March 1862 Nantes, died: 7 March 1932 Paris

In 1906, the French Socialist Party expelled its representative B. after four years in parliament because he had accepted a post in the bourgeois cabinet as minister of public education and culture. In this capacity, he was responsible for the implementation of legislation for the separation of church and state. He was French Premier from 1909–17 (with interruptions), and in 1921/22, 1925/26, and 1929; he was also foreign minister from 1925 to 1932. B. had a vision of a federal union of Europe. He recognized the necessity for German–French understanding and supported the evacuation of the Rhineland, disarmament, and European economic union. The Pact of Locarno of 1925 came into being thanks to the efforts of B., →Stresemann, and J. A. →Chamberlain. In 1926, B. and Stresemann were joint recipients of the Nobel Peace Prize as "politicians of reconciliation and negotiation."

BRÜNING, HEINRICH

Politician
born: 26 November 1885 Münster, died: 30 March 1970
Norwich (USA)

B. studied philosophy, history, constitutional law and economics in Munich and Strasbourg, completing his doctorate in 1914. The following year he volunteered to go to the front. In 1919, he worked with the Prussian welfare minister and subsequent Prussian Prime Minister Adam Stegerwald. He took over from Stegerwald as leader of the Christian League of German Trade Unions. He was a member of the Reichstag as a Catholic Center Party representative from 1924–33 and developed a reputation as an expert in finance policy; he was also a member of the Prussian regional parliament from 1928–30. He was appointed Reich Chancellor on 30 March 1930. His priority as an economist was to overcome the serious consequences of the world economic crisis and get the German economy back on an even keel. His austerity measures and deflation policies were tolerated by the SPD, despite the resulting exacerbation in mass poverty and unemployment (he was known as the "Hunger Chancellor"). In terms of foreign policy, B. hoped to be able to persuade the Allies of Germany's insolvency and hence bring an end to the reparation payments which were regulated by the Young Plan. In terms of domestic policy, B. seriously considered a return of the Hohenzollerns and the introduction of a parliamentary monarchy. When the Reichstag no longer supported his policies, B. continued to govern with the help of emergency legislation supported by the Reich President. However, though B. achieved the re-election of Hindenburg in April 1932, the President engineered B.'s downfall at the instigation of the East Prussian landowners on 30 May 1932. From May to July 1933 he was the last leader of the Catholic Center Party which subsequently disbanded. B. emigrated to the USA in 1934; he lectured at Harvard University from 1937 to 1951 and in Cologne from 1951 to 1955.

BUSCH, ERNST (FRIEDRICH WILHELM)

Actor and Singer
born: 21 January 1900 Kiel, died: 8 June 1980 Berlin

B. came to Berlin from the country in 1927. In Berlin, he made a name for himself as a member of a political cabaret act. He also worked as a singer and stage and screen actor (*Kuhle Wampe*, *The Threepenny Opera*). His friend →Eisler wrote numerous songs for him. Forced to emigrate in 1933, B. participated in the Spanish Civil War, was arrested in France in 1940 and handed over to the Nazis in 1943. Imprisoned until 1945, B. appeared on stage in Berlin again in the post-war period as an actor and singer. He was a member of the East Berlin Academy of Art from 1972.

CAPA, ROBERT

Photographer
born: 22 October 1913 Budapest, died: 25 May 1954
Thai-Binh (Vietnam)

C. (André Friedmann), the West's most important war photographer was self-taught. He studied political science in Berlin and worked as a laboratory technician and photographic assistant for the Dephot picture agency. In 1933 he went to Paris, adopted the pseudonym C., and worked as a freelance photographer. His photographs of the Spanish Civil War, in particular a snapshot of the killing of a Republican, made him famous. C. dedicated himself mainly to war reporting, although he avoided all glorification of violence. He photographed the invasion of China by Japanese troops, the Second World War in North Africa, Italy, France – where he landed under heavy fire with US infantry – and Germany, and subsequent wars in Israel and Indochina. He was killed by a mine while working on a report for *Life* magazine in Vietnam. C. was a co-founder and president of the Magnum agency. The Robert Capa Gold Medal Award has been awarded every year since 1955 for "outstanding photography that requires extraordinary courage."

CHAMBERLAIN, JOSEPH AUSTEN

Politician
born: 16 October 1863, died: 16 March 1937 London

Like his father, colonial minister Joseph C., and his step-brother, Prime Minister Arthur Neville C., Joseph Austen C. was a member of parliament. He was a member of the Conservative Party for 45 years up to his death. He was Chancellor of the Exchequer from 1903 to 1906 and 1919 to 1921. As foreign minister, he was an ardent supporter of the Pact of Locarno and the Kellogg–Briand Pact (1924–29). He was knighted and received the Nobel Peace Prize along with Charles Gates Dawes in 1925.

CHAPLIN, CHARLES SPENCER

Director and Actor
born: 16 April 1889 London, died: 25 December 1977 Corsair (Switzerland)

In 1914, "Charlie" C. went to Hollywood, where he soon created his trademark silent-movie character of the tramp, the gentleman of the road with bowler, mustache, child-like gaze, and a big heart. His comedies always had an element of tragedy and his heroes only held their ground with the courage born of desperation. Films such as *The Kid* and *Gold Rush* were global successes. C. was hesitant about entering the new world of the talking movie: *City Lights* (1931) and *Modern Times* (1936) had music but little or no dialog. C's first "proper" talkie was *The Great Dictator* (1940), in which C. parodied Hitler. C. emigrated from the USA to Switzerland in 1952 as a result of the anti-Communist "witch-hunt." He received an Oscar in 1973 and was knighted in 1975.

CUNO, WILHELM (CARL JOSEF)

Politician
born: 2 July 1876 Suhl, died: 3 January 1933 Aumühle near Hamburg

On 22 January 1922, a basically apolitical person was appointed Reich Chancellor: C., who had a doctorate in law, had been a government adviser since 1910. He organized the wartime Nutrition Office during the First World War and in 1918 became director general of the Hapag shipping company. C. was a man who firmly believed in the primacy of economics over politics. He represented the German government as an economic expert at the armistice, peace, and reparations conferences. His good relationship with →Ebert

contributed to his appointment as Chancellor. Like most of his ministers, C. did not belong to any particular party. His efforts to bring about a revision of the Treaty of Versailles were unsuccessful. In 1923, he called for passive resistance of the French and Belgian occupation of the Ruhr. This gave rise to an increase in inflation and further deterioration of the country's economic situation. Following his resignation on 13 August 1923, he withdrew from politics and concentrated on his work for Hapag.

DIETRICH, MARLENE

Actress
born: 27 December 1901 Berlin, died: 6 May 1992 Paris

It took just one film to make the 28-year-old Berlin woman an international star in 1930: →Sternberg's *The Blue Angel*. After modest initial artistic success "Die Dietrich" (Maria

Magdalena von Losch) became a legend in the role of the nightclub singer Lola Lola. When she followed Sternberg to the USA, he consciously made her into an erotic icon. Dressed in men's clothes, with her dark husky voice and hooded gaze, D. assumed the persona of the vamp. As well as Sternberg, she worked with other directors in the USA, including Ernst Lubitsch and Billy Wilder. She rejected Goebbels's invitation to return to Germany for political reasons and became a US

citizen in 1939. During the Second World War, she gave a number of concerts for American soldiers. In the 1950s, she concentrated on her career as a stage actress and chanteuse and rarely appeared in films. Her last film appearance was in *Just a Gigolo* in 1978. She spent the remaining years of her life as a recluse in Paris.

DIX, OTTO (WILHELM HEINRICH)

Artist
born: 2 December 1891 Untermhaus (now Gera), died: 25 July 1969 Singen/Hohentwiel

Having served on the front in the war, D. reproduced his war experiences in shocking drawings and paintings. Originally strongly influenced by Expressionism, in the 1920s he moved towards Realism at the Düsseldorf Academy of Art, and his paintings were classified with the "New Objectivity" movement. He taught at the Dresden Academy from 1927. Condemned by the National Socialists for his blunt depictions of war and poverty, D. withdrew to "internal exile." After 1946 he created a substantial body of late work, often with biblical motifs.

DÖBLIN, ALFRED

Writer
born: 10 August 1878 Stettin, died: 26 June 1957 Emmendingen (Breisgau)

A doctor and writer, D. found his patients and themes in the working-class neighborhoods of Berlin. As a psychiatrist, he had a particularly perceptive feel for the psychological deformities and depths of the modern metropolis. Having volunteered for army service during the First World War, he made his mark as an Expressionist writer and left–liberal publisher. His first popular work, however, was his novel *Berlin Alexanderplatz*, which was published in 1927 (filmed in 1931 with →George in the main role). Due to its use of film-like montage technique, abbreviated plot sequences, inner monologues, and newspaper excerpts, it is still viewed as the archetypal German urban novel. After the Reichstag fire D. fled Germany and spent some years in exile in Switzerland, France, and the USA. Although he continued to write, D. was completely isolated at this time, not least as a result of his conversion from Judaism to Catholicism. Having returned to Germany immediately after the war, he failed to re-establish himself and in 1953 he moved on to Paris. He was not rediscovered as a writer until the latter years of his life.

DUISBERG, CARL

Chemist and Industrialist
born: 29 September 1861 Barmen,
died: 19 March

Director General of the Bayer paint works from 1912, in 1925 D. became Chairman of the Board of I.G. Farbenindustrie AG, of which he was a co-founder. As the driving force of the Reich Association of German Industry, he supported →Brüning in his efforts to undermine the influence of parliament and establish an authoritarian government.

EBERT, FRIEDRICH

Politician
born: 4 February 1871 Heidelberg, died: 28 February 1925 Berlin

Right-wing extremists would not forgive him the fact that he started his career as a saddler and left-wing extremists for the fact that he ended it in the office of Reich President: E. was one of Germany's most hated politicians. Throughout his tenure in office he was forced to take legal action against personal attacks. This additional burden was also a contributory factor in his early death. After some years spent traveling, E. settled as a publican in Bremen and started his slow but steady climb up through the ranks of the Social Democratic party hierarchy. He was

elected to the Reichstag in 1912 and elected party leader along with →Haase in 1913. The two leaders, and ultimately the party, split over the question of war loans. After the split, E. took over leadership of the SPD parliamentary group with →Scheidemann. In 1918 he joined the leadership of the Berlin January strike with the aim of exercising a moderating influence on the workers, a move which the left interpreted as a betrayal of the working class and the right saw as a betrayal of the Fatherland. This conflict was intensified when E. took over as Reich Chancellor from Prince →Max von Baden. E's aim was to prevent the establishment of a socialist republic in favor of a parliamentary democracy or even a constitutional monarchy. To this end, he entered an alliance with the Supreme Army Command under →Groener. E. managed to gain support for his policy in the Council of People's Representatives. He was elected Reich President by the National Assembly on 11 February 1919. In 1922, the Reichstag extended his period of office by three years. Almost all of E's period in office was characterized by economic and political crises. E. never gained the respect of reactionary middle-class circles and lost the support of the working class because he stood firmly by his alliance with the unreliable military command. He supported →Noske in the quashing of the workers' revolts by the military and although he contributed to the failure of the →Kapp putsch he continued to support its leader, despite the ambiguous role of the army. E. has not gone down in history as an important theorist or statesman but as a party soldier and servant of the state of great personal integrity and loyalty. His collaboration with reactionary forces and the large number of emergency presidential decrees he passed meant that he stood in the way of his own chief political goal, the democratization of Germany.

ECKENER, HUGO

Aviation Pioneer
born: 10 August 1868 Flensburg,
died: 14 August 1954 Friedrichshafen

E. tested the ideas of Ferdinand von Zeppelin in war and peace. He was a co-founder of the German aviation company Deutsche Luftschiffahrt AG in 1909, and by 1914 he had already undertaken 2,000 airship flights. After Zeppelin's death in 1917 he was the driving force of the Zeppelin works. In the 1920s he undertook numerous spectacular trips across the Atlantic, over the Arctic, and around the world. After the *Hindenburg* explosion in Lakehurst in 1937, he returned to his pre-1909 profession of writing.

EHRHARDT, HERMANN

Army Officer
born: 29 November 1881 Diersburg, died: 27 September 1971
Brunn am Walde (Austria)

Lieutenant Commander E. was involved in almost all of the right-wing conspiracies and assassinations of the post-war period. The marine brigade, a voluntary corps of approxi-

mately 5,000 which had the swastika as an emblem on its helmet, was officially founded by E. on 1 March 1919. It fought against Communist insurgents and formed the core troop on which →Kapp relied for his coup d'état. E. was arrested after the failure of the Kapp putsch but was able to flee and founded the secret organization "Consul" in Bavaria (later "Viking Alliance"). These organizations were responsible for the murders of →Rathenau and →Erzberger. E. once again escaped from custody and fled to Austria where he withdrew from political life.

EINSTEIN, ALBERT

Physicist
born: 14 March 1879 Ulm, died: 18 April 1955 Princeton (USA)

In 1905 E., an employee of the patents office in Bern, revolutionized physics with the publication of his theory of relativity. With his formula for the equivalence of mass and energy ($E=mc^2$) and his later quantum hypothesis of light, he radically changed our understanding of the world. He was appointed professor in 1909 and received the Nobel Prize in 1921. From 1914 he worked in Berlin. As a prominent Jew, pacifist and member of the League of Human Rights, E. was treated with hostility throughout the Weimar period. When →Hitler came to power, E. left Germany for the USA. He resigned from his official positions and never returned to Germany. E. was deeply involved in resistance to the Nazi regime. In 1939, he warned the US President that the Germans were building an atom bomb. He later campaigned for the restriction of the use of atomic power to non-military purposes.

EISENSTAEDT, ALFRED

Photo-Journalist
born: 6 December 1898 Dirschau, died: 24 August 1995 Chilmark (USA)

In 1929, haberdashery salesman E. made his hobby, photography, into his profession. He worked for the Pacific and Atlantic Picture Agency and also worked on a freelance basis for a number of publications, including the *Berliner Tageblatt* and the *Berliner Illustrirte Zeitung*. His very first commission, a photo essay about the awarding of the Nobel Prize for Literature to Thomas →Mann, attracted much attention. E's fame spread through his photographs from the Italian campaign in Abyssinia, portraits of artists and politicians, and also photographs of everyday life. The distinctive features of his work are his clarity of composition and the fact that he did not use a flash. In 1935 he emigrated to the USA, where he was appointed to the permanent staff of the newly founded *Life* magazine. He provided more than 2,500 photos for the magazine, including some 90 title shots. He also published in *Harper's Bazaar* and *Vogue*. E. received numerous international awards and is acknowledged as one of the founders of modern photo-journalism.

EISLER, HANNS

Composer
born: 6 July 1898 Leipzig, died: 6 September 1962 Berlin

Philosopher Rudolf E. was too poor to finance his talented son Hanns's musical education. Hanns E. was not able to study composition at the Vienna Conservatory and as a private pupil of →Schoenberg until after his war service. In 1926, teacher and pupil fell out because the Communist E. deemed Schoenberg's new music too complicated and inaccessible for the masses. With his popular workers' songs and choral verse, E. became the leading proponent of the German working-class music movement and it was in this capacity that he collaborated with →Brecht and →Busch. E. went into exile when the Nazis came into power. During this period

Alfred Eisenstaedt

he had some success with his compositions for film. During the post-war period, E. became one of the most important artistic personalities in the German Democratic Republic.

EISNER, KURT

Politician and Journalist
born: 14 May 1867 Berlin, died: 21 February 1919 Munich

SPD member E. (K. Kosmanowski) came to Berlin in 1899 to work on *Vorwärts* on the recommendation of →Liebknecht. He was dismissed from this position in 1905 for being a "revisionist." E. moved to the job of editor-in-chief of the SPD-aligned newspaper *Fränkische Tagespost* and became a citizen of Bavaria. During the First World War, E. became a pacifist. In 1917, he became leader of the Munich USPD (Independent Social Democratic Party) and was imprisoned for some months in 1918 as leader of the munitions workers' strike. On 7 November 1918, E. proclaimed the Bavarian Republic and was elected president of the Workers' and Soldiers' Council. A few days later, he took office as Bavarian Prime Minister and foreign minister. His belief in a peaceful combination of the socialist system and parliamentary democracy gained him enemies on both the left and right. His support for the National Assembly elections was dismissed by the radical left as "betrayal of the Revolution." E.'s USPD suffered crushing defeat in the regional elections of January 1919. E. was assassinated by a monarchist while on his way to the meeting for the formation of the new regional government, at which he intended to submit his resignation. The news of E.'s murder gave rise to a radical swing in the political climate and it was, in fact, the event that triggered the establishment of the socialist republic of Bavaria.

ERZBERGER, MATTHIAS

Politician
born: 20 September 1875 Buttenhausen (Swabia),
died: 26 August 1921 Griesbach (Black Forest)

An elementary school teacher and journalist, E. was elected to the Reichstag in 1903 as a representative of the Catholic Center Party. He immediately made a name for himself due to his ambition, energy, and astute contribution to parliamentary debates.
During the First World War, he was appointed director of foreign propaganda by Reich Chancellor Bethmann Hollweg. Originally a committed supporter of annexation, in 1917 E. concluded that the war could no longer be won. He promoted the cause of "negotiated peace," initiated the Reichstag peace resolution of 19 July 1917, was head of the German armistice commission, and signed the armistice agreement as a German representative. As vice-chancellor and finance minister in the →Bauer government, he implemented fundamental financial reform; giving the Reich financial sovereignty, and simplifying tax collection. A slander campaign led to his resignation in 1920. E., one of the most defamed "November criminals" and "traitors," was shot while walking in the Black Forest by two right-wing assassins from →Ehrhardt's camp.

FALLADA, HANS

Writer
born: 21 July 1893 Greifswald, died: 6 February 1947 Berlin

F.'s (Rudolf Ditzen) success as a writer contrasts sharply with the failure of his personal life, which was plagued by drug and alcohol addiction, his lack of formal educational qualifications, and several spells in prison. It was against this background that his successful work *Kleiner Mann, was nun?* was produced in 1932. F's socio-critical novels also include *Wer einmal aus dem Blechnapf frißt*, which was based on one of his stays in prison. F. adjusted to Nazi rule, as he did to the political situation in the Soviet occupied zone in the post-war period. Having been Mayor of Feldberg, he went to Berlin supposedly to work for the *Berliner Rundschau*, but in fact to be admitted to the Charité hospital psychi-

atric clinic. His autobiographical novel *Der Trinker*, written in code, was not published until after his death.

FEHRENBACH, KONSTANTIN

Politician
born: 11 January 1852 Wellendingen (Black Forest),
died: 26 March 1926 Freiburg

A lawyer by profession, F. was a representative of the Catholic Center Party in the Baden regional government and from 1903 a member of the Reichstag. He was appointed Reichstag President in 1918, and in 1919 he presided over the National Assembly in Weimar. His dignified and even-tempered nature led to him being appointed head of a bourgeois coalition government in 1920. However, the 68-year-old was not up to the heavy demands of domestic and international politics. After 11 months in office, his minority government fell on the reparations issue. F. was leader of the Catholic Center parliamentary party from 1923 to his death in 1926.

FORSTER, RUDOLF

Actor
born: 30 October 1884 Gröbming (Styria),
died: 26 October 1968 Bad Aussee (Styria)

Rudolf F.'s career led him from a stint as a touring actor in Bohemia, via Vienna to Berlin where he made a name for himself in 1920–32 as a Strindberg interpreter. He played Mackie Messer (Mack the Knife) in →Pabst's 1931 film version of *The Threepenny Opera*. He worked in Hollywood and on Broadway from 1937 to 1940. F. later appeared in many theaters throughout Europe and numerous films.

FRANK, LEONHARD

Writer
born: 4 September 1882 Würzburg, died: 18 August 1961 Munich

A pacifist and social revolutionary, F. lived in exile from 1915 to 1918 and from 1933 to 1950. Major literary success eluded him after his first autobiographical novel *Die Räuberbande* (The band of robbers) (1914). In 1918, he became a member of the Munich Revolutionary Council, and he was appointed vice-president of the PEN Club in 1923. In addition to novellas and psychological novels, F. also published a second autobiographical novel *Links, wo das Herz ist* (Left, where the heart is) (1952).

FURTWÄNGLER, (GUSTAV HEINRICH ERNST MARTIN) WILHELM

Conductor
born: 25 January 1886 Berlin, died: 30 November 1954 Baden-Baden

F. composed his first symphony at the age of 17 and by 35 he had established his reputation as Germany's most important conductor, with a unique talent for combining the emotional experience and intellectual penetration of a work of art. After an interlude as successor to Richard Strauss at the Berlin State Opera, he was conductor of the Berlin Philharmonic Orchestra and Leipzig Gewandhaus Orchestra in the 1920s, and also guest conductor with the Viennese Philharmonic and New York Philharmonic Orchestra. In 1934, he resigned from all of his positions in protest against the harassment of →Hindemith. Despite this, however, he remained in Germany and was criticized for this after 1945.

GEORGE, HEINRICH

Actor
born: 9 October 1893 Stettin, died: 25 September 1946 Sachsenhausen

A character actor (Falstaff, Macbeth, Othello), G. was consistently outstanding in artistic

terms although rather flexible in political terms. Dismissed from his position in 1933 due to his Communist sympathies, G. (real name Georg Schulz) came to terms with the new regime and succeeded in obtaining important roles again. In addition to his stage appearances, his roles in numerous films, including *Metropolis* and *Berlin Alexanderplatz* increased his popularity in the 1920s. G. later played leading roles in Nazi films. He was imprisoned by the Russians in Sachsenhausen where the harsh conditions resulted in his death.

GIDAL, TIM

Photographer
born: 18 May 1909 Munich, died: 4 October 1996 Jerusalem

Son of an orthodox Jewish family, G.'s first photographs were of friends from the Zionist movement. From 1929, like his brother Georg Gidal, who died young (born: 13 March 1908 Munich, died: 21 October 1931), he worked as a freelance photographer, mainly on behalf of the *Münchner Illustrierte Presse*. With his direct, natural style of photography, G. (Ignaz Nachum Gidalewitch) was a pioneer of modern photo-journalism. He left Germany in 1933. In 1935, he completed his studies in history, art history, and economics, which he had begun in Germany in 1928, in Basle with a dissertation on "Picture Reporting and the Press." Soon after this, he emigrated to Palestine. His photographs had a formative influence on the London *Picture Post*, where he worked along with Hutton and →Man. His photo essay about Mahatma Gandhi was sold throughout the world in 1940. Having joined the British Army as a volunteer in 1942, he worked as head reporter for the army newspaper *Parade* until 1944. He taught the history and sociology of visual communication in New York and Jerusalem. He published books about photo-journalism and German Judaism.

GOEBBELS, JOSEPH (PAUL)

Politician
born: 29 October 1897 Rheydt, died: 1 May 1945 Berlin

G., who held a doctorate in German language and literature, compensated for his physical disability and failure as a writer with his demagogic talent. G. came to the NSDAP in 1924, and was

quickly noticed by →Hitler who made him *Gauleiter* (Nazi administrative district head) of Berlin. G., who originally belonged to the more social-revolutionary wing of the party, completely submitted himself to Hitler's influence and saw himself as the Führer's "herald." The campaigns initiated by G., for example for the elevation to martyrdom of →Wessel and defamation of →Remarque, attracted as much attention to the NSDAP as his propaganda speeches and articles in the party newspaper *Der Angriff*. In 1928, G. was elected to the Reichstag; he was appointed party propaganda leader in 1930 and Reich Minister for Propaganda in 1933. As propaganda minister, he had complete control of art and the media. He outlawed all artists and journalists who were unacceptable to the party and ordered their work to burned. He had indisputable rhetorical talent, but the content of his speeches was limited to fanatical anti-Semitism and adulation of Adolf Hitler. During the Second World War, as defeats against Germany mounted, he became the protagonist of "total war." Hitler appointed him Reich Chancellor in his will. However, G. followed his idol to his death in 1945, along with his wife and children.

GÖRING, HERMANN (WILHELM)

Politician and Army Officer
born: 12 January 1893 Marienbad near Rosenheim, died: 15 October 1946 Nuremberg

A fighter pilot awarded the *Pour le mérite*, G. became involved in agitation for the NSDAP in 1922. →Hitler commissioned him to set up the Storm Troopers (*Sturmabteilung*, SA): the involvement of the war hero was a matter of prestige for the NSDAP. G. was shot during the November putsch of 1923 and prescribed morphine for pain relief. His addiction to the drug later led to almost complete paralysis. After the November putsch, G. fled abroad and returned after an amnesty. He was a member of the Reichstag from 1928 and was appointed Reichstag President after the elections of 31 July 1932. On 30 January 1933, he became a minister in Hitler's government and shortly after that Prussian Prime Minister and interior minister. He used this position to force officials,

and particularly the police, to toe the party line. After the murders of SA leader Erich Röhm and his supporters, he availed himself of the services of the secret political police force, the Gestapo, which he created. Hitler named him his successor out of gratitude for his loyalty and service. In the following years, G. collected a series of offices of state, including that of commanding officer of the Luftwaffe and commissioner for the four-year plan for the war economy. The defeat of the Luftwaffe in the Second World War and his self-indulgent flamboyant lifestyle discredited him both in the eyes of the public and of Hitler. Sentenced to death at the Nuremberg Trials as a war criminal, he committed suicide the night his execution was ordered.

GROCK

Clown
born: 10 January 1880 Reconvilier (Switzerland), died: 14 July 1959 Imperia (Italy)

The musically talented clown figure "Grock" (Charles Adrian Wettach) became the alter ego of vaudeville artist Wettach. From 1910 to his retirement from the stage in 1954, the "King of the Clowns" performed in this role to millions of people throughout the world. He worked independently of the circus and made solo appearances, also on television. He was director of his own circus from 1951.

GROENER, (KARL EDUARD) WILHELM

Army Officer and Politician
born: 22 November 1867 Ludwigsburg, died: 3 May 1939 Bornstedt (Potsdam)

→Ludendorff's resignation from his post within the Supreme Army Command in 1918 left open the job of organizing the retreat of the German army from the western front. Hindenburg assigned this task to G., the new quartermaster general, who was a gifted expert in field railways. G. convinced Wilhelm II that the army no longer stood by its oath of allegiance and forced him to abdicate. He entered into a pact with →Ebert for the suppression of the Communist uprisings and authorized the use of the volunteer corps (*Freikorps*). In 1919, he supported the signing of the Treaty of Versailles.

G. was transport minister from 1920 to 1923, defense minister from 1928 to 1932, and, concurrently, interior minister from 1931 to 1932, in which capacity he enforced the ban on the SA. This brought him into conflict with his protégé →Schleicher and ultimately led to G's fall from power. G. has gone down in history as a "pragmatic Republican." However, his main priority was the army and its interests and along with →Brüning, he paved the way for German re-armament and had →Ossietzky tried for treason.

GROPIUS, WALTER (ADOLF GEORG)

Architect
born: 18 May 1883 Berlin, died: 5 July 1969 Boston

Work on the design of functional buildings for AEG was a more influential factor in G.'s career than his failure to complete his architecture studies. At the age of 28, he was responsible for the design of the Fagus Werke shoe factory in Alfeld, which became the most important example of the New Architecture in Germany, the "architecture of the industrial age," with its strong emphasis on glass and steel structures. From 1919, he was director of the Bauhaus in Weimar, of which he was also a founder. At the Bauhaus he promoted his concept of the unified work of art, which should be created through a merging of art, crafts, and technology. G.'s approach to architecture was completely functional and he put his theories into practice in his design for the Dessau Bauhaus of 1925/26. He resigned as director of the Bauhaus in the late 1920s and concentrated on his work as an architect (Siemensstadt housing estate in Berlin). Forced to emigrate in 1934, G. went to Great Britain and on to the USA, where he taught architecture at Harvard University.

GROSZ, GEORGE

Painter and Graphic Artist
born: 26 July 1893 Berlin, died: 6 July 1959 Berlin

Having volunteered for army service during the First World War, G. (Georg Ehrenfried Gross) was cured of enthusiasm for war by his experiences on the front. From then on, his art was completely focused on protest and condemnation. In his caricatures and paintings, G. depicted the horror of war and condemned the misery of the post-war period with its crass extremes of poverty and affluence (*The Face of the Ruling Class*, 1921). Many found G.'s attacks on the military, capitalism, and the church intolerable and he was fined several

times for blasphemy, attacks on the army and breaches of public morality. In 1920, he participated in the first international Dada Fair in Berlin. His paintings were classified as part of the "New Objectivity" movement. From around 1925, G.'s style became less cutting and hence also less important illustrator of the Weimar period, G. worked mainly for the Communist publications. He designed books by authors including →Toller and →Brecht. Shortly before the Nazis deported him and removed his work from galleries as "degenerate art," he realized his dream of living in the USA in 1933. He became a US citizen and taught at American universities. He only returned to Berlin a few weeks before his death in 1959.

GRÜNDGENS, GUSTAF

Actor and Director
born: 22 December 1899 Düsseldorf, died: 7 October 1963 Manila

Having trained as an actor in Düsseldorf, G. arrived in Berlin via Hamburg in 1928, where he set new standards with his performance as Mephisto in Goethe's *Faust* in 1932/33. He attracted →Göring's attention; the latter shielded him from attacks on account of earlier left-wing tendencies and appointed him Prussian Councilor of State. G. became a willing servant of the new masters and was promoted to state actor and director. Although G. occasionally helped threatened colleagues during this period, and despite due recognition of his outstanding artistic achievements, his post-war career was overshadowed by the accusation made by Klaus →Mann and others that

he willingly subjected himself and his work to Nazi propaganda.

GUTTMANN, (WILHELM) SIMON

Photo Agent
born: 17 November 1891 Vienna, died: 14 January 1990 London

As a young art critic, G. promoted the work of the Expressionists in Berlin. He avoided service during the First World War by pretending to have tuberculosis and fled to Switzerland, where he joined forces with the Dadaists. In the early 1920s, he came into contact with Vladimir Mayakovsky and the Soviet film industry in Russia and decided to work as a photo agent. From 1928 to 1933, he was director of Dephot (*Deutscher Photodienst*), one of the most important agencies which provided photographs and full text reports for the magazine market. The Dephot photographers included, inter alia, →Capa and →Umbo. After the Nazi seizure of power in 1933, G. was forced to emigrate. In 1940 he fled from the German army on foot across France and later escaped to London. He worked with →Lorant on *Picture Post* from 1944 to 1946. In 1946, G. founded the Report photo agency with →Man, which he ran until his death at the age of 98 years.

HAASE, HUGO

Politician
born: 29 September 1863 Allenstein, died: 7 November 1919 Berlin

Despite being a pacifist, as SPD leader and head of the parliamentary party, H. had to obey party orders and announce the party's support for loans to finance the First World War. As a result of the war he distanced himself from the SPD, resigned from the leadership and became a co-founder and leader of the Independent Social Democratic Party (USPD). Together with →Ebert, he was head of the Council of People's Representatives from November to December 1918. He was assassinated in 1919.

HARDEN, MAXIMILIAN (FELIX ERNST)

Journalist
born: 20 October 1861 Berlin, died: 30 October 1927 Montana (Switzerland)

After ten years working as an actor with a traveling theater, H. (Witkowski) became a critic. As a supporter of the modern theater, he advised →Reinhardt, and with his publication *Die Zukunft* (The Future) (1892–1922) he was one of the most influential theater and literature critics in Germany. Politically, he moved from being an admirer to an opponent of →Wilhelm II. He was severely injured in an attack by right-wing radicals in 1922.

HARTMANN, GUSTAV, ("IRON GUSTAV")

Cab Driver
born: 23 April 1859 Magdeburg,
died: 23 December 1938 Berlin

After 40 years on his horse-drawn cab, H. noticed that his customers were opting to travel in motorized taxis. To prove that his trade had not quite been consigned to history, at almost 69 years of age, on 2 April 1928 H. set off on a journey to Paris and back. H. and his horse Grasmus took weeks to complete the journey but they were greeted with great enthusiasm on their arrival in Paris and back in Berlin. H.'s journey was the inspiration behind one of Hans →Fallada's novels.

HAUPTMANN, GERHART

Writer
born: 15 November 1862 Ober-Salzbrunn (Silesia),
died: 6 June 1946 Agnetendorf (Silesia)

During the Weimar period, H. was one of the most popular German dramatists and a respected artist. His play *Die Weber* (The weavers) (1892) is one of the most important works of Realism. This was followed by the social-critical comedy *Der Biberpelz* (The beaver fur) in 1893, and the tragicomedy *Die Ratten* (The rats) in 1911. In addition to social themes, H. also worked on fairy stories and dark mythical material, for example in *Rose Bernd* (1903) and *Und Pippa tanzt* (And Pippa dances) in 1906. He received the Nobel Prize for literature in 1912. He was an early supporter of the Weimar Republic and wrote an obituary for →Rathenau. Despite being productive to the end of his days, H. was too old to emigrate in 1933, as so many other German artists did. He remained silent with respect to the crimes of the National Socialists and allowed himself to be used in cultural propaganda. Former friends, such as critic Alfred Kerr, who had emigrated, broke off contact with him because of this.

HEARTFIELD, JOHN

Painter, Illustrator, and Stage Designer
born: 19 June 1891 Berlin, died: 26 April 1968 Berlin

Helmut Franz Josef Herzfeld was interested in provocation from an early age. The widespread hatred of England was so repulsive to him that the changed his name to John Heartfield during the First World War. He founded the anti-militaristic journal *Neue Jugend* (New Youth), joined the KPD (Communists) in 1919, and was one of the leading Berlin Dadaists. Here he met →Grosz, with whom he collaborated to bring the art of photomontage to a new level: the ingenious combination of photos, drawings, and other elements was particularly popular in the Soviet Union. H.'s works were also used in the design of covers for books published by the Malik publishing house. He also worked as a stage designer for →Piscator and →Reinhardt from 1920 to 1930. However, H.'s reputation rests mainly on his development of photomontage as a political weapon used in publications and posters against the rise of National Socialism. In 1933, he was forced to flee to Prague where he continued to work for the *Arbeiter Illustrierte Zeitung*. In 1938 he emigrated to England. After the war, he returned to Germany and created stage sets for →Brecht's Berliner Ensemble.

HESSEL, FRANZ

Writer
born: 2 November 1880 Stettin, died: 6 April 1941 Sanary-sur-Mer (France)

After a bohemian existence in Munich and Paris, H. participated in the First World War and became an editor with Rowohlt publishers in 1924. During this time he was also productive as a writer (e.g. *Spazieren in Berlin* (Strolling in Berlin, 1929) and translated the works of French authors into German. His writings were banned by the National Socialists. In 1938, he emigrated to Paris and was imprisoned in a French internment camp in 1940, where he died in 1941.

HINDEMITH, PAUL

Composer
born: 16 November 1895 Hanau, died: 28 December 1963 Frankfurt/Main

H. was not happy with his job as concert-master at the Frankfurt Opera House (from 1915). As a violinist and viola player, he preferred working

as a musician and in 1922 joined the Amar Quartet, which was famous for its repertoire of New Music. H.'s compositions were the key force in music development in Germany from 1921 (*String Quartet*, 1921; *Chamber Music* and *Die junge Magd* song cycle, 1922). He used new forms, tonal systems, and sentence techniques which he presented in spectacular performances (one act opera *Mörder, Hoffnung der Frauen*, 1921; song cycle *Das Marienleben*, 1922; opera *Cadillac*, 1927). From 1927 to 1934, H. was professor of composition at the Berlin Conservatory. During this time he met →Brecht and →Döblin, and →Benn wrote the texts for his oratorio *Das Unaufhörliche*. His work was banned by the National Socialists. He emigrated to the USA via Turkey, taught at Yale and later in Zurich. After his opera *Mathis der Maler*, which was performed in the USA in 1938, H. reverted to a more traditional style.

HINDENBURG, PAUL (LUDWIG HANS ANTON) VON BENECKENDORFF UND VON

Army Officer and Politician
born: 2 October 1847 Posen, died: 2 August 1934 Neudeck (East Prussia)

A veteran of the wars of 1866 and 1870/71, H. was retired as a general in 1911 but reactivated on 22 August 1914 as commander of the 8th Army in East Prussia. The victory over the Russians at Tannenberg, which he planned with →Ludendorff, made him extremely popular. In November 1914 he was promoted to Field Marshall and took over the Supreme Command of the German armies on the Eastern front. In 1916, he was appointed

Commander of all German land forces, the most senior army officer in Germany. In this capacity he was able to exercise an influence on political decisions. In November 1918, he advised →Wilhelm II to go into exile. H. offered his services to the →Ebert government to help deal with the internal unrest. He retired from military office in 1919. In 1925, H. allowed himself to be persuaded by the right to stand for the office of Reich President and was elected in the second election. He was re-elected in 1932, this time as a liberal candidate. Despite being a monarchist, he was loyal to the constitution but dismissed democratic politicians, like →Brüning, at the urging of his cronies and advisers – East Prussian landowners, →Papen, →Schleicher, and his own son, officer Oskar von H. (1883–1960). However, he stubbornly resisted the right's demands to curb the power of the Reichstag. The cabinets of Papen and Schleicher, which relied solely on the authority of the president and were without democratic legitimization, remained unsuccessful. Despite his reluctance, H. allowed himself to be persuaded by his advisers to nominate Hitler as Chancellor in January 1933. An old man, H. was no longer up to the challenge of his office. However, he lent this cabinet an air of respectability and did not oppose its criminal activities.

HITLER, ADOLF

Politician
born: 20 April 1889 Braunau (Austria), died: 30 April 1945
Berlin

When war broke out in 1914, the failed Austrian artist saved himself from personal oblivion by joining the Bavarian army. He was in a military hospital suffering from gas poisoning when the war ended. In 1919, the army sent him as an informer to a meeting of the small *Deutsche Arbeiter Partei* (German Workers' Party) H.'s talent as an orator soon emerged at party meetings. He was admitted to the party and became its leader in July 1921. The NSDAP (National Socialist German Workers' Party), a renamed nationalistic anti-Semitic splinter group of the German Workers' Party, was initially popular only in Bavaria. On 8 November 1923, the party organized a putsch under Hitler and →Ludendorff, which was suppressed by the police the following day. H. was discovered in hiding and appeared in court, where he took the opportunity to make long-winded political declarations, with the result that he obtained valuable publicity which spread his fame throughout Germany. H. used his short spell

in prison – he was released in 1925 after just one year – to start work on his book *Mein Kampf*. On his release he re-established the NSDAP, which had been banned since the putsch, and pursued a dual strategy: officially he supported the idea of continuing the fight for power by legal means but in reality he promoted a campaign of civil war-like violence and terror on the streets staged by the party's military wing, the SA. Against the background of the economic crisis in the late 1920s, the NSDAP became the second biggest party in Germany in 1930 and two years later it was the largest: in 1931, the NSDAP, DNVP and "Stahlhelm" joined forces in the Harzburg Front. Autumn 1932 brought resistance: H. was defeated by →Hindenburg in the elections for Reich President and the NSDAP suffered significant losses in the election. A split in the party was only barely avoided in December of the same year. However, around the same time Hindenburg's associates deemed that H. was the only party leader capable of building a right-wing government with a popular base, and Hindenburg reluctantly appointed Hitler as Chancellor on 30 January 1933. Within a few months, H. had established a complete dictatorship (24 March 1933 "Enabling Act"). His rule was characterized by racism and terror. H. committed suicide at the end of the Second World War, a war which he planned and started.

HOFFMANN, HEINRICH

Photographer
born: 12 September 1885 Fürth, died: 16 December 1957
Munich

H. became a freelance photographer in Munich in 1908. A competent businessman, he achieved his first major success with photographs of the Socialist Republic of Munich. He made no secret of his support for the forces of reaction. Shortly after this he became a friend of →Hitler's – it was in H.'s

studio that Hitler met his wife Eva Braun. H. soon became Hitler's "court photographer." In this capacity, he not only earned a lot of money but also worked on the creation of the figure of the "Führer" as we know it. He was sentenced to five years in a labor camp after the war.

HOLLAENDER, FRIEDRICH

Cabaret Artist and Composer
born: 18 October 1896 London, died: 18 January 1976 Munich

"Falling in love again, what am I to do?" – this song, made famous by Marlene →Dietrich, was only one of the many hits composed by H. He wrote music and words for reviews, cabarets, and UFA films. In 1919 he founded the *Schall und Rauch* cabaret with →Reinhardt and in 1930 the Tingel-Tangel Theater. A Jew, H. fled Germany for the USA in 1933 and was responsible for the music in almost 200 Hollywood films. He returned to Germany in 1956 and worked again in cabaret.

HUGENBERG, ALFRED

Publisher and Politician
born: 19 June 1865 Hanover, died: 12 March 1951 Kükenbruch
(Lipperland)

In his capacities as industrialist, media mogul, and party leader H. helped →Hitler to come to power. In 1891, he was co-founder of the imperialist and nationalist Pan-German League and a committed supporter of annexation during the First World War. In addition to his work as chairman of the board of directors of the Krupp conglomerate, the Prussian privy councilor created a monolithic media empire comprising daily newspapers, news agencies, advertising agencies, UFA (Germany's largest film production company), and the Scherl-Verlag publishing house. From the outset, H.'s editorial policy was anti-republican. He was a member of the National Assembly; in 1918 he

joined the German National People's Party (DNVP) and became its leader in 1928. His chauvinistic and anti-parliamentary propaganda resulted in numerous resignations from the party. H. represented the interests of heavy industry but was also aware of the necessity of winning a majority. Due to his party's electoral failures, he joined the alliance with the "Stahlhelm" and the NSDAP in the Harzburg Front in 1931, a move which ended the isolation of the NSDAP. With →Papen and →Meissner, H. was responsible for the fall of →Brüning and →Schleicher. When →Hindenburg announced Hitler as the new Chancellor on 30 January 1933, H. believed his aims had been fulfilled. He was appointed by Hitler as minister for finance, agriculture and nutrition. H. believed he had achieved his goal of using Hitler and "boxing him in." In reality, after just six months H. was demoted and forced to sell large parts of his business empire, after which he disappeared from the political scene.

JANNINGS, EMIL

Actor

born: 23 July 1884 Rorschach, died: 2 January 1950 Strobl (Austria)

J. played at the Deutsches Theater under →Reinhardt from 1915. In 1918 he achieved his breakthrough in the role of the village judge Adam in Kleist's play *The Broken Jug*. J. Theodor Friedrich Emil Janenz) enjoyed significant success in other roles, including that of Mephisto. He was the first of the leading actors of his time to identify film as a genre in its own right; he became Germany's first film star and worked with Ernst Lubitsch, →Murnau, and →Sternberg (*The Blue Angel*). From 1926 to 1929 he worked in Hollywood and received the first Oscar ever awarded to an actor. When talking movies were introduced, he returned to Germany where he willingly collaborated in the production of Nationalist Socialist propaganda. After the war, the Allies banned him from practicing his art.

JARRES, KARL

Politician

born: 21 September 1874 Remscheid, died: 20 October 1951 Duisburg

J., who had a doctorate in law, became Mayor of Remscheid in 1911 and Mayor of Duisburg in 1914. He was expelled from the Ruhr by the French occupying forces. A DVP member, he was vice-chancellor and interior minister under →Marx from 1923 to 1925. In the presidential election of 1925, he achieved a relative majority of votes with almost 39% but withdrew his candidature, which was supported by the DVP

and DNVP, in favor of →Hindenburg. In 1933, the National Socialists dismissed him as Mayor of Duisburg and he retired from politics to work in industry.

JÜNGER, ERNST

Writer

born: 29 March 1895 Heidelberg, died: 17 February 1998 Wilflingen

The most controversial author of his time, J. lived through 11 decades, eight of which spanned his career as a writer. And yet, J. is judged exclusively on what he published in the 1920s and 1930s. A lieutenant in the First World War who was awarded the *Pour le mérite*, J.'s "diary" *In Stahlgewittern* (1920) idealizes his experiences as a soldier on the front. J. supported a "national, social, well-defended and authoritatively organized" state and in 1930 he published an anti-Semitic essay. This and his glorification of war won him the support of the National Socialists, from whom, however, he soon distanced himself. In the latter years of his life he declared himself to be an "anarchist."

KÄSTNER, ERICH

Writer and Journalist

born: 23 February 1899 Dresden, died: 29 July 1974 Munich

Nowadays, K. is mainly known as an author of children's literature (*Emil und die Detektive*, 1928, *Pünktchen und Anton*, 1931, *Das fliegende Klassenzimmer*, 1932). However, it was not because of his children's stories that the Nazis burned his books. K, who saw himself as a "moralist," had attracted their disapproval with his cabaret texts, contributions in the *Weltbühne* and in the *Vossische Zeitung*, and his satirical novel *Fabian* (1931), which remains an important document of the end phase of the Weimar Republic. K.'s writings were banned and he was arrested several times. After the war, he was editor of the arts section of the *Neue Zeitung* and a youth journal. In 1957, he was awarded the Georg Büchner Prize and he was President of the West German PEN Center from 1957–62.

KAHR, GUSTAV RITTER VON

Politician

born: 29 November 1862 Weissenburg, died: 30 June 1934 Dachau

K. received his title for services to folklore and protection of monuments – this was still possible in 1911. Thus honored, he became President of Upper Bavaria, Prime Minister of Bavaria in 1920/21 and then President again. In 1923, he declared a state of emergency and fell out with the national government due to his reactionary and separatist tendencies. →Hitler forced him to keep quiet about his intended putsch on 8 November 1923 but on the following day, K. had the putsch suppressed. He was murdered in revenge by the National Socialists during the Röhm putsch.

KANDINSKY, WASSILY

Russian Painter and Art Theorist

born: 4 December 1866 Moscow, died: 13 December 1944 Neuilly-sur-Seine (France)

K. came to Munich in 1896 to study and became a student of Franz Stuck. By 1914, he had established a wide network of international contacts, founded *Der Blaue Reiter* "Blue Rider" movement with Franz Marc and →Paul Klee, and written on the theory of art. K. is one of the founders of abstract art and developed new forms and colors. He taught at the Bauhaus from 1922 up to its closure. He emigrated to France in 1933 when the Nazis came to power.

KAPP, WOLFGANG

Politician

born: 24 July 1858 New York, died: 12 June 1922 Leipzig

K., the son of an 1848 revolutionary who emigrated to the USA, did not grow up thinking that he would end up organizing a putsch in an attempt to destroy the first German Republic. He worked as a civil servant and in 1917 was co-founder of the German Fatherland Party, which rejected any form of negotiated peace. A conservative member of the Reichstag from 1917, he never recovered from the collapse of the monarchy. On 13 March 1920 he staged a coup with the support of →Lüttwitz and →Ehrhardt's troops, but he had no mass support behind him. The trade unions called for a general strike and the civil servants remained loyal to the →Bauer government. K. surrendered and fled to Sweden. He gave himself up in 1922 and died in detention. Despite its failure, the Kapp putsch revealed the weakness of the government and legal system. Few of the conspirators were prosecuted.

KESSLER, COUNT HARRY

Writer and Patron

born: 23 May 1868 Paris, died: 30 November 1937 Lyon

Although K. never held a distinguished political office nor wrote an important literary work, he is a key figure in the history of Wilhelmine and Weimar Germany. The son of an ennobled banker and an educated man of the old school, K. frequented the progressive art scene in Germany as a dealer and promoted the work of German and French Expressionists, including →Benn, →Dix, and →Grosz. As a patron, he facilitated the success of the journal *Pan*, the Insel-Verlag, and Cranach-Presse publishers. His experiences during the First World War made K. a committed pacifist. He promoted the idea of the League of Nations and German–French reconciliation. The foreign office sent him on numerous diplomatic missions, where, as a consequence of his liberal attitudes, he earned the nickname of the "Red Count." As a Republican, he opposed →Hindenburg and →Hitler and left Germany in 1933. K. wrote a biography of Rathenau, much-quoted diaries, and memoirs.

Egon Erwin Kisch

KISCH, ERWIN EGON

Journalist

born: 29 April 1885 Prague, died: 31 March 1948 Prague

After working as a local reporter on the German-language daily *Bohemia* for seven years, K. moved to Berlin in 1913. He worked as a reporter and freelance writer in Berlin until 1933 without interruption, not even during military service in the Austrian army, nor during his participation in the revolution in Vienna (commander of the "Red Guard"). K. became one of the most respected socialist journalists of his time: his contributions were published in a wide range of newspapers from the *Rote Fahne* to the *Berliner Börsen-Courier* (a financial paper). As "rampaging reporter" – a nickname taken from the title of the book which made him famous in 1925 – he founded the journalistic form of reportage in Germany and defined standards of authenticity which remain valid today, but did not necessarily keep to the neutrality he himself always demanded. He produced newspaper articles and books on his travels in the Soviet Union, USA, and China. He also published his war diary *Schreib das auf, Kisch* (1922–29) and a collection of reportages *Hetzjagd durch die Zeit* (1926). K, a member of the KPD and an early opponent of National Socialism, was arrested on the day of the Reichstag fire as a Jew and opponent of the regime. He was later released on the request of the Czech government. He participated as a reporter in the Spanish Civil War and lived in exile in Mexico from 1939 to 1946.

KLEE, PAUL

Artist

born: 18 December 1879 Münchenbuchsee (Switzerland),
died: 9 June 1940 Muralto (Switzerland)

K. concentrated on his education and traveled to Tunisia with August Macke in 1914 while his wife supported him. His experience of the North African light had a formative influence on his use of color. K.'s work became well known through major exhibitions and →Gropius invited him to the Bauhaus in 1920. However, K. did not fit in there with his mythical-surreal motifs, and he moved to the Düsseldorf Academy in 1931. While the Nazis removed over 100 of K.'s works from galleries and museums, dismissing them as "degenerate art," he continued to work on many new ones during the last years of his life in exile in Switzerland.

KLEMPERER, OTTO

Conductor

born: 14 May 1885 Breslau, died: 6 July 1973 Zurich

After working in Prague, Hamburg, Barmen, Strasbourg, Cologne, and Wiesbaden, K. was appointed conductor of the Berlin Kroll Opera in 1927. When it was closed in 1931, he worked in the State Opera on Unter den Linden. He was denounced by the Nazis not only as a Jew but also as a supporter of contemporary "degenerate" composers such as →Hindemith and →Schoenberg. He emigrated in 1933 and worked in the USA, Budapest and London as one of the most important conductors of his time.

KOLLO, (ELIMAR) WALTER

Composer

born: 28 January 1878 Neidenburg (East Prussia),
died: 30 September 1940 Berlin

K. (E. W. Kollodzieyski) founded the Berlin Operetta. His traditional farces, lyrical dramas and operettas were extremely successful during the Kaiser's era: Wie einst im Mai, Die Männer sind alle Verbrecher, 1913; Der Juxbaron, 1916. He later composed music for revues and talking movies. He provided finan-

cial security for his creative work through his activities as a co-founder of GEMA and his own music publishers.

KOLLWITZ, KÄTHE

Graphic Artist and Sculptress

born: 8 July 1867 Königsberg (now Kaliningrad), died: 22 April 1945 Moritzburg near Dresden

→Hauptmann's Weavers inspired K. (née Schmidt) to produce her cycle Ein Weberaufstand, and the major theme of her early work was the misery of the urban proletariat. A second theme, pacifism, was added when her younger son fell in the First World War (wood carving Nie wieder Krieg, 1924; the memorial Parents for the Soldiers' Cemetery in Roggefelde 1932). She was appointed professor in 1919 and was the first woman appointed to the Prussian Academy of the Arts. In 1921–24, she was involved in the international Communist aid for the Soviet Union. The National Socialists banned her work, which had achieved an international renown.

KORFF, KURT

Journalist

born: 3 October 1876 Jägerndorf (Silesia),
died: 30 January 1938 New York

K. (Kurt Karfunkel) was editor of the most successful magazine of the Weimar period, the Berliner Illustrirte Zeitung. K. was one of the first editors to recognize the importance of images for the print media, and he used photographs of documentary and general interest as well as entire photo essays in his publication. The design of the BIZ became a model for such publications throughout the world. Like →Lorant, the another key figure in the magazine sector, as a Jew K. had to flee Germany. In the USA he was involved in the development of Life and, shortly before his death, he was hired by the Hearst Group.

LABAN, RUDOLF VON

Choreographer and Dance Theorist

born: 15 December 1879 Pressburg (Bratislava), died: 1 July 1958 Weybridge (England)

L. studied ballet, acting, and painting in Paris and from 1910 founded theater and art institutions throughout Europe. He created the new expressive dance and his own dance notation "Labanotation." From 1930–34 he was director of ballet at the Berlin State Opera. In 1938, he emigrated to Britain. The Art of Movement Studio, which he founded in 1942 in Manchester, is now known as the Laban Centre and forms part of London University.

LANDAUER, GUSTAV

Philosopher, Writer, and Politician

born: 7 April 1870 Karlsruhe, died: 2 May 1919 Munich

Art critic, translator and lecturer, L. was imprisoned several times as the leading representative of humanitarian German anarchism in the 1890s. He came to Munich in November 1918 on the invitation of →Eisner and in 1919 he was People's Representative for Culture during the seven days of the first socialist republic. He was murdered by soldiers when the republic collapsed.

LANG, FRITZ

Director

born: 5 December 1890 Vienna, died: 2 August 1976 Beverly Hills (USA)

L. (Friedrich Lang) worked as a dramatist, director and author in Berlin from 1918. In the early 1920s he was the most successful German film director. He combined the dark, demonic atmosphere of the Expressionist silent movie with almost documentary impressions of the hectic metropolis of Berlin: *Der müde Tod, Dr. Mabuse, Der Spieler, Die Nibelungen.* He predicted the totalitarian National Socialist state in *Metropolis.* His best known talking movie was *M* (1931). L. declined an invitation by Goebbels to remain in Germany and emigrated to the USA.

LEGIEN, KARL

Trade Unionist

born: 1 December 1861 Marienburg (West Prussia),
died: 26 December 1920 Berlin

L., a wood turner by trade, achieved an important victory in 1906: as SPD parliamentary representative and trade union leader he succeeded in securing the independence of the trade unions from the party. He achieved equality between the trade unions and employers through the "Stinnes–L. Agreement" which was reached with →Stinnes on 15 November 1918. In 1919, L. was elected leader of the General German Trade Union Association. The general strike against the →Kapp putsch was called by L.

LIEBERMANN, MAX

Painter and Graphic Artist

born: 20 July 1847 Berlin, died: 8 February 1935 Berlin

When L. founded the Berlin Sezession in 1898/99, he was already well known as an Impressionist. He shifted gradually from craft, beach and sport scenes to portraits. L. was so successful during the Weimar period that he was able to select celebrities for his portraits. He became the president of the Prussian Academy of Art in 1920 and its honorary president in 1932. He resigned from the academy in 1933 in protest against Nazi cultural policy.

LIEBKNECHT, KARL

Politician

born: 13 August 1871 Leipzig, died: 15 January 1919 Berlin

The son of an SPD member of parliament, L. became a member of the Reichstag in 1912. He gained a reputation for his uncompromising fight against militarism, which brought him a prison sentence in 1907 for treason. He was the only SPD representative who refused to ratify the war loans in December 1914. This breach of party discipline isolated him in the party but also attracted other opponents of the war to him. He was imprisoned again for treason from 1916 to 1918. Just after his release, he proclaimed the Socialist Republic on 9 November 1918. L.'s far-reaching revolutionary aims were not realized, however, because the Majority SPD succeeded in placing itself at the head of the movement. L. became a leading member of the Spartacus League and the newly founded KPD along with Rosa →Luxemburg. At the beginning of the Spartacus Revolt in January 1919, he called for the fall of the government. When the revolt collapsed, soldiers from the volunteer corps hunted him down and murdered their defenseless prisoner.

LLOYD GEORGE, DAVID

Politician

born: 17 January 1863 Manchester, died: 26 March 1945
Llanystumdwy (Wales)

L. was a Liberal Member of Parliament for 55 years (from 1890). As Chancellor of the Exchequer (1905–15), he created a modern social legislation, and as munitions and war minister, he organized the British war economy. He became Prime Minister in 1916 but fell in 1922 because he negotiated with

Irish separatists and had alienated France and Turkey with his policy in the East. Thanks to his participation at Versailles, the terms of the treaty were somewhat less draconian than they might otherwise have been. He was knighted shortly before his death.

LORANT, STEFAN

Photo-journalist and Publisher

born: 22 February 1901 Budapest, died: 14 November 1997
Rochester (USA)

As picture editor of the *Münchner Illustrierte Presse* L. (Lóránt Istvánt) brought the photo-journalism of the late 1920s to its high point. Under L.'s influence, the bourgeois →Hugenberg publication became one of the first real magazines and reached a circulation figure of 650,000. As a committed opponent of the Nazis and a Jew, L. was imprisoned for a short term until Hungarian journalists succeeded in getting him released. L. fled to Great Britain where he became editor of the *Weekly Illustrated* in 1934. In 1938 he joined *Picture Post,* to which he succeeded in attracting such reputable photo-journalists as Tim →Gidal. In 1940 he emigrated to the USA where he worked as an editor on very successful historical illustrated books.

LUDENDORFF, ERICH (FRIEDRICH-WILHELM)

Army Officer

born: 9 April 1865 Kruszczewina (Posen),
died: 20 December 1937 Tutzing

When the German army attacked Belgium in 1914, one ambitious and aggressive brigade commander particularly distinguished himself: L. allowed his soldiers to storm the Liège citadel, for which he was awarded the *Pour le mérite.* This victory singled him out for more onerous duties: as →Hindenburg's chief of staff he defeated the Russians in East Prussia and by 1916 he was head of the army. The dynamic quartermaster-in-chief demanded a hitherto unfamiliar level of sacrifice on the part of the German population and interfered excessively in political affairs: as a supporter of the "victorious peace" he engineered the fall of the Reich Chancellor Theobald von Bethmann

Hollweg and enforced the Treaty of Brest-Litovsk. When his spring offensives on the Western Front failed, recognizing the hopeless outlook of the military situation, L. urged the politicians to offer an armistice. In this way, he deflected attention from his own responsibility and created the "legend of the stab in the back." Dismissed on 26 October 1918, he fled to Sweden where he wrote his tendentious *Kriegserinnerungen* (War memoirs). L. was openly anti-Republic and supported first →Kapp and then →Hitler. He was not punished for his participation in the Hitler putsch. He was elected to the Reichstag as a National Socialist representative. In 1925 he was defeated by his former boss Hindenburg in the election for Reich President. L. was not prepared to subject himself to Hitler and increasingly protested against his former ally. In the last years of his life he succumbed to religious sects and anti-Semitic conspiracy theories.

LÜTTWITZ, WALTHER FREIHERR VON

Army Officer
born: 2 February 1859 Bodland (Silesia),
died: 20 September 1942 Breslau

The general with the strange title of "Commander of the Troops in and around Berlin and Commander-in-chief in the Mark" adopted an equally strange tactic in 1918/19: he quashed the republican fighting and Spartacus revolt using voluntary as opposed to regular troops. He saw the revolution as a "crime." In March 1920, as one of the highest officers in the German army, he staged a coup d'etat with →Kapp. While L. established control in Berlin by military means, Kapp failed completely. L. fled to Hungary, was dismissed from office but remained otherwise unpunished for his actions.

LUTHER, HANS

Politician
born: 10 March 1879 Berlin, died: 11 May 1962 Berlin

→Cuno appointed L., the lawyer and lord mayor of Essen, as minister for food and agriculture in December 1922. L. was finance minister under →Stresemann and →Marx. He ended the hyperinflation by implementing currency reform. A "pragmatic Republican," L. was chancellor from 15 January 1925 to 12 May 1926. His achievements include tax reform and the Locarno Pact. Resigning immediately after the Locarno signings, he was quickly recalled to form a short-lived minority cabinet that fell in May 1926. In 1930 he was appointed president of the Reichsbank (Germany's central bank). →Hitler forced him to resign and sent him as ambassador to Washington from 1933 to 1937.

LUXEMBURG, ROSA

Politician
born: 5 March 1871 Zamo (Poland), died: 15 January 1919 Berlin

L. was forced to emigrate to Switzerland at the age of 18 due to her work in Jewish revolutionary circles. She completed a doctorate in economics in Switzerland. She was politically active in Germany from 1898, became a member of the SPD, and spokeswoman for the international left-wing socialists. In 1905, she participated in the Russian revolution in Warsaw. Although L. believed in proletarian revolution and did not believe in the possibility of a peaceful transition from capitalism to socialism, she did not share Lenin's view of the party as avant-garde and his demand for the dictatorship of the proletariat. She believed in the creative power of the masses and in her principle "freedom always means freedom to dissent." L. fought against nationalism, militarism and imperialism. She was imprisoned for years for pacifist agitation during the First World War. During this time she turned her back on the SPD and founded the Spartacus League with →Liebknecht in 1917 and the KPD in 1918/19, of which she was program leader. She advised against the Spartacus revolt because she felt it was too early for such action. Following the defeat of the revolt, she was murdered by soldiers from the volunteer corps (*Freikorps*).

MAN, FELIX H.

Photo-journalist
born: 30 November 1893 Freiburg, died: 30 January 1985 London

The first pictures M. (Hans Felix Sigismund Baumann) published were drawings – in 1927 he was still working as a sports artist for the newspaper *BZ am Mittag*. In the following year he went to *Tempo* as a photographer and from 1929 he allowed his photographs to be distributed by the Dephot agency. His photos were mainly published in the *Münchner Illustrierte Presse* and in the *Berliner Illustrirte Zeitung*. In 1934 he followed →Lorant to Britain and became one of the main photographers for the *Weekly Illustrated*, *Daily Mirror*, and *Picture Post*.

MANN, (LUIZ) HEINRICH

Writer
born: 27 March 1871 Lübeck, died: 12 March 1950 Santa Monica (USA)

M., who came from an upper-middle-class background, gradually evolved into a supporter of "human socialism". From 1900, he published novels dealing with contemporary issues, in which he caricatured the fawning nationalistic citizens of the Empire and later the Weimar Republic: *Im Schlaraffenland*, (*In the Land of Cockaigne*) 1900; *Der Untertan* (*The Patrioteer*) 1918; *Professor Unrat* (filmed as *The Blue Angel*) 1928. Unlike his brother Thomas M., he opposed the First World War and supported the Republic. In 1931, he became President of the literature section of the Prussian Academy. In 1933, he emigrated and continued to campaign against National Socialism through his political writing and novels such as *Lidice* (1943).

MANN, KLAUS (HEINRICH THOMAS)

Journalist and Writer
born: 18 November 1906 Munich, died: 21 May 1949 Cannes (France)

Having left school early, Klaus M. worked as a theater critic in Berlin. He founded a theater ensemble with his sister Erika and Gustaf →Gründgens, who later married Erika, and assumed an anti-fascist position from an early stage. He never forgave Gründgens for not following his lead in this and dealt with the conflict between them in his novel *Mephisto*, which was published in 1936 and was the subject of litigation for many years. He suffered increasingly from the lack of recognition from his father →Thomas M. and committed suicide by taking an overdose of sleeping tablets.

MANN, THOMAS

Writer

born: 6 June 1875 Lübeck, died: 12 August 1955 Zurich

Having abandoned his high-school education, "the vainest author of this century" Thomas M. (Marcel Reich-Ranicki), lived the bohemian high life in Munich at his father's expense. His first short stories were followed in 1901 by his first novel *The Buddenbrooks*, a description of the fall of a bourgeois family into decadence which was inspired by his own family history and won him the Nobel Prize for literature in 1929. The commercial success of the novel and marriage to a wealthy heiress in 1905 provided M. with the means to sustain his upper-middle-class lifestyle for the rest of his days. His next artistic success did not come until 1912 with the publication of *Death in Venice*, which also drew indirectly on personal experience in that the book dealt with his suppressed homosexuality. Unlike his brother Heinrich, Thomas M. greeted the First World War with enthusiasm. In 1918, he published *Reflections of an Unpolitical Man*, in which he portrayed himself as a supporter of a "conservative revolution." He did not openly support the Weimar Republic until 1922, and later campaigned on behalf of the SPD. He lived in exile from 1933 but refrained from expressing an opinion on the political situation in Germany so as not to harm sales of his books there. Only when he was deported in 1936 did he begin to speak out against →Hitler in radio broadcasts and writing. The most important work of his period in exile was *Doctor Faustus*, in which he once again showed himself to be a consummate master of the psychological novel dealing with the contradictions between life and intellect. After the war, M. allowed himself to be feted during visits to West and East Germany but he did not return to live there because he did not trust the new German democracy.

MARX, WILHELM

Politician

born: 15 January 1863 Cologne, died: 5 August 1946 Bonn

Despite heading four governments, the honest but rather dull M. has almost been forgotten. Originally a judge, he was involved in Catholic associations and elected to the Reichstag in 1910 as a representative for the Catholic Center Party, to the National Assembly in 1919, and as leader of his party in 1922–28. He was Prime Minister of Prussia for a short time in 1925 and was defeated by →Hindenburg in the election for Reich President. From November 1923 to June 1924, he led two minority governments as Chancellor and facilitated the economic and political stabilization of the Reich. M. was re-elected as Chancellor after the fall of the →Luther government, first with a minority government and then with a majority coalition involving the Catholic Center,

DNVP, DVP, and BVP parties. He was finally brought down by a Reich education act.

MASSARY, FRITZI

Singer

born: 21 March 1882 Vienna, died: 30 January 1969 Los Angeles

A native of Austria, M. (Friederike Massaryk) came to Berlin in 1904 and became one of the most popular operetta and musical stars for the next 30 years. She could guarantee full houses in all of the city's reputable theaters. After the death of her husband, Max Pallenberg, in a fatal accident in 1934, she retired from the stage. In 1938, she fled the Nazi regime and emigrated to Great Britain.

MAX, PRINZ VON BADEN

Politician

born: 10 July 1867 Baden-Baden, died: 6 November 1929 Salem (near Tübingen)

As his cousin, Grand Duke Friedrich II, remained childless, B. became heir to the Baden throne. An officer, aristocratic liberal, and philanthropist by reputation, he was responsible for the welfare of prisoners of war. He was, however, almost completely unknown when Kaiser Wilhelm appointed him Reich Chancellor and Prussian Prime Minister on 3 October 1918. Two days later he presented a peace and armistice proposal to the US President, which was based on →Wilson's "14 points." He put an end to the submarine war and supported →Ludendorff's dismissal. His cabinet was based on a majority coalition comprising the SPD, the FVP, and the Catholic Center. He collaborated with the Social Democrats in the hope of being able to save the monarchy. To prevent the outbreak of the revolution, he approved the abolition of the three-class electoral system, the democratization of the Reich, and finally the abdication of the Kaiser, which he announced of his own volition on 9 November 1918. On the same day, B. was replaced by →Ebert as Reich Chancellor.

Fritzi Massary

MEHRING, WALTER

Writer

born: 29 April 1896 Berlin, died: 3 October 1981 Zurich

Having started out as an Expressionist, M. was a co-founder of the Berlin Dada movement. In addition to writing for →Reinhardt's *Schall und Rauch* and his own political cabarets, he also published biting polemics against reaction, militarism, and National Socialism. He worked as a journalist in Paris from 1922 to 1928, after which he returned to Berlin. He fled Germany in 1933 and became a US citizen in 1942. He returned to Europe in 1953.

MEISSNER, OTTO

Civil Servant

born: 13 March 1880 Bischweiler (Alsace), died: 27 May 1953 Munich

M.'s memoir, *Staatssekretär unter Ebert, Hindenburg, Hitler* (State Secretary of under Ebert, Hindenburg, Hitler) was published in 1950. The title says it all. As a civil servant, he was able to adapt to his various rulers, and even became a minister under →Hitler in 1937. He earned his place in history as →Hindenburg's office director: he was one of those who urged the old man to appoint →Papen and later Hitler as chancellor in place of →Brüning.

MIES VAN DER ROHE, LUDWIG

Architect

born: 27 March 1886 Aachen, died: 17 August 1969 Chicago

M. was long an exponent of neo-classicism and did not develop a more modern style until the 1920s. In buildings such as the German Pavilion at the International Exhibition in Barcelona he abandoned the use of interior walls and reduced outside walls to geometrical surfaces. M. was one of the first architects to build using only steel and glass. He was director of the Bauhaus from 1930 to 1933. In 1937, he emigrated to the USA where he caused great excitement with his "glass skyscrapers."

MOHOLY-NAGY, LASZLO

Painter and Photographer

born: 20 July 1895 Bácsbarsod (Hungary), died: 24 November 1946 Chicago

Although M.'s photos represent only a small part of his work, they had a strong influence on the new photography. He experimented with perspectives and techniques: he was one of the first to take photographs from the bird's-eye and worm's-eye view and he also took photos without a camera ("photogrammes") by placing objects on strips of film and exposing them to light. He came to Berlin in 1920 where he came into contact with Dadaists and Constructivists. In addition to photography, he worked on sculptures, drawings and design. He taught at the Bauhaus from 1923 to 1928 and fled Germany in 1934. In Chicago, he founded the Institute of Design which he modeled on the Bauhaus.

MOSSE, RUDOLF

Publisher

born: 8 May 1843 Grätz (Posen), died: 8 September 1920 Gut Schenkendorf (Mark)

Having served an apprenticeship as a bookseller, M. laid the foundation stone for his media empire with an advertising sales office in Berlin. He invested the profit from the sale of his newspaper supplement in 1871 in the left-liberal newspaper *Berliner Tageblatt*, which became one of Germany's most respected newspapers under M's nephew →Wolff. He later also acquired the *Berliner Morgenzeitung* and the *Berliner Volkszeitung*, in addition to address and telephone directories. Along with →Ullstein, one of the most important newspaper publishers in Berlin, M. also made a name for himself as a patron. Unlike the Ullsteins, however, Mosse had an open and self-confident attitude to his Jewish origins. The M. family was forced by the National Socialists to surrender its assets in 1933.

MÜHSAM, ERICH

Writer

born: 6 April 1878 Berlin, died: 11 July 1934 Oranienburg Concentration Camp

Before the First World War, the anarchist M. led a bohemian life in Munich, writing satires and songs and later dramas and essays. He was imprisoned during the war as a conscientious objector and pacifist and in 1919–24 for his participation in the Munich socialist republic. Following his release, he edited the anarchist journal *Fanal*, in which he campaigned against fascism and class bias in the legal system. M. was killed in Oranienburg as one of the foremost opponents of the Nazi regime.

MÜLLER, HERMANN

Politician

born: 18 May 1876 Mannheim, died 20 March 1931 Berlin

M. initially worked as a journalist. He was elected to the SPD party executive in 1906 and sent on diplomatic missions by the party. He joined the Reichstag in 1916. As a socialist censor of *Vorwärts*, M. was once beaten up by left-wing workers. In 1918, he joined →Braun's Berlin Workers' and Soldiers' Council, supported the National Assembly, and rejected the Spartacists' demand for a socialist republic. He was appointed joint leader of the SPD with Otto Wels in 1919. As foreign minister in the →Bauer cabinet, he had the task of signing the Versailles Treaty. He replaced Bauer as chancellor after the →Kapp putsch but had to resign after just 72 days due to the defeat in the Reichstag elections. In 1928, he became Chancellor of the last Weimar government with a parliamentary majority based on a Grand Coalition of the SPD, Catholic Center, DVP, DDP, and BVP. His greatest achievement was the acceptance of the Young Plan. The coalition finally fell in 1930 over the reform of unemployment benefit. As the cabinets that followed did not have any democratic legitimization, M's downfall is seen as the beginning of the end of the Weimar Republic.

MÜNZENBERG, WILLY

Journalist and Politician
born: 14 August 1889 Erfurt, died: probably 22 June 1940
South of France

From 1906 M., an innkeeper's son, was active in the socialist working-class youth movement. In 1910, M. (Wilhelm) went to Switzerland; in 1915 he organized an international socialist youth conference in Berlin and was elected secretary by its participants. Following encounters with Lenin he joined the Communists and campaigned against the war. Expelled to Germany in 1918, he joined the Spartacus League in Berlin and the KPD in 1919. Lenin gave him the task of establishing the *Internationale Arbeiterhilfe* (International Workers' Aid), which collected donations for starving Russian children. As editor, M. made the IAH journal into the cornerstone of the quickly expanding *Neuer Deutscher Verlag* (New German Publishers), to which film production companies and the *Arbeiter Illustrierte Zeitung* belonged. The "Red newspaper tsar" put his empire at the service of anti-capitalist and anti-militarist propaganda. He was a member of the Reichstag from 1924 to 1933. After 1933, he was forced to continue his work in exile in France. In 1939, M. was expelled from the KPD as an opponent of Stalin. M. met with a mysterious death in 1940 while fleeing from the German army in France.

MUNKÁCSI, MARTIN

Photo-journalist
born: 18 May 1896 Klausenburg (Transylvania),
died: 14 July 1963 New York

The Hungarian photo-journalist (M. Marmorstein) came to Berlin to work for Ullstein in 1927. His photographs appeared inter alia in the *Berliner Illustrirte Zeitung* and the *Dame*, and also in foreign publications. A Jew, M. had to leave Germany in 1934. In the USA, M. became the best-paid fashion photographer of the 1940s, working mainly for *Harper's Bazaar* and *Life*. He revolutionized the previous artificial rigidity of fashion photography using extreme angles of vision, open-air photography, and the spontaneous effect of models in movement. His

experience as a sport photographer in Berlin was useful here. Although M. is viewed as one of the pioneers of photo-journalism, his photographs were never exhibited as a collection during his lifetime.

MURNAU, FRIEDRICH WILHELM

Director
born: 28 December 1888 Bielefeld, died: 11 March 1931
Santa Barbara (USA)

→Reinhardt discovered M. (Plumpe) in a student production and brought him into his ensemble. After his war service, M. moved to film: he made 14 (now mostly lost) films between 1919 to 1923, the best known of which was *Nosferatu, eine Symphonie des Grauens. Der letzte Mann*, made in 1924, was

distinguished by Jannings's outstanding performance and the use of the "unbound camera." From 1926, M. also worked in the USA. The films he directed there included *Taboo* (1929), filmed in Tahiti: he was killed in an accident before its premiere.

NIELSEN, ASTA

Actress
born: 11 September 1885 Copenhagen, died: 25 May 1972
Fredericksberg (Denmark)

N., who was one of the biggest starts of German silent movies, was born into a poor Danish family. She attended drama school in Copenhagen and came to Berlin in 1910. She mainly played demanding tragic or demonic leading ladies (*Die arme Jenny*, 1911, *Die*

freudlose Gasse, 1925). In the late 1920s, she performed mostly on the stage. She returned to Denmark in 1937, where she soon retired from acting.

NOSKE, GUSTAV

Politician
born: 9 July 1868 Brandenburg,
died: 30 November 1946 Hanover

"Someone has to be the bloodhound" – these were the most famous words that N. ever uttered. N. played "bloodhound" so enthusiastically in 1918–20 that he remains one of the most unpopular Social Democrats in history. The former basket-maker became a journalist and in 1906 a military expert for the SPD Reichstag parliamentary party. N. pursued a clear nationalist and imperialist line in parliament. In November 1918, the party leader sent him as governor to Kiel to quash the sailors' revolt. N. was also responsible for military issues in the Council of People's Representatives; his first act in office was to form a troop, the

Freikorps (voluntary corps) with the help of which he defeated the Spartacus revolt and the Bremen socialist republic. Having been appointed defense minister in the meantime, he imposed martial law in Berlin in March 1919 and allowed strikers to be shot. His policy of mass retaliation discredited N. among the working class. He was betrayed by the military during the →Kapp putsch and had to resign. He was President of Hanover from 1920 to 1933.

ONDRA, ANNY

Actress

born: 15 May 1902 Tarnow (Galicia), died: 28 February 1987 Hollenstedt (near Hamburg)

A Czech comedienne, O. also made films in Germany and Great Britain, including the film *Blackmail* with Alfred Hitchcock. In the 1930s, she was director of her own film production company the Ondra-Lamac-Filmgesellschaft. O. (*Die vom Rummelplatz, Der Scheidungsgrund*) married world boxing champion Max Schmeling in 1933.

ORSKA, MARIA

Actress

born: 16 March 1893 Nikolajew (Russia), died: 16 May 1930 Vienna

A woman of fiery personality, O. (Rahel Blindermann) had major successes in the Viennese theater between 1909 and 1920 as Salome and Queen Christina. She gained a reputation as the most important interpreter of the work of Oscar Wilde and Frank Wedekind. She often made guest appearances in Germany, Paris, and Scandinavia. O. committed suicide in 1930.

OSSIETZKY, CARL VON

Journalist

born: 3 October 1889 Hamburg, died: 4 April 1938 Berlin

O. studied law but failed to qualify and worked as a clerk. Following the Battle of Verdun he became a pacifist and in 1919 he became secre-

tary of the German Peace Society. From 1922, he worked as editor of the *Berliner Volkszeitung*, where he met →Tucholsky. He was dismissed in 1924 because he had stood for election as a candidate for the – unsuccessful – pacifist–radical democratic Republican Party. From 1926, he gained his reputation as an important journalist and editor of the *Weltbühne*. This "weekly publication for politics, art, economics" had considerable influence on the left-wing intellectuals of the Weimar period, of which some (like Tucholsky) provided regular contributions. Despite low circulation and attacks on the majority parties, the journal became the radical–democratic conscience of the Weimar Republic. Ossietzky's critical attitude to militarism and nationalism resulted in him being brought before the courts five times; he was imprisoned for several months in 1932 for an article about the secret re-armament of the German army. He was imprisoned again as an anti-fascist after the Reichstag fire. As a result of an international campaign, the prisoner was awarded the Nobel Prize for Peace in 1936, but was not released. O. died as a result of his imprisonment.

PABST, G. W. (GEORG WILHELM)

Director

born: 27 August 1885 Raudnitz (Bohemia), died: 29 May 1967 Vienna

P. began his career as an actor in Austria, Germany, and Switzerland. He made his directorial debut in 1912 at the German Volks Theater in New York. He was interned in France on his way back to Germany, as the First World War had just started. The advent of the Second World War also surprised him in 1939, thwarting his plans to return to the USA. His most important creative phase lay between these events. He started working as a film director in 1923 and quickly became the main proponent of the New Objectivity movement. In 1925, he had his first film success with *Die freudlose Gasse* (with →Dietrich and →Nielsen). His talking movies *Westfront 1918* (1930) and *The Threepenny Opera* (1931) were popular and critical successes. He lived in France and Hollywood from 1933 to 1938. During the Second World War he worked in Munich and after the war he founded his own film company in Vienna, whose productions included *Es geschah am 20. Juli* (1955).

PAPEN, FRANZ VON

Politician

born: 29 July 1879 Werl, died: 2 May 1969 Obersasbach (Baden)

P., a professional soldier was never able to come to terms with the collapse of the monarchy. As a royalist with good contacts with conservative landowners and industrialists, he was elected to the Prussian regional parliament in 1921. Despite his sympathies for the right-wing DNVP, he joined the Catholic Center Party. His most pressing aims were to drive the SPD out of government in Prussia and reverse social reforms. P. wanted to form a right-wing government including the Catholic Center and NSDAP. He failed to win support for this idea in his own party and resigned from the party. With the support of →Schleicher and →Hindenburg, P. became Reich Chancellor in a "cabinet of Barons" in June 1932, which did not have democratic legitimatization. As chancellor, P. lifted the ban on the SA and SS; in July he dismissed the →Braun Prussian government and assumed power himself. Neither P.'s ministers nor Schleicher were in favor of any other anti-democratic steps and P. was replaced in December by Schleicher. P. got his revenge by plotting with NS-friendly business circles and the old elite against Schleicher and persuaded →Hindenburg to agree on a Hitler–Papen cabinet. Vice-chancellor P. hoped to use →Hitler to achieve his own political ends, but he was dispatched on ambassadorial postings from 1934, first to Vienna and then to Ankara, where he served the Nazi regime until 1944. He was tried and found not guilty at Nuremberg.

PIECK, WILHELM

Politician

born: 3 January 1876 Guben, died: 7 September 1960 Berlin

P., who was originally a carpenter, lost his position as secretary of the SPD party school due to protests he organized against the First World War. Conscripted in 1916, he deserted and did not reappear in public life until the beginning of the November Revolution. He worked at the headquarters of the Spartacus League and

was a co-founder of the KPD. During the Weimar period, P. was a member of the Prussian regional parliament and the Reichstag. Exiled from 1933, he represented the Communist Party leader Ernst →Thälmann, who was imprisoned in Germany. He returned to Germany after the war where he became leader of the East German Communist Party (SED) and the first president of the GDR.

PISCATOR, ERWIN (FRIEDRICH MAX)

Director
born: 17 December 1895 Ulm, died: 30 March 1966 Starnberg

Having served on the front, P. joined the Dada movement and Spartacus League in Berlin. In 1920, he founded the Proletarian Theater for the Propagation of Communism through Agit-Prop and Didactic Plays. He put his motto "art is a political weapon" into action as director of the Central Theater and the Volksbühne. In 1927, he opened his own theater on Nollendorfplatz which, despite sophisticated technology ("total theater" with revolving stage, lighting effects, film and slide projection) and reputable authors such as →Brecht, →Toller, and →Mehring, went bankrupt three times. P. failed to resolve the contradiction of staging proletarian theater to middle-class audiences. He lived in exile from 1933 to 1951. He remained loyal to the aims of political theater as director of the Freie Volksbühne in West Berlin (from 1962) where he directed the premieres of Rolf Hochhuth's *Stellvertreter*, Heinar Kipphardt's *In der Sache J. Robert Oppenheimer* and Peter Weiss' *Ermittlung*.

PLANCK, MAX (KARL ERNST LUDWIG)

Physicist
born: 23 April 1858 Kiel, died: 4 October 1947 Göttingen

Along with →Einstein, P. revolutionized the world of physics around the turn of the 20th century: with his quantum physics he proved that light and heat are not emitted continuously but in small spurts or quanta. In addition to the discovery of the "Planck quantum," the other

Max Planck   Albert Einstein

great service he did to science was to recognize the importance of Einstein. P. received the Nobel Prize in 1918. During the Weimar period he was inter alia president of the Kaiser Wilhelm Society for the Promotion of the Sciences, which was re-established in the Federal Republic of Germany as the Max Planck Institute.

RATHENAU, WALTHER

Industrialist and Politician
born: 29 September 1867 Berlin, died: 24 June 1922 Berlin

As a Jew, R. was barred from becoming an army officer. Instead he started working in his father's company AEG and became its president in 1915. During the First World War, he organized the supply of raw materials for the armaments industry. In →Harden's journal *Zukunft* and his own writings (*Von kommenden Dingen*, 1917), R. provided a theoretical framework for a world of cooperative capital as opposed to the authoritarian Wilhelmine state and demanded economic and constitutional reform to facilitate the development of the technological age. R., who sat on the advisory boards of approximately 100 companies, was also a member of the oligarchy of – as he himself described it – "300 men who all know each other" who controlled the economy of Europe. His contradictory philosophical and political positions left him open to attack from all sides. Thus, he did not succeed in launching a political career until 1921. R. became a member of the German Democratic Party (DDP) executive, minister of reconstruction in 1921, and foreign minister under →Wirth in 1922. He concluded the Wiesbaden Agreement with France, which obliged Germany to make reparations in kind to the French. In the interest of the economy and in view of the futility of new conflicts with the

Allies, R. became the "politician of appeasement." At the Genoa world economic conference he failed to achieve any reduction in reparation demands for Germany. For rational as opposed to ideological reasons he entered the Treaty of Rapallo with the Soviet Union in 1922, which brought an end to the international political isolation of both states and initiated their close economic – and secretly also military – collaboration. The Rapallo Treaty made R. an increasing target for nationalistic, anti-Communist, and anti-Semitic attacks. On the day after DNVP politician Karl Helfferich reviled R. in a speech, he was shot by members of Ehrhardt's "Consul" organization. His funeral was accompanied by large pro-Republican demonstrations.

REINHARDT, MAX

Actor and Director
born: 9 September 1873 Baden (Austria), died: 31 October 1943 New York

R. (Goldmann) made his debut as an actor in the role of an old man at the age of 17. In 1894, he came to the Deutsches Theater in Berlin, founded the cabaret *Schall und Rauch* (later Kleines Theater) and took over as director of the Neues Theater. He made the headlines in 1905 by putting a real forest on the stage for a naturalistic production of *A Midsummer's Night Dream*. As well as being director of the Kammerspiele (chamber plays) from 1906, he

was director of the Deutsches Theater from 1905 to 1920 and from 1924 to 1933. Consequently, almost every prominent actor of the Weimar period worked under R. at some point. With his distinctive feel for atmosphere and his sensitive guidance of actors, he was responsible for the development of the pivotal role of the director in the theater. R. was no theorist and yet he revolutionized the theater by introducing sensory forms of play and using new venues (such as the circus). His experiments may have been too daring for some tastes but, in comparison with the new political theater (→Piscator), R. seemed conventional because he understood art as an apolitical "neutral country." In 1920, R. went to Austria where he directed the Salzburg Festival. He also directed the theater in Josefstadt in Vienna and founded a school of acting, the Max Reinhardt Seminar. He returned to Berlin in 1924 and resumed his role as director of his theater companies until he emigrated in 1933.

REMARQUE, ERICH MARIA

Writer

born: 22 June 1898
Osnabrück,
died: 25 September 1970
Locarno

R.'s (Erich Paul Remark) experiences during his service at the front in 1918 had a profound effect on him and dominated his literary output. After the war, R. also worked as an editor and published short pieces of prose and poems. He quickly achieved international renown in 1929 with the publication of his anti-war novel *All Quiet on the Western Front* (filmed in 1930). His realistic portrayal of the horrors of trench warfare was one of the most debated literary events of the Weimar period and was a complete contrast to the work of →Jünger. The success of the book enabled R. to develop a luxurious lifestyle but also brought him enormous hostility from the right. His books were burned in 1933 as a "literary betrayal of the soldiers in the World War." He was deported by the Nazis in 1938 and forced to spend the rest of his life between the USA and Switzerland. He became a US citizen in 1947. His subsequent anti-fascist and anti-militarist novels (*Drei Kameraden*, 1938, *Arc de Triomphe*, 1946) were commercial successes but did not have the outstanding literary quality of *All Quiet on the Western Front*.

RUGE, WILLI

Photo-journalist

born: 23 October 1892 Berlin, died: 6 November 1961 Offenburg

Ruge was a sensational reporter with a passion for flying. He photographed his own legs while doing a parachute jump and documented two world wars as a Luftwaffe photographer. He also documented the Spartacus revolt from an airplane. His entire archive was destroyed by bombing in Berlin in 1943. After 1945, he worked inter alia for the Burda-Verlag publishing house. He placed advertisements in many newspapers, including American ones, in an effort to find the originals or at least copies of his lost work (particularly from the *Berliner Illustrirte*).

RUTTMANN, WALTER

Director

born: 28 December 1875 Frankfurt/Main,
died: 15 July 1941 Berlin

Originally a painter and friend of →Klee, R. turned to film in 1919 and directed *Opus I*, the first abstract German cartoon in color. His best known work was *Berlin – Symphony of a Metropolis* (1927), a pictorial essay about 24 hours in the life of the city of Berlin filmed in the style of the New Objectivity from unorthodox points of view (e.g. from an advertising column). R. later filmed war propaganda.

SALOMON, ERICH

Photo-journalist

born: 28 April 1886 Berlin, died: 7 July 1944 Auschwitz Concentration Camp

No other photographer had more influence on the development of photo-journalism than S., a doctor of law and former car rental agent and stockbroker. S. came to photography at the mature age of almost 40 years. From 1925, he worked for →Ullstein, mainly on the *Berliner Illustrirte Zeitung*, and from 1928 as a freelance; he also worked for the *Münchner Illustrierte Presse*, *Life* and the *Daily Telegraph*. S. used his Ermanox camera with its photo-sensitive lens (he later moved on to a Leica) to be able to work in interior spaces without a flash. In terms of authenticity and spontaneity, photos produced in

this way were far superior to previous press photography. However, S's outstanding work rested not only on his clever use of the technology but above all on his ability to be everywhere without being perceived as a photographer, giving newspaper and magazine readers access to a whole new world of the courts, diplomatic summits, Reichstag and League of Nations sessions, for S. often worked with a concealed camera. The London journal *Graphic* coined the term "candid camera" in reference to his method. His book *Berühmte Zeitgenossen in unbewachten Augenblicken* (Famous contemporaries in unguarded moments) was published in 1931. As a Jew, S. had to emigrate to Holland, from whence he was deported to the Theresienstadt concentration camp in 1943 and murdered with his family in Auschwitz in 1944.

SANDER, AUGUST

Photographer

born: 17 November 1876 Herdorf (Siegerland),
died: 20 April 1964 Cologne

A photographer, Sander worked for more than four decades on his photo collection *Men of the Twentieth Century*, a systematic and enclyopedic account of German society comprising a comprehensive series of portraits. Parts of this work were published in the volume *Antlitz der Zeit (Face of the Time)* in 1929 with a foreword by →Döblin. He also worked on landscape and architectural photography. His surviving work is housed in the *August Sander Archive* in Cologne.

SCHACHT, (HORACE GREELEY) HJALMAR

Banker and Politician
born: 22 January 1877
Tingleff (North Schleswig),
died: 3 June 1970 Munich

After his economics studies, S., an extremely ambitious and talented son of a businessman, quickly rose in the ranks of the Dresdner Bank, becoming director in 1916. In 1920 he became owner of the Nationalbank für Deutschland. In 1923, his friend →Stresemann appointed him as currency commissioner to tackle the problem of hyperinflation, and in the same year, S. became President of the Reichsbank, the German central bank. With the help of the currency reform prepared by →Luther, he ended the most serious period of inflation ever experienced in German history. S. resigned in 1930 in protest against the acceptance of the Young Plan. Originally a co-founder of the left–liberal German Democratic Party (DDP), S. moved more and more to the right and resigned from the DDP in 1926. He assisted in the establishment of the "Harzburg Front" and helped to make →Hitler acceptable in industrial and financial circles. He served as Reichsbank President under Hitler from 1933 to 1939, economics minister from 1934 to 1937, and general representative for defense finance from 1935 to 1937. S. generated the resources required by Hitler for armament but disagreed with Hitler and →Göring about the way it should be financed; up to 1943, he was a minister without a portfolio. He was imprisoned in a concentration camp after the attempted assassination of Hitler on 20 July 1944 and was acquitted at the post-war Nuremberg Trials.

SCHEIDEMANN, PHILIPP

Politician
born: 26 July 1865 Kassel,
died: 29 November 1939
Copenhagen

S.'s humorous and ironic memoirs draw attention from the fact that the journalist was one of the most prominent German politicians for a decade. He became one of the three SPD parliamentary party leaders in 1913. Elected as party leader along with →Ebert in 1917, he expressed his support for a "negotiated peace." He was Secretary of State in →Max von Baden's government. To prevent the establishment of a socialist republic, S. demanded the abdication of the Kaiser and declared the Republic on 9 November 1918. Along with Ebert, the popular and rhetorically talented politician was a leading force in the Council of People's Representatives. He led a coalition of the SPD, DDP, and Catholic Center as Prime Minister from February to June 1919. He resigned in protest against the "infamous" conditions of the Treaty of Versailles. From 1920 to 1925, he was mayor of his home town of Kassel, but was still a member of the Reichstag. Just as he had fought against left-wing extremism, he now warned against the swing to the right in the Republic; in a controversial speech in 1925, he disclosed the secret cooperation between the German army, the Red Army and radical right-wing military groups. He survived an attempt on his life by the Consul organization (→Ehrhardt) and fled Germany in 1933.

SCHICKELE, RENÉ

Journalist and Writer
born: 4 August 1883 Oberehnheim (Alsace), died: 31 January 1940 Vence (France)

A journalist, S. founded the pacifist Expressionist journal *Weisse Blätter* in Switzerland during the First World War. He worked in Germany again from 1919 and emigrated to France in 1932. The theme of his work was the bridging of German–French hostility to form a culturally unified Europe. He wrote poetry, novels (*Symphonie für Jazz*, 1929) and translations, sometimes under the pseudonym Sascha.

SCHLAGETER, ALBERT LEO

Militarist and Assassin
born: 12 August 1894 Schönau (Black Forest),
died: 26 May 1923 Golzheimer Heide near Düsseldorf

An army volunteer and lieutenant during the First World War, S. could not come to terms with the defeat of the Empire. As a member of the volunteer corps, the *Freikorps*, he fought in the Baltic, the Ruhr, and in Upper Silesia. When French troops occupied the Ruhr in 1923, S. went underground and organized acts of sabotage. He was sentenced to death by a French court-martial for an attack on a railway line. His shooting made the NSDAP member a martyr – and not only for the German right.

SCHLEICHER, KURT VON

Militarist and Politician
born: 7 April 1882 Brandenburg, died: 30 June 1934 Neubabelsberg

S.'s importance must not be judged by the fact that he was chancellor for only 57 days in 1932. He was a member of the Supreme Army Command and a colleague of →Groener and later →Noske. After →Seeckt's dismissal in 1926, Colonel S. was the most important military man in the country. When his patron Groener took over the defense ministry, S. began his precipitous rise in politics: he was promoted early, won the trust of →Hindenburg, and, as a "political general," and thanks to his excellent contacts in political and economic circles, he was one

of the most influential men in Germany from 1929 to 1932. S. pursued the same goal as the "apolitical" Seeckt: the secret rearmament of Germany with circumvention of the terms of the Versailles Treaty. However, in his efforts to attain this goal, he disassociated himself from Seeckt's political "neutrality" and deliberately influenced political decisions through the office of minister for politics, which was created for him. He remained in the background as a string-puller while engineering the appointments of →Brüning and →Papen as chancellor. As defense minister in Papen's cabinet, S. was responsible for the coup d'etat against the SPD government in Prussia. Disappointed by Papen, he formed a presidential cabinet in December 1932. He tried in vain to enter an alliance with the trade unions and the →Strasser wing of the NSDAP. →Hindenburg refused S's demand to abandon the constitution. S. then freed the way for →Hitler to become Chancellor. He was murdered by Hitler's SS a year and a half later.

SCHOENBERG, ARNOLD (FRANZ WALTER)

Composer
born: 13 September 1874 Vienna,
died: 13 July 1951 Los Angeles

An autodidact, S. revolutionized composition techniques. An Expressionist to begin with, he later discovered atonality. The "emancipation of dissonance" led to his twelve-tone technique, the basis of which he developed in Vienna between 1920 and 1923. The new method defined a specific sequence of all 12 tones of the tonal system for each piece of music which was retained throughout the entire piece. From 1926, he taught composition at the Prussian Academy of the Arts in Berlin. In 1933, he went into exile in the USA. His most famous works include the opera *Moses and Aron* (1930–32) and the oratorio *Ein Überlebender aus Warschau* (1947).

SEECKT, HANS VON

Army Officer
born: 22 April 1866 Schleswig, died: 27 December 1935 Berlin

The creator of the Reichswehr or German army was controversial even during his lifetime. →Tucholsky praised his cleverness and farsightedness but also declared him to be "as slippery as an eel and impenetrable," which led to the nickname, "Sphinx." Streets are still named after him and efforts to have them renamed in some towns and cities governed by the SPD are usually unsuccessful. S. participated in the First World War as a

general staff officer. In 1919, he was head of the troops bureau in the defense ministry and the following year was commander-in-chief. Despite this prominent position in the service of the Republic, S. remained a monarchist. He circumvented the Versailles treaty and formed the German army as a specialist army of professionals which would be filled up with volunteers in the event of a war. He organized the army as a "state within the state" and kept it as remote from politics and the Republic as possible. He refused to act for or against →Kapp ("Reichswehr does not shoot at Reichswehr"). →Ebert authorized him to act against the →Hitler putsch and left-wing revolts from November 1923 to March 1924. He was dismissed after a row with defense minister Otto Gessler in 1926. He was a DVP representative in the Reichstag from 1930 to 1932. As a co-initiator of the "Harzburg Front" (1931) he helped make the NSDAP politically acceptable. He acted as a military adviser to the Chinese Nationalist Chiang Kai-Shek from 1934 to 1935.

SELDTE, FRANZ

Politician
born: 29 June 1882 Magdeburg, died: 1 April 1947 Fürth

The fact that he lost an arm in the First World War did not prevent S. from founding the nationalist and militarist *Stahlhelm Bund deutscher Frontsoldaten* ("Steel Helmet Association of German Front Soldiers") in 1918. From 1924, he was leader of Stahlhelm with Theodor Duesterberg (born: 19 October 1875 Darmstadt, died: 4 November 1950 Hameln). In 1931, he led the Stahlhelm into the Harzburg Front. While Duesterberg, who received 2.56 million votes as DNVP candidate in the presidential election of 1932, rejected the NSDAP's "coordination" measures and was hence forced to resign and imprisoned for a short time after the Röhm putsch, S. authorized the integration of the

Franz Seldte   Theodor Duesterberg

Stahlhelm into the SA. S. was minister for labor under →Hitler from 1933 to 1945. He died in prison before being tried for war crimes.

SEVERING, (WILHELM) CARL

Trade Unionist and Politician
born: 1 June 1875 Herfold, died: 23 July 1952 Bielefeld

S. had the typical career of a Social Democrat of his time. He started out as the son of a cigar worker, trained as a fitter, and became a trade union secretary in Switzerland. He then became editor of a Social Democratic newspaper and was a member of the Reichstag from 1907 to 1912 and 1920 to 1923. He was a member of the National Assembly in 1919. As a colleague of →Noske, he was responsible for the overthrow of the Red Ruhr Army in 1920. He was a member of the Prussian parliament or Reich interior minister almost throughout the Weimar period and was a particularly vehement opponent of the KPD. He was dismissed in 1932 by →von Papen and →Braun.

STERNBERG, JOSEF VON

Director
born: 29 May 1894 Vienna, died: 22 December 1969
Hollywood (USA)

After his literature studies, S. (Jonas S.) grew weary of his native city and went to Hollywood where he initially worked as a cutter and assistant. He made his first film *The Salvation*

Hunters in 1925. He discovered Marlene →Dietrich and made her into a world star in his first talking movie, the UFA production *The Blue Angel* based on a novel by Heinrich →Mann. He returned to Hollywood with Dietrich where they made more films together, including *Morocco* (1930), *Blonde Venus* (1932) and *Shanghai Express*.

STINNES, HUGO

Industrialist
born: 12 February 1870 Mülheim/Ruhr,
died: 10 April 1924 Berlin

S. was seen as the prototype of the contemporary industrialist. As a self-made man, he built a mining and energy conglomerate out of nothing and never hesitated to openly exercise his political influence. Through rationalization measures and tight organization in his companies, he achieved high levels of productivity and increased his profits, which he used to buy even more companies. In 1902, he took over as Director of the Supervisory Council of the Rhenish-Westphalian Electricity Works in Essen. By 1910 he had built a business empire. During the First World War, as one of the spokesmen of industry, he demanded an uncompromising peace based on annexation and exploited the Belgian coal and steel industry. When the Empire collapsed, he entered an agreement for tactical reasons with the trade unions through →Legien. During the inflation period, S. succeeded in gaining stakes in over 1,600 companies in a wide range of sectors and established the basis for his infamous reputation as a war and inflation profiteer. His company, Seimens-Rhein-Elbe-Schuckert-Union, disbanded two years after his death.

STRASSER, GREGOR AND OTTO

Politicians
Gregor: born: 31 May 1892 Geisenfeld, died: 30 June 1934 Berlin
Otto: born: 10 September 1897 Windsheim,
died: 27 August 1974 Munich

Like his brother Otto, Gregor became a member of the volunteer corps after his service at the war front and took part in the overthrow of the Munich socialist republic. He joined the NSDAP in 1921, formed the SA, and took part in the

Gregor Strasser

Otto Strasser

→Hitler putsch. After a short term in prison, he became party propaganda manager in 1926–27, and organization manager of the NSDAP in 1928–32. The Strasser brothers formed a "national Bolshevist" opposition against Hitler within the party. Otto resigned from the party in 1930 and founded the competing "Fighting Association of Revolutionary National Socialists," later known as the "Black Front." →Schleicher tried in vain to split the NSDAP with the help of the Strassers. Gregor resigned from all party offices in 1932 and was murdered in 1934 during the Röhm putsch. His brother fled the country and continued to fight against Hitler. He founded an unsuccessful political party in the Federal Republic of Germany in 1956.

STRESEMANN, GUSTAV

Politician
born: 10 May 1878 Berlin, died: 3 October 1929 Berlin

One of the most popular riddles of the Weimar Republic was: "What would have happened if S. had lived longer?" What is certain is that S. worked himself to death and that he was one of the most charismatic democratic statesmen of his time – a time when charismatic and democratic statesmen were in short supply in Germany. S. rose from a humble background to obtain a doctorate in economics at the age of 22, become a union official at 25, and a representative of the National Liberal Party in the Reichstag at 29. During the First World War, S. supported annexation. For this reason his application for membership was rejected by the DDP. Thus, on 15 December 1918, he founded the right–liberal DVP, whose leader he remained to his death. S. was aware that the DVP did not enjoy mass support and came to terms at an early stage with the idea of forming an alliance

with other bourgeois parties and the SPD. He reluctantly acknowledged that there was no going back to a monarchy. He placed his hopes in foreign policy successes, such as the softening of the terms of the Versailles treaty, to re-unite the torn nation. In 1923, he was Chancellor and foreign minister in a DVP–SPD–Catholic-Center–DDP coalition for 100 days. S. ended the Ruhr revolt, gave →Seeckt the power to use violence and had the →Hitler putsch quashed. His government ended the hyperinflation through currency reform. He resigned as Chancellor over a dispute with the SPD ministers but remained in office as foreign minister. He negotiated the Treaty of Locarno with →Briand in 1925, for which both received the Nobel Peace Prize. S. secured Germany's access to the League of Nations in 1926.

TAUT, BRUNO

Architect
born: 4 May 1880 Königsberg (now Kaliningrad),
died: 24 December 1938 Ankara

T. had an architectural practice with his brother Max (born: 15 May 1884 Königsberg (now Kaliningrad), died: 26 February 1967 Berlin) from 1912. As editor of the journal *Frühlicht*, he was one of the early defenders of Expressionist architecture. In 1920, he became involved in the New Architecture. Promoted to head architect of the non-profit-making housing association in Berlin, he reformed residential architecture and built some 10,000 apartments. He was appointed Professor at the Technical University in 1930 and a member of the Prussian Academy of the Arts in 1931. From 1932, he worked abroad and his last post was as a university lecturer in Istanbul. He produced important theoretical writings on architecture. Max T. was mainly known for his work on office buildings. He founded the College of Visual Art in Berlin in 1945 and from 1955 was director of the architecture department at the Academy of the Arts.

THÄLMANN, ERNST
(FRITZ JOHANNES)

Politician
born: 16 April 1886 Hamburg, died: 18 August 1944
Buchenwald Concentration Camp

An uneducated dock worker, energetic, articulate and a trade-union activist, T. was the textbook working-class hero. A deserter, he moved from the SPD to the Independent SPD in 1918 and on to the KPD in 1920. T., who was

particularly popular in Hamburg, quickly rose within the party ranks. He was a member of the Reichstag from 1924 to 1932 and represented the party in the presidential elections of 1925 and 1932. He was elected party leader in 1925, from which time he also represented German Communists on the international stage. T. belonged to the left wing of the KPD. He was loyal to Stalin and had his personal support. The party received up to six million votes (1932) under his leadership. He viewed the SPD "social fascists" as the party's main enemy but also organized the opposition against the NSDAP. He was arrested on 3 March 1933, detained in solitary confinement, imprisoned for years, and finally murdered in Buchenwald concentration camp.

THYSSEN, FRITZ

Industrialist
born: 9 September 1873 Styrum (now Mülheim/Ruhr),
died: 8 February 1951 Buenos Aires

The son of the founder of the Thyssen business empire August T., Fritz T. joined the family business in 1882. After his father's death in 1926 he took over the Thyssen Group and also became trust director of the Vereinigte Stahlwerke (United Steelworks), of which he was a cofounder. He became involved in politics in order to influence social developments after the Revolution of 1918. He provided financial support for →Ludendorff to the tune of 100,000 Reichmarks and in this way financed the →Hitler putsch. He was the first major industrialist to provide financial support for the NSDAP from 1923, promoted Hitler in industrial circles and later became a party member. He wrote to →Hindenburg in 1932 demanding that he appoint Hitler as chancellor. Hitler made him Prussian State Councilor and a Reichstag member. T. clashed with →Göring as he disapproved of the persecution of the Jews and the government's war plans. In 1939, he emigrated to Switzerland and publicly broke with National Socialism (he published a book, *I paid Hitler*, in 1941). He later went to France where he was handed over to the Gestapo in late 1940. He was imprisoned until 1945 and emigrated to Argentina in 1948.

TOLLER, ERNST

Writer
born: 1 February 1893 Samotschin (now Szamocin, Poland),
died: 22 May 1939 New York

An army volunteer, T. was dismissed prior to Verdun in 1917 after a nervous breakdown. In Munich he met →Eisner and →Landauer; under their influence he became a pacifist and joined the Independent SPD. He was a leading light in the Munich Socialist republic and was imprisoned for five years after its failure. He wrote his autobiography *Eine Jugend in Deutschland* (A youth in Germany) and a volume of poetry *Das Schwalbennest* (The swallows' nest) in prison. His plays for the theater, including the scandal-provoking *Der deutsche Hinkemann* (1923) made T. one of the most important dramatists of Expressionism and the New Objectivity (*Hoppla, wir leben!*, 1927). He fled Germany in 1933 and committed suicide after Franco's victory in the Spanish Civil War.

TUCHOLSKY, KURT

Journalist
born: 9 January 1890 Berlin, died: 21 December 1935
Göteborg (Sweden)

Having obtained a doctorate in law and participated in the First World War, T. found his vocation in journalism. He had written before the war, mainly anti-Wilhelmine criticism, and in 1912 he published *Rheinsberg. Ein Bilderbuch für Verliebte*. His main work was, however, written for the *Weltbühne*. T. became its main journalist and was its editor for a short time in 1926 before →Ossietzky took over. T. made a key contribution to the pacifism, anti-militarism, criticism of the law, opposition to reaction and Prussian ideals in the *Weltbühne*. As a member of the Independent SPD, he repeatedly expressed his disappointment in the failure of the November Revolution to fulfill its alliance of intellect and power. T. also worked for other newspapers and was Paris correspondent of the *Vossische Zeitung*. His comic songs and satires, published under the pseudonyms Kaspar Hauser, Peter Panter, Theobald Tiger, and Ignaz Wrobel, were very popular. His biting

critical illustrated book *Deutschland, Deutschland über alles* (1929) which was laid out by →Heartfield, settled his score with the elites of Weimar society. His bitterness about developments in Germany caused him to fall silent in late 1932. The National Socialists deported him, burned his books, and appropriated his royalties. T. committed suicide in 1935.

UDET, ERNST

Army Officer
born: 26 April 1896 Frankfurt/Main,
died: 17 November 1941 Berlin

None of the surviving fighter pilots had shot down more enemy aircraft by the end of the war than U., a squadron leader who was awarded the *Pour le mérite*. After the war, he founded an airplane factory; he worked throughout the world as a test and exhibition pilot and also for film production companies. He was appointed general aircraft master in the newly established

Luftwaffe. Held responsible by →Göring for the failures of the Luftwaffe in the Second World War, he committed suicide in 1941. His death was passed off as an accident by the regime.

ULLSTEIN, RUDOLF

Publisher
born: 26 February 1874 Berlin, died: 2 February 1964
Berlin

Leopold Ullstein founded a newspaper publisher in 1877, whose publications included the *Berliner Zeitung*, *Berliner Abendpost*,

Berliner Morgenpost, and the *Berliner Illustrirte Zeitung*. His sons inherited Germany's biggest newspaper group on his death in 1899. Rudolf U. was director of publishing technology and thanks to his adoption of rotary presses, the company gained a technical advantage over its competitors. U. was a member of the board of Ullstein AG from 1921 to 1933. During this period, with →Korff as its editor, *BIZ* became Germany's most popular magazine with a circulation of 1.8 million. Politically, the U. family was liberal–democratic. In 1934, the family was forced by the Nazis to sell its business. U. fled to Great Britain in 1939 where he worked in a factory. In the 1950s, U. was director of the Ullstein printing works, which he co-founded, and director of the board of Ullstein AG in Berlin.

UMBO

Photo-journalist
born: 18 January 1902 Düsseldorf, died: 13 May 1980 Hanover

U. (Otto Umbehr) took courses at the Bauhaus between 1921 and 1923 and then started to take photographs. He soon became an avant-garde artist with an international reputation on the basis of his portraits, abstract city photos, and "photogrammes." He provided photomontages for →Ruttmann's *Berlin – Symphony of a Metropolis*. In 1928, he co-founded the Dephot picture agency. He worked as a freelance photo-journalist in Germany up to his death in 1980. He was rediscovered as a pioneer of Modernism shortly before his death.

WALTER, BRUNO

Conductor
born: 15 September 1876 Berlin, died: 17 February 1962
Beverly Hills (USA)

In 1894, W. (Bruno Walter Schlesinger) became Gustav Mahler's assistant in Hamburg. He followed his master to Vienna, where he conducted the premiere of Mahler's *Lied von der Erde* in 1911 and his 9th Symphony in 1912. In 1911, W. became general director of

Bruno Walter   Yehudi Menuhin

music at the Munich National Theater and later at the Berlin City Opera. He was appointed →Furtwängler's successor as conductor of the Gewandhaus Orchestra and director of the Viennese State Opera in 1936. As a Jew, he emigrated to the USA after the *Anschluss*.

WESSEL, HORST

Student
born: 9 October 1907 Bielefeld, died: 23 February 1930 Berlin

W. was a law student who joined the NSDAP and SA in 1926. He was active in the fighting against the Communists, fell in love with a prostitute, and was mortally wounded by her pimp. →Goebbels transformed the victim of a crime of passion to a political martyr. The poem "Die Fahne hoch …," which W. wrote in 1929, became the second national anthem after the *Deutschlandlied*.

WIGMAN, MARY

Dancer
born: 13 November 1886 Hanover, died: 19 September 1973
Berlin

→Laban's assistant, W. (Marie Wiegmann) made her first solo appearance as a dancer in 1919 and founded her own school for expressive dance in the following year. She worked as a dancer and choreographer in Dresden and Leipzig, toured through Europe and the USA, and was director of her own dance studio in Berlin until 1967. W. was one of the most influential representatives of free dance and is credited as the creator of dramatic and expressive solo dance.

WILHELM II

Emperor, King of Prussia
born: 27 January 1859 Berlin, died: 4 June 1941
Doorn (Netherlands)

After the death of his father Friedrich III in 1888, and becoming Kaiser at an unexpectedly young age, W. dismissed Bismarck and led a "personal

regime." With his extremely tactless and chauvinistic speeches, he led Germany into a position of isolation on the world political stage, and ultimately also into the First World War. In 1918, he was forced by →Groener – with →Hindenburg's approval – to flee to the Netherlands. →Max von Baden independently announced W's abdication

as Kaiser and – against W's will – as King of Prussia. W. supported anti-democratic movements in Germany from exile; however, →Hitler did not fulfill his hopes of restoration.

WIRTH, JOSEPH (KARL)

Politician
born: 6 September 1879 Freiburg, died: 3 January 1956
Freiburg

W. became a Reichstag representative for the Catholic Center Party in 1914 and remained a member of the party until 1933 with just one interruption. In November 1918, he became finance minister in Baden and in 1920 he was appointed Reich finance minister. In May 1921, W., a teacher by profession, became Reich Chancellor for one and a half years. He had to form a new government in the middle of his period of office: he was also finance and foreign minister for different periods. W. supported a socially responsible, democratic state ruled by law. Despite his personal rejection of the Treaty of Versailles, in his foreign policy he supported compromise and "appeasement" with the West. In the East, he achieved a rapprochement with the Soviet Union through the Rapallo Treaty. He is famous for the declaration he made after the murder of →Rathenau: "The enemy is on the right!" He was a minister under →Müller and →Brüning. He lived in exile in Switzerland from 1933 to 1948. A born politician, he was politically active to his old age in the Federal Republic and campaigned against →Adenauer's Western leanings in favor of stronger links with the USSR.

WOLFF, THEODOR

Journalist
born: 2 August 1868 Berlin, died: 23 September 1943 Berlin

W. began his career as a management trainee in his cousin →Mosse's company. He soon made a name for himself as a literature and theater critic, dramatist, novelist and translator of French. In 1894, he went to Paris as the correspondent of the *Berliner Tageblatt*. W.'s reports on the Dreyfus affair increased the newspaper's circulation and the *Tageblatt* overtook its competitor, the *Vossische Zeitung*. In 1906, Mosse appointed him as editor in chief and over the following years, W. made the *Tageblatt* into Germany's model liberal publication. He succeeded in attracting prominent authors such as →Tucholsky,

→Einstein, and theater critic Alfred Kerr. In the First World War, W. admonished supporters of annexation to take a more moderate line. He welcomed the abdication of →Wilhelm II in November 1918. When he formed the liberal DDP party shortly afterwards, he refused to allow →Stresemann to join, although he later approved of the latter's foreign policy. W. was flabbergasted at →Hindenburg's election as Reich President: "What is one to do with a people which does not learn from its misfortunes, and which time and again [...] allows itself to be led around on a halter by the same people?"

W. resigned from the DDP in 1926 due to a row about culture policy. He identified the NSDAP as the most dangerous opponent of democracy and he appealed to people to vote for the SPD. A Jew and opponent of the Nazis, W. had to flee Germany in 1933. In 1943 he fell into the hands of the Gestapo and died as a result of his imprisonment. A staunch democrat, political analyst, and brilliant stylist, W. is now respected as the most important German journalist of the pre-war period.

ZETKIN, CLARA (JOSEPHINE)

Politician
born: 5 July 1857 Wiederau (Saxony), died 20 June 1933
Archangelskoje (Soviet Union)

A teacher by profession, Z. (née Eisner) married a Russian revolutionary who died soon after the wedding. Z. remained loyal to the workers' movement, became editor of the SPD women's publication *Gleichheit* (Equality), and worked in the women's office of the Communist International. She believed the emancipation of women was directly linked with the "liberation of the working classes." She actively opposed the First World War, became a co-founder of the Spartacus League and the Independent SPD, and a member of the central committee of the German Communist Party (KPD). Z. was a friend of Lenin and spent most of the 1920s in the Soviet Union, although she was a Reichstag

representative between 1920 and 1933. In 1932, as the most senior member of the Reichstag, she opened the session with an appeal for the formation of a united front against the NSDAP.

ZILLE, (RUDOLF) HEINRICH

Graphic Artist
born: 10 January 1858 Radeburg, died: 9 August 1929 Berlin

The son of a Saxon worker, Z. came to Berlin in 1867. He earned his living as a reprographic technician for the Photographic Society and began to publish his drawings of working-class Berlin around 1900. Although Z. mainly portrayed poverty, alcoholism, and homelessness, he was extremely popular even before the First World War that "Zille Balls" were held at the Berliner Sportpalast. The acuity of his observation is backed up by the photographs which Z. used as studies for his drawings.

ZUCKMAYER, CARL

Writer
born: 27 December 1896 Nackenheim, died: 18 January 1977
Visp (Switzerland)

The former army lieutenant did not have much success with his first play *Kreuzweg* and he had to eke out a living as a bar singer. In contrast, his popular drama *Der fröhliche Weinberg* (The Merry Vineyard) (1925), which became the most staged play of the 1920s, was awarded the Kleist Prize. Z. wrote the screenplay for →Sternberg's film *The Blue Angel* and had further exceptional success with his stage play *Der Hauptmann von Köpenick* (The Captain of Köpenick) in 1931. An opponent of the Nazis, Z. emigrated in 1933 and wrote his internationally acclaimed play *Des Teufels General* (The devil's general), which deals with the entanglement of the individual in the National Socialist regime.

Clara Zetkin

THE NATIONAL SOCIALIST "CLEANSING" OF THE ILLUSTRATED PRESS

Immediately after the accession to power of the new Reich government under Adolf Hitler, a veritable witch-hunt of Jewish photojournalists began. Long before 1933, the National Socialists had made what they referred to as the "Jewish Press" into a target for their defamation campaigns. Faced with undisguised threats, many large publishers and German radio started dismissing Jewish employees in March 1933.

The "Reich Ministry for Education and Propaganda" under Joseph Goebbels was founded on 13 March 1933. The "mandatory obligation of persons in the press to the state" began with the establishment of professional associations. The "coordination" of photojournalists was carried out by the "Reich Association of German Picture Reporters", which became the "Reich Association of the German Press" after the "Reich Cultural Chamber Law" of September 1933.

The professed aim of the National Socialists was to "Aryanize" the media as quickly as possible. As the accompanying document of 1933 shows, it was possible for a "German" press photographer to be mistakenly denounced as a Jew without being one: the list contains the acknowledgment and correction of such an error in the case of H. Koch from Hamburg. This process was complete by mid-1934 and was confirmed by the sale of the Jewish Ullstein publishing company and with it the *Berliner Illustrirte Zeitung* to a state trust in June 1934. With the destruction of their professional life, many photo-journalists, editors, and picture agencies which had built up photo-journalism in the Weimar Period into a great institution fled the country: Erich Salomon, Alfred Eisenstaedt, Tim Gidal, Walter Süssmann, Kurt Korff, Stefan Lorant, Simon Guttmann, Rudolf Birnbach ... This list is endless and also contains many whose names are now forgotten.

Above: Dr. Erich Salomon with the camera which made him and his work famous – the Ermanox 35-mm camera. His illustrated book *Zeitgenossen in unbewachten Augenblicken* (1931) is an outstanding document of his talent as a photo-journalist. The internationally renowned photographer emigrated to France in 1933. During the war, he and his family were, however, taken prisoner and transported to Auschwitz where they were murdered.

Right page: *Deutsche Bilder in der Presse*, the list of German, Jewish, and foreign photographers published in *Deutsche Nachrichten*, 2nd August issue, 1933.

Deutsche Bilder in der Presse
Verzeichnis deutscher Pressephotographen

A.B.C., Aktuelle Bilder-Centrale, Inh. G. Pahl, Berlin-Steglitz, Worpsweder Str. 17.

Akademia, wissenschaftliches Korrespondenzbüro, Inh. Dr. L. Kühle, Berlin-Charlottenburg 4, Dahlmannstr. 25.

Argusfot, Inh. Carl Fernstädt, Berlin SW. 68, Hedemannstr. 23.

Atlantic Photo-G. m. b. H., Berlin SW. 68, Schützenstr. 67.

Badetow, Martin, Berlin-Charlottenburg 4, Wielandstr. 16.

Baenisch, Wilh., Heimatbilder, Greifswald.

Bärwinkel, F. W., Stralsund i. Pommern, Frankenstr. 50.

Berger, Emil, Photograph, München, Theresienstraße 30.

Bittner, Hans, Berlin-Charlottenburg 5, Rönnestraße 16.

Bloom, Otto, Berlin-Steglitz, Björnsenstraße 23 a.

v. Blücher, F. A., Berlin-Zehlendorf-West, Bülowstraße 3.

Custon, Albert, Hamburg 5, Lohmühlenstraße 54.

Dietrich, Hans, München, Klenzestraße 41.

Donath, Otto, Berlin-Charlottenburg, Bismarckstraße 19.

Ebert, Georg, Berlin-Lichterfelde, Viktoriastr. 15.

Eberth, Carl, Hofphotograph, Kassel, Hohenzollernstraße 43.

Ehlert, Max, Berlin-Wilhelmshagen, Kirchstr. 15.

Engel, Erich, Berlin NW 21, Dortmunder Str. 9.

v. Estorff, Gustav, Potsdam, Höhenstr. 4.

Feller, Paul, Hannover, Voßstr. 57.

Fotoaktuell, Inh. Frau F. Ruge und Helmut Möbius, Berlin SW 68, Enckestr. 1.

Foto Deli, Inh. Offszanka, Berlin W 62, Kurfürstenstr. 101.

Foto Expreß, Inh. Max Niggl, Berlin-Zehlendorf, Schliessenstr. 34.

Frankl, A. u. E., Berlin-Schöneberg, Hauptstraße 101.

Frege, Horst, Hamburg, Gryphiusstr. 3.

Fritsche, John, Hamburg 36, Neuer Wall 63, IV.

Gerlach, Max, Illustrationsverlag, Berlin S 42, Wassertorstr. 60.

Geschwindner, Karl, Karlsruhe i. Baden, Körnerstraße 48.

Gey, R., Sportphotograph, Leipzig C 1, Brüderstraße 14.

Girke, W., Berlin SW 11, Stresemannstr. 49.

Godel, Willy, München, Theresienstr. 30.

Graeber, Gerhard, München O 8, Orleansstr. 10.

Greth, Frau R., Photographin, Berlin W 15, Pariser Straße 39.

Groß, Alfred, Illustrationsverlag, Berlin SW 68, Zimmerstr. 48 b.

Haeckel, Georg, Illustrationsverlag, Berlin-Lichterfelde, Kaiserplatz 3.

Haeckel, Otto, Photos aus aller Welt, Berlin-Friedenau, Wielandstr. 35.

Hahn, Hans, Berlin W 30, Motzstr. 7.

Hammer, Erich, Dresden A 16, Blumenstr. 106.

Hauschild, Wilhelm, Hannover 1 N, Pettenkoferstraße 11.

Hege, Kurt, Werkstatt für Lichtbildnerei, Essen, Burgstr. 16.

Henschke, Hans, Photoverlag, Berlin SW 68, Markgrafenstr. 78.

Hoffmann, Heinrich, Presse-Illustrationen, Berlin SW 68, Friedrichstr. 214; München, Amalienstr. 25.

Hoffmann, Herbert, Berlin-Charlottenburg 2, Goethestr. 6.

Huhle, Kurt, München, Erhardtstr. 15.

Jacobi, Walter, Darmstadt, Karlstr. 34.

Jäger, Joseph, Frankfurt-Preungesheim a. M., Runkeler Str. 10.

Jung, Hermann, Mainz-Gonsenheim, Kapellenstraße 14.

Junghanß, H. C., Leipzig C 1, Hospitalstr. 12.

Kester, Philipp, Lichtbildarchiv, München, Ungererstraße 12.

Kiesel, Lichtbildner, Berlin W 30, Martin-Luther-Straße 9.

Kindermann, Klaus, Sportbilder, Berlin SW 68, Markgrafenstr. 24.

Klaas, Ludwig, Bad Kreuznach, Baumgartenstr. 46.

Koch, Hans, Sport- und Pressephotograph, Hamburg 30, Hoheluft-Chaussee 131.

Krauskopf, Fritz, Aktualitäten, Heimatbilder, Königsberg i. Pr., Steindamm 64.

Kühlewindt, A., Kgl. Preußischer Hofphotograph, Königsberg/Pr., Vorstädtische Langgasse 39.

Kurth, Helmuth, München 13, Hohenzollernstr. 99/4.

Lantin, Rolf, Inh. Martin Knauer, Düsseldorf, Herderstr. 65.

Licht, E. J., Köln a. Rh., Gereonswall 63.

Löhrich, Max, Pressebüro, Leipzig S 3, Fichtestraße 36.

Lüddecke, Walter, Pressedienst, Berlin SW 11, Trebbiner Str. 9.

Mach, Heinrich A., Sportphotograph, Berlin-Charlottenburg, Schillerstr. 62.

Mai, Paul, Berlin-Neukölln, Friedelstr. 43.

Matthies, Elly, Hamburg-Fuhlsbüttel, Maienweg 271.

Mayen, Axel Dieter, Hannover, Lavesstr. 15.

Menzendorf, A., Renn-, Reit- und Fahrsport, Berlin NW 23, Altonaer Str. 4.

Meyfarth, Willy, Altona a. d. Elbe, Catharinenstraße 31.

Neubacher, Hermann, Hamburg 1, Hermannstr. 11.

Nicolai, Christian, Berlin SW 19, Kommandantenstraße 36.

Nolte, Hennig, Berlin-Britz, Talberger Str. 80.

Nötzoldt, Adolf, Erfurt, Am Johannestor 8b.

P.B.3., Presse-Bilder-Zentrale G. m. b. H., Inh. Brämer & Güll, Berlin SW 68, Friedrichstraße 214.

v. Perckhammer, Heinz, Berlin W 15, Kurfürstendamm 53.

Petri, Paul Hans, Mainz, Heidelbergerfaßgasse 7.

Pfalz-Bilderdienst, Inh. A. Gerspach, Neustadt a. d. Haardt.

Photo-Kühn, Baden-Baden, Friedrichstr. 1.

Plog, Heinrich, Pressephotograph, Ludwigslust i. Mecklenburg.

Pomprein, Rupert, Berlin SW 19, Jerusalemer Straße 8.

Reich, Otto, Hamburg, Schaarsteinweg 4.

Reil, Hermann, Bremen, Lloydstr. 112.

Rehlaff, Hans, Berlin-Charlottenburg 5, Hebbelstraße 2.

Riebicke, Gerhard, Charlottenburg 4, Krumme Straße 54.

Rupp, Alfred, Berlin-Charlottenburg, Wilmersdorfer Str. 163.

Schaller, Hans, Flugsportphotos, Berlin-Wilmersdorf, Babelsberger Str. 46.

Schirner, Sportbilder-Verlag, Berlin SW 68, Kochstr. 13a.

Schorer, Joseph, Hamburg 13, Rappstr. 20.

Schütze, Karl, Hamburg 5, Lohmühlenstr. 54.

Schweig, Gustav, Hamburg, Rellingerstr. 73.

Seifert, Fritz, München, Nymphenburger Str. 66.

Sennecke, Robert, Illustrationsverlag, Berlin SW 11, Hallesches Ufer 9.

Spiehl, Johann, München, Eisenmannstr. 3/4.

Stenzel, Friedrich August, Leipzig, Pfaffendorfer Straße 18.

Stöcker, Alex., Berlin-Friedenau, Wiesbadener Straße 3.

Stüber, Frl. Margarethe, Berlin W 35, Königin-Augusta-Str. 44.

Tiedemann, Wilhelm, Hannover, Auf dem Lohe 8.

Transocean G. m. b. H., Berlin W 9, Friedrich-Ebert-Str. 8.

Tschuschke, Curt, Quedlinburg am Harz, Hindenburgstraße 1.

Ullmann, Curt, Berlin-Halensee, Hektorstr. 19.

Unger, Dr. Hj., Schriftsteller und Bildberichterstatter. Eigene Aufnahmen aus aller Welt. Berlin W 15, Pariser Str. 28.

Voigt, Friedrich, Leipzig, Adolf-Hitler-Str. 142.

Walther, Hedda, Berlin-Charlottenburg 9, Kastanien-Allee 23.

Weber, Alfred, Hamburg 21, Overbeckstr. 3.

Weber, Dr. Friedrich, München, Arcostr. 5.

Weber, Wolfgang, Berlin W 9, Bellevuestr. 6.

Wegner, Otto, Berlin N 4, Chausseestr. 53.

Weiler, Wilhelm, München, Türkenstr. 98.

Weißgärber, Horst, Darmstadt, Elisabethenstr. 50.

Weller, Dr. Peter, Berlin W 30, Nollendorfplatz 9.

Wich, Max, Bildverlag, München 13, Zentnerstr. 44.

Wilmkes, Franz, Kettwig-Ruhr, Umstand 28.

Winkelmann, Walter, Hamburg 19, Eppendorfer Weg 111.

Wißmann, Wilhelm, München 2 C 1, Pfandhausstraße 8.

Liste der Juden und Ausländer

Aktueller Bilderdienst (Biberfeld), Berlin. — Associated Preß, A. P., Berlin. — Beer, Dr., Hamburg. — Biberfeld, Berlin. — Bieber, E., Hamburg. — Binder, Berlin. — Birnbach (Weltrundschau), Berlin. — Block, Dr. Hamburg. — Dephot, Berlin. — Deutsche Presse-Photo-Zentrale (Basch), Berlin. — Deutscher Pressefischer-Dienst (Fodor), Berlin. — d'Ora (Horovitz), Berlin, Paris, Wien. — Eisenstädt, Alfred, Berlin. — Europa-Materndienst (Fodor), Berlin. — Expreß-Matern-G. m. b. H. (Fodor), Berlin. — Fanat, Berlin. — Federmeyer, Berlin. — Fodor-Illustrationsverlag, Berlin. — Glaß, Berlin. — Göndör, Emmerich, Berlin. — Hegy, Ladislaus, Berlin. — Hirsch, Max, Hamburg. — Alpreß, Berlin. — Jeidels, Berlin. — Karasch, Berlin. — Kaftan, Hamburg. — Keystone Biem, Berlin. — Kluger, Zoltan, Berlin. — Köster (alias Glück), Berlin. — Kutschuk, Gregor, Berlin. — Marcus, Elly, Berlin. — Mauritius, Berlin. — Moscigan, Hamburg. — Neofot, Berlin. — New York Times, N.Y.T., Berlin. — Neofot, Berlin. — Nordmart-Photo (Dr. Beer), Hamburg. — d'Ora, Berlin, Paris, Wien. — Pariselle (alias Lo Wegner), Berlin. — Photothek, Berlin. — Presse-Photo-G. m. b. H., Berlin. — Rasmussen, Berlin. — Salomon, Dr., Berlin. — Schaul, Hamburg. — Schlochauer, Berlin. — Süßmann, Walter, Berlin. — Szigethy, Berlin. — Temesvari, Berlin. — Unionbild, Berlin. — Vogel-Sandau, Berlin. — Wallentin, Fred, Berlin. — Wegner, Lo (alias Pariselle), Berlin. — Weltrundschau (Birnbach), Berlin. — Wide World, W. W., Berlin. — Dr. Wolff. — Yva.

*

In unserer ersten Liste war versehentlich der Name H. Koch-Hamburg aufgeführt. Er ist heute an der richtigen Stelle der deutschen Liste genannt.

Index

The index lists all of the people, places, and names found in the text in alphabetical order. The names of newspapers are in *italic*. The page references in *italic* refer to illustrations.

List of abbreviations used in the book

AIZ	Arbeiter-Illustrierte-Zeitung (Workers' Illustrated Paper)
BIZ	Berliner Illustrirte Zeitung (Berlin Illustrated Paper)
BVP	Bayerische Volkspartei (Bavarian People's Party)
Comintern	Communist Internationale
DDP	Deutsche Demokratische Partei (German Democratic Party)
DNVP	Deutschnationale Volkspartei (German National People's Party)
DVP	Deutsche Volkspartei (German People's Party)
IAH	Internationale Arbeiterhilfe (International Workers' Aid)
IB	Illustrierter Beobachter (Illustrated Observer)
KPD	Kommunistische Partei Deutschlands (German Communist Party)
MIP	Münch(e)ner Illustrierte Press (Munich Illustrated Press)
NSDAP	Nationasozialistische Deutsche Arbeiterpartei (National Socialist German Workers' Party)
SA	Sturmabteilung (Storm troopers)
SPD	Sozialdemokratische Partei Deutschlands (German Social Democratic Party)
SS	Schutzstaffel (Protection squad)
UFA	Universum Film Aktiengesellschaft
USPD	Unabhängige Sozialdemokratische Partei Deutschlands (German Independent Socialist Party)

Selected Bibliography

R. Bessel and E.T. Feuchtwanger (eds.): *Social Change and Political Development in Weimar Germany*, London 1981

M. Broszat: *Hitler and the Collapse of Weimar Germany*, Leamington Spa/Hamburg/New York 1987

Gerhard Brunn and Jürgen Reulecke (eds.): "*Metropolis Berlin. Berlin als deutsche Hauptstadt im Vergleich europäischer Hauptstädte 1870–1939*", Bonn/Berlin 1992

"Bilder, die lügen," edited by Stifung Haus der Geschichte der Bundesrepublik Deutschland, Bonn 1998

P. Gay: *Weimar Culture: The Insider as Outsider*, 2nd. edition London 1988

Johann Friedrich Geist and Klaus Kürvers: *Das Berliner Mietshaus 1862–1945*, vol. 2, Munich 1984

Tim Nachum Gidal: *Chronisten des Lebens. Die moderne Fotoreportage*, Berlin 1993

Otto Groth: *Die unerkannte Kulturmacht. Grundlegung der Zeitungswissenschaft*, 2 Vols., Berlin 1960–72

Franz Hessel: *Spazieren in Berlin*, Vienna/Leipzig 1929; "New edition: *Ein Flaneur in Berlin*," with photographs by Friedrich Seidenstücker, Berlin 1984

Bernd Hüppauf: Kriegsfotografie, in: Wolfgang Michalka (ed.): *Der Erste Weltkrieg. Wirkung Wahrnehmung Analyse*, Munich/Zurich 1994

Sigrid and Wolfgang Jacobeit: *Illustrierte Alltags– und Sozialgeschichte Deutschlands. 1900–1945*, Münster 1995

Count Harry Kessler: *Diaries of a Cosmopolitan*, translated and edited by Charles Kessler, Weidenfeld and Nicolson 1999

Gabriele Klein: *FrauenKörperTanz*, Berlin 1992

Eberhard Kolb: *The Weimar Republic*, London 1988

W. Lacqueur: *Weimar: A Cultural History 1918–1933*, London 1974

C. Maier: *Recasting Bourgeois Europe: Socialization in France, Germany and Italy in the Decade after World War I*, Princeton 1975

Wilhelm Marckwardt: *Die Illustrierten der Weimarer Zeit*, Munich 1982

Peter de Mendelsohn: *Zeitungsstadt Berlin*, Frankfurt a.M./Berlin/Vienna 1982

Karen M. Moores: *Presse und Meinungsklima in der Weimarer Republik*, Mainz 1997

Hans Mommsen: *Aufstieg und Untergang der Repubik von Weimar 1918–1933*, Berlin 1998

Rainer Otto and Walter Rösler: *Kabarettgeschichte. Abriß des deutschsprachigen Kabaretts*, Berlin 1977

Detlev J. K. Peukert: *The Weimar Republic, translated by Richard Deveson*, London 1991

Rudolf Pörtner (ed.): *Alltag und Jugend in unruhiger Zeit*, Munich 1993

Bernd Weise: Fotojournalismus. Erster Weltkrieg – Weimarer Republik, in: Klaus Honnef, Rolf Sachsse and Karin Thomas (Eds.). *Deutsche Fotografie. Macht eines Mediums 1870–1970*, Cologne 1997

John Willett: The New Society – Art and Politics in the Weimar Period 1917–1933, London 1978

Heinrich August Winkler: *Weimar 1918–1933. Die Geschichte der ersten deutschen Demokratie*, Munich 1998

Heinrich August Winkler and Alexander Cammann (Ed.): *Weimar – ein Lesebuch zur deutschen Geschichte 1918–1933*, Munich 1997

Weimarer Republik, published by Kunstamt Kreuzberg and Institut für Theaterwissenschaft der Universität Köln, Berlin and Hamburg 1977

Acknowledgements

Quotations which are indicated in the book as "original captions" or "original photo essay text" are translated versions of the original texts that were printed on the backs of the photographs or accompanied the series of photos. These texts were composed either by the photographer or an editor from the agency which distributed the photographs. Hence, these texts reflect the different perspectives of the photo journalists, not those of the publishers who used the photos and the accompanying texts. Whether the texts were edited or actually published can only be established by checking the newspapers and magazines. Our spot checks merely provide a basis for assumptions about this aspect of media history.

All of the remaining quotations are taken from contemporary sources. The publisher made every effort to locate all rights holders and estates before printing this book. Persons and institutions who may not have been consulted and wish to assert their rights to quotations used in the book are requested to contact the publisher so that this can be corrected in future printings.

(t = top, b = bottom, r = right, l = left, c = center)

And As You See …
9 Kurt Korff, in: *Berliner Illustrirte Zeitung*, No. 50, 1919 **11** Holger Böning: "Eine kapitale Ente", in: *Die Zeit*, No. 11, 11.3.1999 **16/17:** Kurt Korff, in: *Berliner Illustrirte Zeitung*, No. 50, 1919 **17 r:** Arthur Liebert: "Unsere Zeitung und unsere Zeit. Eine kulturphilosophische Würdigung", in: *Zeitungs-Verlag*, 27. Vol., No. 26, 25.6.1926, p. 17 **18 c, t:** Kurt Korff, quoted from: Peter de Mendelsohn: *Zeitungsstadt Berlin*, Ullstein, Frankfurt a.M./Berlin/Wien 1982, p. 152 **18 c, b:** Jest van Rennings: *Die gefilmte Zeitung. Werden, Struktur, Wirkung, Wesen und Aspekte der Filmwochenschau* unpublished dissertation, Munich 1956, p. 156 **18 r:** Otto Groth: *Die unerkannte Kulturmacht. Grundlegung der Zeitungswissenschaft*, de Gruyter, Berlin 1960–72, Vol. 2, p. 205 **22** Siegfried Kracauer: "Die Photographie", in: "Das Ornament der Masse", Suhrkamp, Frankfurt a.M. 1963, p. 33 **23** Kurt Korff: "Die Berliner Illustrirte", in: *50 Jahre Ullstein 1877–1927*, pp. 290–291 **24 r:** André Kertész, in: Tim Nachum Gidal: *Chronisten des Lebens. Die moderne Fotoreportage*, Edition q, Berlin 1993, p. 27 **25 li:** Willy Stiewe: *Das Bild als Nachricht*, C. Duncker Verlag, Berlin 1933, p. 87; **r, t:** Gidal 1993, loc. cit, p. 40; **r, c:** ibid; **r, b:** Wilhelm Marckwardt: *Die Illustrierten der Weimarer Zeit*, Minerva Publikation, Munich 1982, p. 113 **30:** Stefan Lorant, quoted from: ibid, p. 123 **31 l/r:** Egon Erwin Kisch: "Ein Reporter wird Soldat", in: Wolfgang R. Langenbucher (Ed.): *Sensationen des Alltags*, Verlag Ölschläger, Munich 1992, p. 58; **r:** Curt Riess: "Weltbühne Berlin", in: Rudolf Pörtner (Ed.): *Alltag und Jugend in unruhiger Zeit*, dtv, Munich 1993, pp. 30–54, p. 54 **34 l, t:** Harry Pross: "Presse – 14 Jahre zwischen Glanz und Ignoranz", in: Hilmar Hoffmann und Heinrich Klotz (Eds.): "Die Kultur unseres Jahrhunderts 1918–1933", Econ, Düsseldorf 1993, p. 212 f.; **l, b/c, t:** Paul Schlesinger, quoted from: de Mendelsohn 1982, loc. cit, p. 362 **35/36:** Kurt Koszyk: *Deutsche Presse 1914–1945*, Coloquium Verlag, Berlin 1972, p. 330 **36 b:** Willy Münzenberg, in: *Der Arbeiterfotograf*, Vol 5, 1931, p. 99 **37:** Joseph Goebbels, quoted from: Michaela Haibl: "Unterhaltung", in: Wolfgang Benz, Hermann Graml und Hermann Weiß (Eds): "Enzyklopädie des Nationalsozialismus", dtv, Munich 1997, p. 181

I was Red in November
44: Bertolt Brecht: "Trommeln in der Nacht", 1922, in: *Gesammelte Werke 1. Stücke*, Werkausgabe Edition Suhrkamp, Frankfurt a.M. 1967, p. 112 **45:** Erich Ludendorff, quoted from: Albrecht von Thaur: *Generalstabsdienst an der Front und in der OHL*, Göttingen 1958, p. 235 **48:** Friedrich Ebert: *Schriften, Aufzeichnungen, Reden. Mit unveröffentlichten Erinnerungen aus dem Nachlaß*, Reissner, 2 Volumes, Dresden 1926, Vol. 2, p. 127 **50 t:** Karl Liebknecht: *Gesammelte Reden und Schriften*, published by Institut für Marxismus-Leninismus beim Zentralkomitee der SED, Dietz, Berlin 1968, Vol. 9, May 1916 to 15 January 1919, p. 594 f.; **b:** Friedrich Ebert, quoted from: Prinz Max von Baden, *Erinnerungen und Dokumente*, 1927, edited by Golo Mann and Andreas Burckhardt, Stuttgart 1968, p. 567 **53:** Friedrich Ebert: *Schriften, Aufzeichnungen, Reden*, loc. cit, Vol. 2, p. 127 **57 c:** Appeal of the KPD Spartacus League and USPD on 5.1.1919, quoted from: *Geschichte der deutschen Arbeiterbewegung*, published by Institut für Marxismus-Leninismus beim Zentralkomitee der SED, from 1917 to 1923, Dietz, Berlin 1966, Vol. 3, Original edition p. 533; **r:** Theodor Wolff: *Der Marsch durch zwei Jahrzehnte*, de Lange, Amsterdam 1936, p. 219 **59 l:** Appeal in Berlin on 1.1.1919, quoted from: *Weimarer Republik*, published by Kunstamt Kreuzberg and the Institut für Theaterwissenschaft der Universität Köln, 3rd edition, Elefantenpress, Berlin und Hamburg 1977, p. 133 **59 c:** Gustav Noske: *Von Kiel bis Kapp. Zur Geschichte der deutschen Revolution*, Verlag für Politik und Wirtschaft, Berlin 1920, p. 67 f. **59 r:** government call for formation of volunteer corps, quoted from: *Weimarer Republik*, 1977, loc. cit, p. 140 **60 t:** Karl Liebknecht: "Trotz alledem!", 1919, quoted from: ibid, p. 147; **b:** Karl Retzlaw: *Spartakus. Aufstieg und Niedergang. Erinnerungen eines Parteiarbeiters*, Verlag Neue Kritik, Frankfurt a.M. 1972, p. 120f.

Germany, Germany...

65: Kurt Tucholsky: *Deutschland, Deutschland über alles*, Berlin 1929, New Edition Rowohlt, Reinbek b. Hamburg 1980, p. 12 a. p. 230 **66 r, t:** Theodor Wolff: *Der Marsch durch zwei Jahrzehnte*, 1936, loc. cit, t. p.; **r, b:** Wolfgang Stresemann: *Mein Vater Gustav Stresemann*, Munich/Berlin 1979, p. 171 **68/69:** appeal from the Bauer government, quoted from: Hagen Schulze: *Weimar. Deutschland 1917–1933*, Siedler Verlag, Berlin 1994, p. 218 **69 r:** General von Seeckt, quoted from: Hans Meier-Welcker: Seeckt, Frankfurt a.M. 1967, p. 261. Cf. Friedrich von Rabenau (Ed.): Hans von Seeckt. *Aus meinem Leben. 1918–1936*, v. Hase & Koehler, Leipzig 1940, p. 221, in which Seeckt's words are "Troops do not shoot at troops". Quoted from: Horst Möller: Weimar. *Die unvollendete Demokratie*, dtv, Munich 1985, p. 146 **70 c:** "Christliche Welt", quoted from: Kurt Hirsch: *Die Blutlinie*, Röderberg-Verlag, Frankfurt a.M. 1960; t.P.; **r, t:** Joseph Wirth, quoted from: Schulze 1994, loc. cit, p. 244 **72 l, b:** Erich Ludendorff: *Meine Kriegserinnerungen 1914–1918*, Verlag Ernst Siegfried Mittler und Sohn, Berlin 1919, p. 622 **74:** Gustav Noske, quoted from: Heinrich August Winkler: *Weimar 1918–1933. Die Geschichte der ersten deutschen Demokratie*, Beck Verlag, Munich 1998, p. 76 **79:** Karl Radek, in: *Protokoll der Konferenz der Erweiterten Exekutive der Kommunistischen Internationale. Moskau. 12.–13. Juni 1923*, Hamburg 1922, Reprinted: Milan 1967, p. 147, pp. 240–245 **80:** Gustav Stresemann, quoted from: Erich Eyck: *Geschichte der Weimarer Republik*, 2 Volumes, Rentsch, Erlenbach/Zurich 1954, Vol. 1 (Vom Zusammenbruch des Kaisertums bis zur Wahl Hindenburgs), p. 441 **81:** Arnold Zweig: *Bilanz der deutschen Judenheit*, Amsterdam 1934, New edition: Querido Verlag, Berlin 1991, p. 68 **83:** Official brochure of the city of Berlin, quoted from: *Weimarer Republik* 1977, loc. cit, p. 172 84 Proclamation of 8.11.1923, quoted from: ibid, p. 277

Those were the Days

95: Leonhard Frank: *Links wo das Herz ist*, Aufbau-Verlag, Berlin/Weimar 1952, p. 113 f. **96:** Henry Bernhard (Ed.): *Gustav Stresemann. Vermächtnis. Der Nachlaß in drei Bänden*, Ullstein, Berlin 1932, Vol. 1, quoted from: Schulze 1994, p. 300 **97 c:** Wolfgang Stresemann: Speech on Briand and Stresemann, in: *Rotarier*, 1974/75, p. 13 **98:** Gustav Stresemann to Karl Jarres, quoted from: Bernhard 1932, loc. cit, Vol. 3, p. 263 f. **100 l, t:** Schulze 1994, loc. cit, p. 295; **l, b/c, t:** KPD Propaganda 1925, quoted from: *Dokumente und Materialien zur Geschichte der deutschen Arbeiterbewegung*, Dietz, Berlin 1975, Vol. 8, pp. 130–133; **c:** Theodor Wolff, in: *Berliner Tageblatt*, 27.4.1925; **c, b/r, t:** Gustav Stresemann, in: Bernhard 1932, loc. cit, Vol. 2, p. 60 f. **103 t, c:** Count Harry Kessler: *The Diaries of a Cosmopolitan. Diaries 1918–1937*, translated and edited by Charles Kessler, Weidenfeld and Nicolson, London, 1971, pp. 265–266; **r, b:** Hindenburg in a speech on the 11.11.1925, quoted from: Erich Marcks u.a.: *Paul von Hindenburg. Als Mensch, Staatsmann, Feldherr*, Berlin 1932, p. 104 **110:** Stahlhelm meeting of 8.5.1927, quoted from: *Geschichte der deutschen Arbeiterbewegung* 1966, loc. cit, Vol. 4, p. 480 **113:** Gustav Stresemann, quoted from: Bernhard 1932, loc. cit, Vol. 3, p. 565 f. **114** Count Harry Kessler:Diaries, loc. cit, pp. 367–368.

We are a Poor Country

117: Kurt Tucholsky: *Deutschland, Deutschland über alles*, Rowohlt, Reinbek bei Hamburg 1980, p. 46 **120 t:** Fritz Wolter: "Die Korrumpierung der Presse", in: *Die Weltbühne*, 24.5.1923, p. 598; **b:** Ludwig Turek: *Ein Prolet erzählt. Lebensschilderung eines deutschen Arbeiters*, Malik-Verlag, Berlin 1930, New edition: Verlag Neues Leben, Berlin 1957, p. 337 f. **122:** Commentary on a furnace and steelworks 1922, quoted from:

Jürgen Kuczynksi: *Geschichte des Alltags des deutschen Volkes*, Vol. 5, 1918–1945, Pahl-Rugenstein, Cologne year as above, p. 31 **135:** Welfare minister Hirtsiefer on 13.10.1928, quoted from: Carl Dietmar: *Chronik Köln*, Bertelsmann, Gütersloh/Munich 1991, p. 369 **141:** Protest note of German Newspaper Publishers' Association on 3.11.1928, quoted from: Marckwardt 1982, loc. cit, p. 98 **144:** Comments on statistics on nutrition and luxury foods for 1920–1923, quoted from: Kuczynksi, year as above , loc. cit, Vol. 5, p. 374 **147:** Adolf Münzinger: *Der Arbeitsertrag der bäuerlichen Familienwirtschaft*, Berlin 1929, 2nd Vol., p. 811f.

So You Want to be Rich?

149: Joachim Ringelnatz: "Komm, sage mir, was du für Sorgen hast", in: *Ausgewählte Gedichte*, Rowohlt, Reinbek nr. Hamburg 1987, p. 140 f. **151 r, t:** Arthur Rosenberg: *Geschichte der Weimarer Republik*, 1935, New edition edited by Kurt Kersten, Frankfurt a.M. 1961, p. 171; **r/b:** Hans von Seeckt: "Heer im Staat", 1928, in: *Gedanken eines Soldaten*, Verlag für Kulturpolitik, Leipzig 1935, p. 23 **154 t:** Franz Hessel: *Spazieren in Berlin*, Verlag Dr. Hans Epstein, Vienna/Leipzig 1929; New edition: *Ein Flaneur in Berlin. Mit Fotografien von Friedrich Seidenstücker*, Das Arsenal, Berlin 1984, p. 193; **b:** A director of the Hamburg housing department, 1927, in: Sigrid und Wolfgang Jacobeit: *Illustrierte Alltags- und Sozialgeschichte Deutschlands. 1900–1945*, Verlag Westfälisches Dampfboot, Münster 1995, p. 336 **159:** Fritz Huschke von Hanstein: "Fritz des Kleinen Pferd hieß Spatz. Das Rittergut an der Werra – Eine Jugend auf dem Lande: politikfern, aber stramm deutschnational", in: Pörtner 1993, loc. cit, pp. 233–249. p. 241 and 245 **164:** Dr. P. Buttenwieser, 1930, quoted from: Kuczynski, year as above, loc. cit, Vol. 5, p. 121 **167:** *Soziale Praxis*, volume 9, Berlin 1923 **173:** Wolfgang Stresemann: *Mein Vater Gustav Stresemann*, Herbig, Munich/Berlin 1979, t. p. **182:** Werner Picht and Eugen Rosenstock: *Der Kampf um die Erwachsenenbildung 1912–1926*, Quelle & Meyer Verlag, Leipzig 1926, p. 49 **191 l:** Dr. Schmidt, in: *Strafvollzug in Preußen*, published by Prussian Interior Ministry Mannheim/Berlin/Leipzig 1928, P. V; **r:** Staatssekretär Hölscher, in: ibid, p. 3 **192:** Agnes Neuhaus, in: *Strafvollzug in Preußen*, published by Prussian Interior Ministry, Mannheim/Berlin/Leipzig 1928, p. 117 **195:** Carl Zuckmayer: *Als wär's ein Stück von mir. Horen der Freundschaft*, S. Fischer Verlag, Frankfurt a.M./Hamburg 1969, p. 286

So That's the Way the World Is...

209: Bertolt Brecht: "Der Aufstieg und Fall der Stadt Mahagonny", Berlin 1928/29, in: *Die Stücke von Bertolt Brecht in einem Band* Suhrkamp, Frankfurt a.M. 1978, p. 203–226, p. 213 **210 c:** Stephen Spender: *World within World*, Hamish Hamilton, London 1951, p. 131 **210 r:** Gottfried Benn, quoted from: Detlev J. K. Peukert: *Die Weimarer Republik*, Suhrkamp Verlag, Frankfurt a.M. 1982, p. 186 **213 t:** Walter Gropius: NEUE BAUHAUSBÜCHER, Bauhausbauten Dessau, 2. unchanged edition, Gebr. Mann Verlag, Berlin 1997, quoted from: *Bauhausbauten Dessau. Bauhausbücher 12*, Munich 1930, p. 11 **214:** Max Greil, quoted from: Magdalena Droste. *Bauhaus 1919–1933*, Cologne 1993, Benedikt Taschen Verlag, p. 113 **218:** Tilla Durieux: *Eine Tür fällt ins Schloß*, 1927, Silver & Goldstein, Berlin 1989, p. 223 **221:** Erich Mühsam: Unpolitische Erinnerungen, in: Helmut Kreuzer. *Die Boheme. Beiträge zu ihrer Beschreibung*, Metzler, Stuttgart 1968, p. 17 **222 t:** John Heartfield/George Grosz, in: Der Gegner, quoted from: Manfred Brauneck (Ed.): *Die rote Fahne. Kritik, Theorie, Feuilleton 1918–1933*, Fink, Munich, 1973, p. 63 **223 b:** Karl Deutsch: "Die Maschine als Bühnenelement", in: *Weimarer*

Republik 1977, loc. cit, p. 788 **224** Ernst Toller: Ein deutscher Hinkemann. Antikriegsschauspiel, 1923, quoted from: Ernst Toller: *Hinkemann. Eine Tragödie, Dramen der Zeit* 1954, p. 95; New edition: *Gesammelte Werke in fünf Bänden*, edited by John M. Spalek and Wolfgang Frühwald © 1996 Carl Hanser Verlag, Munich/Vienna **225:** Ernst Toller: *Eine Jugend in Deutschland*, 1933, p. 161, New edition ibid © 1996 Carl Hanser Verlag, Munich/Vienna **226 t:** Max Reinhardt: "Auf der Suche nach dem lebendigen Theater", 1924, in: *Ich bin nichts als ein Theatermann. Briefe, Reden, Aufsätze, Gespräche, Auszüge aus Regiebüchern*, edited by Hugo Fetting, Henschel-Verlag, Berlin 1989, p. 228f. © Dornier Medienholding, Berlin **226 b:** Hugo von Hofmannsthal: Jedermann. Das Spiel vom Sterben des reichen Mannes, *Dramen*, S. Fischer Verlag, Frankfurt a.M. 1969, Vol. 3, b.P. **229 l:** Elias Canetti: *Die Fackel im Ohr. Lebensgeschichte 1921–1931*, Carl Hanser Verlag, Munich/Vienna 1980, p. 282 **229 r:** Alfred Döblin: "Der Geist des naturalistischen Zeitalters", Dezember 1924, in: *Schriften zur Ästhetik, Poetik und Literatur* © 1989 Walter Verlag, Düsseldorf/Zurich, P. 188 f. **230 t:** Albert Einstein: "Über den Frieden. Weltordnung oder Weltuntergang", in: *Menschenrechte*, 11.11.1928, quoted from: Otto Nathan und Heinz Norden (Eds.), Verlag Herbert Lang & Cie., Bern 1975, p. 111; **c, t:** Heinrich Mann: "Sinn und Idee der Revolution", speech 1918, in: *Münchner Neueste Nachrichten*, No. 607, 1.12.1918; **c b:** Thomas Mann: "Von deutscher Republik", lecture 1922, in: *Berliner Tageblatt*, No. 469, 17.10.1922; **b:** *Berliner Tageblatt*, No. 469, 17.10.1922 **232 l:** Max Reinhardt: *Ausgewählte Briefe, Reden und Schriften*, edited by Franz Hadamowsky, Prachner, Vienna 1963, p. 91 © Dornier Medienholding, Berlin **233 r:** Konrad Haenisch: "Warum feiern wir Gerhart Hauptmann?", in: *Die Volksbühne*, No. 3, 1922, pp. 34–36 **234:** Arnold Zweig: Bilanz der deutschen Judenheit, Querido Verlag, Amsterdam, 1934, quoted from:*Bilanz der deutschen Judenheit. Ein Versuch*, Reclam, Leipzig 1991, p. 210 **237:** Käthe Kollwitz: *Tagebuchblätter und Briefe*, edited by Hans Kollwitz, Gebr. Mann Verlag, Berlin 1949, p. 100 f. **239 l:** Yehudi Menuhin, in: Otto Friedrich: *Morgen ist Weltuntergang. Berlin in den zwanziger Jahren*, Nicolai Verlag, Berlin 1998, p. 215 **239 r:** A spectator at the premiere of the opera Wozzeck by Alban Berg on 14.12.1925, in: ibid p. 222 **243:** Rudolf von Laban: The Mastery of Movement, London 1950, quoted from: *Die Kunst der Bewegung*, Wilhelmshaven 1996, p. 7 **247:** Mary Wigman: *Deutsche Tanzkunst*, Dresden 1935, p. 10 **249 t:** Friedrich Hollaender: Das bist Du!, in: Rainer Otto and Walter Rösler: *Kabarettgeschichte. Abriß des deutschsprachigen Kabaretts*, Henschel-Verlag, Berlin 1977, p. 98; **b:** A critic on Hollaender, in: ibid p. 100 **251:** Elisabeth Bergner: *Bewundert viel und viel gescholten... Elisabeth Bergners unordentliche Erinnerungen*, Bertelsmann, Munich 1978, p. 90 **252:** Josef von Sternberg: *Ich, Josef von Sternberg*, Erhard Friedrich Verlag, bei Hannover 1967, p. 140 f. **254:** Fritz Lang: "Wege des großen Spielfilms in Deutschland", in: *Literarische Welt* 2, No. 40, 1.10.1926, p. 3

Happy Days are Here Again

257 Comedian Harmonists: *Wochenend und Sonnenschein* , Duophon, Berlin 1930, Original title: *Happy Days are Here Again*, from the film: *Chasing Rainbows* (1929), Text: Jack Yellen, Music: Milton Ager © Ager, Yellen & Bornstein Inc., New York **259:** Herbert Marcuse: "Der affirmative Charakter der Kultur", 1932, in: *Kultur und Gesellschaft I*, Suhrkamp, Frankfurt a.M. 1980, p. 68 **260 t:** Two young female textile workers describe their Sunday outings, quoted from: Kuczynski, year as above, loc. cit, p. 344 ff.; **b:** Interview mit Albert Joost, in: Bernd Polster (Ed.): *"Swing Heil". Jazz im Nationalsozialismus*, Transit Verlag, Berlin 1989, p. 95 *263:*

Franz Hessel: Ein Flaneur in Berlin, loc. cit, p. 186 f. *267:* Tilla Durieux: *Eine Tür fällt ins Schloß*, loc. cit, p. 179 *269:* Rudolf Kayser: "Amerikanismus", 1925, in: *Vossische Zeitung*, No. 458, 27.9.1925 *270:* Eduard Bernstein: Die Geschichte der Berliner Arbeiter-Bewegung, Vol. 3, Berlin 1910, quoted from: Gerhard Brunn and Jürgen Reulecke (Eds.): *Metropolis Berlin. Berlin als deutsche Hauptstadt im Vergleich europäischer Hauptstädte 1870–1939*, Bouvier, Bonn/Berlin 1992, p. 88 **271 t:** George Grosz, quoted from: Cay Rademacher, Der Schnee der Zwanziger, in: *GEO Spezial*, Berlin, No. 1, February 1999, pp. 134–142, p. 134; **b:** Carl Zuckmayer: *Als wär's ein Stück von mir*, S. Fischer Verlag, Frankfurt a.M. 1980, p. 328 **273:** Franz Hessel: *Ein Flaneur in Berlin*, loc. cit, p. 48 f. **279** A friend of vaudeville, quoted from: Wolfgang Jansen: *Das Varieté. Die glanzvolle Geschichte einer unterhaltenden Kunst*, Berlin 1990, p. 179 **282:** Ludwig Jürgens: *Sankt Pauli. Bilder aus einer fröhlichen Welt*, H. Köhler Verlag, Hamburg 1930, p. 5 **285:** Egon Erwin Kisch: "Ein Abend in St. Pauli", in: Welt am Abend, 4.2.1931, in: *Mein Leben für die Zeitung 1926–1947. Journalistische Texte 2*, Aufbau Verlag, Berlin/Weimar 1983, p. 261 **287:** Franz Hessel: *Ein Flaneur in Berlin*, loc. cit, p. 263 **289:** Count Harry Kessler: *Diaries*, loc. cit, p. 417.

The System is Collapsing!

293: KPD appeal, quoted from: Kurt R. Grossman: *Ossietzky. Ein deutscher Patriot*, Kindler, Munich 1963, p. 233 **295:** Ludwig Kaas: Speech to general assembly of German Catholics in Freiburg, August 1929, quoted from: Rudolf Morsey: "Die Deutsche Zentrumspartei", in: Rudolf Morsey and Erich Matthias: *Das Ende der Parteien*, Droste, Düsseldorf 1960, p. 291 **298:** Stephen Spender: *World within world*, loc. cit., p. 129 f **301 l:** Schleicher's radio broadcast of 15.12.1932, in: *Akten der Reichskanzlei. Kabinett v. Schleicher*, pp. 141–145. p. 141, in: Eyck 1954, loc. cit, Vol. 2, p. 503 **302 t:** SPD election appeal, in: *Vorwärts*, No. 335, 20.7.1930 **b:** Adolf Hitler addressing the Reichsgericht 1930, in: Friedrich A. Krummacher and Albert Wucher: *Die Weimarer Republik. Ihre Geschichte in Texten, Bildern und Dokumenten*, Desch, Vienna 1965, p. 306 **305:** Joseph Goebbels: Wege ins Dritte Reich. Briefe und Aufsätze für Zeitgenossen, Munich 1927, pp. 26–29, quoted from: Ulrich Höver: *Joseph Goebbels: ein nationaler Sozialist*, Bouvier, Bonn/Berlin, p. 81 **306:** Ernst Thälmann at the KPD party conference on 10.6.1929, *Protokoll der Verhandlungen des XII. Parteitages der Kommunistischen Partei Deutschlands. Berlin-Wedding 9.–16. Juni 1929*, Frankfurt a.M. 1975, P. 75 ff. **309:** B. Nelissen Haken: Stempelchronik, Hamburg 1932, quoted from: Kuczynski, year as above, loc. cit, p. 107 **310:** Willy Münzenberg, Speech on day of solidarity 1931, in: *Weimarer Republik*, 1977, loc. cit, p. 575 **312 t:** Oberst Kühlenthal, in: *Documents on British Foreign Policy, 1919–1939*, Edited by E. L. Woodward and Rohan Butler, Second Series, Vol. 1, Crown Edition, London 1947, P. 479; **b:** Adolf Hitler: *Mein Kampf*, Vol. 1, 1925, Eher-Verlag, Munich 1934, p. 197 f. **313 l:** Joseph Goebbels,

quoted from: Wilfried Ranke: *Propaganda*. pp. 34–49, p. 41, in: Benz 1997, loc. cit; **r:** Joseph Goebbels, quoted from: Winkler 1998, loc. cit, p. 445 **317:** Sir Horace Rumbold: in: Eyck 1954, loc. cit, Vol. 2, p. 490f. **318 t:** SA song, in: Peter Longerich: "Die SA", in: Heinrich August Winkler and Alexander Cammann (Eds.): *Weimar – ein Lesebuch zur deutschen Geschichte 1918–1933* Beck, Munich 1997, p. 318; **b:** "Roter Wedding" group fighting song, in: *Mit Lenin! 50 Kampflieder*, Verlag Junge Garde, Berlin 1929/30 **320 l:** KPD memo, quoted from: *Die Generallinie. Rundschreiben des Zentralkomitees der KPD an die Bezirke 1929–1933* Introduced and edited by Hermann Weber, Düsseldorf 1981, pp. 526–534; **r, t:** Heinz Kühn: *Widerstand und Emigration. Die Jahre 1928–1945*, Hoffmann und Campe, Hamburg 1980, p. 49; **r, b:** Arkadij Gurland: "Tolerierungsscherben – und was weiter?" In: *Marxistische Tribüne* 2, No. 12, 15.06.1932, pp. 351–356, p. 352 f. **323 t:** tenants council, 1932, quoted from: Johann Friedrich Geist und Klaus Kürvers: *Das Berliner Mietshaus 1862–1945*, Prestel, Munich 1984, Vol. 2, p. 421 **324 t:** Joseph Goebbels: *Die Tagebücher von Joseph Goebbels. Sämtliche Fragmente*, edited by Elke Fröhlich on behalf of the Institut für Zeitgeschichte and in association with the archives of K. G. Saur, Munich 1987, Vol. 2, . 271 © 1987 Cordula Schacht, attorney **326:** Schleicher's radio broadcast of 15.12.1932, loc. cit, p. 141 **327:** Carl von Ossietzky, quoted from: *Weimarer Republik*, 1977, loc. cit, p. 403 f. **328 t:** Theodor Wolff: "Was tut Lehmann?" In: *Berliner Tageblatt*, 18.09.1932, in: Bernd Sösemann (Ed.): *Theodor Wolff. Der Journalist. Berichte und Leitartikel*, Düsseldorf/Vienna/New York/Moscow 1993, pp .337–341, p. 337 and 340 f.; **c t:** Joseph Goebbels: *Tagebücher*, loc. cit, Vol. 2, p. 331 f.; **c b:** Reichspräsident Hindenburg, quoted from: Thilo Vogelsang: *Reichswehr, Staat und NSDAP. Beiträge zur deutschen Geschichte 1930–1932*, Stuttgart 1962, p. 440; **b:** Ernst Breitschied, in: *Anpassung oder Widerstand? Aus den Akten des Parteivorstands der deutschen Sozialdemokratie 1932/33*, quoted from: Schulze 1994, loc. cit, P. 145 f.

Strolling in Berlin

331: Franz Hessel: *Ein Flaneur in Berlin*, loc. cit, p. 273 **332 l:** ibid, p. 275; **r:** Egon Erwin Kisch: "Berlin in der Arbeit", in: *Mein Leben für die Zeitung*, loc. cit, p. 37 **335 t:** Walter Mehring: *Das Ketzerbrevier*, Claassen Verlag, Düsseldorf (now Munich) 1921, p. 28; **b:** Karl Baedeker (Ed.):*Berlin und Umgebung, Handbuch für Reisende*, Karl Baedeker Verlag, 19th Edition, Leipzig 1921, p. 39 and 46 **337 t:** Franz Hessel: *Ein Flaneur in Berlin*, loc. cit, p. 94; **b:** Erich Kästner: *Fabian*, Deutsche Verlags-Anstalt, Stuttgart 1931, Original edition, p. 273 **341 l:** Translation of "Solang noch Untern Linden", marching song from the revue "Drunter und Drüber", Musik: Walter Kollo, Text: Herman Haller and Willi Wolff © 1923 Vuvag, Berlin; quoted from: Walter Kollo: *Chorusbuch, Dreiklang – Dreimasken Bühnen- und Musikverlag*, Berlin/Munich 1978, p. 59 f.; **r:** Walter Benjamin "Die Wiederkehr des Flaneurs", in:

Die Literarische Welt, Vol. 5, No. 40, 4.10.1929 **342:** Gustav Radbruch: Referat über die Rechtspflege, in: Artur Kaufmann (Ed.): *Gustav Radbruch. Band 13. Politische Schriften aus der Weimarer Zeit. 2. Justiz, Bildungs- und Religionspolitik*, C. F. Müller Juristischer Verlag, Heidelberg 1993 **345:** Berlin skit on a song from the Operetta *Gasparone* by Karl Millöcker (1884), quoted from: Walter Kiaulehn: *Berlin – Schicksal einer Weltstadt*, Biederstein, Munich/Berlin 1958, New edition: dtv 1981, p. 237 **350 l:** Carl von Ossietzky, quoted from: Walther Kiaulehn: *Keine Zeit, keine Zeit, keine Zeit!* In: Winkler/Cammann 1997, loc. cit, pp. 149–151, p. 150; **r:** Fritzi Massary, in: *Die Dame – Ein deutsches Journal für den verwöhnten Geschmack*, quoted from: Herman Glaser: *Das Automobil. Eine Kulturgeschichte in Bildern*, Beck, Munich 1986, p. 24 **353:** Friedrich Kroner: "Das Auto meiner Frau", in: Christian Färber (Ed.): *Die Dame – Ein deutsches Journal für den verwöhnten Geschmack. 1912–1943*, Berlin 1980, p. 148 **359:** Paul Michaelis: *Der Robinson der Robinsons. Eine humoristische und sozialistische Erzählung für die Arbeiter- und Fortbildungsschul-Jugend*, Verlag der Leipziger Buchdruckerei AG, Leipzig 1921, p. 45 **360:** Franz Hessel: *Ein Flaneur in Berlin*, loc. cit, p. 8 f. **363 l:** Heinrich Zille: "Mein Lebenslauf. Aufgezeichnet für die Akademie der Künste in Berlin", in: *Kunst und Künstler*, Vol. 23, Berlin 1925, p. 62 ff.; **r:** song, quoted from: Winfried Ranke: *Vom Milljöh ins Milieu. Heinrich Zilles Aufstieg in der Berliner Gesellschaft*, Fackelträger, Munich 1979, p. 300 **365:** Intellectuals on the Stammtisch, quoted from: Georg Wedemeyer: *Kneipe & politische Kultur*, Centaurus-Verlagsgesellschaft, Pfaffenweiler 1990, p. 24 **366:** Advertising slogans for widows' balls, in: Franz Hessel: *Ein Flaneur in Berlin*, loc. cit, p. 47 **367:** Franz Blei: "Beweise für die Liebe", in: *Lehrbuch der Liebe und Ehe*, Avalun-Verlag, Hellerau bei Dresden 1928, p. 112 **369 t:** "Das gibt's nur einmal", from the UFA film *Der Kongreß tanzt*, Music: Werner Richard Heymann, Text: Robert Gilbert © 1931 Ufaton-Verlag, Berlin/Munich; quoted from: *Das große Schlagerbuch, Deutsche Schlager von 1800 bis heute*, edited by Monika Sperr, Munich 1978, p. 161; **b:** Irmgard Keun: *Gilgi, eine von uns*, Universitas Deutsche Verlags-Aktiengesellschaft, Berlin 1931, p. 9 **370:** Franz Blei: "Sexuelle Not der Eltern", in: *Lehrbuch der Liebe und Ehe*, loc. cit, p. 17

From Adenauer to Zuckmayer

405: Theodor Wolff, commentary on Hindenburg's election in 1925, in: *Berliner Tageblatt*, No. 197, 27.4.1925 **406:** C. A. Kanitzberg: "Der neue Weg", in: *Der Photofreund*, Berlin 1933 **407:** "Deutsche Bilder in der Presse", in: *Deutsche Nachrichten*, No. 32, 2. August edition, 1933, p. 7 f.

Picture Credits

Most of the illustrations not listed here originate from the Swedish television archive, SVT Bild, Sveriges Television AB, Stockholm, © SVT Bild/Das Fotoarchiv

© Bildarchiv Preußischer Kulturbesitz, Berlin: p. 392 r/photo: Nina v. Jaanson; p. 406
© Ullstein Bilderdienst, Berlin: p. 380 t, r; p. 383; p. 385 l; p. 390 r; p. 393 c; p. 395 r; p. 396 c, t; p. 403 r
© VG Bild-Kunst, Bonn 1999: George Grosz, *Der Aufwiegler*, p. 222; Max Liebermann, *Selbstporträt*, p. 392 b, l

Endsheet: "Berlin Newspaper City 1918–1933": Berlin I, Map from Chapter: Berlin and Potsdam, from: *Deutschland in einem Band. Kurzes Reisehandbuch von Karl Baedeker. Mit 25 Karten und 73 Plänen*, 4th edition, Karl Baedeker, Leipzig 1925 © Karl Baedeker GmbH, Ostfildern

Thanks

The Weimar Republic is a product of intensive teamwork. This book could not have been written without the thorough and expert research on press photography carried out by my colleagues Tove Kleiven and Brigitta Werner at the Swedish television archive SVT-Bild, Sveriges Television AB. Thanks to their efforts, this invaluable treasure trove has been rediscovered, explored, and presented for viewing.

Torsten Palmér

It is possible to collaborate on a project like this even from a great distance: many thanks to my colleagues in Stockholm – Torsten Palmér, Tove Kleiven, and Brigitta Werner. Thomas Morlang and Andreas Schäfer assisted me in the literature research and read each draft of the text. As always, Dr. Volker Guckel threw a critical eye on the second-last version of the text. My three assistants also deserve particular thanks for their "positive vibrations": Regina Berkowitz, Nora Britt Edda Neubauer and Lynn Inger Carlotta.

Hendrik Neubauer

For support in the research of the biographies, Patrick Bierther would like to thank Daniel Magilow, Olivier Lugon, Patricia Edgar, and their colleagues from the photographic collection of the SK Stiftung Kultur, Cologne; Brooke Henderson, Getty Museum, Los Angeles; Rainer Laabs, Ullstein gumbo, Berlin; Dr. Margret Heitmann, Salomon Ludwig Steinheim Institute for German–Jewish History, Duisburg; Karin Weber-Andreas, Berlin; Jola Merten, *Berliner Morgenpost*, Berlin; Silvia Volpato, Essen.

The publishers would also like to thank Regine Ermert for proof-reading and generation of the index; Astrid Roth and Matthias Rebel for researching the historical sources; Astrid Schünemann for picture research and Sybille Carmanns and Annette Ocker for their practical support in the coordination of the project and final proof-reading stages.

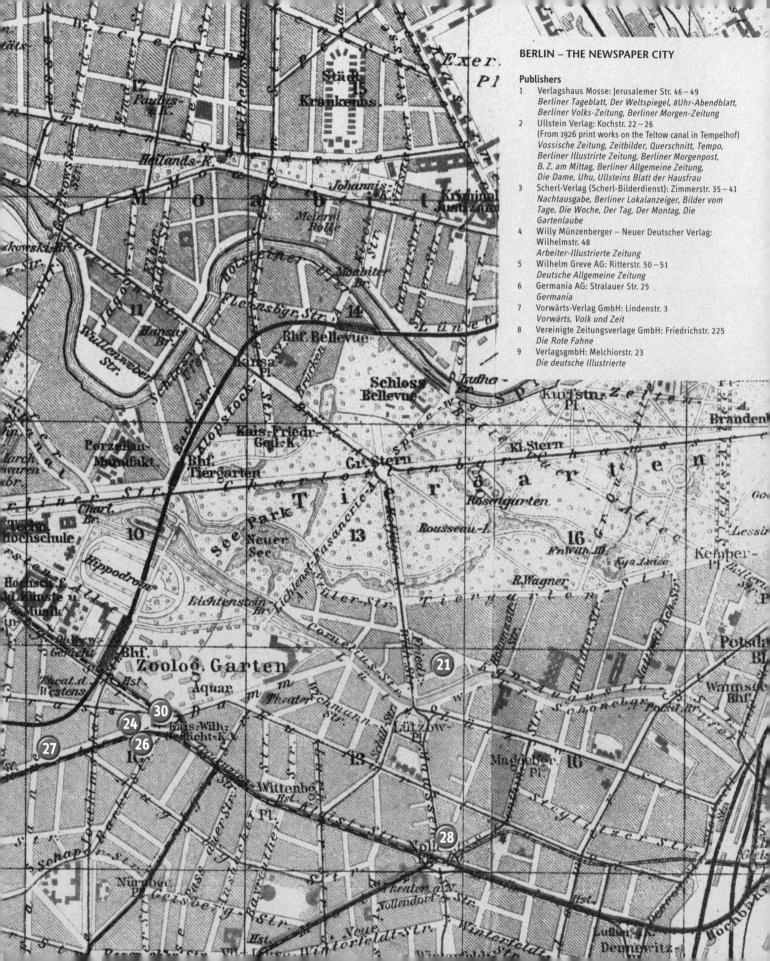

BERLIN – THE NEWSPAPER CITY

Publishers

1 Verlagshaus Mosse: Jerusalemer Str. 46–49
   *Berliner Tageblatt, Der Weltspiegel, 8Uhr-Abendblatt,
   Berliner Volks-Zeitung, Berliner Morgen-Zeitung*
2 Ullstein Verlag: Kochstr. 22–26
   (From 1926 print works on the Teltow canal in Tempelhof)
   *Vossische Zeitung, Zeitbilder, Querschnitt, Tempo,
   Berliner Illustrirte Zeitung, Berliner Morgenpost,
   B. Z. am Mittag, Berliner Allgemeine Zeitung,
   Die Dame, Uhu, Ullsteins Blatt der Hausfrau*
3 Scherl-Verlag (Scherl-Bilderdienst): Zimmerstr. 35–41
   *Nachtausgabe, Berliner Lokalanzeiger, Bilder vom
   Tage, Die Woche, Der Tag, Der Montag, Die
   Gartenlaube*
4 Willy Münzenberger – Neuer Deutscher Verlag:
   Wilhelmstr. 48
   Arbeiter-Illustrierte Zeitung
5 Wilhelm Greve AG: Ritterstr. 50–51
   Deutsche Allgemeine Zeitung
6 Germania AG: Stralauer Str. 25
   Germania
7 Vorwärts-Verlag GmbH: Lindenstr. 3
   Vorwärts, Volk und Zeit
8 Vereinigte Zeitungsverlage GmbH: Friedrichstr. 225
   Die Rote Fahne
9 VerlagsgmbH: Melchiorstr. 23
   Die deutsche Illustrierte